MW00718795

The Cornwallis

Family History

1225 - 2006

by

Rev. N.B. Cryer

Copyright © The Lord Cornwallis

ISBN 1-904446-07-8

Published by Quacks Books

The author asserts the moral right to
be identified as the author of this work

British Library Cataloguing in Publication Data
Rev. N.B. Cryer, 2006
The Cornwallis Family History
1225 - 2006

All rights reserved. No part of this publication may be
reproduced, stored in a retrieval system, or transmitted,
in any form or by any means, electronic, mechanical,
photocopying, recording or otherwise, without the prior
permission of the copyright holder.

Printed by Quacks Printers
7 Grape Lane, Petergate, York, YO1 7HU

Rt. Hon. Lord Cornwallis, OBE, DL

Contents

CHAPTER 1

"Unearthing the Roots"

It was late in the evening of 5 January, 1209, that Isabella of Angoulême, the second wife and Queen of King John, gave birth at Winchester to a second son. He was named Richard, somewhat ironically, after his uncle Richard 'Coeur de Lion' who had died 10 years previously. A partial cloud was cast over the boy's childhood for among the King's numerous illegitimate progeny there was already another Richard de Warenne, Lord of Chilham, Kent, born some 15 years or so earlier, who had already been admitted to knighthood and was married by the time Prince Richard was aged 6. The latter's first English biographer (in 1947) remarks that "there are a number of references in the records which may refer to either (son), as well as a few which have become firmly attached to the biography of Richard of Cornwall". (Denholm Young, p. 2) Happily for our purposes the references that might be doubtful are not such as to affect our story though the continuing use of the name Richard in the next generation requires careful attention.

It would not be useful here to recount at length the story of Richard, the Earl and later 'King of Almayne', when two others have done this adequately already. What has to be done, however, is to recall some aspects of the early part of his life which materially affect the Cornwallis family history and which suggest where and why the affairs of the family began to develop as they did.

I turn first of all to the calendar of events which tell us about Richard's movements and whereabouts in his years of early manhood, bearing in mind that in those days it was a case of much earlier physical development than has been customary until fairly recent times. I begin in the year 1225 when, on 2 February, shortly after his 16th birthday, Richard was knighted by his brother, King Henry III, at Westminster. A few days later he had had bestowed on him the recognized seigneurial rights over Cornwall which had been his father's before him, though at this stage they were to be exercised only 'during the King's pleasure'.

In March he was one of a commission of three appointed to recover the province of Gascony, by assisting the folk there and the neighbouring Poitevins against the French. The expedition set off on Palm Sunday, the very day of the commissioning. That the young man was still being 'reared' was shown by the fact that his earlier tutor, Roger d'Acaster of York, was in his accompanying household.

14 months later Richard returned home and was warmly welcomed by his brother. This was in May 1227 and in August he was officially styled Earl of Cornwall and Poitou at Westminster. We know that he began to take an active and early interest in his western estates because there is now the record of his first official visit to the principal properties. On 9 July we learn that he came up to Court from Devon to plead his case concerning one of his Cornish manors. He was informed of a plan to have him detained in London and as a result he secretly left the city and never drew rein until he had reached Reading. His household followed him the next morning and the whole party then proceeded to Marlborough. There they met the company of William Marshal, Earl of Pembroke, who was not only Richard's sworn ally and friend but was in due course to become his father-in-law.

Richard was thereafter in close touch with several of the senior barons and spent much of the rest of that year in the Midlands. Denholm Young, however, also tells us that "For the next <u>two years</u> he received not infrequent marks of favour, but his <u>doings or whereabouts cannot again be traced</u> until the Breton campaign of 1230". (p. 14) He may, however, have been in Ireland on the Kerry campaign for some part of 1228.

From April 1230 Richard was setting off again to France but after a fruitless campaign, and the onset of a disease in the English army which affected the King and his brother, Richard returned in October. It was in time to learn of the death of Gilbert de Clare, Earl of Gloucester, and within 5 months the Earl had recovered his health sufficiently to court and then marry Isabella, third daughter and co-heir of William Marshal, who was the widow. The wedding took place on 30 March 1231 at Fawley near Marlow in Buckinghamshire.

"Isabella Marshal", says Denholm Young, "like all Richard's wives, was a woman of wonderful beauty, but she was older than Richard, for she had already been married to Gilbert de Clare for 14 years and had borne him six flourishing children. Her marriage with Richard of Cornwall was to be no less fruitful though their first son, John, was born and died in 1232 and a sister, Isabella, was born about September 1233 and died a year later.

These two events created a problem for Richard, who, after 4 years of marriage, had a wife who was no longer young and had still not produced an heir. We know that Richard at this time sought the Pope's permission to obtain a divorce but this was refused and only the birth of a son, Henry, cleared the air. He at least was to survive childhood though he did not outlive his father for he was sadly murdered at Viterbo in 1271. It was another 5 years before Isabella gave birth once more in Launceston Castle, Richard's favourite residence in Cornwall, but this time she too died with her baby Nicholas. It was January, 1240.

It is thus clear that in the middle years of this decade Richard was eager to produce offspring especially as Henry III was childless until the birth of the future Edward I in 1239. Yet Richard of Cornwall had by no means been regularly at the side of his consort and at the age of 31 he was already a widower.

As for his subsequent movements we know that in 1232 he was on campaign in Wales with his brother-in-law, William Marshal II. The latter's father had died in 1231 as the result of an illness contracted at the time of Richard's wedding. During the next 7 years Richard is found more and more in the baronial camp though he was no longer in favour of resistance to the Crown. After all, he might himself be the wearer of it if his brother's line ceased. When at last a new Prince of Wales arrived, 17-18 June 1239, any suggestion of contention with his brother ended and, as we shall now note, Richard was duly rewarded for his loyalty. He was "still young and handsome and great hopes were entertained of him". (Denholm Young, p. 22)

The second feature of these early years in his life is Richard's steady acquisition of wealth. He was widely believed to be the richest man in England by his middle age and this was partly achieved by both the steady accumulation of properties and their rights, as well as the careful management of such privileges as custody and wardship which he was granted by the Crown, even if these were of only a temporary nature. He was, as has been already mentioned, very jealous of anyone whom he thought to be withholding rights and lands that were properly his.

When, for example, he had been given suzerainty over the County of Cornwall, albeit at the king's pleasure, at just 16 years of age, he only allowed six months to pass before he requested the control and revenue of the Cornish tin mines. Following his 18th birthday (1227), when the Earldom was formally confirmed but he was still not permitted to enjoy his revenues 'as of right and without hindrance from any', he was soon engaged in dispute about the meagreness of his endowment. He began what was to be a bitter dispute over some eight Cornish manors granted by King John to a certain Waleran Teutonicus (or Tyes). It is significant for our purpose that whilst six of those manors were reallocated the one about which no stated conclusion was declared by the King's mandate was Tamerton near Saltash, on the Cornish border with Devon. We shall soon see why Richard could well have had a special interest there.

It was not until the time of his first marriage, in 1231, that Richard was given the full and complete right to his Earldom and all within it, and it was at this point also that he received the honours, in fee, of Wallingford in Oxfordshire and Eye in Suffolk. He also received the very lucrative wardship of the Theobald Walter lands at this point and that included the management of some widespread properties in Ireland. If one consults the Butler Family History (4th edition, p. 8) we are given some idea of what this meant.

"Going from father to son, each of the first five Chief Butlers was called Theobald, which invites confusion, and each, as was the wont with feudal magnates, feared God, fought hard, married well and, except for the first Butler, died young.

"Out of his vast estates in Ireland and England, the first Butler founded (three abbeys and one monastery) and married Maud Vavassour of that Yorkshire family which was reputed never to have married an heiress and never to have had to bury a wife." The descendant of the 2nd Butler, the 3rd Earl of Ormond, inherited further considerable estates in Ireland and England. It is inconceivable that Richard who had this wardship did

3

not himself benefit by procuring some permanent presence on the other island.

This latter benefit was even more enlarged when in 1231, on the death of his father-in-law, William, Earl of Pembroke, Richard was granted custody of the Braose lands in England as well as the estates of a further Theobald Butler in Ireland. It is also intriguing to note that when Richard's brother-in-law and friend, Richard Marshal, was threatened with dispossession the latter's constables in his nine Irish castles held out against royal control and Richard could thus count on another foothold in that land. (p.6)

Before ending this part of our story we need to record that by 1231 Richard was at last confirmed in the rights to his mother's dower which meant, amongst other things, the possession of manors and property in many English counties and not least in London. His increasing loyalty to the Crown also resulted in the grant 'in demesne' of Warin Basset's lands in Cornwall, the full profits from the Stannaries, or tin-mining courts, and the wardship of the estates of the young Baldwin de Lisle in Devon, Hampshire and the Isle of Wight.

Not only could we continue this series of grants almost indefinitely throughout Earl Richard's life but we have the complete list of those properties in England which Richard bequeathed to his son, Edmund. What that list reveals confirms what is most relevant to the Cornwallis story. Richard was by 1240 the owner of a substantial number of properties and land rights in London, Norfolk, Suffolk, Northamptonshire, Oxford and Hampshire quite apart from his tenures in Cornwall and Ireland and many other parts of the kingdom. The significance of all this will be revealed as our story unfolds.

It only remains to introduce some acquaintances of the young Earl whom he met when he made his first tour of his Devon and Cornish domains. They were members of a family that was already well established in these western parts and whose manors lay directly in the young Lord's path.

No sooner have you crossed the river Tamar, that ancient border between England and the Duchy of Cornwall, than you are within sight of one of the earliest Norman strongholds in that area. Trematon stands high aloft, on the summit of one of a rather jumbled group of hilltops that lie behind Saltash. Placed on a steep hill for purposes of inaccessibility it had long been a place of defence in ancient times. It became a baronial castle granted to the first Earl of Cornwall, Robert of Mortain, soon after the Conquest. Originally of the usual 'motte and bailey' type, like Totnes and Launceston, it was steadily improved until it fell into the hands of the eventual 14th century 'Royal Duchy' administration. Thereafter it was to remain untouched until it eventually became the 'private' ruin that it is today, quietly persisting with its great gateway and outer walls but overlooked by the more modern home of a local gentleman.

The name of the family that occupied this castle in the 11th to 13th centuries was derived from the local landscape for the words 'Vallis torta' referred to the narrow winding valley that descends from Trematon to the south. At the time of the Domesday Survey a Valletort was already holding the fief which also included thirty-nine manors and owed service to the Count of Mortain. By the 12th century we know that this property was in the hands of a Reginald Valletort and Saltash history records that he at this time confirmed to the town its existing rights and immunities. The age of the locality is also reflected in the name of the site on which his castle stood. Trematon comes from the Cornish 'Tre-madern' which meant 'The town of the King', an appropriate derivation in view of its later being part of a royal Earl's or royal Duke's patrimony.

We also know that Reginald had one son, Roger, who was of age in 1140 and some accounts of the family line claim that he married Joan, the daughter of the then Earl of Cornwall, himself called Reginald. Whether this was the case, or whether this claim has been confused with another event soon to be described, is not for us to pursue here. What matters is that the Valletorts had already become one of the important families in Cornwall, and in the century that was to follow the descendants of Roger were to extend their branches into the Devon manors of Modbury, Tawton, Clyst and Inceworthy.

It was during their tenure of Trematon that the outer wall, or enceinte, was constructed as well as a fine keep/tower on the 'motte', and finally the gatehouse. By the end of the 13th century, in the reign of Edward I, all these additions to the site had been completed. The castle was as secure as it would ever be and the efforts of the Valletorts were appreciated by their overlords. Richard, Earl of Cornwall, as early as his first tour in 1227, certainly expressed satisfaction with the work done by his Valletort contemporaries and he knew what he was talking about.

"Richard's early years had been spent at Corfe Castle in Dorset and this may have inspired his lifelong interest in castle-building. His work survives at Tintagel and Launceston (and he) left behind at Ascalon elaborate fortifications which were to serve as a defensive base for further crusades." (Dorothy Winkless) In 1289 the last surviving male of this Valletort line was to hand back the castle to Earl Edmund and that is why it appears in his list of possessions.

That Richard had further occasion to know what he was talking about is confirmed not only by the fact that he often visited the place but that he became intimately associated with a lady who bore this family's name. After attaining his majority he is recorded as having made a further tour of his Cornish properties in 1230 and sometime within the following two years we have evidence to show that he was the father of at least one son, and possibly two, born out of wedlock to a Joan de Valletort.

Joan was the daughter of a John de Valletort who was Lord of the Manor of Tawton and one record has it that she was first married to a cousin, Ralph de Valletort, one of Roger of Trematon's great-grandsons. That this was so is revealed by the record of a Fine (224: Assize Rolls H.III) where we read that the Manor of Inceworthy and 200 acres were held 'by Alexander and Joan Okeston by gift of Ralph de Valletort, first husband of Joan and brother of Roger, whose heir he is'. That this was no mean inheritance is also indicated in this record which states that Roger had bequeathed Inceworthy with "all appurtenances as well in demesnes, arable lands, services of freemen, villeinages, woods, meadows, pastures, ways, paths, waters, ponds, mills, fisheries, pessages, etc" and these were to pass to Ralph's heirs if he and Joan have no children.

It appears that Ralph died without offspring and Joan had married again. Her new husband, Alexander de Okeston, had been granted the Valletort manor of Modbury and his wife was in her own right recognized as Lord of Inceworthy in Milbrook. The Modbury manor passed at Sir Alexander's death to his son, James de Okeston, but as he died without an heir the property became that of his sister, Joan Plantagenet, who married Sir Richard Champernown. In due time and at the mother's death this couple were to receive also the manor of Inceworthy. Meanwhile Joan, as the widow of Sir Alexander, was to have yet another suitor.

That Joan de Valletort was a lady of grace and charm seems undoubted. Already a mother and twice a widow she must have possessed some special qualities to be able to capture the attentions of one whom we have already noted was susceptible to women of peculiar beauty. What is important for our purpose is that not only was there some romantic attachment between the young royal Prince and this West country widow but that eventually at least three, and possibly four, healthy children were produced as a result of what some regard as a lasting liaison. Others however think that such a brood was produced through attachments to more than one lady.

Let us at this point recall that at three definite points in Richard's early manhood there is a significant silence as to his whereabouts. These periods are the summer of 1227 during which he made his first sortie into Devon and Cornwall, most of the years 1228 to 1230, and in the years 1233 and 1234. That Earl Richard was in Cornwall and Devon for most of these stretches is a reasonable assumption since he was always a man to care for his possessions and the Stannaries, in particular, demanded his careful attention at this time. Mention has been made of his constant desire to build up his financial resources and it was the attention which he gave to his lands and revenues in these years that allowed him the luxury of becoming a German 'Emperor' in the years ahead. If to that task there was added the very pleasurable pursuit and company of an attractive and healthy child-bearing concubine, just when he was avid for children to bear his name, then it is hardly surprising that he should lie low from time to time and see his 'familia' develop.

The names of three of these illegitimate offspring are recorded in several places and not least in the Dictionary of National Biography (Vol. XVI). The first, Richard de Cornubia, was born around 1230, and, with a wife also called Joan, daughter of John, Lord St Owen was to launch a family that still bears the name Cornwall. He himself was to die in battle before the end of the century and his line through Geoffrey, his eldest heir, ended in the next century. That from a younger son, Edmund, continued and thus were created the Cornwalls of Burford in Shropshire and of King's Nymet in Devon. This latter line was to produce Lord Fanhope and the Cornwalls of Berington, Herefordshire. There were at least two other sons but they were both monks. William, who was actually the first/born, eventually became Prior of Beaulieu Abbey and then Abbot of Newenham in 1272. In 1275 we note him being fined 2s for 'default of the New Forest' and in 1288 he abdicated due to blindness and returned to Beaulieu where he continued until 'a great age'. Nicholas, the youngest boy, was also first a monk at Beaulieu but then passed all his other days at Newenham under his brother's rule. It may be worth noting that the coat of arms adopted by this branch of the Earl's offspring was 'Ermine a lion rampant gules ducally crowned or a bordure sable bezantée'. We shall have to attend to the details of the first Richard's inheritance shortly as it materially affects our subject.

The next child, albeit third in time of birth (c.1236) was a daughter Isabella, also called 'de Cornubia'. She is probably the lady who was eventually married to Maurice, Lord of Berkeley, but we cannot here pursue her further story. It is the second and fourth children who are rather of most importance to the Cornwallis family record.

The first of these two boys was Philip de Cornubia, and the first to be called also 'Le Cornwaleys', who was born around 1232/3. He was early destined for the ministry of the Church and when he was 12 or 13 influence was brought to bear on the Cathedral authorities at Lichfield so that Philip, even at this tender age, was granted occupancy of the newly-created prebendal stall of Ruitone (or Ryton). A year or so later Richard of Cornwall was granted £600 by an unknown Archdeaconry 'for the purposes of education' whilst in 1248 the Earl was granted an 'indult' to hold 'an additional benefice on the petition of the Archbishop of Lyons'. An 'indult' suggests that the income thus generated was to be devoted to the education of a 'puer' (or boy) being trained for Church service. It looks very much as if Philip's career was being guided by an astute financial mind such as his 'natural' father possessed.

That children thus born out of wedlock could be accepted for a Church career is confirmed by a Papal letter of 1239 in which dispensation is given to "Roger, clerk, a 'nephew' of the King and of Richard, Earl of Cornwall, already dispensed on account of illegitimacy, to be promoted to a bishopric if canonically elected thereto".

By the time his father died in 1272 Philip le Cornwaleys was already well established. He was frequently the official go-between of the Bishop of Winchester and the Archbishop of Dublin and in 1285 he was even sent on a special mission to Rome. At the age of around 60 (1293) he became Archdeacon of Winchester as well as Rector of West Meon in that diocese, whilst in May of that year a mandate is issued by him giving corporal possession of Selborne Priory to the Dean of Aultone (Alton). There is also an interesting sealed document of the same month approving the grant of the parish of Great Weldham to the Prior and Convent of Selborne. The oval green seal shows Archdeacon Philip at prayer, with three saints alongside. Three years later he was described as Rector of St Just-in-Penwith, Cornwall, and in 1301 he was given a licence to convey lands in that Duchy. He died in office in 1304, just beyond his 70th year.

Yet that was not all. In 1265 there is mention in one of his letters of two nephews who are known as Walter and John de Sancto Austolo, that is of or from St. Austell. They are commended to his attention and one of them, John, was specially looked after since he also was bound for the priesthood. In 1285 when his uncle was already well-regarded in the Winchester diocese this boy, now 24, was granted the benefice of East Meon, the neighbouring parish to the one his uncle was to occupy 9 years later. Yet why these boys were called 'of St. Austell' is an even more intriguing part of our story.

It concerns their father, Walter de Cornubia, probably the last child of the Valletort connection. This part of our story begins by noting that whilst Earl Richard spent Christmas 1239 at Winchester he set off soon thereafter to visit his properties in Devon and Cornwall in order to set new boundaries. This was important as he was to depart on a 'Crusade' that began later that year. It would appear that the Earl established something more than just landmarks: he helped conceive this other Cornwaleys called Walter (born 1240), but this time the boy would not become a priest, but the founder of yet another line. It was the two boys, his namesake Walter, and a younger child, John, who were in due time to be the results of his own marriage to a lady called Cristina.

It is at this point that we must consider the arrangements made by their father for the futures of Richard and Walter de Cornubia. We can learn to some extent what those were from the list of estates owing fees to Earl Edmund or his widow, Margaret, second daughter of the 2nd Earl of Gloucester. What we particularly learn is that Richard was amply provided for with the manors of Eure in Buckinghamshire, Esthall in Oxfordshire and Thumek in Lincolnshire. Other evidence points to there having been a further property which was in his gift, the Manor or 'Court' of Saint Stephen's in Brannell, otherwise briefly called Branel. This had first belonged to his father, the Earl Richard.

Richard was therefore well provided for and it is to be noted that when he died fighting for Edward I in 1296 Eure and Branel were beqeathed to his son Geoffrey whilst Edmund was given Esthall and Thumek. It was thus that the Cornwall branch of Earl Richard's 'familia' were provided for. But what happened to Walter? Did the fact that he was an 'afterthought' born some ten years after his now well established eldest brother and with a sister and 'priestly' brother arranged for, create a special problem for his royal parent? We can guess that his coffers were now seriously stretched as a Crusade and then a bid for the German Crown were undertaken?

What we know, and this we gather from the estates list of Edmund, is that in 1301 the Earl Edmund's widow, Margaret, laid a plea before the King's Justice as follows: "Branel. The said Margaret seeks 1/2 of the manor and of the advowson of the church as her dower against Walter de Cornubia; who says that the said earl (Edmund) gave the same to him and his heirs and he offered the earl's charter which testifies this . . ." Judgement was at that stage withheld but on Margaret repeating her plea three years later it was stated in a royal 'Extent' that the manor and the advowson of the church at Branel were the rightful property of the said Walter de Cornubia.

What does all this suggest? We know for sure that it was certainly the intention of Richard de Cornubia to leave the Court/Manor of Branel to his eldest son. There is even evidence to show that one of Geoffrey's children, also called Geoffrey, was born at Branel c.1275 and that he went on to become a Carmelite friar. Yet the death of Geoffrey without assignable issue meant that Earl Edmund was able to reallocate what then reverted to him as part of his father's original property. That he knew all about the 'natural siblings ' in his family is undoubted and he would be aware that the youngest of them in Cornwall, Walter, had been given the advowson of the church at Branel as well as a place there to grow up in. We know for instance that the core of this property comprised two farms and a mill. If therefore this was where the first 'Cornwaleys' family was established and where the boys, Walter Junior and John were born and brought up then it is not at all surprising that when the manor came once more into Earl Edmund's gift he should award it to the son, Walter, who had now succeeded his father.

What still needs to be explained is that St. Stephen-in-Brannell, as it is now more simply called, is just 4 miles to the west of St. Austell. In the period with which we are dealing the extent of the manor included most of the land now included between Probus in the west, St. Mawan to the east, St. Denis to the north and Creed to the south. Looked at on the map it is half of the area that might in those days have been called the jurisdiction of St. Austell. This no doubt provides the explanation of why the younger Walter and John were called 'de Scto. Austolo'. That was the area to which they belonged and where they had grown up. In a very real sense Walter Junior was to remain a St. Austell landowner. It was a place where the 'Cornwaleys' members first established a home. That could well be why in his latter days Archdeacon Philip, the uncle, made one more gift to his native land. He endowed in perpetuity a chantry in the Church at St. Austell. He was, I suggest, acknowledging where the members of his family first belonged and where they, like himself, should be constantly remembered.

CHAPTER 2

Taking Root

We do not know precisely when the first Walter le Cornwaleys died but we do know that Cristina le Cornwaleys, his widow, appears on the London Hustings Rolls (H) for the year 1283 and he must therefore have died before that date. What this further suggests is that leaving his son, also Walter, to raise his family in the heart of Cornwall at Branel, Walter and his wife had become householders, if not more, in the City of London. This is further confirmed by two more references to Walter le Cornwaleys on the same Rolls in 1273 and 1276. Nor is this all.

In a volume entitled "Memorials of London Life in the 13th, 14th and 15th centuries (1276-1419)" written by Henry Thomas Riley (and published by Longmans Green in 1868) we read that in 1277/8 a 'Roll of Felonies committed and misadventures that happened in the City of London' was compiled. Therein we note the phrase, "Walter le Cornwaleys and John Adrien being then Sheriffs" (p. 17). Later in that book (p. 376) we learn that the same Cornwaleys, also called 'L'Englys', was a member of the Vintners' Company and represented Broad Street Ward on the Common Council from 1278 to 1281. We may also note a Henry le Waleys who was a Cordwainer and Mayor in 1283 (see pp. 263, 375). We shall return to this name a little later.

It is true that the names Cornwaleys or Engleys are not found amongst the few Aldermen mentioned in the Guildhall records of that time but Walter is described as 'Alderman of that Ward' in connection with some property in the parish of St. Margaret's, Lothbury (see Ancient Deeds A 2261). As this was mentioned during the tenure of the Mayoralty by one, Rokesle(y), and at the time when Romdeve and Wyatter were Sheriffs it means that his membership of the Common Council in this capacity would be between September 1280 and September 1281. The parish of St. Margaret's includes portions of Broad Street and Coleman Street and since Walter L'Engleys was chosen towards the end of the Sheriffs' year to fill a vacancy in Broad Street Ward caused by the death of the former Councillor, W. Bukerel, this may account for no official notice being made of the change.

In the light of all this information it now seems as if the first Walter le Cornwaleys died around 1281/2 as this would account for his not continuing in this Common Council position and for the introduction of another name in the Broad Street Ward seat. His widow was therefore quick to substitute her name for his in the records since that would ensure certain rights and privileges. What is even clearer is that the family were already, within one generation, closely connected with the City of London and this makes the subsequent emergence of Thomas Cornwaleys (or Cornewayle) as a Sheriff almost a century later immediately more understandable. Yet before we come to that illustrious member of the family line there is much more that we can say about the intervening growth of this family.

The reader may recall that in the first chapter mention was made of the fact that some historians believe Earl Richard to have had some illegitimate children by other ladies. As we now begin to discover other names and dates attached to Cornwaleys men, and maidens, which are contemporary with Walter and his sons that inference begins to grow into a likelihood.

Before we turn to the detail of these further names I must first deal with what some might regard as an alternative solution to the fairly sudden emergence of a whole spate of persons called 'Cornewaleys'. This contention is that the term 'Cornewaleys' was not a generic term pointing to relationship from a common ancestor but rather a contemporary method of distinguishing a person's place of origin. It is true that there were such terms in use in England at this period. 'Englys' and 'Waleys' appear in the City records of the day and could certainly suggest that either the person was English or Welsh - though the word 'waleys' like the word 'Wales' still meant 'stranger' or 'foreigner'. It is therefore perfectly possible that the term 'Cornewaleys' could be interpreted as 'a stranger (or incomer) from Cornwall' and have no more significance than that. What persistently militates against that interpretation here is the limitation of the name to areas where there is a definite link with Earl Richard and the cessation of the term's use once we have a name firmly established, as with Thomas Cornwalleys (or Cornwallis), the Sheriff of London in 1374. (In this connection see also the evidence of changing surnames in Southampton, pp. 32ff below.)

Thereafter the name 'Corn(e)wal(l)eys' has only one meaning - a member of a distinguishable family which can be shown to be interrelated. Yet this is only 4 or 5 generations after the term first appears. I believe this to be too much of a coincidence and I therefore propose to work on the supposition that Richard, Walter, Philip de Cornubia and Isabella did have brothers and sisters who were born of Earl Richard by other 'spouses'.

Let us begin with what was probably their first family tree:

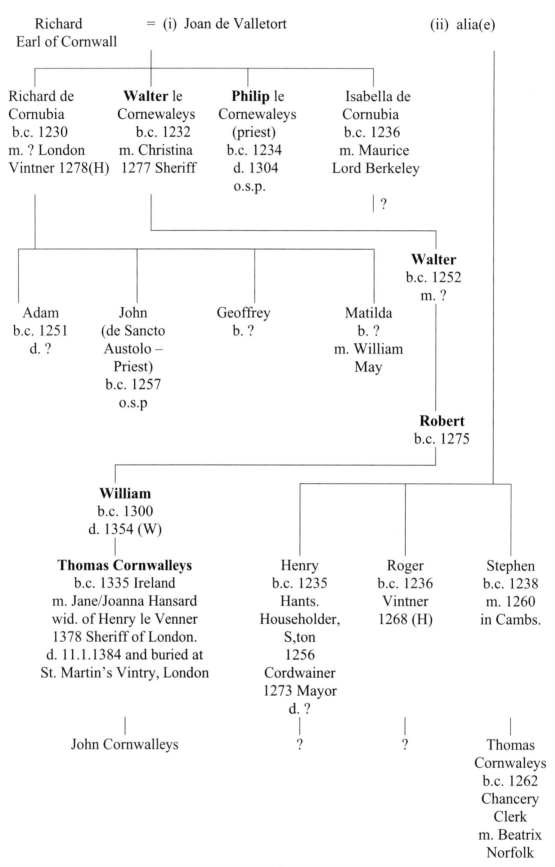

The London evidence in the 14th century

An American genealogist, G. Andrews Moriarty, writing in the 1956 volume of the 'New England Historical and Genealogical Register' made the following interesting observations:

"The family of Cornwallis first appears in London in the first half of the 14th century in the person of William Cornwallis, a London citizen and merchant, living in the parish of All Hallows, Stanyng. Little is known about him, but he apparently also owned property in the London parish of Stebenheath (now Stepney) where his immediate successors were extensive property owners. There are over 400 deeds relating to the London properties of the family at the Guildhall . . . and the late Mr. Walter Rye printed and published (in *The Genealogist*, new series, vol. iv, pp. 98ff) a very valuable group of deeds relating to their London property, once preserved in the family's muniment room at Brome Hall, in Suffolk.' (p. 121)

As we have already seen this statement is no longer the whole truth because evidence is now available showing that an ancestor of William Cornwalleys was already beginning to establish the holding of London property by the 1270s. This fact the more explains why, by the middle of the 14th century, this particular branch of the family was already somewhat advanced in the property market. These things do take time to build up and if we are correct then the efforts made by William had already been well grounded in the work of his father, Robert, and his grandfather Walter, whom we mentioned at the outset of this chapter. What is undoubted is that when William made his will at Stepney on 26 August 1354 he asked that his rents be applied for "the provision of masses for the souls of the testator and his wife, Alice". Such a provision itself shows that William must have been a man of means since such a bequest could only have been made by someone who had a certain surplus of funds. The will (recorded in the Hustings Wills Vol. 1, p. 680) also reveals that he was a widower at the time, his wife having predeceased him, and it adds that his kinsman, John Tintagel, (was this one of his wife's family?), was to be guardian of his son, Thomas. Since this means that Thomas had not yet reached adulthood, albeit by 1359 he is registered as a member of the Vintners' Company, he must have been born between 1333 and 1338.

Before we turn to the much fuller and better documented life of Thomas Cornwalleys it would seem proper if some indication were given of how and from where we obtain the information relating to other members of the Cornewaleys family in the late 13th and early 14th century. Our starting point has to be the Hustings, or early voting, Rolls from the City of London archives. These reveal the following names:

Adam de Cornewaleys	1276	(H.8/3)
Christina, widow of Walter	1283	(H.14/91, 92, 157)
Matilda, daughter of Richard	1305	(H.34/17)
Richard, Vintner	1278	(H.9/69)
Roger, Vintner	1278	(H.9/69)
Walter, called be Cornewaleys	1276	(H.8/5)
Walter le Cornewaleys	1283	(H.14/91, 92, 157)
Walter, Skinner	1298	(H.28/22)

As a further confirmation we have an extract from the Bridge House Deeds which are now kept in the Guildhall archives. Whilst these are specially useful for the family's London concerns after 1400 we do have one item (B/9) that is dated in early 1273. It reads:

Indenture: Grant by John de Breynford, Chaplain, to Adam de Montacute and Alicia his wife of his tenement in the parish of St. Mary Magdalene, Old Fish Street, lying between the tenement of the same John towards the South and the tenement belonging to Geoffrey de Lung towards the North and the king's highway towards the East and the tenement formerly belonging to Adam le Cornwaleys towards the West for an annual rent . . .

> Witness: Sir Walter Heremy, then Mayor
> John Horn & Walter be Poder, Sheriffs.

The last mention of Adam in Guildhall records is 1300 but of course there is no guarantee as to whether that signified his death. Other members referred to in the foregoing trees are mentioned other Guildhall records as follows:

> Henry   1256;   Stephen 1260;   Robert   1291.

How the family had begun to acquire property in and around the City is clearly indicated when we examine the background of inheritance that was to lead to the establishment of Thomas Cornwalleys, William's son. We are able to follow the sequence by examining the documents found in the Brome property muniment room.

To assist in understanding the story at this point another short genealogical tree may help:

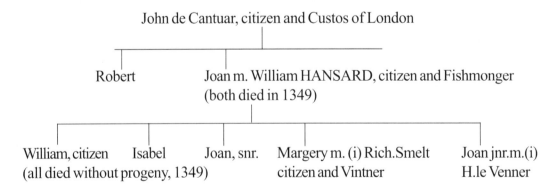

Henry le Venner, citizen and Vintner, also died in 1349 and his widow married another Vintner, Thomas Cornwalleys, sometime before 1368.

Joan's inheritance came in the following manner. In 1272 Richard de Exemue, citizen of London, died leaving a will that required his wife to find a chaplain for masses in St. Dunstan's 'versus Turrim' (towards the Tower). In 1286 his son, also Richard, granted to John de Cantuar all that land with houses and 'schop' in the parish of St. Dunstan 'versus Turrim' which were of Robert de Garscherche.

In 1330 Richard de Gloucester deeded 13 acres of meadow in Middlesex to William Hansard, Senior and 3 years later Edmund Crepyn deeded 4 acres of meadow in Old Ford to William. William had, as we have noted above, married Joan, the daughter of John de Cantuar and in 1338 Robert Cantuar, Joan's elder brother, mortgaged to William, who now lived in the parish of St. Dunstan 'versus Turrim', a garden in St. Botolph's without Aldgate.

Meanwhile in 1335, Mary, now the widow of Edmund Crepyn, deeded to William Hansard her dower rights in the lands she had in Stepney, where William and Robert Cornewalleys had already acquired property, and also at St. Mary Magdalen in Middlesex.

Just prior to his death, as also that of his wife and 3 eldest children, all of them almost certainly dying due to the heavy onset of the Black Death in the late 1340s, the land at Old Ford, the tenement and curtilage at St. Botolph's without Aldgate, now Aldersgate, all the lands and houses which are shown to have come to William Hansard, Junior through marrying Alice Trentemars, and finally 86 acres of prime land in Stepney, were deeded to Henry le Venner and William Hansard's younger daughter Joan. Yet Henry le Venner also perished with the plague in 1349 and his widow was left with a sizeable inheritance and no children. Nor was this all. In 1350 Richard Smelt, husband of Joan's immediately elder sister, Margery, as well as other Fishmongers of London, deeded to Joan, as a widow, all the lands, tenements and appurtenances in St. Botolph's, at Old Ford, Poplar and Stepney.

Moreover, at or just before the time Thomas Cornwalleys married Joan le Venner (or Fanner) we see that he too was engaged in extending his inherited wealth. In 1359 he buys a 'messuage' with garden in St. Botolph's from Adam and Margery Pope; and in 1360 a tenement in the same parish from William de Essex. It is no surprise therefore to learn that by the mid-1360s Thomas was a resident of St. Botolph's parish, established principally in the wine trade, and seeking to represent his Vintry Ward in the Court of Common Council. By 1376 he was an Alderman, as also in 1379, 1381, 1383 and 1384; a Sheriff in 1378; and by 1380 he was a Burgess for London in the House of Commons. He died on 4 January 1386.

The Irish connection

We cannot leave Thomas Cornwalleys entirely at this point because not only shall we have to encounter him in connection with the life and activities of his son, John, but there remains an intriguing aspect of his origins which no-one has seemingly addressed hitherto. I refer to the claim that he was born in Ireland. Why this should have been and where it may have taken place has intrigued me ever since starting this family trail and I now want to suggest a possible solution to the 'mystery'. I have to add that a more conclusive answer to these questions is unlikely to be achieved until I have examined sources that are only available in Dublin, Kilkenny and Waterford (or Wexford?) and that I have so far not been able to arrange.

In the article mentioned earlier by G. Andrews Moriarty there is the following statement:

"The old pedigrees state that the family originated in Ireland, but no proof of this is forthcoming and it seems more likely that their place of origin was the county of Cornwall." (p. 123)

For the family as a whole there can I think now be no doubt as to its Cornwall, if not Cornish, provenance but the Irish connection is recognized and in the accepted armorial tree of the family it states more precisely that Thomas Cornwaliss was 'born in Ireland'. Why and how could that be?

There are, I believe, three factors which conduce to such a possibility. They are: the development of family fortunes, the advantages of being colonizers and the dangers of plague at home. I propose to examine each of these factors in turn and then to suggest why what we have discovered would lead to the likelihood of Thomas's Irish 'birth'.

It is manifest that following the decease of Earl Richard and his son, Edmund, the members of the Cornwall and Cornwallis families would have to fend for themselves in establishing both their place in Society and their personal fortunes. I indicated in chapter 1 that whilst there would be some lesser manors that might be allocated as the starting places for their development these would only be available so long as it pleased the Earl Richard's direct descendants. Edmund, Richard's heir, was dead by 1300 and thereafter the Crown assumed the Duchy of Cornwall as a Royal prerogative for the King's eldest son. It may well have been that event that sharpened the awareness of the various members of the Cornewalleys branch that they would have to discover their own self-made sources of income. Considering their origins there were really only five lines to follow: profession of arms, profession of faith, landholding and management, property (and city government) or trade.

There is, in the earliest records available, not the slightest indication of any involvement of the family in military service. Though this would change with time we can at once dispense with any notion of finding a Cornwallis in this particular field for the next 200 years. It was not the same with the sacred ministry. Examples have already been provided of several men who chose this vocation. It was not the way to make the family fortune, however, since even if a mediaeval priest had a concubine and offspring they could not inherit whatever favours or incomes he might enjoy in his lifetime.

That landholding and estate management were within their sights at an early stage soon becomes obvious but unless land is inherited it has to be sought and purchased and neither profitable marriages nor estates can be claimed without some financial standing. It was thus, I believe, inevitable that without descending into 'artisanship' or 'craftsmanship', both of which were then very closed shops in any case, the only viable options in the years after leaving Branel were property acquisition in the City of London - or some such city elsewhere - and engagement in trade. It was to both of these ventures that the second Walter le Cornewaleys turned his attention and his hand and from which the subsequent successes of the family grew. And we know that the trade was largely, though almost certainly not only, in wine.

What has to be accepted as part of the Cornewaleys picture at this stage is a comparative silence about the activities and the whereabouts of the descendants of Walter le Cornewaleys, Junior between 1270 and 1340. Bearing in mind that this covers just the period when any expectation of special assistance from near-Court or eminently-noble circles was decreasing or ceased it is not unreasonable to presume that Walter Junior would have encouraged his son (or sons) to stretch their wings and look for opportunities of advancement wherever they might be found. One of the most likely places was Ireland.

We know that Richard, Earl of Cornwall, had by 1246 surrendered all his direct 'rights' to the forfeited Irish lands of the Marshals, Butlers and de Braose over which King Henry III gave him the guardianship from time to time. Yet we also know that Richard had endeared himself to his 'temporary' wards and their tenants and that not least by his marriage to the daughter of William Marshal he was persona grata in at least the south-eastern parts of that island. Anyone who could claim relationship to him in the succeeding half-century might not be without benefit in trying to establish legitimate business activities in that area. But what opportunities for work and expansion of trade were there in Ireland between 1250 and 1350?

It is here that we begin to discover that there were indeed prospects for immigrants or colonizers across the Irish Sea at this time. Let me quote from one of the latest histories of Medieval Ireland by A.J. Otway-Ruthven (1968):

"By the end of the 13th century, as the evidence already cited shows, in many areas settlers of English descent formed at least half the population, and sometimes considerably more, and all along the east coast, in the inland counties of Leinster, in south Tipperary, Waterford, and parts of Cork and Limerick there had been a relatively heavy immigration . . .

"Where did the settlers come from? Many of the greatest men, Strongbow himself, the de Lacys, and others, came from the marcher lordships of south Wales . . Other settlers came from Devon and Cornwall (Deveneys and Cornwaleys are both names commonly found); from Lancashire, like the de Salmesburys of Moycarkey, who must have come with the Butlers from their Lancashire lands; from Derbyshire, like the Dowdalls of co. Louth, whose name was originally Douedale (or Dovedale) . . .

17

There were "clearly very considerable inducements drawing men to Ireland" and one of these was that the "establishment of towns was of great importance. Reference has already been made to the many villages which had the elements of an urban constitution but towns proper were a very different matter, and were to be one of the main bastions of Norman power . . . Those important enough to be centres in which customs were collected under Edward I (1272-1307) were, in order of the magnitude of the sums collected, New Ross, Waterford, Cork, Drogheda, Dublin, Youghal . . . New Ross and Waterford each regularly produced more than twice as much as any other port, but this concentration of export through the ports of the south-east declined in Edward's later years.

This author goes on to outline "the brisk and lively trade in the hey-day of the colony" by showing that the main staples, from which tolls could be levied to erect walls and bridges, were wine, salt and foodstuffs, with horses, cattle, wool, cloth, iron, tin and timber as additionally significant items. This picture is enhanced by the material produced in E.C. Curtis's book, 'History of Mediaeval Ireland from 1086 to 1513' (1938). He writes:

"The principal import trade was in wine, and the amount shipped to Ireland from the royal dependencies of Anjou, Acquitaine, and Gascony was very great. Not only was there enough to supply the king's castles in Ireland, the justiciar's expeditionary forces and the private cellars of ecclesiastics, Norman barons and Gaelic chieftains, but large quantities were from time to time re-shipped to supply the Welsh castles and the armies led into Wales and Scotland . . . In January 1300, 3,000 hogsheads of wine were ordered from Ireland to be sent to Skinburness. Waterford seems to have had the largest share in this trade, but all the other principal ports participated in it in greater or lesser degree . . . . (and) contrary to what might be supposed . . . Ireland in the latter half of the 13th century and the beginning of the 14th exported large quantities of grain. As early as 1225 the Mayor of London bought 1,000 crannocks of wheat from the 2nd Earl William Marshal (sic) in Ireland, and there are other examples of the private export of grain to England, Scotland and France . . . For all the (military) expeditions to Scotland to the end of Edward's reign (1300-1307) large supplies of similar victuals were obtained from Ireland." (pp. 275ff) Here, surely, was a ready-made niche for a merchant family wanting to make its way.

There was also the help of the Church. It was just at this time that another Cornewaleys was regularly being sent on missions to Ireland and the Continent by the Bishop of Winchester, John of Pontoise. Uncle Philip, as he would be known to Walter Junior's children was not an Archdeacon for nothing and one can be quite sure that if there were any way in which he could make contacts, promote the family name or carry messages across the water he would be both able and willing to do so. It is worth recording that in 1282 Cardinal Benedict Gaetani, who was to become Pope Boniface VIII in 1294, appointed Philip to be one of his Chaplains, whilst in 1287 the Bishop of Winchester nominated him as his Proctor when the Bishop could not attend Convocation. His was a position and a voice of some consequence and what is made very clear by Curtis is that it was just at this time that the Irish Church was being drawn closer to England and hence Rome and the importance of official 'visitors' from England was at its height.

In the light of all these factors it is increasingly my conviction that without weakening their purpose of seeking a more established position in the City of London the Cornwalleys's net was spread over one or more of these trading outlets in south-eastern Ireland, as we shall shortly see was also the case in the port of Southampton. Waterford, with its links to the Butler family, seems especially likely as the second export city of importance though Wexford with its Marshal connections has also to be considered. I can well see Robert being despatched to such a centre to expand the family's trade revenues and then requiring his son William to spend a period out there. What is certain, according to Clarencieux King of Arms in 1561 is that William's son, Thomas, was born in the Emerald Isle.

The third factor which cannot be overlooked is the very real threat of famine and plague that began to affect Western Europe in the early 14th century. Philip Ziegler in his standard work on 'The Black Death' reminds us that "there were famines in England in 1272, 1277, 1283, 1292 and 1311. Between 1315 and 1319 came a crescendo of calamity. Almost every country in Europe lost virtually the whole of one harvest, often two or three. The lack of sun hindered the production of salt by evaporation and thus made still more difficult the conservation of what meat there was. In England wheat more than doubled in price . . . Nor was this the end: 1332 was another disastrous year for the crops and the period between 1345 and 1348 would have seemed uniquely unfortunate in any other century."

It is in the midst of all this catastrophe that we again set the facts which were recorded above about the provisions supplied by and through Ireland. Here was one of the countries that suffered least prior to the final access of the Black Death in late 1349. Away from the cities and insanitation of Britain and Europe its comparative healthiness and viability as a food store must have made its prospects as a trading and dwelling centre seem the more attractive. What again seems to have been more than likely is that by a measure of segregation from the pains and problems of London Robert, William and Thomas were able to survive where whole families like the Hansards were largely wiped out.

That the members of the Cornwaleys family who might have been involved in Irish trade left the island never to return in that guise is also a fact. They must have left by 1350 or even a little earlier. Their reasons for doing so would be self-evident.

"By 1333 the young King (Ed. III) abandoned the thought of coming to Ireland in person and turned his warlike genius first against the Scots and next against the French. It was a fatal decision for the English interest in Ireland. The colony was at the crisis of its fate . . ." (p. 214, Curtis, op. cit.)

Though the new Viceroy, Darcy, ruled sufficiently well to calm any major revolt this fragile peace lasted only until 1341 when a new ruler, Sir John Morice, sought to replace existing officials with Englishmen whose estates were **wholly in England**. Such men were thought likely to be "more honest and impartial, more efficient and less easily intimidated" but such was the Irish and Anglo-Irish reaction that the Latin Annals of Eire record that 'the Land of Ireland at this moment stood at the point of breaking for ever from the hands of the King of England'.

As trade also had begun to decrease in what was a general decline in the economy of Western Europe it was obviously not the moment to extend one's commitments. If, alongside that pattern of affairs, William had begun successfully to acquire property and standing in Stayning and Stepney, as well as a firm trading base in the City, then it might be time to bring his effects - and his young son - home to England and for good. How he could be sure of avoiding the dreaded effects of the Plague is not known. We are told, for instance, that it caused 3 out of 7 benefices held by the Abbey of Westminster to become vacant by the spring of 1349 and all 8 Wardens of the Company of Cutlers to be dead by the autumn with 4 Wardens of the Goldsmiths. We even learn that the Abbot of Westminster took refuge in his country home at Hampstead but was still an early victim and 27 other monks accompanied him to their graves. That the family did in fact survive is itself note-worthy but the devastation in both Ireland and London meant that a somewhat different society was about to emerge. It was no coincidence that many more properties were for sale in the 1350s and 1360s and those who could acquire them were able to build a much more stable future.

One last effect of the plague is worth noting for it has some bearing on our later story. "William of Wykeham", writes Ziegler, "wishing to cure 'the general disease of the clerical army, which we have observed to be grievously wounded owing to the small number of the clergy, as a result of Pestilence'. . . founded New College to repair the deficiency. But New College owed more to the Black Death than the inspiration for its creation. According to tradition, backed by Thorold Rogers, New College garden was the site of Oxford's largest plague pit, an area formerly covered by houses but depopulated by the epidemic and converted to its grisly purpose." Purchased by William's agent such an investment's "increasing value must have done much to solace future generations for the tribulations of their ancestors". (p. 263)

The Southampton properties

If we have sought to establish by deduction a Cornwalleys trading presence in Ireland we need do no more in the port of Southampton than state what is evident from local records. Before we come to that evidence however it may be as well to establish just how significant Southampton was in the period with which we are here concerned.

By 1226 the Cinque Ports were at the height of their prosperity and jealous of the rise of other harbours that might rival their service to trade. One writer on early Southampton tells us that there were already complaints by Southampton merchants that their cargoes had been seized unlawfully. In this same year the bailiffs of Winchelsea were ordered by the King's Justices to release a ship belonging to one, Colman of Dover, which was carrying hides to the Hampshire port. On 4 May 1252 the Cinque Ports were admonished by King Henry who addressed a writ to the barons on behalf of Southampton and Portsmouth ordering the former not to seize cargoes that the latter's merchants sought freely to deliver and in the century that was to follow we read that Genoese carracks preferred Southampton to Sandwich as London's outport. The approach to Southampton was eased by double tides which prolonged high water for 4 hours and thus bore these heavy vessels up the estuary with ease to the sheltered anchorage below the town walls. From Southampton there was also an easy route to London overland. To the north-west the road through Salisbury gave easy access to the great wool and cloth producing districts of the Cotswolds, while the Italian agents purchasing tin in Cornwall could despatch it in local vessels from the Cornish harbours to the greater port of Southampton.

There was even a plan to establish the main Italian staple for wool in this town until the London merchants entered their objections. This was not a case of 'sour grapes'. Many London merchants did business in Southampton, some through agents, in all sorts of commodities, and in the wine trade theirs was the largest share. It was certainly a place for men who were desirous of 'growing in trade' to become established.

The interest of Richard, Earl of Cornwall, in the area is marked first by a grant of the church of St. Keverne in Cornwall to the Abbot and Chapter of Beaulieu Abbey for his own soul and that of his father, King John. This interest is reinforced when c.1240 Richard makes an annual grant of 10 marks to the Abbey for the soul of his late wife, Isabella of Gloucester.

Nor is this all. In the 'God's House Cartulary, Southampton' (edited by J.M. Kaye, 1976) we read that c.1220-1225 Master Roger of Hampton grants all 'his lands, rents and buildings in Southampton to God's House' and at the same time acknowledges that he pays 'iii solidi' for 'the land belonging to the Earl of Cornwall and that next to it' - a note with the text says that this property is not identified.

However, in 1230 John, son of Ralph Hampton, makes a further grant to Walter le Flemyng and acknowledges 'ii solidi' for the house of one, Reginald Cornubiensis - and now a note states that this was a tenement numbering 467/8 on the High Street just above New, or English, Corner, an area called 'The Shambles' hitherto. (p. 71)
(The location of this tenement is seen on p. 2 of 'Southampton 1454')

On the next page there is mention of tenements 471/2 in the same street, these being held by Isabella Norther who was a tenant successively of Reginald and Richard Cornubiensis who paid 'vi solidi' to God's House: whilst in the next item the mention of St. Lawrence's parish further identifies where these 'Cornwaleys' occupants lived.

The tenement No. 500 opposite All Saints Church is also mentioned as being occupied by an Alicia be Mondenard who paid rent to Henry, son of Richard of Cornwall, and thus we are again in touch with the Henry de Cornubia (or le Cornwaleys) mentioned c.1235 as having been born in Hampshire.

This branch of the family grew. In the 1260s there is a sale recorded in the Cartulary of the Abbey of St. Denys, Southampton, which involves a Hamund (or Hamon) Cornubiensis. He is here agreeing to pay the widow, Marchebrune Burdin of Portsmouth, a lump sum of 11s and an annual sum of '1/4lb cummin' to purchase the house for which he used to pay 12d rent.

What is of further interest is that in the next entry we learn how Hamund, with the agreement of his wife, Alicia, donated as alms to the Church of St. Denys the 12d annual rent which he used to pay to the widow, Marchebrune. We even learn that the house was 'in suburbio Suth't' which meant outside the walls of the town, and 'in East Street by the causeway on the right as one goes to St. Mary's Church'. (p. 76)
(One can plot this property as being by the Nos. 70-71 on the 1454 map).

That this is not an isolated family reference is revealed later on in the same Cartulary (p. 134) where we are told that from 1233 to 1252 a certain Nigel Character paid 12d annually to the Priory for tenure of a house in Above Bar Gate which stood between the houses of Roger Whit(e) and John le Cornwalais (sic). The two families figure again in another entry for the period 1253-1258 when John Burgeis and his wife, Cecily, pay John Marcial (Marshall) "for a tenement and curtilage 'in suburbio' outside the North (or Bar) Gate on the west of the Street between the house lately held by Baldwyn le Whit(e) and that of William le Cornwalleis (sic) . . ." The rent is 'ii solidi' to God's House and 3d to the parish of St. Lawrence.

To complete the local 14th century picture we learn that William le Cornwaleys had a daughter, Cecilia, who in 1327 paid 3d rent for the house which she had obviously inherited from her father and which she shared with a Cecilia Felemet. A map of the St. Denys Rentals in 1349 actually shows where this property stood in Above Bar and in relation to the present street system. It is fascinating to see that whilst she lived at No. 16, No. 2 was called Little Hampton, a Henry Flemyng lived at No. 5, Baldwin Le Whyte at No. 12, the clergy of St. Mary's at No. 14, and a Thomas Neel in No. 17. It was a William Neel who had been a witness to grants made by Hamon le Cornwaleys almost a century earlier, whilst an entry in the city records states that from 1350 to 1625 when the rent was written off No. 14 was described as the 'garden of St. Mary's precentor between the houses first of Baldwyn le Whit and William le Cornwaleys. 10a was already a tenement called 'Brasyers' owned by the College of William Wykeham at Winchester.

It can be seen that the family was perhaps more extensive in this late 13th and early 14th century than might previously have been imagined. When to this list we add a Michael le Cornwaleys, an attorney who is negotiating the sale of land at Whippingham in the Isle of Wight at Candlemas in 1272, and a Geoffrey de Cornubia who in May 1315 is paying homage to King Henry for the bands of Margaret his wife, the daughter and co-heiress of Hugh de Montmorency, deceased of Salop, we know that our search is probably far from over. What is clear is that members of the family were beginning to reproduce in abundance and that property and trade were now their lively concern.

CHAPTER 3

Spreading the Roots

The continuing London roots

John Cornwallis (though still usually recorded as Cornewaleys) was a citizen and merchant in London like his father. We do not know exactly when he was born though we have already seen that his parents, Thomas and Johanna (or Joan), married sometime before 1368. It is likely, however, that his birth was between 1362 and 1365 because in 1383 we have a Deed recording a transaction for 20 marks for 4 acres in the parish of Stebenheath (Stepney) made between John and his parents. This would suggest that the former had by this time reached a legal age and that he was therefore between 18 and 21 years old.

The City and its life into which he was born has, in the last century, been very fully described as a result of much more complete research into 14th and 15th century documents. John would, for example, have heard his father explain the positions of Sheriff and Alderman, those having been already attained in the family. Originally the Wards of the City "were in the hands of the landowners, and the alderman was still very much in the position of a 'lord of the manor'. His office was at first always, and still usually, hereditary. These 'barons' of the city, as they were often called, formed amongst themselves an oligarchy, and ruled the merchant guild, an association which had control of the civic government, the revenues, and the trade regulations." Such was the case in the time of Walter le Cornwaleys when there was also the confusion of having aldermen of the wards and also of the guilds.

All this changed when in 1327 Edward III granted the charters that established the 12 great Liveries, which included the Vintners. Whether these bodies were the direct successors of the guilds is a matter still to be resolved though it is obvious that at the outset some of the actual members of the Liveries were those who had hitherto been guildsmen.

As these Companies flourished with their royal recognition so the City officers whom they elected also grew in importance. In 1354 Edward III granted the right for silver maces to he carried before the Mayor and Sheriffs whilst two pillars or posts were permitted to be set up outside the homes of not only these citizens but also of each alderman. The pillars were painted gold for the Mayor whilst the others had gilded or coloured ones and on these posts were displayed the Royal Proclamations which passers-by might only read after removing their caps in respect. It is no surprise therefore to read in 1421 that a complaint was laid against John Cornwallis that the posts outside his house in Aldgate Without were causing obstruction to the movement of carts in what was an increasingly busy thoroughfare. It would appear that the posts erected in his father's time as Sheriff were still in place.

Concern for public well-being was the nub of the Alderman's duties. Besides assessing the arms of all within his Ward this officer had to be assured that any gate in his jurisdiction was manned by 12 strong men during the day and by 24 at night. He was responsible for their regular inspection at sunrise and sunset to ensure that the men were present, and to help in this task Bedels (or Beadles) were appointed who kept the names and addresses of all who made up the guard. Possible dangers in the unlit streets constantly occupied the citizens' minds and it was having a strong Alderman in each Ward that mainly suppressed disorder. In 1370, moreover, there was the threat of a French attack and the Livery Companies were given the especial task of defending the riverside area from the Tower to Billingsgate. The Vintners, of which John's father was then a member, were required to mount guard each Friday, along with the Pelterers or Poulterers.

Mention of this possible attack should remind us that it was not Cheapside or Eastcheap, Thames Street or the Strand which was the highway of the City, but the Thames itself: and because larger craft could not pass through London Bridge Billingsgate long surpassed Queenhithe in the number and importance of its ships and the size of its trade. The threat of a landing there by the French was particularly acute.

Yet John's father would no doubt have described how in 1356 the bad state of the roads just outside the City Gates was tackled and a toll was levied on all carts and horses using them to enable repairs to be undertaken. In 1358 the Sheriffs of Middlesex and London were commanded 'to cleanse the streets from dirt and all impurities and to gravel Bishopsgate and Aldgate against the coming of the body of Queen Isabel, the King's mother'. Constant attempts to keep the London streets cleaner occurred during John's lifetime and in 1389 Parliament issued a proclamation requiring that "no person whatsoever should presume to lay any dung, guts, garbage, offals, or ordure in any street, ditch, etc. upon the penalty of £20" - the equivalent of a then Master Mason's annual pay. It was also arranged that carts should call at people's houses, and carry off their refuse in barrels, to be used in the country as manure.

Do we wonder that those who could do so would steadily move eastwards from the inner city to live in more salubrious surroundings? Eastcheap, where the family at this time had property, was a noisy place. People stumbled over baskets of hens, ducks and geese, and were deafened by the screeching of all the birds that flew beneath the heavens seeking scraps. Here cooks were for ever preparing roasts and stews, and the air reeked with a wholesome scent of crackling. The Cheap was the very beginning and end of the world. Everyone who would meet anyone gathered there. Such at least is the description given by Sir Walter Besant in his book on 'Medieval London'.

It was in Thomas and John Cornwallis's day that the familiar 'frame' houses of strong and thick oak, folded in with plaster, began to be built on the south side of Cheap. Rising to three or four storeys they were covered with carved woodwork and would display on their fronts the sign of the trade or even the arms of the Livery Company to which the owner belonged. When, as in the case of Thomas Cornwallis, the owner was granted his coat of arms these too would be carved or painted above the door. Yet as the family moved into Stepney their house also would grow. There would now be a gateway, with its posts before it, and an inner courtyard with rooms arranged around it.

For a member of a merchant household such as the Cornwallis's the day would start early. A light breakfast, in the modern French style, but with milk, mead or ale, would be taken and then the family would attend Mass, either in St. Botolph's, Holy Trinity or at a private celebration in their own home. We know that by 1379 Thomas Cornwallis employed a private chaplain named Richard and this priest actually lodged on the premises. This might even have meant that there was a small chapel with a priest's room attached.

The rest of the morning would then be spent in an office at the house or somewhere in the Vintry Ward, or overseeing work at the busy riverside. A little example of what business occupied Thomas is shown in the Close Rolls for September 1372 when Thomas is one of the merchants requesting permission for a ship that had brought wines from Bordeaux to be allowed free passage immediately. Permission is given provided the ship does not sail close to Sandwich until the King has safely embarked there for a trip to France. By 11 a.m., the fashionable dinner hour, the business day would be over and a merchant's attention could now be given to his family or City duties. Civic banquets or an evening meal with the household would usually take place at around 6 p.m. and by 9 the way to bed beckoned, unless some special event occurred.

One other feature of merchant life deserves mention. Being wealthy and pious the merchants were continually rebuilding, beautifying or enlarging the 103 churches within and without the walls. The mere fact that there were so many churches indicates that many of them were very small and with minute 'parishes'. In the area of the Vintry so well known to the Cornwallises there were 5 parishes in an area 1600 feet long and only 400 feet wide along the edge of the river. None of these parishes covered more than 4 acres and St. Martin's, where Thomas and John were buried, comprised exactly 1/3 acre. The church buildings had first of all been wooden structures, with walls made up of trunks cut down the middle and laid one upon the other. The first Norman inhabitants started to erect stone chapels but it was only now, in the mid-14th century, that there was capital to spare for improving these tiny dark churches. Within the next hundred years the benefactions of the City merchants were to provide higher roofs, stained glass, richer furnishings and chantry chapels with priests and singing boys.

That this family took its part in this transformation is proved by various entries in the registers of churches in differing areas of the City. In 1359, 1363 and 1379 Thomas Cornewaleys granted a year's rent from various of his tenement properties for the upkeep of St. Botolph's without Aldgate; whilst in 1383, just prior to his death, he allocated to St.

George's in Eastcheap the rents from adjacent buildings that he owned. His son, John, was to confirm this gift later and he had already granted £5 per annum for a chantry 'de Jesore' at St. Martin's Vintry as well as contributing to new building at All Hallows Gracechurch and St. John's Walbrook. John is also noted as one of the parties who in 1412 agreed to allocate the rents of tenements alongside St. Botolph's without Aldgate for the erection of a chantry to pray for a distinguished local citizen.

Whilst John thus assumed his father's mantle as a church benefactor he is specially to be commended for his concern in another direction. In 1406 a complaint was laid before the Mayor, Aldermen and Common Council by William Cressewyck, John Cornwallis and John Westone regarding the housing of women prisoners in Newgate gaol. They contended that the women were housed in too small a chamber and that when the women wished to relieve nature they were compelled to cross another cell called the Bocardo where were housed some of the worst male prisoners. They did this "ever to their great shame and hurt". The petitioners requested the City Fathers for a plot of land adjacent to the gaol where they would erect a stone tower with proper facilities to be used solely for the securing of women prisoners. Their request was granted on the sole understanding that the City be at no expense in its erection and that it be employed for women only. Such concern for the desperate in the early 15th century is not that frequent and is all the more commendable. Was it also due to the public interest of such citizens that in 1416 the lighting of the City streets was at last made compulsory?

Yet if the family were concerned about the houses of God and the housing of prisoners they were no less aware of their own property responsibilities. Recognizing that the Cornwallises reflect the general tendencies amongst their contemporaries it is worth noting what Kevin McDonnell says in his fascinating book about 'Medieval London Suburbs':

"Far and away more significant than the 'foreign' settlers were the Englishmen of standing who built up estates for themselves or purchased suburban seats in the eastern suburbs. From the 13th century onwards Londoners and courtiers with money to invest looked to the opportunities which awaited them outside the City. Many examples of this practice are to be found." (p. 126) The Cornwallises were no exception.

In May 1370 we have an indenture between Henry Venner, the son of Joanna Cornwaleys by her first husband, his mother and Thomas certifying that Henry grants and releases the estate of Erdgode le Popeler and other plots in Stepney to them since the former property had been a gift to Joanna from certain men here named. It was even probable that this manor had been held earlier by the Black Prince. Notwithstanding this acquisition we also learn that in February 1384 William Kenyon, Thomas's chaplain, was appointed by John's parents to deliver 'seisin' or possession of 4 acres mentioned above and now called 'Bollmede' in Oldaforth (Aldgate). It seems very likely that this step was in order to secure a separate dwelling place for John's mother since his father was to die within the year. In May 1388 we have a deed issued by a John Branyll, citizen and butcher of London, granting a parcel of land with a garden in St. Botolph 'extra Algate juxta Turrim' which was alongside the lands of the widow, Joan Cornwaleys. In view of what we learnt in the last chapter about the siting of the Cornwallis estates in or near the City it seems very clear that this was the area in which they now felt most 'at home'.

This is further confirmed by other events. On 6 February 1417 William Colville, Esq., along with others, appointed 2 persons to secure possession for John Cornwallis of a manor called 'le Bernes' in the parishes of St. Botolph without Aldgate and Stepney. A British Museum MS. informs us that this was an extensive estate involving three parishes, St. Botolph without Aldgate, Whitechapel and Stepney, and we know that John was still in possession of it in 1429. What is even more interesting from a family point of view is that John's only surviving daughter, Catherine (or Katharine), was to marry this same William Colville (or Clovyle) of Hanningfield, Essex, having been his ward under her father's will. The Colevilles had been in Essex for over 200 years and around 1270 we learn that a Master William de Colvill is receiving a gift from Warren Mownkensey in West Hanningfield. It is also to be noted that a R. de Coleville was a survivor of the Battle of Senlac and thus, as with the Tyrells whom we shall meet later, the Cornwallis roots were expanding in the true Norman soil from which they themselves came.

It is worth reminding ourselves that Stepney "at the time of the Conquest and for long after was a centre of fashion . . . If the Abbot of Westminster had the manor of St. Margaret's extending west from the wall to Chelsea, the Bishop of London had a counter-balancing estate in the east: for Stepney extended from Aldgate to the River Lea, and from the Thames to the northern hills" (or Hackney). This was called the 'lord's hold' and from the Bishop's list of tenants "we gather that some great men of the court, some of the City and some of the Church lived here".

W.J. Loftie in his book on 'The History of London' goes on to say that "these great persons lived either about Bishopsgate, outside the wall, or at Stepney itself, near the Church of St. Dunstan". This St. Dunstan's was of course 'in-the-East' and is not to be confused with the St. Dunstan's-in-the-West in Fleet Street.

Another glimpse of Stepney's status is given by the fact that "in 1299 Edward I held a Parliament in Stepney at the house of the Mayor of London, Henry le Waleys. The Mayor's country house must have been a palace." It is therefore not inappropriate to recall that in November 1280 Walter le Cornwaleys was a co-witness with Henry le Waleys to a transfer of property in Stratford, just beyond Stepney. It can thus be seen that for the Cornwallises to have property in this area was both determinate and appropriate.

It is as well to remember, of course, that Stepney was nothing like what we see today. As a map of as late as 1610 indicates, it was a countryside of arable pasture and meadowland though the fields nearer to the river became marshy and waterlogged after the disastrous floods of 1394 and this may account for Joanna Cornwallis wanting to forego any residence in her Poplar estate. Incidentally this retreat from the river is reflected in the name 'Stepney' because it derived from Stibba's Haven, but by the time of the Domesday Survey it was already known as Stibenhede or Stibba Haven's heath and the first parish church was set back well away from the riverside.

27

"At the beginning of the 14th century", writes McDonnell, "the bishop, as landlord, was actively concerned with the cultivation of the demesne, and his estate, administered as a single unit, appears to have been a typical arable estate of the south-east of England. By the second half of the century, however, a complete change had taken place. The manor itself had been divided and was accounted for in two divisions by the reeves of Stepney and Hackney . . . The landlord now interested himself only in the hay harvest off a few meadows and leased, or 'farmed', the rest of the demesne. The active entrepreneur had become a rentier." Why this happened is not known for certain but it is more than likely that the volume of demand for leases in the suburban area may have had a compelling effect.

The new development in the manor of Stepney meant that the work of the Bishop's officers also changed. Under the reeve or bailiff were the bedels whose importance was enhanced as the monetary element in the economy became paramount. If, as seems clear, the bedel was responsible for the collection of rents then by 1400 he must have been answerable for the greater part of the Manor's income. It was no doubt a profitable but also a demanding task even if not of long duration and to ensure that only those most capable and trustworthy were appointed the office was an elected one. In 1407 John Cornwaleys, as himself a significant holder of Stepney property, was elected bailiff of Stepney but asked to be excused and was ordered to lose 3 acres of wheat standing in Fannesfield. In March 1426 he similarly refused to act as bedel and was this time required to lose 5 acres of meadow at Longmede and elsewhere. In the full recital of John Cornwaleys's properties we learn that the additional areas were 8 acres in Heherbury (Ebury), 4 acres in Fannesfield and an acre each in Homefield and 'Justyngacre', where 'jousting' traditionally took place. The forfeited lands were granted to a Roger Pynchepole, Esq., of Essex on a 100 Years lease. Since John was at this stage some 60 years of age it is understandable that he had no desire to undertake any further arduous duties of administration.

We can discover from the Guildhall records something of the process by which John Cornwalleys had built up his properties in the eastern end of the City. We note that in 1394 he was one of the purchasers of dwelling houses in Old Jewry in the parish of St. Olave, and in July 1403 he, along with others, had acquired tenements in the parishes of St. Leonard and St. George, Eastcheap. In 1416, however, when he is clearly designated as John Cornewaleys, Esq., Senior, he was selling out to four gentlemen, Lewis Monteney, his two brothers and a Thomas Walsingham, Esq., all his lands in Pudding Lane, St. George's parish, in Berewardislane, at All Hallows, Barkingchurch, as well as the lands in St. Dunstan's-in-the-East and elsewhere within the City. It seems clear that having by then interests further afield to which we shall shortly turn he was now consolidating the Cornwallis holdings in what we are told was then a countryside with fair hedges and long rows of elms and other trees. Davey in his 'Pageant of London' further describes the area:

"The wide space outside Bishopsgate remained open country until far into the 17th century. Bishopsgate Street Without boasted a continuous line of houses on both sides of the way but the back windows all looked on to open fields. The same may be said of the double line of houses that joined Aldgate to the village of Whitechapel (so called from a little white chapel dedicated to St. Mary Matfelon) a place of popular pilgrimage . . ." Bearing in mind both the memory of what living in the heart of the City had meant in the days of pestilence and the fact that land values were rising again as a fresh generation of citizens sought to establish themselves within the Walls John's negotiations seem to prove that he was a foreseeing merchant and a wise landowner. When to his previous commitments we add the fact that he was a husband, a father, prospective Suffolk Lord of the Manor, and still only a leaseholder of the Bishop of London, it is easier to understand his purpose. In reducing the number of his City holdings and refusing the Stepney offices he was still wiser for he had 10 more years to enjoy before he died in 1436. Stow's notable 'Survey of London' records that he was buried at St. Martin's in the Vintry in that year.

It is at this point in the story that certain queries arise. Some of them concern dates relating to the members of the family that carry on the succession and these in turn directly affect the issue of when and how exactly the family became attached to the Manor of Brome. When we have tried to solve these matters we are still left with the most intriguing query of all: why of all places was Brome chosen as a possible estate to be acquired through marriage? It is necessary to address all these puzzles and seek a satisfactory solution to them before we can emerge into the much clearer and more fully documented periods that follow.

The hitherto accepted pedigree or line of descent taken from the 'Visitation of Suffolk' for 1561 states quite clearly that Thomas Cornwallis, latterly the Sheriff, was the parent of a John Cornwallis who died in 1446 (although the year is also given as 14 Henry VI which is in fact 1436/1437) and was buried in St. Martin Vintry. It also confusingly states that John's will was dated 10 August and proved 22 August 1446 (sic). It further affirms that John was the father of another Thomas who was his eldest son and heir and who died in 15 Henry VI or 1437. This latter statement is especially bewildering when we look at the following documents contained in the London Deeds Collection at the Guildhall.

On 23 February 23 Henry VI (1445) a Thomas Cornwaleis (sic) grants to Thomas Brightfield of London "all that his mansion in the parish of St. Martin in Vintry, next 'Narowlan super Celars'. . . to hold from the Nativity of St. John the Baptist next following for 63 years at 14s. rent. Power of re-entry on non-payment of rent. The Landlord covenants to repair and keep wind and water tight". It is not without interest that an attached endorsement states that Thomas Brightfield is to make the following improvements to the house at his own cost: a new kitchen chimney, a lead cistern for a new privy in the wall alongside Narrow Lane, and a couple of freestone windows with iron frames. Yet all this is recorded as taking place 8 years after the date on the family tree stating when this Thomas Cornwaleys is supposed to have died.

There is more. On 4 April 1464 the executors of the Will of a certain William Taverner, citizen and girdler, re-granted to Thomas Cornwaleys all the properties which had been granted to Roger Pynchepole (see above) from whom they were inherited by

Taverner. In February 1472 Thomas Cornewaleys, Esq., let to William Sygrym, citizen and Foyster (or maker of wooden saddles), "all that his great messuage called 'le Bernes' in the parish of St. Botolph's without Aldgate together with the great field called 'Homefeld' in the parish of Stepney, and which now covers 50 acres of land and meadow. The tenant may dig up one acre of sand each year but he is not granted the use of the dovecote and the great chamber or 'gallery' above the hall". It can be seen that this Thomas was a man of means and his property was expanding and increasing. The roots were spreading.

Moreover, a deed for 12 March 1477 states that "Thomas Cornwaleys, son and heir of John Cornwaleys, deceased, late of London, grants to Sir Thomas Mountgomery (sic), kt, John Clopton, esq., Humfrey Tyrell, esq.," and 4 others his dwelling called 'le Horschede' in the parish of St. Mary Matfelon without Aldgate. This latter was the ancient church which was mentioned previously. An endorsement also refers to the lands owned by Thomas Cornwaleys in the Whitechapel parish.

These documents certainly point up some problems of the Brome 'tree' dating. If this latter Thomas was the son and heir of John Cornwallis the London merchant whom we have been describing then the date of his death as given on the 'tree' is incorrect and he lived until at least mid-1477. G. Andrews Moriarty, in the work referred to earlier, states that this Thomas actually died on 26 May 1484 and also adds that he was born by or before 1420. This seems both possible and reasonable since it means that Thomas would be over 60 when he died - a very commendable age in those days. Yet if this was the case then this eldest son of John Cornwallis was born when his father was at least 55 years of age, which seems somewhat unlikely.

Of course we are well aware of the still high rate of infant mortality at this period and this could explain the late birth of this second Thomas. Could it be, however, that as Moriarty suggests there was an intermediate generation, another John, who predeceased his father, the merchant, and thus left the succession to a grandson Thomas? The likelihood of this being the case is first, as we have noted, that the John Cornwaleys mentioned in the transactions above was designated 'Senior' which would be meaningless unless there was a John 'Junior': and second, that when we have mention, in 1477, of 'Thomas, son and heir of John Cornwaleys, deceased', this is directly related to a property that is close to, but not connected with, John Senior and the John here referred to is 'late of London' and not 'of Brome', even though John Cornwallis, Senior had become Lord of Brome some 70 years previously.

There is, however, another possible scenario. Could it be that John Senior was not the father but the older brother of this Thomas and that when he died Thomas became the eldest son and heir of their father, John Senior? I make my own view clear in the 'tree' that will accompany this chapter but certainly the recognition that there was another John, either as an elder brother or the father of Thomas who was lord of Brome does largely clarify the whole matter. I say largely because there are still two puzzling facts.

One is that if Thomas was the next lord of Brome in 1436 then he was made a knight of the Shire in 1441/2 and yet in the London Deed of 1472 it is Thomas Cornwaleys, who lets his property of 'le Bernes' to a tenant, and in 1477 he is still without his knightly prefix in a Deed which distinguishes Sir Thomas Mountgomery from other esquires. A Shire knighthood did not count in London legal matters and the honour was simply a temporary appointment with no lasting prefix.

The other puzzle has to do with another London Deed of 5 Henry VII of 1489. Here we read of John Cornwaleys, son and heir of Thomas, Esq., deceased, granting "to Richard Vannell his manor of Bernes, situate in the parish of St. Botolph, Stebenhithe, and the B(lessed) Mary of Whitechapel". This was on 13 November and yet, surprisingly, on the 14th we note that Vannell "re-grants to John Cornwaleys and Elizabeth, his wife, the same manor to hold to them and the heirs of the said John for ever". That this was all to do with the one family there can be no doubt for the locations are now all familiar ones. Yet the Brome 'family tree' does not mention a John at this date or his immediate brothers Edward and Robert, but passes directly to William the youngest son of Thomas. These omissions will be corrected in the 'tree' that will shortly follow but what they suggest is that if they could be omitted from the 'line' between one lord of Brome and another then there is no reason why there could not have been an omission between John Cornwallis 'senior' and his apparent successor, Thomas. The 'tree', in other words, is incomplete.

Before we show the more complete succession, however, we need to answer the remaining questions as to how and why these members of the Cornwallis family, apparently solid and successful citizens and merchants of the City, linked themselves with the Suffolk estates of Brome and Ode (or Oakley). The way in which they became connected can be first and more easily explained.

The Suffolk Roots

The connection begins in 1400 with the marriage of John Cornwallis, the son of Sheriff Thomas, and Philippa Bucton. She was the daughter and co-heir of Robert Bucton, sometimes called Sir Robert for he too was a Knight of the Shire and Member of Parliament for Suffolk between 1393 and 1400. It was through his mother, a Braham, that Robert acquired the rights to the Manor of Brome which Philippa was to inherit when her father died in 1408. For the purposes of our story, however, there is more that we ought to know about Sir Robert Bucton if we are to appreciate fully how and why the fortunes of the Cornwallis family came to be associated with the otherwise largely unknown Suffolk village of Brome.

Robert Bucton (or Bukton) came of a family that was of North Yorkshire origin and in 1278 a Geoffrey de Buketon was on a jury that was to give judgement regarding some sheep of the Abbot of Whitby. In 1303 Robert de Bukton of Settrington, near Malton, owed 11 marks to a William de Thorntoft and pledged his lands and chattels in Yorkshire in the event of non-payment. In 1309 the Close Rolls also tell us that Arnold de Bukton was owing a ½ of a knight's fee in Muston which is near Filey, and William de Bukton owes ½ of a knight's fee for Buketon (or Buckden) in the heart of the Pennine country. It would appear that this is the source of the family name. Of their northern connections therefore there can be little doubt and that these connections remained is shown by the fact that in March 1382 a John de Bukton of Settrington is acting as witness in a case at Skirpenbeck near to Stamford Bridge whilst in 1396 a Peter de Bucton is a royal legal officer (or escheator) for Yorkshire and is approving the transfer of a messuage and 1 acre from an outlaw, William Barton of Stamford Bridge, to the Warden of the King's Chapel of St. George which stood below York Castle.

In the course of the century, however, one branch of the family moved to the Midlands for in 1342 a Thomas Bukton was Escheator for Northamptonshire and in 1344 he, now a Knight of the Shire, and John de Waldegrave, owe the Earl of Northampton the sum of £340. Another branch reached East Anglia because as early as 1313 a Thomas de Bukton is acknowledged by the Crown as the heir of the lands of Thomas de Bottisham which lie along the road from Cambridge to Newmarket and in 1396 we are meeting our Robert de Bukton, a Knight of the Shire for Suffolk, who in 1398 is exercising a royal writ.

From other sources we know that friendly relations were established between the Buctons and the De la Poles when some of the latter family's members were becoming Mayors of Kingston-upon-Hull. Of them Sir Walter Besant has written as follows:

"William De la Pole, a merchant and Mayor of Hull, was made a Baron of the Exchequer. His son, Michael De la Pole, became 2nd Earl of Suffolk and Lord Chancellor. His being a merchant did not detract from his honour, for who knows not that even our noblemen's sons have been merchants? Whence it follows that mercatura non derogat nobilitati - trade is no abatement of honour". As we saw in the last chapter this principle is fully borne out in the story before us.

The continuing connection of the Buctons and the De la Poles is proved by a Close Roll entry for 1388 in which Michael De la Pole, Kt., Lord of Wingfield and Patron of the church at Stradebrok, in Suffolk is affirmed in his claim on the advowson there by three witnesses – Sir William and Sir Robert Mounteney (or Montenay) and Robert Bucton. It may be recalled that the Montenays were involved in a London property transaction with the Cornwallises whilst Robert's profession is revealed in 1394 when, in the case of a Richard atte Style, Robert Bucton, Escheator for Suffolk, states in the Court of Chancery that the £40 due by Richard for a debt had been paid.

A later instance of the lasting connection between the Buctons and De la Poles is given when in 1417 Philippa's brother, also Robert Bucton, gave evidence in an enquiry at Eye regarding the age of William De la Pole, 4th Earl of Suffolk. Robert stated that he had been present at the parish church of St Andrew, Cotton, in 1396 when the said William was being baptized. Robert had held the bridle of the horse belonging to William's godfather, William of Burgate. Robert Bucton, Senior was doubtless one of the party present at the ceremony.

We also know that as a soldier and patriot Robert had also served with and for the

Percy family of Northumberland. His relative and fellow Escheator, Peter de Bukton, was in 1383 the witness to a grant by Henry de Percy of the Manor of Leconfield, near Beverley, whilst in 1384 Robert is named with Thomas Percy and others as one of the Conservators of the Truce of Brittany, he having been made Warden of the Castle at Brest. In April 1399 he is appointed attorney to Thomas Percy who was then Seneschal of England.

There is mention of a Robert Buckton in Geoffrey Chaucer's work, "Envoi", and the poet there describes this contemporary as being from Goosewold in Suffolk. Chaucer was, we know, the keeper of the King's Staple, not least in Stepney, and was persona grata with the Royal family. It is thus interesting to record that Queen Anne of Bohemia, the wife of Richard II, made Robert Bucton one of her Esquires with the tenure of Gosewold in her Lordship of Eye and we should also note that there is an ancient site of a moated house once known as Goswold Hall in the parish of Thrandeston which lies close to Oakley and Brome. What should prove no surprise is that in the extensive list of manorial properties held by Edmund, son of Richard of Cornwall, the estate which comes next to Brome is "Gosewode: Fee held by John de Gosewaude".

Mention of the regal Lordship of Eye would also explain why in September 1401 Robert, the father, was given the 'life' appointment as Constable of Eye Castle and keeper of the King's gaol within it. Moreover to help us tie up other threads, we should observe that a Robert Bucton, either the father or more likely the son, was on 13 October 1405 made Deputy Buteler for Ipswich and Colchester under Thomas Chaucer, whilst Robert, Senior, had at least 2 Norfolk connections - as Warden of the Castle at Buckenham, to the east of Norwich, and Lord of Babingley Manor, near Castle Rising.

As we thus begin to discover a much fuller picture of a substantial landholder and royal law officer as opposed to a merely local squire whose daughter was to marry John Cornwallis we may still wonder what it was that brought the two families into touch with each other. It is worth remembering that the main Cornwallis residence at Aldgate Without was on the direct and most frequently used route from Essex and Suffolk to the City and it is not without relevance to note that Geoffrey Chaucer was to acquire the lease on all the tolls that were levied at the Aldgate entrance to the City. But the connection of the Buctons and the Cornwallises is graphically illustrated by a Close Roll entry of 10 July 1362 which reads as follows:

"To the Escheator in Yorkshire. You are not to interfere in the messuage and 10 bovates in Aclam which came to the King by reason of the death of Robert Cornwaleys of Aclam and by reason of the nonage of Thomas, son of Robert Cornwaleys, cousin and heir of the said Robert. He holds by knight's service of William de Roos, Alice and Isabel, next heirs and sisters of the said Robert having died." The Escheator was John de Bukton and of him we read in 1371 that 'he was to be relieved of the additional office of Collector being so busily employed on other royal business.'

Where the northern Robert Cornwaleys came from has yet to be revealed but it shows that the Buctons and the Cornwallises were already aware of each other and in the King's 'mind'. As a lawyer Robert Bucton had numerous professional contacts in London which may have led to Thomas the Sheriff and himself meeting there.

Turning to John's generation we know that in 1386 Bucton was arranging a loan in the City to cover his undertaking to raise 1000 marks for the Royal Exchequer from the County of Suffolk. Even more to the point we have in the City Letter Book 'A' a note that in 1389 John Cornwallis was surety in the granting to Henry Venner, his half-brother, of guardianship of the orphan son of a John Bryklesworth and in 1397, when Henry Venner has died, this boy received £20 from John Cornwallis as Executor for Henry. Alongside this relationship we have the Close Roll entry for January 1394 stating that William Venner, elder citizen and merchant of London and uncle to the Henry above, made a gift of all his goods and chattels to Robert Bucton and William Venner, his son. Strange as the bequest may seem it at least reveals a connection between the Buctons and Venners and hence no doubt with John Cornwallis. In 1390 Robert Bucton, Senior, was appointed the King's Justice for holding pleas in South Wales and may thus have frequented City society more often and again met John Cornwallis. We know too that in 1397 Philippa Bucton came of age and was taken to meet the Queen as well as being present at certain banquets in the City. Was it in connection with this visit that she would also at last have met her future husband?

Whilst these events go some way to answering the question as to how the Cornwallises and Buctons might have known each other the principal query still remains. Even if it was by chance that they crossed each other's paths what was there to encourage any development of such an encounter to the point of union between their two houses? Surely there must have been other likely heiresses whom the Sheriff and his son might have met? What then was it about the Buctons that led to their being the ones to be preferred? At a time when the Cornwallis family was determinately seeking to extend and establish its roots for the future why should a family from that part of Suffolk secure their favour?

The answer, I believe, lies in the new situation that was created when the Cornwallis family had reaffirmed its social identity by the award of arms to Thomas the Sheriff. Some further words of Sir Walter Besant are worth stating (p. 222):

"In those days, we must remember, there was the greatest jealousy over the right to bear arms. The Heralds' Visitation continued into the seventeenth century. A man could no more assume a coat of arms than he could - or can now - assume a peerage . . . The aristocracy of the City were brothers and cousins to the gentry: perhaps the lesser landed gentry of the country. Let that fact be borne in mind all through our History . . ."

The Cornwallis family would now be still further aware of certain factors that could materially assist its future. One of these was any association with properties or areas of the country that had been linked with their earliest progenitor, Richard, Earl of Cornwall. When, therefore, they encounter another rising family that has a legitimate claim on at least three localities that figure in the portfolio of Earl Richard's, his 3rd wife's or his son

34

Edmund's possessions, and which were not claimed by other Cornwall descendants then it would seem both wise and natural to allow these matters to weigh in the balance as against other possible alliances.

These were not times when romantic fancy dictated marriage settlements or liaisons. Robert Bucton, Senior, is himself an example of prevailing custom. He acquired an interest in Eye by his own endeavours and royal contacts but Brome came to him through his father's marriage to the Brahams whilst by his own marriage to Anne, the daughter and co-heiress of Sir Robert a Tye, he had acquired the Manor of Oakley, which lies next to Brome and in which incidentally he preferred to settle down. His gravestone was eventually removed from the church interior and laid in the ground outside but his true memorial is the 60 foot Church Tower which he caused to have erected about 1380.

Settling At Brome

For the Cornwallises the way back into something of their 'natural' heritage was by marriage into such a family. It has not to be forgotten that two further factors were influencing John Cornwallis at just this time. One was that whilst they might be substantially well off in terms of possessions they were only landholders by long lease in Stepney and there would be a longing to achieve freehold status. Also the very area in which they resided, albeit it was to remain mainly rural for another 200 years, was beginning to see a steady increase in population – from about 2,200 in 1300 to over 5,000 in the 1500s - and the suitability of the Lea Valley for developing trades was clearly evident. For those who had already forsaken the inner City for a more rural environment the natural inclination was to seek a landed property of their own in the surrounding counties. There is ample evidence to prove this point for in 1421 John Cornwaleys is amongst others in purchasing the rights to properties and church advowsons in Sulham, Tilehurst and Purley, Berks. whilst in 1422 he is part of a further purchase from the Carews in many parts of Surrey and Kent. John's intentions were crystal clear.

Nor is it fanciful to consider that with his own legal awareness and royal contacts Robert Bucton may have seen in the Cornwallis connection the most fitting fulfilment of marriage for his daughter. It is not by chance that in the present Brome Church there are displayed the arms of the Braham, Tye, Bucton and Cornwallis lines whilst not overlooking those of the Butlers with their Irish connections.

In 1408 Sir Robert died and the Manors of Brome and Oakley were bequeathed respectively to Philippa and her brother, Robert. Philippa's husband, John Cornwallis, was now to be a Suffolk landowner and country gentleman as well as a London merchant. He was, as we know, determined to lay a firm foundation for his family's future. The birth of a son, also named John, who in his turn could, by 1420, have produced his own first born confirmed that the family had a future. The fact that John Cornwaleys, Junior, did not survive his father was not unique. In the years that followed this pattern in the family was repeated not infrequently. Yet the succession was to be maintained and the roots would be still more widely spread.

It would seem that the only dwelling available for the new lord of Brome and his family on their Suffolk property was little more than what had been there from Saxon times when a Dame Goda had occupied a moated and aisled structure known as Ling Hall. This was situated in an embanked area to the east of the present church site though sadly there is no trace of it today. For John Cornwallis and his new wife their main home would still have been in Stepney and when they came to visit their country estate it may have been a case of sometimes staying as Robert's guests at 'The Grove' which was the Oakley manorial residence and a house with which Philippa was already familiar.

That through the Bucton connection the new couple were steadily more involved in East Anglian affairs is true as we shall see shortly but it is not to be thought that this interest only began from the time of John's marriage. In 1393 Agnes, the daughter of John Grauncete, Junior, of Hokynton (now Oakington), Cambridgeshire, granted to John Cornwaleys, his heirs and assigns the 'quitclaim' to 6 messuages, 67 acres and 16 1/2 acres of meadow in Cottenham and Hokynton. This was a sizeable property.

It was equalled in 1422 when William Coggeshall who had given John Dorewarde of Essex the manors of 'Esthall, Pakelisham and Marsh' (now Eastend, Paglesham and Marsh, north of Southend-on-Sea) reallocated them to John Cornwaleys, John Tyrell and two others, all with their heirs and assigns. John Cornwallis is no newcomer to the area, therefore, but in 1425 a claim was laid by a Sir John Falstolf of Norfolk and others against John Tyrell and his wife Catherine, John Cornwallis and Edward Tyrell, for the manor of Haryngby, whilst in 1433 John is granted a fief just across the border with Norfolk. The roots were indeed spreading and the Cornwallis name was becoming known in the north Suffolk and south Norfolk areas.

In view of the transactions already referred to it should come as no surprise that when a future family liaison was considered for Thomas, the second Cornwallis lord of Brome, it was from the Tyrell family that the bride was chosen. She was the co-heir of Edward Tyrell of Downham close to Hanningfield in Essex, and with the help of her dowry Thomas Cornwallis was able to extend materially both the influence and the range of the Cornwallis estates. He would be aware that his father had already set a pattern when in 1419 he had, along with John Tyrell, bought land and the local advowsons connected with the Manor of Bromfordes near Newendon. Moreover this family link brought the descendants of the Earl of Cornwall once again back into the circle of those Norman families who could claim to have come with William I. It was, after all, a Tyrell who had asked that he might lead the centre column of the attack in the Battle of Hastings and Sir Walter Tyrell II was ordered by the Conqueror to marry the Anglo-Saxon heiress, Alicia Gifford, so that both her family's lands and their allegiance should come firmly within Norman control. It was thus that the Tyrells who stayed in England settled in Essex, initially at East Horndon, now Horndon-on-the-Hill, and Langham, just north of Colchester.

Whilst it is well to remind ourselves that at least during this Thomas's lifetime the business interests of the family in the City continued to be maintained we have already noted his lease of the house called 'le Bernes' because he was presumably settling into the country home in Suffolk and the demands of his growing number of manors claimed a greater measure of his and his sons' time. Trade had, as with so many other families then and since, created the foundation for a successful country existence and it was only when this had been satisfactorily established that life as country gentry and nobility could flourish.

Thomas Cornwallis became an Elector for Essex in 1442, a position explained by his having become possessed of the manor of Butlers in Basildon, which he held as a member of the Manor of Stortford which also belonged to his earlier landlord, the Bishop of London. In 1447 and 1453 he was Elector for Suffolk, and a Knight of the Shire as already mentioned in 1449/50. We know too that he was acquiring land in Stuston and Thrandeston, as well as inheriting the Manor of Oakley following the death of Robert Bucton, Junior. The roots were spreading even further.

They continued to grow until the end of his life. In 1468 Thomas is recorded as backing an £800 bill of a Sir John Marney for paying a fine to the Crown and in 1473 he received a pardon for his part in the affair and is then described as 'of Brome, Bartilesden and London'. The Bartilesden reference is because under the 1477 Will of Sir John Marney of Buckinghamshire he is seen to have been a fee-holder under that gentleman who now confirmed the above-named property to him. To show that this was not plucking a bow at a venture we learn that Sir John's brother, Sir William Marney of Essex, had a daughter, Alice, who married Sir James Tyrell of Heron some 25 years later.

It can thus be seen that Thomas, 2nd Cornwallis lord of the manor of Brome, certainly played his part in extending the family roots and seeing them firmly established. When we consider the members of the family that survived him this description of his efforts seems to be even more justified.

As was shown above Thomas and Philippa had four sons and a daughter. Of the last of these sons, William, and his sister Catherine, we shall speak at more length in the next chapter but we cannot end this one without commenting on the contribution of John, Edward and Robert who, though they produced no offspring, made their own contribution towards retaining the estates of the family and securing them for their sibling.

John Cornwallis assumed the mantle of his father in 1484 when he had already married an Elizabeth Baude, reputedly of Bedfordshire. Initial research into her family reveals that in 1369 a Nicholas Baude of Standon in Hertfordshire paid 10 marks to confirm his claim to lands and chattels of a manor in Kent whilst by 1373 a William Baude was a Knight of the Shire for Hertford. A century later, in 1470, a Ralph Baude, Esq., claimed rights in the manor of Chelsyn, Hertfordshire., and was also appointed a J.P. in the county. A John Baude was also appearing as a 'gentylman of London'. In view of the family interest in dynastic concerns it is unlikely that the eldest son would have either wished or been allowed to unite with a family that did not have substantial properties or a standing in their county. Since we know that John Cornwallis continued his father's title as Lord of the Essex Manor of Bartilsden it is not unlikely that that may have been his residence whilst his father was alive and that would set him closer to the life and affairs of

Hertfordshire/Bedfordshire. A little more research on the Baudes will no doubt easily explain the matter.

That this John was prepared to devote his major attention to the country estates that came to him after his father's death seems to be proved by his continuing to lease the Stepney properties, which he and his wife were presumably not intending to occupy, and because he does not seem to figure in City affairs as his predecessors did, nor does he carry any duties of a Shire nature. The fact that he was without offspring and that his wife, who outlived him, may have born more than one child who died in infancy, might suggest that he was eager to ensure a proper inheritance for his successors. His life span of over 50 years, together with the occupancy of Brome for over 20 of them, helps to re-inforce the view that he was no mere cypher in the family reckoning and perhaps should have his name and contribution more firmly recognized. Nothing can do this better than the contents of his well-thought-out Will which was approved after his death in 1506. Its opening is typical of the period and reminds us that England was still a devout Catholic land:

"In the name of God, Amen. I, John Cornewaleys, Esquyer, bequeathe my soule to Allmighty God, our Ladie, Sent Marke & all the holie companye of hevyn, and requyre my body to be buryed in the Chauncell of the Church of our Ladie of Brome . . . before our Ladies nygh (niche) to the walle of my Chapell there . . ."

His devotion is further remarked in a bequest of 24 marks sterling for the next 4 years so that a priest should 'syng for my soule, my faders, moders, and all my goode friendes and all Christen soules'. Yet he is far from otherworldly: he gives 6s 8d to the parson for 'my tithes and other duties negligently forgotten' and leaves 20s each for upkeep of the bells and the repair of the church fabrics at Oakley, Stuston, Thrandeston and even Bartyllesden in Essex. When to the above grants you add his detailed gifts of money or crops to the Monks and church of Eye Abbey and the parishes of Oxen, Diss, Scole, Palgrave, Billingford and Papley you even more recognize that his especial contribution to the extending of roots was in establishing the Cornwallis presence and influence in the immediate vicinity of the now established centre at Brome. That was a vital legacy for the future.

That Bartilsden and London may have been the original homes of John and Elizabeth is emphasized by the provision of the residue of the goods and chattels of those dwellings being placed at the disposal of his widow and it is interesting that Elizabeth and his youngest son, William, are 2 of the 3 executors.

Of his family he is clearly mindful for he leaves his niece Elizabeth Foxmer £10 and her sister Anne £10.6.8d, with £10 also for his niece Elizabeth Cornwallis, William's daughter. To his brother and 'heir at Lyng Hall', Edward, he specially bequeathes his precious Chapel items - 'My grete Masse Boke, vestiment of silk, a chalise and corporalls case' - whilst the list of places and objects connected with the Hall itself gives a further insight into what life for a country gentleman entailed in those days. 'All table footings and brewhouse or bakehouse fittings; one whole plough, a cart and 5 horse; the gilt goblet and cup of my father's, the latter with a cover; and in the chamber over the parlour he speaks of a 'fether' bed, a tester, curtains, coverings, bolsters, 2 pillows and 1 layer of blankets. The then modern comforts of manor house living were still sufficiently new to enumerate.

Nor did this next lord of the manor forget non-family members. He gives Elyn Barker 'my servant' 6s 8d, Agnes Fastell £10 for her marriage and his godson, John Reve, 20s, and as a form of codicil, 'I bequethe to the Abbot of Bury myn ambulling nagge that I bought of John Revet'. The whole document is redolent with careful attention to the possible needs of those who survive him and suggests that he earned no less a place than others in the ongoing story of the Cornwallises of Brome.

He had obviously set an example to his brother, Edward, who took up the reins from 1506 to 1510. What part the other brother, Robert, played in affairs is not altogether clear but an entry in the Close Rolls for 1511 mentions both Edward and Robert Cornwallis as having made sureties of 100 marks and here the latter is stated to have his residence at Prittlewell in Essex. We know that he married a daughter of the Mountney family and that for one brief year he succeeded Edward but as John's Will above does not mention him and an Inquisition of 1510 shows that William was also recognized by law as Edward's heir it would appear that that there was no hesitation in William taking over as Robert died without issue. What is clear is that Edward made no alterations to the properties owned by the family and one example of this is given by Copinger, the reputed author of a history of Suffolk Manors. He describes how the estate of Thrandeston was first vested in Thomas Cornwallis before he died in the 1470s, thence transferred to John and later Edward, after which it was faithfully entrusted to William. Of Edward there is no doubt more to be learnt but at least we know that in 1511 he was the holder of land in Hook, Yorkshire, and in the year of his death he had been appointed to the Royal Household as "Sewer to the Chamber Extraordinary".

It is thus evident that he had maintained a literal 'tradition' and by the time William finally assumes the lordship of Brome he was also in possession of Hoo Hall, Hoxne, Woodhall and Yaxley, a London and a Yorkshire property. The roots had spread very extensively but also very closely indeed. The next generation had an inheritance of which they could be justly proud.

CHAPTER 4

Developing the Tree

In 1961 a Mr Alan Simpson wrote a series of essays entitled "The Wealth of the Gentry" relating to East Anglian families. One of those essays entitled 'The Courtier' began as follows:

"The Cornwallises were one of those families which rose from the squirearchy to the peerage, under the Tudors and Stuarts, by cultivating a connexion with the court over several generations. They acquired, so to speak, a hereditary interest in a household office, and they seem to have had the qualities of bravery, tact and competence that were needed to catch the sovereign's eye. The founder of the family was a fourteenth-century merchant, a sheriff of London in 1378, whose heir was settled as a squire on the borders of Norfolk and Suffolk by the beginning of the fifteenth century. A century later they were still squires, but the lordships of Brome and Oakley had been enlarged by lands in the neighbouring towns, and William Cornwallis, a younger son who succeeded three childless brothers, was a substantial figure among the clients of the house of Howard when he died in 1519." (p. 142)

On the face of it this might seem a fair summary of what has so far been written in this family history though four comments must be made to preserve a truer record.

The first is that the origins of the family are manifestly a century older than is indicated here and the rise of Thomas the Sheriff owes at least as much to his family predecessors in Cornwall and the City of London, if not also in Ireland, as to his own considerable energy and wit.

The second significant matter is that this family originated from the highest royal circle and never lost sight, I believe, of what might be deemed their natural place in the service of the realm. It was not so much a new seeking of recognition by the monarch as regaining their due acknowledgement as valuable members of a family that always recalled its royal origins and was discreetly and constantly ready to serve the ruler's cause. It was not a case then of seeking honours so much as revealing their natural claim to them.

Thirdly, and most pertinent to our present stage of the story, we need to recognize that William Cornwallis succeeded brothers who were not quite the cyphers that the above passage might suggest and who strove, as we saw, to maintain and extend the already sizeable interests that their father and grandfather had established. These 'childless brothers' held the reins of manorial office between them for 26 years whereas William only held them for 9. Some kind of proportion needs to be restored and recognized.

And fourthly, we shall begin to see that contrary to any previous impressions the task of consolidating and extending the Suffolk property was neither as straightforward nor as simple as the above passage from Mr. Simpson's studies suggests. Oakley and Brome were not quite as homogeneous as they at first seemed.

Let us be clear however about one thing. In undertaking his unexpected responsibilities William was certainly no fool. He was obviously respected for his judgement by both the family and by others. We have seen that his elder brother, John, chose him as an Executor of his will and in 1499 we note that he was an auditor approved by the Royal Justices. This was to assist in settling the affairs of the then local De la Pole family when Edmund De la Pole was served with a Bill of Attainder and his possessions had been seized by the Crown. William clearly had a good head on his shoulders and one that was recognized by people in authority. Copinger reports of him that 'he was among those gentlemen of the county of Suffolk who were certified in 1501 to have an estate sufficient to support the degree of a Knight of the Bath, several having to take that order on the creation of Henry, Prince of Wales. In 1513', he continues, 'he was among the principal persons of that county of Suffolk nominated by Act of Parliament as most discreet persons, as justices of the peace, or assessing a subsidy of £163,000 by a poll-tax for defraying the expense of taking Terouanne and Tournay'. (p. 241)

He also married well and was fruitful to boot. He and his wife, Elizabeth Stanford, had eleven children of whom more will be said later. (See the family tree at the end of this chapter.) William's wife's family, the Stanfords of Bedfordshire, were already known in public circles. In 1343 a William and an Edmund de Stanford (or Staunford) appear as citizens and merchants of London and in May 1355 it is noted that William has the right to a tenement in the parish of St. Lawrence in Thames Street in the City. A Robert de Stanford is named as a witness in 3 cases at Rotherhithe in 1344, 1348 and 1349 but, more significantly the Close Rolls reveal that in July 1350 a Thomas de Stanford was about to set out for Flanders to buy merchandise as 'had John de Cornewaleys who was already in that land'. That the two families were therefore already acquainted seems clear but the records then begin to multiply with Stanford references so that three branches of that family emerge. One in the City and Middlesex, one in East Anglia and one in Bedfordshire. How these branches were related cannot he entered into here but it is surely worth remarking that by the year 1450 the Cornwallis and Stanford families were quite likely to have encountered each other in more than one area of the south-east.

For our immediate purpose we need to record that in November 1466 John Stanford, son and heir of John Stanford of Ixnyng (Ixworth?) in the county of Suffolk, renounced all rights to messuages, lands and woods, etc. in Clifton and 'Maperdesale' (now Meppershall), in the county of Bedford which another John Stanford, Citizen and Mercer of the City of London, had recovered by writ against a William Stanford. This grant was made to the latter John Stanford and three others, together with 'all the lands, rents, reversions and services in the towns and parishes of Clifton, Meperdsale, Stanford, Polanger and the Overhoo (?)'. A glance at the map will reveal that these places lie just to the north-west of the present Hitchin and Letchworth but over the Bedfordshire border. It is clear that it was a daughter of the John Stanford, citizen and mercer, the owner of 'Gemys, Jempsis or Sanford manor at Stackden' (Stagsden near Bedford) that married William Cornwallis of Brome and she brought with her family links in Suffolk and Norfolk.

Of the eldest son of this marriage, John (later Sir John), a great deal more will have to be said in due course but before we consider him let us in turn look at William's sister, Catherine, and the kind of life experienced around Brome in the late 15th century; then at the growth of the family properties, including the connection with the Howards and the growing interest in Eye; and lastly at the other children whom William sired. The story may now seem to become more complicated but this is because the family tree was becoming strong and healthy and many more facts start to become available.

One source of these further facts is the 'Book of Brome', one of those literary oddities that contribute to the richness of our English heritage. Almost certainly unknown today by 99% of our population, including even most of those who reside in Suffolk, it is yet a valuable item of social and literary history because it so naturally reflects the period in which it was compiled. Lucy Toulmin Smith, the eventual editor of the 1886 printed version, describes how 'a small paper ms. volume was lately put into my hands by Dr. G.H. Kingsley, who found it while turning over the interesting papers connected with the 'manor of Brome, in the muniment room attached to the land-agent's office of that place'. (p. 1)

She also added (p. 2), 'there is, however, no mention of Brome in the volume; the local entries chiefly relate to Stuston (or Sturston), a neighbouring Suffolk village, and to Scole, which lies in Norfolk . . . This book probably came into the Brome muniment room in consequence of the united (Cornwallis) ownership in four neighbouring manors, of which Brome finally became the more prominent. Robert Melton (who kept) the accounts was a Stuston man and, as shown hereafter, was probably Steward of the Cornwallis property and the adviser of the family. He wanted to put down his notes of manorial dues and other matters relating to Stuston leet and court baron law, and finding this volume only half filled with poetry, used it for the purpose.'. Hence its title:

'A Common-place Book of the 15th Century, containing A Religious Play and poetry, Legal Forms and Local Accounts.'

Whilst the book may be said to be only indirectly connected with the Cornwallis family it reveals not a little the concerns and interests of those who lived in such a place at the period before and during which William was its lord. Melton was a co-executor with Robert and William of the will of their elder brother, John, who was Lord of Brome, Stuston, Okely and Thranston (sic).

The most direct connection of this work with the family is the specific reference to Catherine, the sister of William, who 'married Francis Froxmer (or Frewsmere),Esq., of Essex, and of whom was born a daughter, Elizabeth. It is not unlikely that as John Cornwallis left £10 to this niece Robert Melton's accounts of 1507/8 may in part have been a carrying out of his executorship in this regard.

We are told, for example, that 'This byll witnessith of sweche money as I, R. Melton, reseyuyd (received) of Mastras Froxmer for serteyne cornne yt I, R. Melton, solde (be)longyng to the seyd M. Froxmer from Candylmes in the xxiij yere of the reigne of Harry the vij (A.D. 1507/8) on to mydsummer neste after that.' (p. 174)

Where exactly the Froxmers lived has not yet been discovered though we have seen that the Froxmers were a family in Essex. It is possible that Catherine, being the only surviving sister of William, may have been offered a tenancy of one of the 'Cornwallis' manors. What is certain is that Robert Melton dealt with a clientele in all the neighbouring districts known to the Cornwallis family and he is unlikely to have gone too far in both gathering and selling 'Mastras Froxmer's cornne'. The area he worked in is bounded by Diss, Scole, Eye, Stuston and Oakley. (See again the map at the end of this chapter)

What the book also provides us with, of course, is much detail on the farming possibilities that faced William and his like. This part of the country relied heavily on its barley crops though there was also trade in malt, 'mesclin' (a mixture of wheat and rye, and later referred to in Yorkshire as 'maslin bread'), oats and pease, whilst the local measures used were the 'coomb (or cumbe)' and the bushel. We note too how the local 'gentry' went to Norwich for more ambitious shopping, to buy a bonnet of velvet, a frontlet of satin, or the materials for a gown of tawny cloth. We also see that medical aid had to be largely of the self-help variety and the last item in the volume is a recipe for a remedy to help the recovery from yellow jaundice.

Alongside these glimpses of the more humdrum aspects of daily living at the time, and in such a part of England, we also have examples of the more diverting practices that were currently enjoyed - the puzzles and poems that were devised or recited, examples of the prayers and devotional texts, including even a carol, that would highlight the seasons of the Christian Year. Most valuable of all are two other items. The first is the text of one of the less well known, indeed rare, Mystery Plays, called 'Abraham's Sacrifice of Isaac', which, with a smaller cast, could be performed either in the hall of 'a Manor House such as that of Ling Hall at Brome or in the square of a country town like Diss or Eye. We know that there were two guilds at Diss, those of St. Nicholas and Corpus Christi, which could have undertaken the production of such a play. What is so remarkable is that though we are aware that a larger set of such plays was performed in Norwich at this time this is the first complete text of such a drama in this part of England.

In a copy of the local parish magazine for November 1936 there was reproduced an article called 'Nikke's Lane' which referred to some of the occasions when Bishop Richard Nikke of Norwich cane to visit the Cornwallis family at Ling Hall. One of the incidents there referred to was in November 1519 when 'he rode into the village along with Archdeacon Thomas (Cornwallis) . . . All were getting ready for a village feast, to be provided by the kindly Squire (William). The bishop stayed a day or two and seemed interested in what was going forward. He wheeled the sick squire in a chair to see the Play that aunt Froxmer was presenting along with Bob Melton of Stuston and his brother John, the parson of Brome. (The Squire's daughter) Katharine too was in the play. She was the 'ram-caught-in-the-thicket' and folks said 'nobody cou'nt a' said ba'aa better'ner, not even down in Lon 'on'. But Squire was taken worse, and the bishop had to hurry away for the Martyr's Feast at Bury. And now you must be told: it was on that very day - St. Edmund's Day, that Squire William breathed his last, and they buried him at Oakley."

The other main item appearing in this Book of Brome is 'a curious religious catechism or dialogue between the Emperor Adrian and Christ under the form of a child' (sic). This poem, called 'Epotys' (a shortened English form of Epictetus), and probably compiled in the early 14th century, had not previously been printed in England and its appearance therefore proved of great interest to those interested in knowing about the religious, theological, and ethical attitudes of the English Middle Ages. Here we have in everyday language the teaching of the time about fasting, penance, the fall of Man and his redemption, heaven, hell and the Trinity. Another extract from 'Nikke's Lane' puts all this in context:

'Squire (William) was a straight, good man, devoted to the Faith he professed; he didn't talk about his religion, but he was not ashamed to go on his knees in the House of God and give worship to Whom worship is due'.

It is indeed easy to forget that this was still a very Catholic society with a great emphasis on the pattern of the Redemption as the structure for all its activities. This adherence to the Old Church will before long become a significant feature of the Cornwallis story and when it does we will need to recall that this was no sudden allegiance. The Book of Brome leaves no reader in any doubt that Church, State and home were closely and intricately interwoven. It was the attempted readjustment of that intimate association that was to lead to disturbances not only in the country at large but in this family in particular.

The Book of Brome also illustrates clearly the judicial requirements still attaching to those who were the landed 'Lords' of the English countryside. Here we have the 'Articles of Enquiry' at a Court Baron and a Court Leet which continue the ancient administration of public welfare by local justice and responsibility. The Court Baron was the local Lord's court and consisted of his free tenants as the adjudicators, with the Lord's Steward as registrar and presiding officer. This mainly dealt with issues of landholding and trespass, or the failure to render due rents and charges. Local knowledge in such matters will be seen to have been vital.

The other body was the Court Leet which dealt with felonies and misdemeanours, offences and nuisances about which the law of the land was clear and precise. The Lord of the Manor here presided as a type of magistrate who must, if the case so required, refer the matter to a still higher tribunal. In both processes the Lord of the Manor was expected both to be aware of what was transpiring in his demesne and required to provide the means whereby justice could be dispensed and enforced. For the likes of William Cornwallis, at just this juncture of his life, the Book of Brome shows the burden of responsibility which he and his peers had to bear. There was more to being a landowner than enjoying the fruits of the earth, the privileges of a better house and status in society. There were duties that were perpetual and for which the lord was alone answerable.

Such was the inheritance that devolved upon William and his son at Ling (or Lyng) Hall and before we consider the lesser/known members of the family that also first dwelt there we ought to review the history of that manor and its surrounding properties.

A brief mention was made in the last chapter of the dwelling which stood on a moated site to the south-east of the present church building. Whilst somewhat changed from its earliest days it was still the home of Squire William though we are told that he would have preferred a house nearer the 'Hoo' of Oakley. He continued to reside there however because, as he said, 'John (his brother) wished it so in his will'. The existence of this aisled building and the fact that the lower section of the present church tower is of Saxon construction dovetails with the mention of Brome in the Domesday Survey. Here we learn that there were two Saxon Freewomen and landholders in the locality, Dame Coda (or Goode) farming nearly 300 acres around Brome and Mistress Leusida at Hoo in Oakley. Their two properties were part of the vast estates held by Edric of Laxfield, the third largest landholder in Suffolk prior to the coming of the Normans. Dame Goda may well have been the original occupant of the first building called Ling Hall whilst Leusida lived on the site later called Hoo Hall. It is also clear that the 8th century wooden church at Brome had been by now replaced with a stone nave and tower, one of the 43 round ones still extant in Suffolk. The church at Oakley retained a nave half of which was timber-built until the 14th century when Robert Bucton was to add the first stone tower.

To complete the Oakley story the Bigods, Earls of Norfolk, took over the Manor of Oakley (or Hoo Hall) as the first Norman owners but the Crown confiscated their rights through insurrection under Henry III and in 1294 the Rector of Oakley was being presented by a Goscelin de Lodne. His daughter married Ralph de Hoo and their son, who was patron in 1333 and 1360, was John de Hoo of Laxfield. Until 1401 the patron was then a Joan Bacon of Brome, after which the now familiar Robert Bucton makes his appearance.

Even this, however, is not the whole story. There was also another small property called the Manor of Beauchamps in Oakley Woodhall. The eldest daughter of Goscelin de Lodne married William de Beauchamp who thus gave his name to this property and it remained in that family until it was acquired by the Bacons of Erwarton (see below) in the 14th century. By subsequent negotiation William's son, the later Sir John, acquired it from Joan Bacon and it was only in 1519 that the whole of the Oakley estates were finally in Cornwallis hands. This included the small church of Oakley Parva though that fabric fell into disuse before Sir Thomas inherited it in 1544.

When we now turn to Brome what has equally to be grasped is that there were in fact three manors - one of Ling Hall which has just been mentioned, another called 'Brome' or 'Erwarton', and yet another named 'Monk's Brome'. It is because many writers about Suffolk have assumed that the Ling and Brome Mall manors were always one, as indeed they became after 1550, that certain facts in the records have been both misunderstood and misrecorded. Let us now attempt to set the record straight.

After the Conquest the Manors of Ling Hall and Brome also became the property of the Bigods and a Norman extension to the nave of Brome Church, revealed by the arcades of that period on the north side, shows one effect of the new Norman masters. Roger Bigod, the 4th Earl, was at one stage a close friend of Richard, Earl of Cornwall, but when Bigod joined De Montfort in the uprising against King Henry III Earl Richard had to decide where he stood and, because he gave his support to his royal brother, he was allocated some of the Bigod's lands in Eye and the lands around, including those at Brome. It is worth noting that the Castle of Framlingham also at this time reverted to the Crown for later redisposal. The Cornwallis family 'founder' had thus an early interest in the Brome, Oakley and Eye areas.

The Earl's tenure was only for a limited time and by 1263 we read that Hugh de Cressy died in possession of the Manor of Ling Hall and thereafter the property eventually became part of the inheritance of the Barham family through whom it passed, as we saw in the last chapter, to Robert Bucton. It was thence that by 1400 this manor became the first Cornwallis Suffolk possession. Brome, however, was only partially theirs.

The next Brome property had a different history. This encompassed the ground later used for the erection of 'Brome Hall'. The Bigods having forfeited their rights by insurrection Bartholomew D'Avillers I held Brome Manor in 1213 'by serjeanty of the King' and there are still deeds showing this family name as attached to some of the local manor fields. Richard Davillers next inherited and died in 1269. He left what was now known as Erwarton Manor to Bartholomew II together with what had become from 1253 free warren, a fair and market in Brome. John Davillers inherited in 1287 but it was the tenure by Bartholomew III, who held the manor until 1330, which reveals that it was still held of the King and for the service of "leading 200 men of the counties of Suffolk and Norfolk to the King's wars in Wales and paying their expenses at 4d a day for 40 days after which they will be at the King's expense".

Of Bartholomew's 4 daughters, who were under age when he died, the third, Margaret, died early; the second, Cecilia, married and bestowed her share to provide for her mother; the fourth, Joan, married first Bartholomew Bacon and secondly Sir Edmund Barkley but neither husband produced issue. Isabella, the eldest daughter, eventually acquired the whole property and married Sir Robert Bacon about 1350. This hitherto unremarked tenure of the other manor at Brome is intriguing in the light of the Bacon connection with Brome 200 years later.

It was via their daughter, another Isabel, that the title to the property passed to the Calthorpes of Burnham Thorpe in Norfolk and thence to a Sir Philip Calthorpe who married Jane Boleyn, the aunt of the famous Queen Anne, and their daughter married Sir

Henry Parker, K.B. It was the latter's sale of this manor to Robert Hyde which ensured its passing into the hands of William Cornwallis's grandson, the renowned Sir Thomas. It was thus only in 1550 that the two principal manors of Brome became the rightful property of this family.

It is when we understand this succession of 'owners' that we can begin to make sense of something else that at first seems so mystifying. Why, one has to ask, if the Cornwallises had acquired Oakley and Brome from the time of the Bucton marriage were they patrons of the Oakley living from 1412 but not of the Brome one until 1549? All however is now revealed and anyone who studies the list of Incumbents in both places can see the reasons for the patrons there named.

In the essay by Alan Simpson with which this chapter opened there is a detailed account of the properties which William Cornwallis's heir possessed in 1540 and, when compared with what was stated as his father's properties at the end of the last chapter, this list reveals that there had been added the Norfolk manors of Titteshall (now Tivetshall) and Thorpe Cornwallis (now Thorpe Abbotts) to the north and east of Scole respectively. To these were added Mellis, Rowton and Hyxley (Bixley?) in the nearer Suffolk vicinity. The significance of the two Norfolk properties is that they explain the remark of Mr. Simpson about William Cornwallis being 'a substantial figure among the clients of the House of Howard'. William was obviously holding these manors as a result of negotiations with the Dukes of Norfolk, whilst his son, Sir John, followed in his footsteps by acquiring from the Howards the further property of Brome Priory (or Monks Brome) to increase the main Ling Hall holding.

The Howards had of course passed through a very uncertain period when their loyalty to Richard III had to be exchanged for acceptance by the new House of Tudor but by the time William Cornwallis is their 'client' they had been reinstated by Henry VII and their principal properties of Tendring Hall, Ashwellthorpe and Framlingham Castle were all once more occupied by some Howard branch or other. Tivetshall was one of the holdings of Ashwellthorpe, the home of the Earl of Surrey, and it is therefore in no way surprising to learn that William's son, John, inherited homage duties connected with such a tenure and was soon serving in the Earl of Surrey's expedition to France in 1521, even though only two years after he had succeeded his father.

What is also interesting in the compared lists of properties – and not least when one adds the list of 1548 which followed the inheritance by Sir John's son, Thomas Cornwallis - is that from time to time some of the family properties were probably allocated, for as long as they might be required, to some of the younger members or relatives of the family. Which brings us naturally to these younger siblings.

The second son of William and Elizabeth was Thomas who became a priest. He had been at Eton and was admitted to King's College, Cambridge as a scholar in August 1517 when he was 18 years old. He obtained his B.A. in 1519 having already gained a Fellowship and was made deacon in Ely Cathedral in the same year, being priested 2 months later. He was presented in turn to the livings of Oakley and Thrandeston which were in the family 'gift' and where, says one source, 'he became the revered and much loved shepherd of the flock committed to his spiritual care'. He was eventually and additionally appointed as Archdeacon of Norfolk in 1543 by William Reppe next Bishop of Norwich. His need of stipend and living accommodation was therefore taken care of and it is worth remembering that it was to Thrandeston that his mother came to live after the death of her husband in 1519. Thomas was her named executor and was himself buried at Thrandeston in 1557.

It was his next brothers who might eventually have needed a property. Whether any of the manors of Hoxne, Woodhall and Yaxley were so granted is not known but it is noteworthy that by 1558 Woodhall was again in the hands of Sir Thomas, but Hoxne and Yaxley were still held by others. Edward seems to have followed in the footsteps of his older brother by accepting service in a royal household, and held from 1550 a grant for life of the office of Groom Porter. He married, though we have not yet found out whom, and he had a son Thomas who married Katharine, the daughter of Lord Southborough(?). It is unlikely, however, that he would have needed an establishment especially as he had died by May 1568.

William, the fourth son, married and left a son, William, who was buried at Hengrave in 1565 but nothing else is known about him and it may be that he was a discreet gentleman farmer who cared for corn and cattle at somewhere like Hoxne. His youngest brother, Francis, is mentioned as residing in Peckham which was then in Surrey and the link with Surrey is confirmed by his burial in Camberwell in 1565. He took on the post of Royal Groom Porter after his brother Edward died.

The daughters seem to have been reasonably provided for. Elizabeth married a gentleman named William Singleton; Prudence was the wife of Roydon Eden; Edith married William Barwick, Esq., of East Grinstead, Sussex; Afra married Sir Anthony Awcher (or Archer) of Ottenden in Kent and had four sons, John, Edward, William and Thomas. Katharine, whose name was mentioned earlier in connection with the local performance of the Mystery Play, entered the nunnery at Elstow just south of Bedford. It will be recalled that this was her mother's home county.

The author of the article 'Nikke's Lane' has some further comments on this daughter. He recounts how shortly after the death of their father Katharine and Dorothy were riding down Nikke's Lane when there approached a number of horsemen with a lady in their midst. All dismounted and the two sisters seemed to know these people for they went straight up to and spoke to the lady who was heard to say something about 'your promise'. For, to be sure, the village folk had gathered round and were quick to discover that 'Old Nick' was in this; and that the lady, who turned out to be the Abbess of Elstow, was come to take their young 'Miss Katharine' away. Indeed, after taking farewell of her widowed mother, they were not long in departing' - and the compiler of these reminiscences concludes, 'It behoves us to say that no more saintly child ever gave herself to serve God's holy Church. Often after that she was seen in her native village, ministering with such tenderness among the sick and suffering - winning such a name for piety and good works that St. Catherine's Day, in the minds of our people, became, at a later date, associated with her memory'. If it seems strange to read that a nun returned to her home village to carry on her good works it should be remembered that this was the period when the monasteries and convents were dissolved and their occupants dispersed. This reference reveals what happened in one case but also reminds us that the family were personally involved in national events.

Nikke's Lane too began to be viewed in a more pleasant light when it was at last realised that Bishop Nikke's influence was actually for good. 'After all', says our parish author, 'I think he gave them the Fair ground, abutting on the lane.'

The sister Dorothy who was mentioned as riding with Kate married a John Hede (or Head) who was also from Kent.

Having now reached the point where sons and daughters were leaving their widowed mother for their own homes and ways of life, it is high time that we met the next 'head of the family'. It would seem appropriate to hear the provisions that William made for this family before he died. His will was dated 8 November 1519 and it need be no surprise that he first requires that his body be buried in the church of St. Nicholas, Oakley since it was to be another generation before either bodies could be laid to rest in, or effigies arranged for, the church at Brome. Nonetheless William, as a true Catholic, bequeaths 6s 8d to the high altar at Brome, albeit at Oakley he leaves only 3s 4d to the high altar but provides at the latter for 'an honest priest to sing for his soul and all his friends' souls for the space of one year, and that 8 marks 6s 8d be given him for wages'. There can be no doubt about the Catholic orthodoxy of this Squire.

To his wife, Elizabeth, he granted the manor of Bixley (Hyxley?) for life as also her own inheritance in Bedfordshire. If his sister-in-law, the widow of his elder brother John, should predecease Elizabeth then the latter was to have the use of their London property, Barones, in Stepney though the rents connected with that tenure were to be used for fulfilling the rest of his will. He gave legacies to his daughters and thereafter the residue of his lands was to go to his son and heir John and to his heirs male. The Bishop of Norwich was to supervise this testament and William's widow and Thomas Goolding, clerk, were to be the executors.

William was buried at Oakley as he had wished and at the east end of the chancel is a gravestone bearing the Latin inscription that again asks for prayers to be said for his and his wife's souls. Elizabeth was to live another 17 years and in her will asked that she be buried in the chancel of Thrandeston parish church.

It is now time to look at the member of the family who was to take the family on its next stage of growth in both local and national status. John Cornwallis was born, as one can well imagine, without the most promising of prospects. He was the first son of his parents but his father, albeit shrewd and well-regarded, was the youngest son of his own father and there was every possibility that his brother John could have had heirs who would have taken on the Suffolk and other properties. It is therefore not at all surprising that the John whom we are now considering sought a career and was in 1511 (at age 20) the same John Cornwaleys recorded in the Patent Rolls as Captain of the Crown's vessel 'Jamys' which had a crew of 123 men and cost the Exchequer £132 p.a. – a responsible assignment.

Sailing, after all, was part of the inheritance that earlier merchant members of the family had shared and it was not the last time that a Cornwallis would distinguish himself at sea. Little could John have imagined, when he enlisted for a mariner's tour of duty, that it was to be just this experience that would bring him a due measure of fame and distinction. It was an added bonus that he was able to bring this maritime experience to bear when called upon by the Lord Admiral of England – the Earl of Surrey – to provide a due complement of fighting men for an expedition to France. That he was prepared for the task that was then set him might otherwise seem somewhat odd. He was not, however, just a leisured country squire. He was a young yet experienced sailor and commander and when, following the costly but abortive diplomatic approach to France at the 'Field of the Cloth of Gold', Henry VIII demanded an attack upon those across the Channel John Cornwallis was among those ready and willing to serve.

In her book on the Howards, 'The Lion and the Rose', Ethel Richardson tells us that having received his further patent from the Emperor so that he might command a joint sea and land force Thomas, Earl of Surrey, 'appeared suddenly, without any warning of his approach, off Cherbourg, and, landing there on June 13, 1521 made a rapid raid over the countryside. He then went back to Portsmouth, and as quickly returned, for on July 1 he landed again, near Morlaix. He took the town and sacked it, burnt 17 ships and amassed immense booty returning, this time, to Southampton.'

Something of the intensity and impact of the whole expedition can be grasped even from this excerpt and it was after engagement in such circumstances, and when he had distinguished himself in leading a landing party at Morlaix, that John received the honour of knighthood from the Lord High Admiral. This was the first step to such honours for the family. Temporary honours of knighthood had attended some of his forebears as they represented a county constituency. Now the family had a lasting knighthood conferred on one of its members.

Nor was this the only reward he earned. In 1542, after further royal service, but specifically granted as a continuing recognition of his Morlaix exploits, King Henry VIII granted him in fee tail the manor of Titteshall in Norfolk which was part of the proceeds from the closure of the Abbey of Bury St. Edmunds. This was all the more acceptable since 18 months before the Morlaix expedition Sir John had at last entered upon a patrimony that he could never have expected to enjoy. The right, and the means, to be a country gentleman were at last his to command. His betaking himself to war and to life-risking service is the more commendable. It was to set a tone for others and not least for Sir John's own eldest son, Thomas.

Nor can it be a matter of surprise for us that when he again returned to Suffolk and to family life he should achieve further successes as well as his marriage to Mary, the daughter of Edward Sulyard (or Sulliard) Esq. of Otes, Essex. The latter was a J.P. and member of Lincoln's Inn as well as the son of one who was at some time the Governor of that Inn, the Tutor to the Prince of Wales, later Edward V, and Lord Chief Justice of the Court of Common Pleas. This meant that the Cornwallis family had made further beneficial connections not only with the County but also the Court. Moreover the link of the now well-established family of Sulyard with the town of Eye was not likely to be lost on any senior Cornwallis member and as Sir John was already taking steps to enlarge the patrimony he had inherited this might well be the moment to ponder the attraction exercised for the Cornwallises by this Suffolk borough.

In the perspective of local involvement there was always another whole dimension that had to be reckoned with. This was the field of local politics and it is here that Henry, one of Sir John's sons, begins to turn our attention to the town and communities of Suffolk, including that of Eye, just two miles south of Brome.

In the recently published first detailed history of Eye by Clive Paine we discover some facts which are far from irrelevant to our story. Before the Conquest Eye was part of the vast property belonging to that Edric of Laxfield to whom reference has already been made and who was the largest landowner in Suffolk after King Edward the Confessor and the Abbey of Bury St. Edmunds. Such an extensive holding was reallotted by King William I to his principal lords and it was William Malet, who had had the task of burying King Harold at Battle, Sussex, who was the principal recipient of such lands, including Eye. He increased the height of the island (or 'eye') site, built the castle and established a market. This was so successful that by the time of Domesday 25 trading burgesses resided around the market place. Such improvements also attracted the 'royal eye' and on the death of William Malet in 1071 some of the properties of the Honour reverted to the Crown although his son, Robert Malet, still retained 75,000 acres.

After 1106 the title of the Lord of the Honour of Eye was held by Royalty or noble families and even for a short time by Thomas à Becket. King Richard increased the garrison in 1192 and by 1215 there is mention of the 'King's Prison at Eye'. Yet the crucial period for our attention was from 1230 to 1344 when the Honour was first granted by King John to Richard, Earl of Cornwall, and thereafter to Richard's only legitimate heir, Earl Edmund. To complete the story the Honour was then held by the de Ufford family from 1344-1382, the De la Poles from 1398 to 1513, and by Charles Brandon, 1st Duke of Suffolk, husband of Mary Tudor, from 1514 to 1538. With the exception of the Commonwealth period the Honour was once more in Royal possession until 1697 but thereafter it was granted to Charles, 3rd Lord Cornwallis, of Brome, whose family had been Stewards of Eye since at least 1632.

It is into that interesting sequence of tenures that the earlier links of the Cornwallis family with Eye have to be fitted. The apparently determinate family policy of recovering in some fashion a link with the royal forebears who once held title to London or Suffolk properties again appears in the presentation of Henry Cornwallis as the Member of Parliament for Orford in 1532, a seat he held until 1553. Though it might be another century before a Cornwallis might represent Eye the marriage of Sir John and Mary Sulyard was a step in the right direction and the service that Sir John's eldest son was to render as Sheriff for both Norfolk and Suffolk could only enhance both his family's profile in the area and prepare the way for later claims of local influence.

As a landowner Sir John was also successful. The first of his bailiff's accounts that we have suggest that he had doubled his rent roll in five or six years and by 1540 the various properties were bringing in a clear annual income of about £115 a year. By the time he died the net income from land had risen to £200 per annum. This was achieved mainly by the regular new land purchases which were made, such as Monks Brome which he bought from the Duke of Norfolk. Similar new acquisitions were made in each of the following years though Palgrave was assigned to a member of the family and we have seen that the Roxne and Yaxley manors remained in other hands. The sums that were acquired from Court fees and fines were not large on the whole though there was a windfall from Titeshall in 1542 but this may have been due to the impact made by a new and vigorous lord.

Nor is it to be forgotten that in both London and elsewhere there were Cornwallis interests that were being managed by Sir John. In the London Bridge Accounts for 1538 we note that an annual quit rent of £45 was paid to Sir John Cornwaleys, Kt. from "a Tenement at Tower Hill near to the Minories and late held of Jo. Higgyns, butcher . . ." (p. 173) What is therefore certain is that by the time Thomas was to inherit he was to be worth no less than £300 a year, a very respectable patrimony for a squire in 1544. Sir John had managed his local affairs well.

Yet as was suggested at the outset of this chapter Sir John Cornwallis was not content with being a landed gentleman. His interest in a Court appointment had no doubt been stimulated by the example of his uncles or great-uncles, Edward and Robert, William and Francis, but the Sulyard connection, and possibly a suggestion or even recommendation of the Howard family members, could have helped. What is clear is that having set his own house in order in the late 1520s and early 30s he was in 1538 appointed as a Steward of the Household of King Henry VIII's one and only illegitimate son, Prince Edward. His retention of this office up to the time of the Prince's death six years later bespeaks both his dedication and his ambition. He had a sufficiency of status and income to maintain a place at the court of the next monarch and he was certainly making it much more likely that subsequent members of his own and later generations of the family would be considered for like appointments. We know, and will be showing in the next few chapters, that what he and his uncles had begun was a foundation of some substance.

All in all then Sir John Cornwallis is a notable figure and he could depart this life in the confident knowledge that he had served both his kin and his kingdom well. His will, dated 10 April 1544 reveals the care and attention to his possessions and his progeny that we would expect.

With a natural piety he 'commends his soul to Almighty God and the whole company of heaven' (which suggests a natural familiarity with the usual liturgy of the day) and requests that his body be buried 'with Christian burial, where it shall please God to suffer him to depart this world'. Why exactly he was at Ashridge in Buckinghamshire – once the site of Ashridge Abbey near Berkhamsted – when he died is a query which noone has hitherto been able satisfactorily to answer. What does not seem to have occurred to anyone is the fact that Richard, Earl of Cornwall died at Berkhamsted in 1272 and his son, Earl Edmund, not only died there in 1300 but at Ashridge Abbey. They were both buried at Hailes Abbey which Richard had founded and which, like Ashridge, had recently suffered closure and destruction. With the family memory as strong as we know it to have been and with the dissolution of so much that linked their ancestors past with the present could it be that Sir John, knowing that he was possibly approaching his death, wanted to close his life where both those early ancestors ended theirs? What might seem morbid and necrophiliac to us was not necessarily such to persons then. Another suggestion may be that he was there conducting royal business with the Princess Elizabeth whose residence this was and we certainly know that he was on good terms with her. His desire to be buried there also has its peculiar fascination. What is clear is that his wishes were respected and it is in Berkhamsted that there is a tomb where his bodily remains were interred though he is also most vividly recalled by the effigies of himself and his wife – he bearing his Steward's white wand – in the parish church of Brome. More must be said about this, however, in the next chapter.

Of his substance and concern as a local landholder there can be little doubt for he next instructs his executors to 'distribute within one month after his decease a sum of £5 to be divided equally among all the poor householders in whichever nearby towns his lands lie. His son and heir, Thomas, receives all the furniture of his houses at Broome, Frense (Fersfield?) in Norfolk, 'or elsewhere within the realm of England' and likewise all his cattle, corn, &c. so long as he gives his two younger sisters, Anne and Mary, 'their double marriage apparel', which presumably means a sum which would be twice the cost of their marriage dowry. Nonetheless, Sir John was not asking Thomas to write a blank cheque because he adds: 'according to the degree of every such person or persons they should marry withall'. In the event Anne married a Mr. Thomas Kent of Suffolk whilst Mary became first the wife of William Hales in Devonshire (a name which again conjures up memories of Richard, Earl of Cornwall's Abbey) and then Roger Warren who owned and lived in a house of renowned beauty at Newbourne, near Woodbridge, Suffolk. These girls also received 300 marks as additional marriage portions and if one or other died before marriage then their portion went to the other.

The value of good clothing was never lost sight of in these days and to his eldest daughter, Elizabeth, here referred to as 'Hasset' since she married John Blennerhasset, he gave his wife's gown of black satten (sic) whilst to his daughter-in-law, the wife of son Thomas, he bequeaths the gown of black velvet which was his wife's. To his son, Henry, the M.P., he leaves his own gown of tawney (sic) taffeta. (It is worthy of a footnote that the daughter of the Blennerhassett couple above was the grandmother of that John Throckmorton who was a pioneer in Providence, Rhode Island.)

Henry Cornwallis is always said to have lived in and around Brome though noone seems to have known precisely where. It could be that he was the member of the family to whom Palgrave was assigned, at least for his lifetime, because when he died in 1598 he was buried at Brome and his presence is remembered by a fine monument close to the

Cornwallis tomb. It shows him kneeling in prayer beneath a classical arch and with two lines of Latin inscribed beneath. They may be translated thus:

"In this state I came in, that thus I might depart,
For let there be no doubt that he who is born must die"

On the other hand he and his family may have occupied Ling Hall when it was vacated after the erection of the 'Elizabethan' Brome Hall c.1560.

What is certain is that Henry first married into a strongly Papist family, the Rokewoods of Euston, who were to be closely linked to the Gunpowder Plot, and Anne, his wife, bore him two children. She died in April 1565 and lies buried in Norwich Cathedral because her mother belonged to the important family of Wychingham in North Norfolk. Henry was then married again, this time to Anne, daughter of Edgar Calibut, another devoutly Catholic family of East Rudham, near Fakenham, Norfolk.

On his son Richard Sir John bestowed his ward, Margaret Lowthe, whom Sir John had 'bought of my Lord of Norfolk'. She was the heir of Lionel Lowthe of Sawtry, in the county of Huntingdonshire, and had her own property and house at Cretingham. That she came of substantial stock is confirmed by the fact that in 1419 one of her forebears who was a Citizen of London and Goldsmith, as well as being elected Alderman, was called on to share with some others a payment to the King of 1000 marks. Richard was either to marry her himself 'if they both will be so contented' or he was to have the advantages and profits accruing from her marrying someone else. Richard did in fact choose the first option and seems to have been happily united with the lady. As a bachelor he lived at Okenhill Hall in Badingham but after his marriage the couple resided either at Earl Soham Lodge or at Creting Hall. What these locations reveal is the intimate link between the Cornwallises and the House of Norfolk, whose ward Margaret had first been.

It now transpires that what may have been thought was a temporary grant from the Bishop of the advowson and presentation to the Archdeaconry of Norwich was no such thing. It belonged to the family for the time being and Sir John wills that "when it falls void (as it would do when his brother Thomas died) his executors present his (fourth) son, William, to it, if so be he takes upon him priest's orders; but if he be not minded so to do, that he should have the nomination thereto'. We know that William matriculated as a Pensioner from Gonville Hall, Cambridge in Michaelmas 1544 but there is no further information about his being ordained.

Nor did Sir John forget his brothers in this final disposal of his goods. Archdeacon Thomas was apparently considered well enough endowed but not only were substantial gowns bestowed on his siblings, Edward and Francis, but it was added for William 'that he should have an annuity of £5 for life out of the lands at Broome, payable at the four usual feasts, as also his board with his son Thomas, or on refusal a further annuity of £6.13s.4d'. This nephew Thomas is registered as a Fellow Commoner at Gonville Hall, Cambridge who matriculated at Michaelmas, 1546. The executors of this will were Lady Blennerhasset, to whom he left 'his gilt cup, with the cover', and John Blennerhasset, his son-in-law.

Into possession of all his other goods, moveable and immoveable, with all his manors, lands, &c., in the counties of Norfolk, Suffolk, Middlesex, London and Yorkshire there now comes Thomas Cornwallis. Born in 1519 just as his grandfather died we know so much less about his education and early religious development, save that whilst his father might be content serving an 'Anglican' Prince his mother came from a dedicated and devoutly Catholic family. The impression of her influence was to last.

It could be that he was provided with a private tutor before he was entered at Lincoln's Inn but he was thereafter introduced to the management of the Cornwallis estates if only because his father was already busily engaged with Court matters by the time his eldest son was 19. It is worth recalling also that Thomas's childhood was at just the time of the 'King's Great Matter' and with a direct line into Court service he was unlikely to be unaware of all that was taking place regarding the King's subsequent marriages. He also had an uncle who was an Archdeacon, an aunt who was a nun who had been separated from her nunnery, and a growing relationship with families that were also determinedly Roman Catholic – both the one into which his brother, Henry, was to marry but also that from which was to come his own bride, Anne Jerningham. Of that family, and of Thomas's own fortunes as he became Lord of Brome and Oakley in his own right, we shall tell in the next chapter. What is clear is that the name Cornwallis was now one that carried its own distinction both locally and further afield. The family had arrived. It was now up to its members to reveal their undoubted qualities.

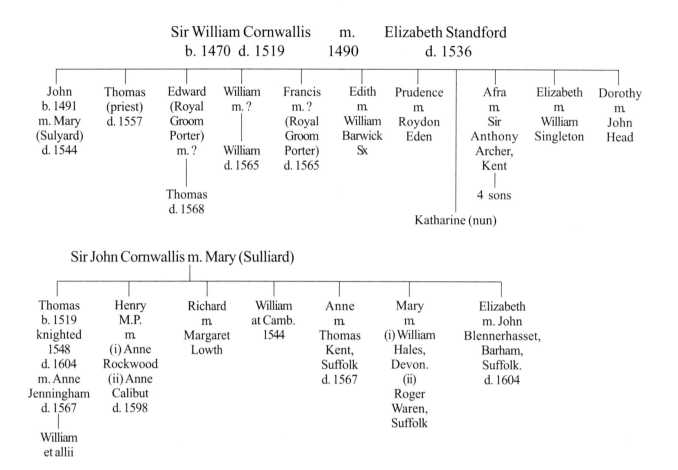

Sir William Cornwallis m. Elizabeth Standford
b. 1470 d. 1519   1490   d. 1536

John	Thomas	Edward	William	Francis	Edith	Prudence	Afra	Elizabeth	Dorothy
b. 1491	(priest)	(Royal	m.?	m.?	m.	m.	m.	m.	m.
m. Mary	d. 1557	Groom		(Royal	William	Roydon	Sir	William	John
(Sulyard)		Porter)		Groom	Barwick	Eden	Anthony	Singleton	Head
d. 1544		m.?	William	Porter)	Sx		Archer,		
			d. 1565	d. 1565			Kent		

Thomas
d. 1568

4 sons

Katharine (nun)

Sir John Cornwallis m. Mary (Sulliard)

Thomas	Henry	Richard	William	Anne	Mary	Elizabeth
b. 1519	M.P.	m.	at Camb.	m.	m.	m. John
knighted	m.	Margaret	1544	Thomas	(i) William	Blennerhasset,
1548	(i) Anne	Lowth		Kent,	Hales,	Barham,
d. 1604	Rockwood			Suffolk	Devon.	Suffolk.
m. Anne	(ii) Anne			d. 1567	(ii)	d. 1604
Jenningham	Calibut				Roger	
d. 1567	d. 1598				Waren,	
					Suffolk	

William
et allii

Map of properties referred to:-

    Tivetshall

Fresfield   Thorpe Abbotts

          Diss   Scole

Redgrave   Palgrave

               Oakley   Hoxne   Wingfield

   Thrandeston   Stuston

   Mellis

              Brome

   Yaxley   Eye   Laxfield

               Occold

                     Earl   Framlingham

        Cretingham   Soham

CHAPTER 5

The Tree begins to Spread

In any family of note there are periods when both personalities and events seem to be blessed with a particular brightness. That might already be said to have been the case with the Thomas Cornwallis who firmly established the family's City status in the 14th century but it can certainly be claimed for his namesake who inherited the estates in and around Brome and elsewhere in the year 1546. It is to him as the new Lord of Brome and to his wife and family that we must now turn.

Anne, who became his wife in 1545, was the daughter of Sir John Jerningham of Somerleyton, Suffolk. The family were originally called Jernegan and claimed Danish extraction, settling first in Horham not far from Brome and where they had property. Subsequently they obtained an estate at Somerley Town in Lothingland, just north of Lowestoft, by marriage with the FitzOsbornes, and where Somerleyton Hall stands to this day. It is not without relevance to our story to record that Anne Jerningham's grandmother was a Margaret Bedingfield, and Anne's sister, Eliza, married Sir John Sulyard of Wetherdon. The links with all these families had no small influence on Sir Thomas's future.

Of this union there were six children - John, William, Charles, Elizabeth, Alice, and Mary (or Anne). John was the firstborn and we know that he was baptized as the son of Thos. Cornwallis, Esq. on 8 September 1547 at Oakley. Sadly he died before his teens and that is why William is today referred to as the eldest son.

With William and his brother Charles we come to an increasing and continuing line of Cornwallis sons who are usually sent to Cambridge, though a few go to Oxford. "It is important to remember that the university community was not large and that the number of students was not sufficiently great to preclude general acquaintance and development of friendship across college lines. It has been suggested that apart from the presence of unmatriculated gentlemen commoners Cambridge did not have many more than 160 students prior to 1553 with St. John's being the largest college with about 30 students and most colleges having 10 or less. In addition to the relative intimacy of university life, one should also keep in mind that many of the students were barely into their teens. They were at the university during a period of their lives when the deepest and most enduring friendships were formed." (Winthrop Hudson, *The Cambridge Connection*, p. 41)

Moreover at just the time when Sir Thomas's sons and grandsons went up the principal influences at Cambridge were an exploding interest in humanist and classical learning, a common Protestant religious orientation and an insistence on a reformed method of pronouncing Greek. Such was the milieu into which these boys entered.

William, born in 1548, is recorded as having been taught at home before matriculating at Trinity College, Cambridge, as a Pensioner and as early as 1560, and he was still registered as a resident student in Trinity Hall in August 1564. His brother Charles, born a year or so later, was also at Trinity College and matriculated as a Fellow-Commoner in 1566. As we shall see in due course the latter obviously benefitted greatly from his education and, having no certainty about his prospects as a landed gentleman, also set his sights on a career in government service.

Alice, baptized in Oakley Parish Church on 23 August 1552, married Richard Southwell of Woodrising, Norfolk, of a devout Catholic family which was also one of the richest in the land. Richard's mother was Bridget Copley whose father was a man of vast possessions in the City, Sussex and Surrey, in which latter county he had the presentation to two seats in Parliament for the manor of Gatton. Through the Copleys the Southwells became cousins of the Cecils and of the Bacons, through the Belknaps and the Cokes. Richard was the eldest brother of Robert Southwell, the 'new poet' of the Elizabethans and a notable martyr-priest. In like manner Elizabeth, born in 1553, was to marry Sir Thomas Kitson, the heir of another Catholic family, and she became the Lady of Hengrave Hall, which had been built by Sir Thomas Kitson's father, a successful London merchant, as recently as 1525. Though its craftsmanship is still impressive it is only a third of the size of the original structure and it was here that Elizabeth was buried in 1602.

After Sir Thomas had buried his wife in St. Mary's, Brome, on 28 May, 1581 he related very closely to his two younger daughters as the following letter suggests:

"Sir Thomas (Kitson) is not yet delivered of his complaint wherewith he hath been very sore grieved these three days. My daughter (Lady Kitson), thanks be to God, is well of her cullock (colic), but her face is yet very lean and speckled. My daughter of Bath hath made her a new straight-bodied gowne of black velvett. It becometh her person well, but it becometh not my weake purse to bee at this charge." (1583)

Leaving aside for the moment the reason for this hint of Sir Thomas's straitened means at this stage we might note that his third daughter, Mary, had been married to William Bourchier, 5th Earl of Bath, but the union not having pleased the Earl's family he was compelled to dissolve it in the Ecclesiastical Court. He was to marry again, this time with the daughter of the Earl of Bedford but Mary was allowed to retain the title, Countess of Bath, when she returned home. She resided at Thorpe Abbots Hall near Brome Parish Church where she was buried on 17 May 1627.

Though we shall follow the progress of the two sons later it is now time to consider the estate of the new Lord of Brome. As was suggested in the last chapter the worth of Thomas's father was "solidly established by the amount he had put into land and the provision he was able to make for his younger children". (Simpson, op. cit., p. 143) Sir John's records do not reveal exactly how much might be the income from the London and Middlesex properties nor from the profits of farming at Brome where northern cattle were fattened for market and there was a foldcourse for sheep. It was however on a firm basis that the new Lord began his tenure and whilst he might soon learn that his religious leanings would not benefit him under the young Edward VI or Queen Elizabeth, both of whom he outlived, he was nevertheless knighted in 1548 in King Edward's court at Westminster.

It was in this capacity and as a Justice of the Peace that he found himself in 1549 faced with an uprising led by the tanner, Robert Kett, some of whose relations later dwelt at Oakley. Together with the Marquess of Northampton, Lord Sheffield and other gentlemen he was required to crush the disturbance and though at first they managed to secure Norwich it was retaken by the rebels and Kett even erected his rude throne beneath the so-called 'Tree of Reformation' on the City's hill. Sir Thomas was captured and the bravery with which he faced his imprisonment, until John Dudley, Earl of Warwick brought the rebellion to a peaceful conclusion, rightly earned him further notice by the Crown.

He was also soon to find himself singularly well placed at a crucial moment of Tudor history, which we ought briefly to recall.

"When a summons to come to her dying brother's bedside reached Mary (Tudor) at Hunsdon, probably on July 5 (1553), she obediently set out on the journey. She had not gone far – she was at Hoddesdon on the London road – before she received an anonymous warning . . . that Northumberland's message was a trap . . . .

"Now if she was to save herself, let alone her chances of becoming Queen, she must act with speed and decision . . . After sending a brief word to the Imperial embassy, she turned aside and, with no more than half a dozen loyal companions, rode hard and straight down the Newmarket road for Kenninghall in Norfolk - one of the Howard properties. She had friends in the eastern counties and there, if it came to the worst, she would be within reach of the coast and rescue . . .". Sir Thomas Cornwallis J.P. was one of those friends as a devoted tenant and servant of the the Howards.

"Northumberland despatched a party of 300 horse under the command of his son, Robert, with orders to pursue and capture the Lady Mary and on Sunday, 9 July, he finally showed his hand. The Bishop of London, preaching at St. Paul's Cross, referred to both the princesses as bastards and fulminated especially against Mary as a papist who would bring foreigners into the country. Also on that Sunday the Lady Jane (Grey) was officially informed of her new status . . . (and) the heralds were going round the City proclaiming Queen Jane but, noted the Greyfriars Chronicle ominously, "few or none said 'God save her'". The sullenly silent crowds in Cheapside and Ludgate that summer evening set the pattern for the rest of the country. The English people . . . had always had a soft spot for Mary Tudor and, even more to the point, they had come to loathe the whole tribe of Dudley for greedy, tyrannical upstarts . . .

"Meanwhile, King Harry's daughter had reached the comparative safety of Kenninghall and on 9 July had written defiantly to the Council, commanding them to proclaim her right and title in her City of London . . .

"Every day that Mary remained free would undermine her opponents further and disquieting reports were beginning to come in about the support rallying to her. The 2nd Earl of Sussex and his son Thomas were on the way to Norfolk, while the Earl of Bath and men like Sir Thomas Wharton, Sir John Mordaunt, Sir Henry Bedingfield and Henry Jerningham, as well as other substantial gentlemen with their tenantry - not to mention 'innumerable small companies of the common people' were already helping to swell the numbers at the little camp now established at Framlingham Castle (another House of Norfolk property), a stronger place than Kenninghall and nearer the coast . . .

"During the next few days the faces of those left behind in the Tower grew steadily longer as word arrived that Mary had been proclaimed in Norwich and that the town had sent her men and weapons. Even more worrying were the reports of desertions and dissensions in Northumberland's forces. Then came a shattering piece of news – the crews of six royal ships, sent to Yarmouth to cut off Mary's escape route, had gone over to her in a body, taking their captains and their heavy guns with them . . . and (so) between 5 and 6 in the evening of 19 July at the Cross in Cheapside amid scenes of hysterical excitement" Mary was proclaimed the rightful Queen . . . '. At Framlingham Mary's first act as Queen had been to order the crucifix to be set up again in the parish church where a Te Deum was sung . . .". (Alison Plowden, *The House of Tudor*, pp. 153ff)

From this impartial and well researched account it can be seen why Sir Thomas was 'in the right place at the right moment'. He began the new reign as one who could assemble forces which enabled the monarch to save her throne and as the inscription on his tomb reminds us he was eventually to die 'in the especial grace and trust of his mistress at her untimely death'. What is certain is that loyalty to the direct royal line characterized the whole of his life and not only did this immediately earn him the gratitude of Queen Mary but it was to temper his treatment later under Queen Elizabeth. John Bossy in a recent book (2001) entitled "Under the Molehill" states that as Queen Mary's Comptroller of the Household he "protected Princess Elizabeth from persecution by her enemies. This service secured him a quiet life during Elizabeth's reign . . .". (p. 72)

What we also note is that amongst the persons specially mentioned as rallying to the new Queen's camp at Framlingham was the present head of the Jerningham family into which Sir Thomas had married. In the 1350s there is a reference to a John Jernagan and property in the area of Brome so some connection then with the Cornwallis family was already likely. Sir Richard Jerningham was a Privy Counsellor to Henry VIII and a Sir Robert was knighted, like Thomas's father, on a battlefield but this time by Charles Brandon, Duke of Suffolk. The Henry Jerningham mentioned above was the owner of Costessy Park, Norfolk, as well as being a Privy Counsellor to Queen Mary, and of this family's religious allegiance we are reminded by the fact that in 1584 Henry's son was criticized for his recusant behaviour by a Commission of Suffolk Protestant gentry. As a more recent history of Suffolk puts it:

"Although East Anglia did not have a strong Roman Catholic movement like that in the north . . . many substantial families, like the Bedingfields of Bedingfield, the Sulyards of Haughley Park and the Rokewoods of Euston and Stanningfield had large parts of their estates confiscated (under Elizabeth) and leased out for the benefit of the Crown. Only in the Lothingland area, where the Jernegan family held sway, were recusants able to maintain their power and freedom for any length of time."

Of Thomas's close connection with the Catholic camp there could thus be no question and whilst Mary was on the throne his future seemed both assured and promising. He was soon nominated to the Privy Council and his wife, Anne, became one of the Ladies of the Royal Bedchamber. In 1553 Sir Thomas was despatched with Sir Robert Bowes to negotiate the Treaty of Edinburgh concerning the border with the Scots and on his return found himself pricked as a Sheriff for Norfolk and Suffolk.

It was in February the next year that Sir Thomas was given another assignment. In the company of William, Lord Howard, and Sir Edward Hastings of Loughborough he was given the task of bringing the Princess Elizabeth from Hertfordshire to London. The fact that Sir Thomas was on royal business at Ashridge may have reawakened memories of his father and certainly this mission reinforces the view that it was for a meeting with the possible heir to the Throne that his father had come to this place. The invitation to leave her secure home and make an uncertain journey whose destination was the Tower might explain why the Princess protested that she was sick or feigned illness and we know that she particularly asked 'that her lodging in the Tower might be more removed from the water and its unhealthy effects' than had been the case on the previous occasion. It was no doubt a triumph of kindliness and tact by her visitors which resulted in the journey being undertaken at all, albeit by easy stages of only 8 miles a day. It was also probably the courtesy and consideration with which she was treated on this occasion which led to Elizabeth harbouring no lasting grudge, at least against Sir Thomas. As Winthrop Hudson has put it: (op. cit., p. 15)

"Those who sustained her with help, friendship, or affection in her times of trouble were persons she did not forget in later years."

Of Sir Thomas's continuing care for Elizabeth's welfare we are given evidence by Copinger in his monumental work on the 'Manors of Suffolk'. We are there told that he opposed the plan in the Privy Council to send Elizabeth out of the country with a view to excluding her from the succession, 'alledging (sic) that the people of England would take it very ill, nay, would not at all endure that the next heir to the crown should be conveyed out of the land'. That Sir Thomas, for all his Catholic convictions, was not enthusiastic about the Spanish alliance seems clear from some of the reports made on him by the Spanish envoys. In May 1558 Count Feria was reporting to King Philip that Cornwallis was one of the most influential men in the government and ought to be one of the negotiators in any dealings with the French but he added that he was always making difficulties about everything. This certainly confirms what was said earlier about Sir Thomas's primary allegiance being not to the faith of his ruler but to the proper royal succession.

Of his courage in dealing with local uprisings yet another trial was made when later in 1554 he was chosen with others to treat with Sir Thomas Wyatt, the leader of a serious rebellion in Kent. This had arisen over the likely effect of Queen Mary's Spanish marriage and reflected significant anxieties amongst many of the population about the likelihood of the Inquisition's influence spreading into England. The State Papers reveal that Sir Thomas and the others were especially charged 'to disclose to Wiatt the motives of her marriage with Prince Philip'. At the conclusion of this episode, which at one point looked like being a real threat to Mary Tudor's rule, when Wyatt had been arrested, tried and executed, Sir Thomas was made one of the group on the Queen's Council charged with garrison-maintenance, and was further rewarded with the post of Treasurer to Calais under his cousin, Sir Thomas Wentworth. In terms of a career all seemed set fair.

The marriage of Queen Mary to King Philip of Spain took place in that same year and both the Queen and many of her people looked forward to the emergence of an heir. The relationship of the royal couple, however, did not mature and by 1556 Philip was again normally resident in Spain. Mary grieved over her husband's constant absence.

"Then, at the end of March, 1557, Philip did come back. It was for a short visit only, with only one objective – to drag England into the everlasting Franco-Spanish war . . . The year 1558 opened with a military disaster. The war in France had begun promisingly with the Anglo-Spanish victory of St. Quentin, but then things went less well and, finally, very badly indeed, culminating in the news that Calais had fallen to the French – 'the heaviest tidings to London and to England that ever was heard of'." (Plowden, op. cit., p. 158) The town of Calais and its surrounding Pale might no longer have been of much strategic importance but as the final remnant of what had once been England's Continental empire it represented a great past. Its loss was regarded as a national humiliation and more than one historian has recorded that Mary was said to have died the following year with 'Calais' engraven on her heart.

Sir Thomas had informed the Queen in July 1557 of the inadequacy of the Calais defences and he relinquished his post two months before the town fell to the French. The connection of his name with the final surrender has therefore been perhaps too easily assumed. Indeed it would seem that no blame whatsoever attached to him as far as the Crown was concerned and in the following Spring he was even suggested as one of those who might try to secure the return of Calais from the French. Moreover his appointment in December 1557 to be Comptroller of the Queen's Household is difficult to understand if his earlier service had been in any way reprehensible. On the contrary, both his loyalty to the monarch and his trustworthiness in business matters seem to have been fully vindicated.

Sir Thomas's religious stance during Mary's reign seems to have been both personally devout and politically discreet. In a letter sent from Calais to Sir William Petre on 6 March 1555 he explains that in his haste to set off for France he had forgotten to ask the Queen to provide a replacement for the present incumbent in that town. The Rev. Dr. Serles was considered by him to be 'a man so rude, unlearned and barbarous, as the like was never heard in the place of a preacher'. Hence 'for the advancement of God's glory, the Queen's proceedings, the estimation of learning and the people's conversion it had been better her Majesty had spent £300 than such an unlearned man should have come among the people'. He asked that Archdeacon Harpsfield or 'some other grave learned man' might be sent with haste ' to repair this man's hurt'.

In matters relating to the often mentioned persecutions of Mary's reign it would seem that Sir Thomas was only once involved in a major case of this kind. The Council required him, together with Sir Nicholas Hare, to examine a William Flower who had seriously assaulted and wounded a priest who was administering the Sacrament in St. Margaret's Church, Westminster. They were to inquire if he had any associates and why he had round his neck a placard with the words 'Deum time, idolum fuge' (Fear God and avoid any idol). If Flower persisted in his 'heresy' the Bishop of Winchester was to proceed against him on that ground and the Justices of the Peace for Middlesex were then to have his right hand struck off on the day before his execution. One suspects that Sir Thomas, whilst dutiful in the discharge of his commission, was not unhappy to be called upon no further. What might also be mentioned is that he was remarked in the Council to be one of those who openly opposed the introduction of Bills relating to religion without Parliament having foreknowledge of them.

His Parliamentary career began with his acquiring a Suffolk county seat on the elevation of Wentworth to the peerage. In 1553 he became M.P. for Gatton in Surrey, the borough owned by the Copley family, but he cannot have been happy with this nomination since he was included by this appointment amongst those 'who stood for the true religion' which here referred to Anglicanism.

Accordingly, and fittingly in view of the family's origins, a seat was found for him at Grampound in the Duchy of Cornwall. He obtained this because the previous occupant, Thomas Prideaux, moved to another seat whilst Bodmin, which the Prideaux family also held, was filled by Cornwallis's kinsman, John Sulyard. After Sir Thomas's return from Calais he became once more a Suffolk M.P. sharing this honour with the Speaker-designate, William Cordell, and during this last period of service he was a frequent bearer of Bills to the Lords.

That Sir Thomas gained greater rewards from his Court appointments than earlier members of his family may be true but that he made excessive profits from them is unlikely if only because they were of comparatively short duration. Nonetheless there are, in the Fitch MSS at Ipswich, two provocative verses of that period. One ran:

> "Who built Brome Hall? Sir Thomas Cornwallis.
> How did he build Brome Hall? By selling of Calais."
> and the other: "Sir Thomas Cornwallis, what got ye for Calais?
> Brome Hall, Brome Hall, as large as a Palais."

What then is the truth of the matter? From the accounts in the Iveagh Collection at Ipswich we can discover all the sums involved and without going into too great detail the result seems to be as follows.

In the last 5 quarters of the actual tenure of the Calais Treasurership the arrears and income (though the latter included several thousand pounds' worth of grain and provisions) amounted to £45,000. Thomas, Lord Wentworth, claimed £880 for his establishment, Sir Anthony Aucher, the chief marshal, was given £300 for his, and Sir Thomas claimed it in 1793. Most of this latter was spent on personnel and in the final assessment the Treasurer was still owing £3485 though this was remitted by a royal warrant of 4 April 1558 on the grounds that this amount was in the hands of the Treasurer's deputies when they surrendered to the French. It could not be said, therefore, that Sir Thomas had benefitted unduly. However, we also see that he did have a year as Comptroller in 1558 and payments due to him in that capacity came in even after he had relinquished that office. From the figures provided for this period we learn that Sir Thomas would have had a final sum of almost £4,800.

To achieve this figure he must also have had several stewardships and wardships and we know that in October 1558 he secured a licence to buy and export 600 sacks of wool for the next 6 years, a privilege which would almost certainly have been sold off to some merchant. Two weeks later he received the manor of Wilton in Cleveland for a yearly rent of £50 and only 5 days before he surrendered his office he was given another Suffolk lease of 30 years on the manor of Walsham, which he at once sold to Sir Nicholas Bacon, the new Lord Keeper. This was not the first nor would it be the last link with that particular family.

As one commentator remarks, however, "From this level of affluence, which reflected the profits of office, the descent was rapid. With Sir Thomas retired to the country the cash defrayed was £1061 in 1560, £1533 in 1561, £1138 in 1562 and £1212 in 1563." (Simpson, op. cit., pp. 148ff) Certainly Sir Thomas would have had a longer and even more distinguished public career if Queen Mary had not died in November 1558. Yet his connection with the old order was too close for him to be similarly employed in the next reign. On the other hand it does seem that he had been remunerated sufficiently for him to contemplate making a new home.

It was between 1562 and 1569 that he, Lady Cornwallis and those children who were still with them moved to the house at Thrandeston so that provision could be made for a much more suitable family dwelling. This was to be a brick mansion with curiously ornamented chimneys and costing the then very considerable sum of £1000. It was to have a lofty great hall or dining chamber wainscotted in oak to a height of some 10 feet whilst the roof had exposed timbers in the style of a church roof. A large stained-glass window was to be at one end displaying several of the arms connected with the family whilst at the other, in the style now familiar in an Oxbridge college hall, there would be a gallery over the screen that included the entrance. Behind the screen there was to be the butler's pantry with stairs to it at both ends of the passage.

From a late 19th century account of Suffolk country houses we are even told that above the wainscot were whole length portraits of Queen Mary and her consort, Elizabeth, Mary of Scotland, Sir Thomas More and his wife and Lord Burghley. On the staircase leading to the later more private dining room and sleeping apartments there would

Sir Thomas Cornwallis of Brome, Suffolk

Brome Hall in the County of Suffolk, one of the Seats of the Rt. Honᵇᵉˡ Charles Lord Cornwallis Lord Lᵗ. of the Said County Baron of Eye &c.

66

eventually be other portraits including those of subsequent monarchs, of Sir Thomas himself and Lady Bacon with three children.

Yet the splendour of the mansion was reflected in the fact that there was a private chapel on the ground floor with a window looking out onto the lawn. It had cushioned seats furnished in silk and one for the clergyman of rich purple velvet was marked with the date 1550. As can still be seen in other private chapels elsewhere the body of the chapel, hung with tapestries showing scenes in the life of Christ, was separated by a carved Gothic screen from that portion occupied by the servants.

Whilst the interior of this new home may have delighted and satisfied those who dwelt there the main impact of this new Hall on the general public was made by the setting of the house in its extensive grounds. An impressive drive with three parallel lines of trees on each side led to the entrance porch at the centre of a U-shaped set of buildings that formed the core of the Hall though to the left of the drive there was an ample stable block in its own courtyard and beyond them lay the Home Farm, one of two such originally connected with the estate. There were further dwelling areas behind the right wing of the main block and an impressive clocktower rose above the entrance door. Had you climbed up into the tower you would have seen six large areas that were to be the formal, flower, kitchen and fruit gardens, with wide areas of parkland extending into the districts of Oakley and Eye and including the Brome Park Farm and the Long Pond of which traces still remain. The terrace walks around the lawns and ornamental pool, with their later topiary, must have been an increasing delight to Sir Thomas.

Yet it was not only the new hall and its grounds that were built and enhanced by Sir Thomas at this time. He also built a Dower House and created the Cornwallis 'chapel' of the Parish Church. That there was a need for a Dower House there is no question. His father had been preceded by three brothers who left widows behind even if his own mother had gone to Thrandeston with his uncle Thomas. The house which he now provided had its own special dignity and much later was to become first another Rectory and then the Hotel which it is today. It stands beyond the Church and on the right of the village lane.

In the first year that the family moved into the new house Sir Thomas turned his attention to rebuilding the north aisle of the Parish Church where some of his ancestors were buried. A stone tomb bearing the marble figures of his parents was erected even though the mortal remains of those displayed had been interred elsewhere. Seeing it today surrounded by the memorials of their immediate successors it is difficult to imagine the impact that its introduction must have made on those who regularly worshipped here. That it marked not merely the status of the Cornwallises as the principal local landowners but now also their patronage of the living must have been evident. Moreover it recorded not only the dignity of those whose effigies were revealed but the family connections of the Cornwallises who had occupied the Manors of Brome hitherto.

The inscription below the figures and on the upper panel around reads:

"Johannes Cornwaleis miles willmi Cornwaleis Armiger filius in domo principis Edwardi oeconumus: et uxor ejusdem Maria Edwardi Suliarde de Essex Armigeri filie, qui quid Johannes, 23 Aprilis anno Domini 1544 obiit Astrugie Incomitatu Buckingham cum ibidem princeps Edouardus versaretur." (Translation: John Cornwallis knight and son of Sir William Cornwallis, steward in the household of Prince Edward: and his wife Mary, daughter of Sir Edward Sulyard of Essex; which said John died on the 23 April A.D. 1544 at Ashridge in the county of Buckingham where the same Prince Edward was living.)

Beneath this inscription are ten panels around the tomb and eight of these show armorial bearings relating to their children as follows:

North side: 1. Cornwallis impaling blank; (for William the priest?)
            2. Cornwallis impaling Rokewood and Wychingham; (Henry)
            3. Cornwallis impaling Lowthe; (Richard)
West end: 1. Cornwallis impaling Jerningham; (Thomas)
            2. Blennerhasset impaling Cornwallis; (Elizabeth)
South side: 1. Kent impaling Cornwallis; (Ann)
            2. Halse impaling Cornwallis; (Mary)
            3. Blank impaling Cornwallis: (an unborn child?)

On the wall facing the recumbent figures are the arms of Sir John himself.

Nor was this all. As Sir Thomas's grandfather had provided the nearby St. Nicholas, Oakley with a fine South Porch over 50 years previously so now he provided the same feature for St. Mary's. The tree was spreading.

During this period of the construction of a new family home to the south-east of the village Sir Thomas, who was now in his forties, seems to have both savoured and enjoyed his role as a country gentleman and squire. A letter sent to Francis Yaxley, Clerk of the Signet, Sir William Cordell, the Master of the Rolls, describes how Sir Thomas and his daughter, the Countess of Bath, with Lord Windsor and his wife, have been with him and 'have been making merry'. Visiting the homes of his brothers and children as well as spending some time in town at his London home occupied him, and hunting was also an activity in which Sir Thomas took great delight. We also have a letter of Sir Thomas to Yaxley, begging to be excused attendance in a Court deputation which was to wait upon the Prince of Sweden during a visit to England. He gave as one of his pressing commitments the need to oversee personally his building projects at Norwich and it is intriguing to note that the person who sold the original property there, the Chapel in the Field, to Sir Thomas was another Catholic, a William Yaxley, related to Francis. He would know that Sir Thomas's plea was quite genuine.

That the close attachment which had existed between the Cornwallis family and that of the Howards continued is proved by Sir Thomas becoming a feoffee of the Duke in 1569. It is therefore somewhat surprising that Norfolk could not persuade him to become more active in local politics especially as he had obviously withdrawn from all his parliamentary duties. However farseeing Sir Thomas might have been in realizing that the

Howard 'connection' might not be wholly beneficial – as the trouble over the projected marriage of the Duke of Norfolk with Mary, Queen of Scots was soon to show – it seems even more likely that, knowing the probable financial burden that he and his wife would have to face as Catholic recusants, not to mention the outlay on his building projects, he would now need to resume his personal and close control on the next development of the family properties. If this was the way he was thinking then it was very wise indeed as events were to show. Alan Simpson, in the study already referred to, has pointed out just how necessary it was for the Master to be in charge.

In each of the villages where Sir Thomas had inherited estates from his father further additions were made in the first decade – Davillers in Brome, Beauchamps in Oakley, Ampners in Thrandeston and the Manor of Palgrave. This last-named was a gift from Queen Mary and the patent of 27 March 1555 states that it was given to both Sir Thomas and his wife 'without fine or fee'. A reversion of the same date was that of the manor of Westhorpe with its two parks and this was expressly granted for 'services to the queen, especially in the rebellion against her at Framlingham and for the labour and costs he had been at in the town of Calais . . .'. In addition we note that there were increased rents from Kilverstone, the Barnes (Barones) house in London, a tenement in Needham Market and a mass of lands and tenements in Basildon, Essex. By 1560 it is likely that an increase of up to £50 a year was coming from the new or re-negotiated rents. (op. cit., p. 146f)

Whilst Sir Thomas was living in London or abroad his receiver and accountant, the farmer Edward Goulding, was living in and renting Ling Hall. That he was a good steward seems evident from the account we have for a period ending in 1557 where we see that an amount of at least £700, not counting arrears still due, was a truer annual income from the tenanted estates. What is clear from the time of Sir Thomas's 'retirement', however, is that the previous territorial expansion by leaps and bounds had stopped". A new but small manor in Scole was acquired, a Norwich town house, called Chapel in the Fields, was bought from Yaxley, leaseholder of the deposed Archdeacon Spencer, and smaller acreages still in Brome and Oakley were added but all these amounted to no more than £100 per annum increase. The Wilton property was perhaps the most profitable acquisition, especially when the old Castle there was demolished and the development of mineral rights was attempted, but in the 35 years that were to elapse before Sir Thomas died in 1604 his income from land rose only from £700 to around £1100 per annum and this was during a generally inflationary period. The judgement of Alan Simpson at this juncture is worth recording:

"On the whole, he (Sir Thomas) cannot be said to have been unlucky in the structure of his empire, whether we look at properties like Ling Hall and Hoo Hall which had been in the family since the early fifteenth century, or at his father's purchases during the dissolution of the monasteries, or at the rewards which he got for his own services. They all bore up well. Indeed a survey such as this may suggest that the difficulties of 'mere' landlords in a period of inflation have been exaggerated, but of that we can better judge when we turn to the other side of the story – the cost of living." (op. cit., p. 157)

Before we come to that reckoning it might be as well if we catch up with what had happened to Thomas's brothers and then his sons.

Of Henry's marriages mention was made in the last chapter and of his first marriage to Anne Rokewood of Euston there were two children – Thomas Henry who was to remain unmarried and Elizabeth of whom we at least know that she was alive in Norwich in 1565. In 1532, at the age of 23, this brother was presented to the seat for Orford, and held it until the end of 1553. In view of his marriage alliances it is hardly surprising to learn that he followed Sir Thomas's example in rallying to Mary Tudor at the outset of her reign. For his 'service at Framlingham' she gave him an annuity of £136.0s.8d and he was further employed by the Crown in August 1554 in conducting negotiations at Padua along with Sir John Cheke, Sir Thomas Wriothesley and other exiles.

In 1555 he was back from the Continent and was commanded to assist his brother, Richard, in searching for an escaped prisoner in Suffolk. Though he had a few other commissions he seems to have withdrawn from public affairs after Queen Mary's death, and lived a very private life at Coxford Abbey, Norfolk, for the next 40 years. We know from his own son, Richard, who was born to Henry's second wife, Anne Calibut, and who was admitted to the English College in Rome in 1598, that Henry was reconciled to the Catholic Church shortly before he died. Nonetheless Henry, like his brother, asked to be buried in Brome Church, as he was in 1598, 'happy to be saved by Christ's passion only, and numbered among the elect. He provided for his surviving children and left an annuity of £4 to his brother, William Cornwallis, a seminary priest who was then a prisoner in the 'Clink' at Southwark. His executor and residuary legatee, Thomas Henry Cornwallis, proved the will at Norwich on 4 July 1599.

To complete this section of the family we should note that the son, Richard Cornwallis, mentioned above, had himself only submitted to the Catholic Church in 1595 through the influence of one of his Calibut half-brothers who was also a mission priest in England, aided by the more well-known Jesuit and escapee from the Tower, Fr. Gerard. Having been educated at school in Norwich and admitted as a pensioner at Caius College, Cambridge, Richard matriculated in 1585, took his B.A. (1588) and M.A. (1592) before becoming a Fellow 1592-6. He was ordained under the name 'Richard Fincham' in 1599 and sent to England in 1601 and so it is possible that he could have called on Sir Thomas, before the latter's death. One interesting point is that Richard's pseudonym 'Fincham' was the name of the place in Norfolk from which came Elizabeth Farnham, the first wife of his cousin, Sir Charles Cornwallis, and it was in the latter's house in Spain that Richard eventually died in 1606. It seems touching that though their religious allegiances were representative of the sharp divisions of the time yet family affection and concern still weighed heavily with them both or could it be that there is another 'hidden' story here? Some facts later suggest there was.

Richard, Sir Thomas's next brother, was first a country squire who began by living at Okenhill Hall at Badingham and in 1553 he is executor for a William Forth of Butley, some 10 miles away. After his marriage the need to manage his wife's properties meant that they resided either at Earl Soham which was even more closely associated with

Framlingham Castle, or at Cretingham. We have already noted that he was also in Royal service and in 1553 we read in a Privy Council document that he was charged with other duties, albeit still relating to his native county. Writing to William Dansell the Council directed that "the ordnance and munitions remaining within the 7 bulwarks at Landguard, Harwich and Marsey be conveyed by sea to the Tower by order of the bearer, Richard Cornwallis, and delivered to the Ordnance officers between this and Midsummer or as soon as maybe. You are to deliver him an imprest of £50 for the charge and carriage thereof and for the wages of 6 persons who have attended in the several bulwarks, unpaid from Christmas last, with receipt for the same".

This engagement reinforces another reference inferring that Richard was associated with his elder brother, Sir Thomas, when the latter was given a place on the munitions and garrisons group appointed within the Privy Council. As in the case of his two elder brothers the end of Mary's reign meant withdrawal from the scene in favour of persons more favoured by the Elizabethan party. He died in 1581 and was buried at Shotley but not before he had seen his part of the family line well established.

His wife, Margaret, bore him seven children – John, Thomas, Joanna, Elizabeth, Anne, Katharine and Grace. The girls all married save Grace who was buried at Erwarton in 1563. Anne married a Thomas Dade of Tannington, just north of Earl Soham, and she was left the manor of Shotley. Their daughter, Audrey, connects the family with the Garneys of Mickfield. Katherine married into the Wriothesley family and in 1584 seems to have been living at Badingham and thus may be presumed to have inherited this property after her father's death or when she married.

The elder son, John, lived at Earl Soham and married twice. His first wife was Catherine Blennerhassett and she bore him five children. Of these the following are known:

Philip who was born at Londham Hall, Pettistree, near Wickham Market and 4 miles south of Cretingham, on 15 September 1578. He was at school in Brandeston, next door to Cretingham, and was admitted as a Pensioner at Caius, Cambridge on 10 October 1594. He died 7 June 1601.

His brother, Thomas, was also born at Pettistree and attended the school at Brandeston, becoming a Pensioner at Caius on 1 December 1596. In April 1600 he was admitted to Gray's Inn and subsequently married Mary Grimstone, sole heiress of Edward Grimston, of Bradfield, Essex. He was M.P. for the County in 1623 and lived at Okenhill Manor and Earl Soham before dying in 1627 without issue.

There is mention of one other student from Suffolk who matriculated from Trinity, Cambridge in 1597 and who could obviously have been a yet younger brother especially as all the other known sons of the various branches are accounted for but as this entry gives no name this has to remain pure speculation.

We know also that when Thomas died without issue he bequeathed his Manor of

Sulyards in Cretingham to his sister Elizabeth, wife of Thomas Corderoy from Hampshire. Of the other sister we as yet know nothing. We know also that the father, John, had as second wife Elizabeth Wolsey but she bore him no children before he was buried at Cretingham in 1615.

Of John's brother, Thomas, we happily know a little more. He is recorded as having been a scholar of Oxford and was eventually granted his M.A. in 1605, the same year that he was knighted. He had occupied the office of Groome Porter to Her Majesty Queen Elizabeth and he still held this post under King James. He married Elizabeth, daughter of a Richard John Molleneux (or Molyneux) of Sefton in Lancashire (now a district of Liverpool) though the latter also had land in Thorpe, Nottinghamshire.

This union produced at least sons of whom the first, called John, died in childhood. It was the second, also called John, who continued the line by a further marriage with the Grimstone family. Rather than explain this continuity by more narrative it will probably be more helpful if we reproduce this section of the spreading family tree.

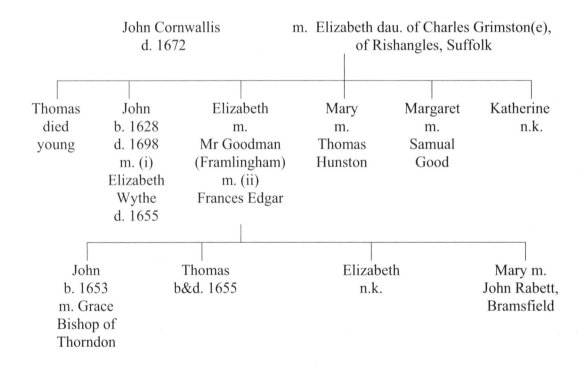

William, Sir Thomas's 4th brother, was born in 1524 and matriculated as a pensioner from Gonville Hall, Cambridge in Michaelmas term, 1544. His career both at and after university is not presently known but he clearly did not feel at home in the now strongly Reformed atmosphere of Cambridge and it is hardly a surprise to see him next referred to in Sir Thomas's 'Book of Evidences' as having been ordained a Catholic priest at Swessyon (Soissons) in France. That he returned as a missionary priest also seems clear since by an Act of Parliament made on 23 November 1561 'he was exiled from this realm to live in perpetual banishment'. Exile may seem to us a severe enough penalty but bearing in mind that the most common fate suffered by these 'visitors' was death by hanging and quartering it might be thought that William had at least some friends at Court. Nevertheless he was again back in England around 1592, was re-arrested and then examined in prison. He there declared that he was 66 and that he had been made a priest by authority from the Bishop of Rome. His niece, Lady Elizabeth Kitson, appealed to Elizabeth Cecil, asking her to use her influence to arrange that 'her poor unkle might be removed to such public prison where we that be so neare him may exercise the libertye the lawe giveth having a regarde to frendshipe Kindred and Charitye'. She adds, interestingly, 'The cause why he returned was extreme want and did therfor rather chose to subiecht himself to the lawe heer, than to become more miserable ther'. (Hengrave MMS. 66(2) Cambridge Univesity Library).

The essential quality of 'loyalty to the Crown' (the Bloody Question as it was then referred to) was tested and to this query Fr. William gave the following and somewhat unexpected reply:

"Methinketh that the pope, by his catholic authority, . . . may not proceed to excommunicate or accurse our sovereign lady, and thereupon pronounce her subjects to be freed and discharged of their obedience to her. Moreover if any pope should send an army into this realm, to establish the catholic Romish religion, I would in that case fight against any such army to the uttermost of my power, on her majesty's side." Whilst this must have been a most satisfactory response William was kept in gaol until 1600 but was then, on account of his age and infirmity, and the discretion which had been shown by Sir Thomas, released by the Council to be confined to his brother's house "wherein wee doubt not but in regard of the favour which ys shewed him he will have care to carry him selfe in such a dutyfull sort as there be no occasion of scandall".

As Sir Thomas, like his other brother Henry, had been paying William an annuity that grew with the years there was little extra burden on the family purse caused by this arrangement. William is also mentioned in Sir Thomas's will and was to be kept in some care and comfort before, as the Parish Register at Brome records, he died there on 23 July 1608.

Turning to Sir Thomas's sons again we perceive that the family tree began to spread in several new directions.

The years immediately following William's time at Cambridge were crucial ones for though we do not know all the details it is clear that on three counts there was a growing division of outlook between father and heir. Whether it was the influence of the Reformation teaching and contacts at Cambridge and/or the uncertainty of his father's status, brought about as a result of his former allegiance to a Catholic monarch, it is clear that whilst Sir Thomas, Dame Anne and their daughters held steadfastly, if without undue bigotry, to the 'old faith' William was henceforth to declare his attachment to Queen Elizabeth and her ecclesiastical 'settlement'. It was to her Court that he found his way in 1570 and as one contemporary commentator put it, 'he lost his youth and £20,000 in service there'. The mention of such a sum refers to William's love of gambling which was to affect at least his middle years. That he found life in such circles more to his taste than that of a country squire was doubtless another cause of disaffection between his father and himself and we know that when the young man had married Sir Thomas wrote to Cecil to express disapproval of both his new daughter-in-law and of the young couple 'living about the City instead of leading a country life'. Could it have been, that wise as Sir Thomas so often proved to be in many things, he simply could not understand his now eldest son's less than enthusiastic attitude to the country life given the fact that his father looked as if he would be in charge at Brome for a very long time. Certainly that seemed to be the case and Sir Thomas was in his 85th year and William in his mid-50s when at last the latter inherited.

What is also somewhat puzzling is the fact that Sir Thomas should have expressed to Lord Burghley his dissatisfaction with the marriage which his heir had contracted. For William's first wife was Lucy Nevill, a co-heiress, of Sir John Nevill, 4th Baron Latimer. Lucy's step-grandmother had been none other than Catherine Parr, and her elder sister, Dorothy, had already married William Cecil's eldest son Thomas. One suspects that Sir Thomas did not like this heir marrying so obviously into the Protestant camp but it would seem to speak volumes for the relationship between Cecil and himself that Sir Thomas's opinions do not seem to have provoked any undue disharmony. We shall have occasion before long to see that such good opinion of each other, and no doubt the family tie, was of no little benefit to Sir Thomas.

Let us however complete the story of William and his children. The date of William's first marriage is not known exactly but was probably when, or even a little before, he attained his majority. What, however, are we to make of the fact that their first child, William, died young in 1566/7 and was buried at Hengrave. Was he born before wedlock?

From the Brome register, but contrary to what is in printed genealogies, it appears that the couple had other Sons, Thomas and John, and then 4 daughters, Frances, Elizabeth, Catherine (or Cornelia) and Anne (though some printed sources say Dorothy). Thomas was baptized at Brome on 10 January 1572 and then seems to have been buried, also at Brome, on the 20th following. John was baptized on 19 February 1573 and was educated at a school in Highgate in North London, where we know that his parents later had a house. He was admitted a Commoner at Caius College, Cambridge in January 1589, grew to manhood and for a brief time became an M.P. for the County of Suffolk but never married. He is said to have been killed when a block and tackle being used to help build a new gallery at Brome fell on his head. He was buried at Brome on 1 November 1594.

His sisters did marry and all of them with some distinction. Elizabeth married first Sir William Sandys, son of Edwin Sandys, the Archbishop of York, and brother of the Sir Edwin who was a founder of the colony at Virginia. She then married Richard, Viscount Lumley but from neither union were any children produced. Catherine married Sir Richard Fermor of Somerton and their daughter Lucy married into the Petre family, which created yet another link with the Cecils.

Anne married Archibald, 7th Earl of Argyll as his second wife and was responsible for his becoming a Catholic so that after her death he enlisted in the service of the King of Spain. The eldest child born to them was James, later Lord of Kintyre and Earl of Irvine. Anne is also mentioned in *THE COMPLETE PEERAGE* as being an authoress of note in her day, a trait in the family which we shall particularly discern in the next chapter. She produced for her husband a book of Sentences, culled from the Latin works of Augustine and translated by her into Spanish. So valued by the Earl was this work that when he died in his London home in Drury Lane in 1638 this work was found upon his person. Frances, the eldest daughter, became the wife of a noted Ipswich gentleman, Sir Edmund Withypole (or Withipool), who soon became High Sheriff and later Deputy Lieutenant of the County.

The mother of these girls, Dame Lucy Cornwallis, whose own sisters included a Duchess and a Countess, must have been gratified by these connections, especially the latter ones, and no doubt enjoyed visits to her daughters before she was buried in Brome Parish Church in May 1608.

Sir Thomas, we know, was particularly delighted by the link with the Withypoles of Ipswich. It may be recalled that Sir Thomas served with Lord Wentworth at Calais and it was one of his daughters, Dorothy, who was the mother of Sir Edmund, Frances's husband. The couple's marriage took place in April 1595 at St. Botolph's, Bishopsgate, in which parish the Cornwallis mansion of Barones (or Barnes) stood. It is to be remarked that the third and fourth Sons of Edmund and Frances were baptized at Brome where Frances, who was then 27, had doubtless come to give birth, having already lost her first boy who died in his first year. Henry Withypole was baptized on 31 August 1602 and Edmund on 10 April 1606.

Sir Thomas also seems to have smiled warmly on his daughter Dorothy for he granted her and her noble husband the use of the London house both during and after his lifetime. We know this because in 1615, when William himself had died, his executors, his brother Charles and Sir Edmund, called in the tenure of the London house from the Earl of Argyll and his wife so that alternative provision for William's dependants could be made. This was important because whilst William could rejoice that his girls were well provided for by marriage his own affairs, and especially in his later years, were never really of the happiest. But before we come to that story in the next chapter it is necessary that we say something further about William's brother, Charles, and also complete the record concerning their father's 'estate' in the last quarter of the century.

Charles Cornwallis benefitted, as we remarked earlier, from the education which he received and on deciding, like his elder brother, that a life serving the Crown was more likely to suit his talents and situation he was soon highly esteemed for his eminent abilities. His main home was at Beeston House to the north-east of Norwich and it is therefore not surprising to learn that his first wife, Elizabeth, was also a Norfolk girl, the daughter of Thomas Farnham of Fincham, which lies in West Norfolk beyond Swaffham. Of this marriage two boys were issue, William and Thomas, and though we shall have much more to say about this William also in the next chapter it will, I think, be helpful if we here insert another mini-family tree to show how the family spread from these two boys.

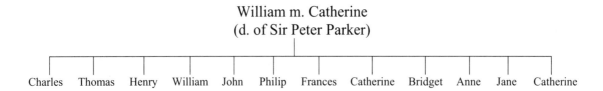

William m. Catherine
(d. of Sir Peter Parker)

Charles   Thomas   Henry   William   John   Philip   Frances   Catherine   Bridget   Anne   Jane   Catherine

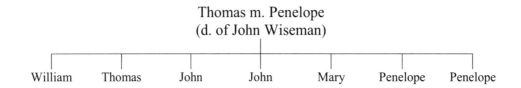

Thomas m. Penelope
(d. of John Wiseman)

William   Thomas   John   John   Mary   Penelope   Penelope

From among all these numerous offspring much more will be said about the boys when we have dealt with the affairs of their fathers and grand-father in the next chapter but it is particularly worthy of note that William's eldest girl married into the well-known Norfolk family of Paston. Her husband was another Thomas and his father was Sir Edmund Paston. She was the first of a few in this branch of the family who were eventually buried at Burnham Thorpe where the living was in the gift of the Parker family and where, it should be recalled, a Rev Edmund Nelson, father of a certain Horatio, was Rector over a century later. The Cornwallis link with Norfolk was being still more firmly established.

Charles Cornwallis, the grandfather, was married twice more. His second wife was Anne, daughter of Thomas Barrow and widow of Ralph Shelton (Skelton or Selden), who died in March 1617, and his third wife was Dorothy Vaughan, who was not only the daughter of Richard Vaughan, Bishop of London, but also the widow of John Jegon, who had been Bishop of Norwich. What must have given Sir Thomas great satisfaction before he died was to see Charles knighted by King James at the Charterhouse in May 1603. Charles's brother, William, had also received that honour in Dublin after the battle of Offaly in the 1599 Irish campaign when he was dubbed by the Earl of Essex on 5 August. It can thus be seen that whatever difficulties their father may have had with the Elizabethan State the sons were plainly accepted as faithful and loyal servants of the monarch.

Sir Thomas, by contrast, certainly had his problems. The mention of a portrait of Lord Burghley in the new Hall that he had built at Brome serves to remind us that though the portrait could not have appeared until some time after 1571, when the peerage was bestowed on William Cecil, a relationship between him and Sir Thomas had been established from about 1550. Whether the two men had been first introduced by Sir

Thomas's father through Court circles or whether they met when Cecil was a secretary to the Earl of Warwick at the time of the Wyatt rebellion we cannot be certain. What is clear is that Cecil was so consummate a politician that whilst he was 'accommodating', and even dissimulating, under Queen Mary he yet emerged in Elizabeth's reign as the new monarch's most trusted and intimate adviser. Various papers reveal that Cecil had performed certain services in 1557 for Sir Thomas and Thomas, Lord Wentworth had once asked that his cousin (Sir Thomas), might be furnished with information regarding a house on the Thames owned by the Duke of Somerset for whom Cecil worked.

Moreover there are always matters that have to be cleared up when any new government takes over from its predecessor. In late November 1558 Sir Thomas and Edward, Lord Hastings are already writing to Cecil as the new Secretary of the Queen's Council asking that there might be some recompense to Ludovicus Nonnius, a physician who came from Spain to attend the late Queen. A year later Sir Thomas was thanking Cecil for his letters and sending him 22 partridges of which some were also to be a gift to Sir Robert Dudley. The latter, wrote Sir Thomas, has not spared 'to utter his good respect and favorable opynyon of me in a right good presence'. In a later missive we find gratitude for a similar expression of goodwill from the Lord Treasurer, and as late as 1566 Sir Thomas is saying, "Though I know that innocence does not always keep men out of trouble yet I would think my poor estate sure and safe enough as long as I have your (Cecil's) friendship". Some have also averred that his kindness to the young Elizabeth counted in his favour.

As we shall see below this kind of contact might not bring complete protection from the molestation suffered by recusants in the remainder of the century but it probably ensured that he might expect a more kindly and sympathetic hearing from those in high places. But first we must pick up the story of his landed properties and the costs of running the many concerns which were his after 1560.

"The loss of Sir Thomas's (government) office in November 1559 obviously simplified the problems of management. We hear no more of his house near the Charterhouse in London, or of Copthall, Essex, where he had also resided. He retired to East Anglia and divided his time between his seat at Brome and a town house in Norwich . . . . For about a decade (until 1570) the annual statement was drawn up by the steward, Simon Goldingham, or his successor, Edmund Oldham; but then Lady Cornwallis carried the responsibility until her death in 1581. During this period they seemed to have dispensed with the services of an officer who was solely the 'steward of household'; we find one man combining the jobs of steward and receiver, and after Lady Cornwallis's death. it was this officer who took over." (Simpson, *op. cit.*, p. 159)

The system of bookkeeping was fairly straightforward. Quarterly books provided the items that could be transferred to 'books of titles' which categorized the different types of expenditure and from these the annual accounts could be drawn up. These were presented under three main heads. They were 'foreign', building work and husbandry. The 'foreign expenses' were the most diverse and included taxes, the ransom of a captain who was captured at Calais (£316), marriage portions and trousseaux (£488 in 1570), expenses of executors, annuities (as for brother William), an unsuccessful effort in 1592 to dig for coal at Wilton (£39.11s.1d), travel costs, and annual allowances for his heir (from £130 to £230 between 1572 and 1597). What is specially striking is the fact that whereas the 'spending money' or amount allowed for incidental purchases to the officers of the estate dropped steadily from £2300 in 1558 to £887 in 1569 there is hardly any such amount allowed thereafter. Matters were becoming serious once the Brome building project was completed.

Nonetheless Sir Thomas was not about to give up on building. The recent Archdeacon of Norfolk Miles Spencer, who had also been dean of the college called Chapel in the Fields at Norwich, had overseen the dissolution of the medieval property but had retained the central dwelling house. After his death it was his nephew, William Yaxley, who inherited it and sold it to Sir Thomas for £400 in 1571.

In 1573 extensive work was begun with a new gallery, a porter's lodge, a new dining hall, a better kitchen and a courtyard paved with Purbeck stone. All this cost between £700 and £800 and was completed by 1579. Yet even this was not the end. From 1583 until 1596 other forms of building work were undertaken – a new wing at the Norwich house, and towers, another courtyard, a mill, a park, a granary, a dairy and a fresh gallery at Brome (hence the fatal scene for grandson John). The new tomb for himself in Brome Parish Church was begun and the first almshouses in the parish were provided. In all this aspect of Sir Thomas's enterprises must have cost close to £3000 and that did not include the charges for masons and carpenters which were paid for by his son, Sir William. What is noteworthy is that there seem to have been very few extravagant items. Whilst £105 was spent on the Chapel Chamber in 1597 (£61 for a bed and £44 for hangings) this was not at all usual. The annual expense under this head was somewhere between £20 and £50, at least after Sir Thomas had surrendered his State appointments. By the same token the amounts spent on fresh meat, game and dairy produce fell from over £200 to as little as £20 in the 1560s and when it again rose it was much more due to steadily increasing agricultural prices. On the other hand the costs of buying cattle and sheep remained high but after his return to countryside pursuits it is clear that he had to replenish and retain his livestock.

The amounts paid to staff and individuals merit our notice. "Quite apart from bed, board and livery, (servants) lived in a society where high and low expected to be tipped. Ninety per cent of the 'gifts and rewards' were tips – a steady stream of small sums, seldom exceeding a pound, bestowed on cooks, musicians, tradesmen, household officers, wayside poor, and all the innumerable people 'bringing presents and taking pains'. The other 10 per cent might have to be dignified with another name, if only because they were given to equals or superiors. They also cost more. The wedding gift, the New Year's gift, the gift to kinsmen and allies, the ring of gold set with a very fair turquoise (£13.6s.8d) and 12 yards of satin (£7.4s.0d) which were given to my Lord Bishop after being billeted on him, and the three and a half yards of taffeta (£2) which his chaplain expected." (Simpson, *op. cit.*, p. 169) It is in this context that we recall the somewhat plaintive remark about his daughter, the Countess of Bath's black velvet gown. 'Gifts' must have seemed endless at times.

There was also of course the wages bill which fluctuated between £140 and £200 a year and as a sample of this charge the £146 of 1577 included the following annual payments:

> William Deal for selling land, £10; Henry Cornwallis, brother, £10;
> William Cornwallis, brother, £10; Margaret, relict of Richard, £20;
> Charles, younger son, and Anne his wife, parcel of jointure, £70;
> Mary, younger daughter, for her exhibition (?), £20; John Thurston,
> lawyer, £1; The subseneschals of Norfolk and Suffolk, £1 each.

There was also, of course, the cost of providing marriage portions for the girls and a capital sum or land for the boys. When Elizabeth married Thomas Kitson in 1561 the portion was £600, the trousseau £160 and £11 was distributed to the household officers at Kenninghall, where the Duchess of Norfolk, whom Elizabeth had served as a lady-in-waiting, presided over the marriage arrangements. Similarly, when Alice married Richard Southwell of Horsham St. Faith's, in 1570, the portion was 1000 marks and the trousseau £83. Frances, one granddaughter, was also given a portion of 1000 marks and another, Elizabeth, a gift of £200. As part of Charles's second marriage jointure he and his wife, Anne, were given the benefit of the Manor of Kylverston, Norfolk, worth about £30 p.a.

If these might be considered 'normal' expenses there were others that were the result of the uncertain circumstances in which Sir Thomas and some of his family found themselves as Catholics in the Elizabethan age. No sooner had the building work at Brome been completed than a new state of affairs erupted. The arrest of the Duke of Norfolk on the suspicion that he had proposed marriage to Mary Queen of Scots meant that there was a round-up of all his clients and associates and in 1569 Sir Thomas had become his feoffee. Simpson writes of this period (p. 172):

"Sir Thomas left Brome on 10 October 1569, with a party of six men, and reached the court at Windsor, via Newmarket and St. Alban's, on the 12th. There he was first examined 'upon some articles touching the Duke of Norfolk' and being found 'not to be in any weye touched with any disloyalty towards his Prince' was then questioned 'upon matier of religion and being found to embrace the Catholique faith now termed papistical and refusing to come to the church to communicate in prayer according to the religion and lawe sett fourth and established', he was committed to the custody of John Jewell, Bishop of Salisbury, while his lady was ordered to remain at Brome." It was virtual house arrest.

He was in Salisbury from 29 November to 6 June and even accompanied the Bishop on a Visitation of part of his diocese. Presumably the Lords of the Council hoped that regular conversation with the foremost Anglican apologist of the day would encourage Sir Thomas to conform. At last however he returned to the custody of the Dean of Westminster in London for a further two months and it is from this short but important period that we have a correspondence between Dean Goodman and Cecil which more fully reveals where Sir Thomas stood on these matters of religion.

The Dean was obviously far from satisfied with the way the Anglican divines had handled the disputation. Yet despite Sir Thomas's present inability to be persuaded Dr. Goodman was hopeful that he might be won over. Sir Thomas approved much in the new forms of worship, especially it being in the vernacular, but like Sir Thomas More earlier and Edmund Campion later he wanted all this to be confirmed by 'General Authority', which for him was the approval of the Church of Rome. On the other hand Sir Thomas wanted several things reformed according to the practice of the early Church and he expressly repudiated the temporal claims of the Papacy, as we recall his priestly brother was to do. Hence the Dean urged that Sir Thomas's conscience should be respected. He wrote:

'I have seldom knowen any of that syde so wyse and so conveniently learned, more reasonable in Conference, or more nearour to conformity.' As Sir Thomas thought so highly of Cecil the Dean urged Cecil to use his personal influence but to treat Sir Thomas gently and not least as he had been suffering from severe pain in his teeth for 3 days.

Cecil accordingly wrote and we have Sir Thomas's reply. After thanking him for his kindly approach Sir Thomas remarks that he was facing the greatest crisis of his life 'havyng now matter in hande, that towchythe me nearest of all that I ever hade sythe I was borne'. He regretted that he could not deal with Cecil's points in detail, having already written on them to the Bishop, but had to affirm that they did not meet his particular difficulties. He believed that the anger of the monarch and the danger that it involved were terrible but he asserted that 'the danger toffende (sic) Almyghtye God ys, or owghte to be, more Weghed then all the perylls in the Worlld besydes'. It was this, and this alone, that had kept him from conforming, whatever anyone else might say.

If this seemed to be the prelude to still stronger opposition Cecil was to be surprised. Sir Thomas wished to clear himself of any suspicion of infidelity to the Queen. He wished the Queen knew all the thoughts of his heart and of his love for her 'ffrom the tyme I knew hyr fyrst as a childe'. He would apply himself to obey her laws in matters of religion 'as Almyghtye God wyll gyve me grace to be further persuadyd' and he would defend her against all foreign princes. He was not well in mind or body and he asked Cecil to see that 'at the Fyrst I be drawne no Further then to cumyng to Chyrche wheare I wyll use my self (by Godes grace) to want offence to eny menne and not by devyse to be pressyd further, wyche myght make me eyther an hypocryte or desperate . . .'. Such no doubt was the kind of mental struggle that must have gone on in the minds of many Catholics of the day. They wanted to assert their loyalty as Englishmen but they really had deep religious affiliations which affected their conscience. Sir Thomas had gone as far as he could.

Meanwhile his son-in-law, Sir Thomas Kitson, who had admitted that he had not received communion for 4 or 5 years past though he had heard sermons at the Sheriff's assize, was completing his term of close arrest at his London house. Pardoned at last in August both Thomases were escorted back to Brome by a party of 20, which included their wives and servants as well as William Cornwallis, the elder son.

This absence of ten months cost £305, including riding charges £128, apparel £38, physic £3, gifts and rewards, £84, and of course the fabrics for the Bishop and his staff. And this sort of absence from Brome was not a one-off. In 1574 he had to make a 'voyage to court about June to shewe himselfe to the Quenes Majestie' and there was another for a similar purpose in 1578.

Yet another sojourn in Town was connected with the sorry business relating to Mary Cornwallis's precipitate marriage at Hengrave with the young Earl of Bath who was then still a student at Cambridge. The marriage was arranged by Sir Thomas Kitson but the intervention of the Earl's mother meant that the Earl left his new wife after two weeks and Sir Thomas made an appeal to the Privy Council which entailed his being in London from October 1579 to May 1580. The reason why there had been a break in his building activities is now clear.

A committee under the chairmanship of Lord Burghley urged the Earl to accept Mary Cornwallis as his wife but he now steadfastly refused. His mother was urging him to reject Mary on the grounds of 'disparagement through marriage with a Catholic'. The legal case that ensued seems to have cost Sir Thomas upwards of £1200, more than the cost of building Brome Hall, and this despite the fact that Sir Thomas Kytson, who was a wealthy man, put his town house in Austin Friars wholly at the disposal of his father and sister-in-law throughout their stay. Another visit to London to help Sir Thomas Kytson in the marriage settlement of his daughter with Lord Cavendish and then a leisurely inspection of the Kytson lands in Devonshire may have been more of a holiday (for Lady Jane Cornwallis had died in 1581) but it still meant absence away from East Anglia.

Not that life back home was easy even when he could be there. Bishop Edmund Freke had been translated from Rochester to Norwich in 1575 and at once found himself faced with a strong Puritan faction, including many of the Justices of the Peace, albeit some of those on the bench were also strong Catholics. The Bishop was a rather weak man dominated by an overbearing wife and he was now somewhat overborne by the Puritan group who levelled specific charges against individuals including Sir Thomas.

They alleged that the Bishop had allowed Cornwallis to impose a favourable Chancellor on the diocese when it was known that Sir Thomas's own secretary, Laurence Bedingfield, had now become a monk at the Carthusian monastery in Brussels. Sir Thomas, it was also said, attended church and sat in the manorial pew but when others were on their knees he continued to sit reading from some book which, if it were what was later found there, was a psalter used for the adoration of the Virgin. Moreover, it was claimed, he had bestowed benefices on papists, non-resident clergy and those who were unlearned. Considering his strictures on the chaplain at Calais this latter seems unlikely unless 'unlearned' here meant non-Reformed'.

They also claimed that at dinner with the Bishop at Ludham in 1578 the Bishop had complained of being short of funds and thus was looking for a move to Worcester. To prevent this his fellow-diners, Sir Thomas, William Paston, Martin Barney and Miles Corbett, had each proffered £10 p.a. to prevent this departure and this, it was asserted, constituted undue influence upon the prelate to the detriment of others. At about the same time they lodged another complaint that the servants of both the Bishop and Sir Thomas had dined and wined so well that 'they reeled home well tipled to the offence of all good people'. Freke, they said, 'could spie out from the furthest of his dyocesse some mynysters of the ghospell for omyttynge the least dutie and yet could not spye out any one masse of so many in Norfolk and Norwich'

In March 1582 Lady Elizabeth Kytson was writing on her father's behalf to no less a person than Sir Philip Sydney who replied as follows.

"Madam, I have . . . dealt with Mr. Secretarie (Walsingham, Sydney's father-in-law) for his favour toward Sir Thomas Cornwallies. Truly, Madam, hitherunto I can obtain no furdre than this, that there is a present intention of a general mitigation, to be used in respect of recusants; so as he may not, he saith, prevent her Majesties dealing therein . . . but assures me that there is ment a speedy easing of the greatnes of your burden . . . I, owing a particular dutie unto Sir Thomas, (am) . . ." She had a similar letter the same day from Fulke Greville who had also spoken up on Sir Thomas's behalf.

The government certainly kept their eye on Sir Thomas and when a Fr. Hugh Hall was questioned in 1583 he admitted that at Ralph Sheldon's home in Worcestershire at harvest time the year before he had talked of religion with 'the gentleman' who had asked if Hall were so fully in the church as he might do the office of priest. When Hall answered that he had not done such office of late Sir Thomas asked him to say mass but 'he refused saying he knew not how Sir Thomas stood'. He further denied that he had ever offered a mass at any Cornwallis or Kitson wedding and he did not know William the son. The approach mentioned above by Sir Thomas is probably explained by the fact that whilst he and Kytson were at Sheldon's they heard of the death of Kytson's daughter, Lady Cavendish, and it is likely they wanted Hall to say a mass for the repose of her soul.

Sadly matters in this sphere were now to get steadily worse for the rest of the 1580s. In 1584 the Bishop of Norwich was commanded by the government to inquire into the practice of Sir Thomas since, though he had continued to prove his loyalty to the Crown, he had once more stopped attending his parish church. The Bishop sent his reply straight to Cecil and we have the next letter from Sir Thomas to him. It closes as follows:

"My lord, I have not long to live, neither do I desire or hope for any fortune of the world (God is my judge), nor other happiness, than with a quiet conscience to end the rest of my days in mine own house, . . . where I would live so privately, as my behaviour nor example should offend or hurt anybody. My lord, if ever my service and poor friendship unto you in times past did deserve praise . . . let me taste the fruit of your favour and credit . . .".

He was now 65 years of age and clearly resolved not to attend Anglican services. In 1585, however, when the Suffolk recusants were asked to contribute to the cost of forming 'a troop of light horse' the name of Sir Thomas is head of the list of 13 (as giving £50), along with William Yaxley and Edward Sulyard. For a time he was unmolested.

Yet in 1587-9 there was an even more serious disruption to his way of life. It was now the time when Mary Queen of Scots was nearing her execution, and obviously still plotting her escape, but it was also the time when wind of the proposed Armada attack on England was being received at Elizabeth's court. Even Burghley could not risk any favours at such a moment and Sir Thomas's account book tells us the story:

'. . . . about the beginninge of July he made a voiage to London to obteyne favor in payment of the mulct (or fine), A penall statute imposeth upon Recusantes', one estimate of which is suggested as being £270 p.a. which was the equivalent of his household provisions for Brome and the house in Norwich. 'But the same Sir Thomas his case . . . . not sortinge to such spedie ende as was hoped of, the said Sir Thomas returned to his house in Brome VII September, and havyng disposed of his houshold affayres made another iorney to London in the ende of October for fynishinge his said suyte . . .'. It took longer than expected and he was ordered to lodge with a Revd Mr Taylor in Wood Street until, along with other Catholics, he was brought before the Archbishop of Canterbury and the Commissioners of Matters Ecclesiastical. They committed him to the custody of the Bishop of London. After one day and two nights 'he was by favor of my Lord Treasurer upon suyt to him made, removed to the house of Mr Blague in Lambith'. The Revd Mr. Blague was one of the Queen's Chaplains who was later to become Dean of Rochester. Little could Mr. Blague have imagined that within 2 centuries one of his prisoner's own stock would be occupying the Archbishop's Palace down the road.

Burghley must have so many times spoken up in his defence that Sir Thomas had just written to him, "I shall lay up this amongst many other assured demonstrations of your love and friendship showed me in this change of time . . .". Despite such support it now seemed that his 'defence' was fading. In November 1587 he was committed to prison. Being very sick he was once more placed at Mr. Blague's house but not recovering was allowed to go to his son-in-law's and thence again to Mr. Taylor's in Wood Street. It was now 1589 and, the Armada threat having been disposed of, he was allowed to go about the City as far as Highgate where William lived. At last, in 1589 and at the age of 71, he was again permitted to return home and all restrictions on his movement were cancelled.

Though the stress and the disturbance may have affected his health he was now to spend the last 15 years of his life undisturbed. As an example of his known integrity the Muster of 1598, in which the Sheriffs of East Anglia were required to confiscate the horses of all recusants, was not applied to him 'Forasmuch as he hathe byn and so contynneth ann aubedient and true servaunt unto her Majestie . . .'. His indebtedness to both the Cecils, for the Lord's son was now also on the scene, never ceased for in 1599 his daughter Lady Kytson was treated very leniently by the authorities albeit a registered recusant, whilst her 'Sister' by marriage, Anne, the second wife of Charles, was also in the same situation. She wrote to Sir Robert Cecil in 1602: "I understand by my son Cornwaleys (the bearer, probably William) who, upon the first intelligence of my being indicted at these last assizes in Suffolk, attended upon you, your honourable offer of means to free me." This leads one to wonder if her being a Catholic was perhaps the reason why Richard 'Fincham', the priest-son of Henry Cornwallis, was made so welcome at Charles's home when the couple were in Spain? Could it also be that the choice of the name 'Fincham' was because Charles's first wife had also been of the 'old faith'?

We are given some interesting glimpses of Sir Thomas in his declining years by looking at a few of his last activities. Two of these are brought to our notice in a revealing article of the Suffolk Institute of Archaeology about Sir Thomas. The first concerns the priest-son of a Humphrey Yelverton of Bawdsewell, Norfolk:

"Charles Yelverton was admitted to the English College in Rome in October (and) after taking his degree at Cambridge he lived with his uncle Charles and then, 'by reason of the persecution', he stayed first with Anthony Bedingfield and then at a doctor's house in Winston, Suffolk. (Winston is near Cretingham) After that he went to Mr. John Bedingfield of Ridgfield where he stayed a year . . .' and when I saw that all the clouds had dispersed and all cause of alarm had gone, I appeared in public again. Then Sir Thomas Cornwallis, knight, sent for me and invited me to stay with him, and there for three or four months I repeated the breviary with him . . .". (p. 255)

Reading and study were certainly two of the occupations of this ageing Suffolk gentleman. In a little set of letters written by Sir Thomas to John Hobart, the brother of the first Chief Justice under King James, there are real clues to finding out the kind of life he was living.

"I have bought two fair maps to furnish my gallery and am also devising to purchase the globe of the earth and the heavens for though I be going out of the world yet am I desiring before I leave it to have some further acquaintance and knowledge thereof (such as) the learned Jesuit Josephus Acosta in his India Discourse reciteth . . . .", or again,

". . though I now be an old man and ready to leave the world yet doth not age example (exempt?) me from that old rule 'Est natura hominis novitatis avida' (It is in man's nature to be eager to learn something new) but that we still desire to know the world's affairs." He remarks that Sir John Fortescue had given him a 'Calendar or Concordantia Religionis et jure' in a book of last year's impression set out by M. Laurentius Riseberginus of the abridgement of the Turkish histories. He had noted on p. 193 that there was another concordance mentioned and he would like this if it could be found. Not exactly the lightest of reading, yet perused with care like the following work:

"In the latter end of the (Saturnalia by Lipsius) you shall find divers figures of the players in Rome both on horseback and on foot. Amongst the which (I think it be the IVth or Vth figure) you shall see a coach with 2 wheels and 2 horses to draw it with . . . I cannot conjecture how it is holden up. I would gladly have such a one to ride about my park but the workmen here cannot discern with what device it is carried. I pray you therefore repair to Mr. Cavendish (who made a coach for her majesty to go as well on water as land) and take his opinion of it . . . if you can get me a model made of it, I doubt not but our workmen here can do it according to the pattern." That was in 1592.

His devotional reading was just as keen. "Likewise buy for me Bishop Fisher's Psalms which you may buy in quires and bind up with Vincentius (Against the prophane novelties of all heresies) . . . and if some of the Church History be come forth I pray enquire the price and how many years it containeth . . .".

In the letters too there is a comment on those abroad who were endeavouring by political action to bring about change in the religious position of this country. He wrote:

"I am very sorry and so (I am sure) be all good Catholics of these lewd libels. It will but exasperate matters. They be out of the way themselves and therfore do not regard what we endure."

The context was probably the appearance in Lyons of a book in Latin by Fr. Robert Persons fiercely attacking the English Crown for its proclamation of 1591 against the missionary priests. Whilst Sir Thomas was the brother, the uncle and the kinsman by marriage of three of these very priests he was so jealous of his reputation as a loyal subject of the Queen that he did not go out of his way to make his home, like some, a centre for these seminary or Jesuit 'visitors'. No doubt he was able from time to time to go to Mass at the houses of his Suffolk friends but he was also determined to convince the government of where he stood politically.

That he was an 'old believer' there can be no doubt as some of the words at the start of his Will, dated 25 March 1604, declare:

"I commit my soule to God and to his deerlie beloved sonne Jhesus Christe . . . and to oure blessed Ladie St. Marye the Virgin and to all the holye companye of heaven" and yet, despite his obvious allegiance to Catholic teaching, he was a faithful and conscientious patron of the several livings which he had both inherited and acquired. Whatever the attacks of the Norwich Puritans there is clear evidence that in Brome and Oakley, Thrandeston and Stuston, the clergy were carefully and prayerfully appointed. What Sir Thomas would have been especially aware of was that in Brome, for example, the clergy had more souls to care for. In 1524 when he was a child there were 29 adult taxpayers in the village. In the year 1603 there were 80.

Even in the very church which he was latterly unable by conscience to attend for worship he still left his own monument and that of his wife, Anne. The inscription, interestingly, was composed and prepared by him before he was interred there and whilst it has no religious, it does have a clear political, message:

"Here lies Sir Thomas Cornwallis, son of Sir John, who was of Queen Mary Her privey councell and Tresurer of Caleys and after Comptroller of her Household in special Grace and Trust of his Mistress who untimely lousing her life he retired himself home to this Towne where he spent the rest of his own privately and loyally all the Rayne of Queen Elizabeth her sister and died heer the second year of King James the 26 December 1604 in the 86 year of his age."

Facing the couple, as they lie with their hands folded in prayer and their feet on the side of a stag with spreading antlers, there hangs the great stone shield of Sir Thomas with its 16 quarterings. The mere listing of the arms denoted (from left to right) is an eloquent portrayal of the way the family Tree had spread – Cornwallis, Tye, Bucton, Tyrell, Butler, Braham, Stamford, Mapershall, Jerningham, Harling, Kelvedon, Ingoldsthorpe, Mortimer, Clifton, FitzOsbern and Hakesworth.

Speaking of the family one little puzzle at this point remains. In a codicil to his will as late as 6 November 1604 Sir Thomas mentions 'Robert Cornwaleys whoe hath verye diligently and paynefully attended uppon me all the tyme of my sicknes'. No such name appears in any list that I have been able to discover so far. That he was a close relative seems clear and that he was probably a single man able to devote this kind of constant service to his respected kinsman also appears likely. My only conclusion is that he was either a cousin, the son of Francis Cornwaleys, his father's brother, who had gone to live in Peckham and had a family there or he was a nephew, a son of Richard Cornwallis of whom we may have but a limited genealogy.

What seems clear is that Sir Thomas was able to die in dignity and kindly attended in his 'new' home. He had his family around him and he could know that despite the tribulations he had borne the prospects for the future were sanguine. As Alan Simpson has remarked.

"Nor was this a man who was compromising his standards to preserve his solvency. He built himself two houses, did all that was expected for his children, preserved his credit among the first families of the county, and had himself interred in a suitably impressive tomb. As a 'mere' landlord the retired courtier seems to have managed well enough."
(*Op. cit.*, p. 178)

CHAPTER 6

A Tree with Noble Branches

So Sir Thomas had finally been buried. His ceremony may have been only a local event but it would nonetheless be a special occasion as we know all burials of gentlemen in that age to have been. As one writer has put it:

"Funerals were taken seriously in Tudor England. When a ritual was appointed for all the ordinary occasions of life there was nothing informal about the manner of leaving it. A decent burial cost a fortune. At the moment of death, embalmers and surgeons, carpenters and masons, drapers and sempstresses, (clergy) and choristers, cooks and butlers, and whole troops of ordinary servants sprang into action, while the poor looked hopefully on . . . . Over it all a costly authority was wielded by those professionals in punctilio, the College of Arms. No young nobleman ever squandered in an evening's dice (playing) a fraction of what it would cost to bury him. The marriage of a daughter might run it close, but a visit from the Queen, which could devour £100 a day, had to be cruelly prolonged to enter the same class. It was not until Puritanism laid its icy hand on idle ceremonies that funerals shrank into their modern frugality, and the days receded when a year's income from a dozen manors might vanish in the vault." (Simpson, *op. cit.*, p. 22)

Sir William Cornwallis, the new Lord of the Manor of Brome, must have been grateful that there were certain factors that would have tempered the costs that might have been levied. His father's longevity, and hence the absence of many of his father's contemporaries who had predeceased him, the restraint that must have attended the death and interment of a recognized recusant and a tomb already provided by his parents, would all have reduced the charges on him as the already ageing and rather more impecunious heir. For truth to tell Sir William was not inheriting a landed 'empire' as extensive as that which his father had received in 1544 nor was he himself the most gifted of property managers.

This is not to imply that Sir William was at this stage without reasonable means though he might well claim that he had lived most of his adult years in a state that a gentleman might call 'impecunious and insecure' as well as being somewhat physically unwell. In 1575 we find him writing to Cecil from Paris regarding a journey which he had made through Germany with his cousin, Kitson.

They had initially intended to visit the baths at Venice for 'the cure of an imperfection of 4 years in my left side, whence has proceeded the whole of my disorder'. However, on approaching Italy they heard such news of disease in the northern Italian cities that they turned north, visited Spas there and were now in France. This suggests that the relationship of William with the Queen's Secretary was a familiar, and no doubt promising, one and both his wife's and his father's relationships in that quarter might prove to be of advantage.

By 1594, however, having already incurred the Queen's displeasure for leaving Court in 'a foolish fit of discontent' William was again in disgrace for having a quarrel over cards with a Surrey recusant named Charles Arundel, an incident which almost ended in a duel in Islington Fields. He withdrew from Court again and offered his Highgate house to Sir Robert Cecil at a bargain price, 'praying his constant favour, good opinion, regard and remembrance if he should see any door open of place or profit for me to enter of'.

In 1597 the Crown Domestic papers record a communication from Sir William to Secretary Cecil. He says that it were 'better to be out of Court than out of countenance, though not being well is the cause of my absence'. He claimed to have deputized for his older cousin during 16 years in the post of Groom Porter in the Royal household, a post, it will be recalled, that had been held by several of his family' predecessors. He now asked for the reversion of the post "should God dispose of my elder cousin . . . and that as Her Majesty would not make me one of her Council, yet if she will one of her Court, by this means I may have a poor chamber in Court, and a fire, and a title to bring a pair of cards into the privy chamber at 10 o'clock at night and so that I might be about her Majesty . . . .".

He did not get the post but Cecil went to some lengths to bring him into Parliament that year, proposing first Ripon and then, on a rearrangement of seats at his disposal, the Cornish borough of Lostwithiel. This latter proposal worked and it has to be said that Sir William was no mere passenger in the House of Commons. He was appointed to several committees where he served with dedication including those on monopolies, the Poor Law, the allocation of Norwich diocesan lands and those of two brothers called Culpepper, as well as a joint conference with the Lords on methods of defence. A Culpepper link reappears later in our story.

Mention of defence should remind us that in 1599 he was in Ireland serving under Robert Devereux the 2nd Earl of Essex. Professor Neale reminds us that "by the end of August 1598 England's hold on Ireland had become extremely precarious; even Dublin, the seat of government, was threatened; and as there was the constant threat of Spain sending help to the rebels, a resolute attempt had to be made to overthrow Hugh O'Neill, 2nd Earl of Tyrone and reconquer the country." (*Queen Elizabeth*, p. 357) The help of any gentry in this urgent enterprise would be greatly valued and it is not surprising that after the crucial battle of Offaly that helped relieve Dublin William Cornwallis and others should be knighted by a grateful Essex.

Shortly afterwards Cecil obtained some small office for Sir William though the recipient was to declare later that it was 'never worth the wax' of the seal on the document that confirmed his tenure.

Even after his father's death, when he was both entitled, and more often likely, to reside at the new House in Brome, his name is mostly linked with the Hampstead property which he reoccupied and he preferred the life of the City to that of a country squire. He hoped, vainly as it turned out, that James I, who was now on the throne, would restore his fortunes with an appointment. He pleads in one letter that his estate was 'shrunk and shaken with so many years' service to a prince, utterly without reward' but elsewhere his constant references to frequenting taverns and losses at cards would suggest that 'princely occupations' were not the only or main cause of his difficulties. He hoped that the monarch would have sent him in 1605 on a mission to Venice that was in fact entrusted to Anthony Standen but, disappointed once more, he now wrote to Cecil informing him that he was too poor to attend at Court and was therefore obliged to forsake the King's service.

We do know that almost until his death, and in an effort to establish extra income, he was involved in property deals like the purchase of Brokes Manor in Ipswich but in 1609 he sold it to Gilbert Havers, a wool merchant of London. There were also other ploys. In 1606 he received a royal grant permitting him 'to hold divers fairs at Scole in Norfolk' and in 1607 a letter to Lord Salisbury informs us that Sir William was to be allowed a grant of up to £700 from the bullion seized from false coiners in Essex. Should the proceeds from this seizure come to more than that amount the remainder was to be placed in the King's coffers and Sir William was to be given the grant of a parsonage or some other reward to compensate him for the transfer. By his own admission he was constantly short of ready funds and therefore we should not be at all surprised that when he died on 13 November 1611, aged 58, at the old family home in Bishopsgate he left debts totalling £3,968. The full circumstances of his estate will become clear when we look at his last Will and Testament shortly.

Yet the story of his last years was not one of disappointment and despondency. In 1608, shortly after the death of his first wife, Lucy, and aware that he no longer had sons to inherit and carry on the family name, Sir William married again. Whom he chose is clearly stated on the tomb that exists to this day in Oakley Church and which he requested to be 'made for myself on the right side of the chancel'. Why exactly this situation was chosen rather than in the chapel at Brome has so far not been discovered. It could have been a matter of space for the memorial that was first erected was so bulky that even in Oakley Church it was eventually rearranged by Sir Edward Kerison. What had been two large side panels covered with Latin text were resited so that today the original north panel forms a reredos for an altar and the south one forms the front face of the altar itself.

The north black marble panel describes how for 'those who have eyes to see' this memorial records that the remains of Sir William Cornwallis 'lie covered here ready for resurrection'. The names of his first wife and all their children then follow. On the south panel we have the following words:

"After he had lost his male heir he turned once more to matrimony and made a most successful marriage with Jane Meautys. She was the daughter of Hercules Meautys, one of the noble squires who were in attendance on Queen Elizabeth and who was himself son of Sir Peter Meautys of the County of Essex. Jane's mother was Philippa, daughter of Richard Coke of Giddy Mall, also a Knight of that County. Jane Meautys bore her husband an only son, Frederick Cornwallis of Brome, Knight and Baronet, but she did not think it fitting as a devoted mother to forsake her son, a living reminder of his father, and at her own expense she arranged for this monument to be erected, the tribute, surely, of a fond wife to a loving husband."

These are generous words, as the monument is a generous gesture when one appreciates that the couple were only married for under three years and the husband requested in his will not merely this memorial but one for his great-grandfather, also William Cornwallis, who was buried here but with a simple stone. Moreover, the ample recognition of William's first wife and the marriages of all their girls, albeit again mentioned in the Will, reflects the quality of Dame Jane, whilst the quantity of fulsome Latin reveals what, in her letters, we shall shortly see as a proper claim to belong to the literary Cornwallises of the 17th century.

Dame Jane was no doubt not only in love with Sir William but was evidently conscious of what standing his family already had in English society. She would appreciate this because her own family background was of a shorter but similar quality. Her great-great-grandfather, John Meautas (also spelt Mewtas or Meutis), came originally from Normandy, via Calais, to become Secretary in the French tongue to King Henry VII. His son, Philip, married Elizabeth Foxley of Northamptonshire and their eldest son, Peter, of Westham in Essex was knighted, sent as an ambassador to France by Henry VIII and was a Gentleman of the Privy Chamber. The family were by now clearly enhancing their reputation with the Crown.

Philip had 3 children, one of whom was Jane's father. Her uncle, Henry, the eldest son, married Anne Jermy of Brightwell, Suffolk, whilst her aunt, Frances, married Henry Howard, 2nd Viscount Bindon. It thus seems very likely that through one or both of these alliances Sir William would have been introduced to Jane at some City, Suffolk or Howard gathering. Jane's elder brother, Thomas, was also made a knight at Whitehall in 1610, an event which would have delighted both Jane and her new husband.

The above monument also mentions the child of this brief but happy union and we shall see that his birth was to be the spur to one of the most remarkable periods in the family history. Though we shall detail the story of Frederick's career somewhat later we ought here to see what provision his father made for his son and heir apparent.

During the latter's minority Dame Jane was to be his guardian and she was to have 'the profits of the Manors of Brome, Ocley, Stuston, Thrandeston and Palgrave, and of all the manors, lands and premises in the counties of Suffolk and Norfolk'. Moreover, she was to 'employ the same for the payment of my debts' but in such fashion that 'all my household stuff, plate and furniture in my mansion house at Brome may be preserved until Frederick my son shall be 21'. Thereafter the heir was to recompense his mother and her executors for the debts paid and services rendered or Dame Jane was to have an equivalent sum from the sale of the Brome House contents.

It is interesting to note that he assigned to Dame Jane for her lifetime 'the manor of Wilton and its park at Cleveland, Co. York, and the advowson of the Rectory, church or chapel at Wilton, and all other messuages, lands and rents in Wilton, West Cotham, Lakisby, Lasinby and Pinchinthorpe, Co. York. Those who might have tenure of these properties during Frederick's minority are Thomas Darcy, son of the 3rd Lord Darcy of Chiche, Sir John Sulyard of Wetherden, Thomas Cornwaleis (sic), son and heir of John Cornwaleis of Soame (or Earl Soham), Suffolk, and Henry Dade, one of the Sons of Thomas Dade of Tannington. Just to show how William was keeping things 'in the family' we note that Thomas Dade was the husband of Anne Cornwallis, the daughter of William's uncle Richard.

Finally, Sir William granted 'To the poor, at or about my mansion house in the parish of St. Botolph without Bishopsgate, London, £10, to be distributed when my body shall be removed from thence to the place of my burial (and) To the poor of Brome and Ockley £40'. He also mentions his personal servants, Robert Morsse, William Crowe, Christopher Nandicke and Walter Warde as 'best acquainted with my estate and I desire them to assist my executors, to each of them £10'.

After the due witnessing of the Will there is a detailed list of the outstanding debts which include amongst others 'Mr Rooksley £1000, Lady Carewe and cousin Win. Cornwaleis £400 each, Mr. Peter 'Vanlow (or Van Loo) and Mr. Wivell £315 each, Lady Killigrew and Mr John Grave £210 each, with Mr. Acton, a silkman, £200, Thomas Saunders for wood £40 or so and Mr. Blount £60 annually for life'. That at least his accounts were kept in good order is abundantly plain and his widow had little doubt as to the situation she faced.

Before we continue with this premier line of the family, however, we need to turn again to Sir Charles Cornwallis who, with his sons, kept the Cornwallis name firmly in the Royal and public eye whilst Jane's son, Frederick, pursued his way to reach full manhood by 1630.

We have already noted that Charles Cornwallis married three times. The Fincham family into which he married in 1576/7 when 21 was made up of devout Norfolk Catholics with strong roots in their native heath and we have already noted that a cousin of Charles who became a Catholic priest was not only given the 'Fincham' name as a pseudonym but was also well received later in the Cornwallis household in Spain. In 1577 (November 21) Charles Cornwallis of Fincham, Esq., is recorded as granting some parcels of land there to a neighbour, William Guybon, and similar sales took place to the same person in 1581. The names of the children by his first wife were recorded in the last chapter and we shall come to them in more detail when we have traced the latter part of their father's career.

Following his wife Elizabeth's death c.1590 he seems to have taken special care regarding his further marriages and in each case he was to acquire connections with interesting relatives.

Anne, his second wife, was the daughter of Thomas Barrow of Barningham, Suffolk, and this latter was the grandson of Richard, of Wynthorp Hall, Lincolnshire. Anne had already been married to Sir Ralph Shelton, a member of a notable Norfolk family which had risen to especial prominence in the 1530s when Sir Rafe's aunt, Mary Shelton, a woman of some literary talent, was at one point even considered as the fourth wife of Henry VIII, following the sudden death of Jane Seymour. Her father, John Shelton, acquired Carrow Priory, Norfolk, at the Dissolution and thus established still further the family's fortunes in that county. Interestingly, Mary Shelton ultimately married into the Heveningham family and it was lands forfeit by William Heveningham in the 1570s for the sum of £1200 which had also helped to provide the young Charles Cornwallis with funds. Anne's elder brother, Thomas Barrow of Shipdenham (or Shipdham) in Norfolk, married a Mary Bures of Acton and one of his sons was Henry, who was executed in London for association with the Rookwood who was involved in the Gunpowder Plot.

During this period of his life Sir Charles was still managing to live as a Norfolk squire and in 1588 he contributed £50 to the defence of the County. In 1587 he sold his share of Kilverstone manor and in 1591 leased the manor of Trimley from Thomas Cavendish before that gentleman's fatal voyage to the American colonies. In September 1594 the property appears as part of a marriage settlement for his eldest son along with Hapsley (now Hemley?), Newbourne and the advowson of Newbourne Parish Church. In 1597 Trimley was sold to Robert Barker of Ipswich by his Trustees though whether this was in order to raise cash or purchase something else is not yet clear. Certainly Sir Charles continued to do business in land for in 1601 he was the subject of a fine on the manor of Hemley (sic) laid by Eliezer Duncon.

Sir Charles's third wife, Dorothy Jegon (née Vaughan), must have been a person of some considerable character. She was the daughter of Richard Vaughan, Bishop of London 1604-1607 and her first husband John Jegon had been Bishop of Norwich 1603-1618. By the second marriage there had been no children but Dorothy now had a son, Charles, to whom we must come later. Sir Charles also acquired a brother-in-law, Thomas, who was Archdeacon of Norwich and his son, John, Rector of Sible Hedingham, married a Rebecca Copinger. It was from her family that there later emerged the author of the mammoth work, 'The Manors of Suffolk', which is a major source book for all local family histories. In addition Sir Charles acquired step-children, one of whom, Robert Jegon of Buxton, married Margaret Robinson, one of the notable Yorkshire family.

Sir Charles was clearly of a much more stable disposition than his elder brother and being a second son he early realized that he would have to fend for himself as we have already noted. He was a manifestly more capable scholar, a trait which we began to discover afresh in his father during that parent's last years. In the 'Gentleman's Magazine' for 1826 Sir Charles is spoken of as 'Highly esteemed for his eminent abilities' and the fact that he was knighted by the newly enthroned King James in July, 1603, and then almost immediately despatched to Spain as ambassador, reflects on his qualities.

When one considers that his father was still alive and a recognized, albeit patriotic, recusant; that his first wife belonged to a recognizably Catholic family in East Anglia; and that Spain, still smarting from the rebuff of the Armada and the less promising state of Ireland as a base for attack, was hardly an easy land in which to play politics, the assignment of Sir Charles must have been due to personal traits that James and his advisers could wisely perceive. That Sir Charles was chosen to serve abroad when on the one hand his uncle and a recently acquired nephew were allied to the Rokewoods, whilst on the other his uncle and cousin were members of that Catholic clergy who were found to be involved with the Gunpowder Plot in 1605, seems either providential or beneficial. Whichever it was Sir Charles took his opportunity with both hands and until 1609 he was able to serve his King and Country with distinction.

His negotiations in that Embassy form a very prominent feature of this first Stuart reign in England and the Letters which relate them and which fill a large part of the second and third volumes of Winwood's Memorials are written with uncommon talent and clarity. What they reveal of their author is a feeling heart, a moral disposition, a warmth of true patriotism but also a constant uneasiness at the small-mindedness and sheer selfishness of the Court he had to serve. In particular he was very active in protecting British merchants from interference by the Inquisition and was constantly stressing the need for the home government to support more vigorously English commercial interests. It no doubt required all the diplomatic skill he possessed to submit his reports. What is somewhat surprising to anyone who takes the trouble to enquire into the duties which he undertook on his country's behalf is why his name is so little referred to in histories of the period.

He was recalled from this diplomatic task in 1609 and his secretary, Francis Cottington, was briefly appointed in his place. In the following year he was entrusted with another Court employment which required both the utmost discretion and integrity.

It is not always realized by the English public that just as King Henry VIII had an elder brother, Arthur, who did not survive so also did Charles I have an elder brother. This was Henry Stuart, Prince of Wales, who was provided with his own household in 1610 on his attaining the age of 16 and his investiture as Prince of Wales. Sir Charles was appointed his Treasurer, and governor of this new establishment, with a salary of £80 a year 'and diet or bo(a)rdwages'. For an English monarch still seeking to be accepted the management of his heir's affairs was a serious and crucial matter and not least when it became evident that father and son were of somewhat different temperaments.

King James, it is now agreed, was 'so well read and instructed in a wide variety of learning that he could . . . have professed several subjects at university level . . . . A man so brought up would want his son trained in the same manner, and from an early age Henry of Stirling was wont to send his father a Latin letter on regular occasions'.

Yet though Henry was a dutiful child and did as he was bid he was by his mid-teens beginning to reveal a character of his own. He was a good son in the sense that he was willing to learn from his father and undoubtedly studied the precepts laid down in James's remarkable work, "Basilikon Doron" (or The King's Gift) with the subtitle "His Majesty's Instructions to his dearest son, Henry the Prince". This was presented to Henry when he was 9 years old and proved so popular generally that it was the first English prose work to be immediately translated into French, German, Dutch and Danish. It appeared in a second, public edition a few days after the death of Queen Elizabeth and was avidly received by English readers since it offered some guide to how their new monarch viewed the role of kingship. Its emphasis on a middle path between Papists and Puritans in religion and on the King's role as a father of his people, owing allegiance to God and noone else, reflected what was James's own belief. The fact that James did not always practise the courses of behaviour, e.g. sobriety and self-control, which he here laid down was, however, increasingly noticed by his son. It is a matter of record that whilst Henry always had respect for his father he was never overtly intimate, and in fact found the tokens of affection that were paid by the King to some of his closest favourites a matter of distaste. We know too that Henry strongly objected to bad language and kept poorboxes in his various homes to receive the forfeits of those who swore in his presence. It is not known how much the poor benefitted when his father paid him a visit.

The fact is that Henry may not have been an intellectual but he had a fair measure of intelligence and a keen, alert mind. He even had a library arranged for him at St. James's Palace. His mind's bias, however, was practical with the result that his interests were quite different from those of his father. Whilst James might have rejoiced at Henry's interest in history he would have been less pleased at Henry's 'real bent for the arts of war. This had first shown itself when as a small child he had delighted in playing at soldiers; but it developed more seriously than such childish trends usually do, and with adolescence it became his main pre-occupation. He did well at subjects useful to soldiers, such as mathematics and cosmography . . . and (was) even allowed a special instructor in the theory and practice of fortification.

'He seems to have been different from his father in almost every possible way for whereas James was almost a cripple and incapable of any physical activity but riding, Henry was a straight-limbed, well-proportioned youth who . . . took the greatest pleasure in sport, especially tennis, athletics and swimming. At sixteen or seventeen he is said to have spent five or six hours a day in armour, practising the use of weapons. (He) walked a good deal in order to prepare himself for long marches (and) even the Prince's musical tastes had a martial flavour. No music was so pleasant in his ears as the sounding of the trumpet, the beating of the drum or the roaring of the cannon'. (Morris Marples, *Princes in the Making*, pp. 81-86)

He was no less interested in the Navy 'and accompanied by Phineas Pett, the Master Shipwright at Woolwich, he visited the Fleet. At the early age of 14 he knew more about ships than his father or the members of the Council and he was allowed to have an armed yacht constructed for his use. Henry had an admiration for a man whom his father kept in prison – Sir Walter Raleigh, and visited him on several occasions. The famous remark, "Only my father would keep such a bird in such a cage" was made openly by the Prince and on another topic, a proposed marriage for him with a Catholic princess, he is reported as stating that "two religions shall never lie together in my bed". (L.G. Pine, *Princes of*

94

Wales, pp. 112-115. An excellent portrait of Henry is found opposite p. 96.)

There seems to be no doubt that Henry was beginning to become very popular and was someone on whom the country began to set a new hope. His very name conjured up the remembrance of a Henry V who had subdued the flower of French knighthood and a Henry VIII who could oppose the Papacy. Court Masques which were requested by Henry, written by Ben Jonson and staged by Inigo Jones stressed these themes. Like Henry of Monmouth this prince at the age of 17 requested that he might be allowed to preside over the King's Council and thus share the executive power of the monarch – a request that was refused because his father's jealousy had by now been aroused. What is certain is that Henry's potential as a future ruler was already being recognized.

'Early in 1609 a Cornishman, Richard Connack, wrote to the Prince as Duke of Cornwall humbly petitioning him to give his mind to the affairs of the duchy. Henry at once examined his rights as Duke, discovered his rents were much in arrears, and ordered his agents to collect all outstanding dues. He also wrote to Connack suggesting that so diligent an antiquary might be interested in studying the other honours and monetary grants accorded by kings to their sons.' (Alan Palmer, *Princes of Wales*, 1979, p l0lf) Was it coincidence that as with that earlier such Prince, the later Edward VI, a Cornwallis should again be a close guide of a Duke, if not an Earl, of Cornwall's affairs?

Prince Henry's increasing abilities and activities, however, must have been a source of concern and embarrassment to his personal advisers for whilst they were naturally eager to promote his qualities and skills as a future King they were also employees of the Crown and could not risk the danger of any serious rift between their protégé and the King. Sadly a solution to their problem came sooner than expected. In 1612, before he was even 18, the Prince's health began to fail and a chill caught after playing tennis led to a bout of typhoid fever that proved fatal. That the problem of a possible breach could perhaps have existed seems to be suggested by the fact that Henry's parents only paid one brief visit to the dying Prince and then went away to bear their grief, or any other feelings in separate palaces.

How is it that we know so much about this heir to the throne? The answer is that not only was Sir Charles Cornwallis a remarkable adviser, confidant and governor for the Prince in the management of his household which comprised some four to five hundred persons but he was also a recorder of all that he observed and learnt about the Prince during his time of service. This record is contained in two eulogies written by him in the years that followed and which were published, the one in 1641 and the second in 1644. It is here that we discover what kind of a monarch we might have had.

The first publication was entitled "A Discourse of the most Illustrious Prince, Henry, later Prince of Wales. Written Anno 1626 and Printed for John Benson to be sold at his shop in Saint Dunstan's Churchyard". It is here that we learn of Sir Charles's obvious antipathy to the idea of his royal charge's marriage to a Princess of Savoy and the close attendance which he kept on Prince Henry throughout the final illness.

The second work was much longer and promised a much more detailed revelation. It was headed:

"The Short Life and Much lamented Death of that most magnanimous Prince
       HENRY, Prince of Wales,
Wherein the whole manner of his life and especially of his sickness
       and cause of his death is set forth at large.
Written by Sir Charles Cornwallis, Treasurer of His Highnesse Howshold,
    a man very intimate with him in the whole course of his life and
       at his death."

What is of as much interest as the fact that Sir Charles was the person privileged to have preserved this unique acquaintance with this Royal Prince is the Foreword that was appended to this volume. It was written by no less a person than Nathaniel Bacon and was addressed to "The High and Mighty Prince Charles, Prince of Wales, &c." It reads:

"Sir, Finding this manuscript amongst others I could not passe by it as I did the rest. The subject thereof being so rare a Prince, as it may seeme worthy your Highness perusall. In reading Him you may read your self: the titles of Honour were the same with yours: your titles of Vertues the same with his, as you are the Mirror of the age, which that you may still continue, shall ever be the prayer of

Your Highness most humble Servant, Nathaniel Bacon."

If, as now appears to have been the case, the Crown desired to draw a judicious veil over the attainments and possible prospects of Prince Henry following his death, it is not at all strange that Sir Charles, who was so obvious an admirer of the Heir apparent, should have delayed both the completion and the publishing of such panegyrics. It is even more revealing that Sir Nathaniel Bacon clearly indicates by his words that though the longer work had been completed some time before 1627, its publication was again delayed until Charles I's son, another Charles, was invested as Prince of Wales. Such a moment, when this Prince was about to go into protracted exile, and his father to face the ultimate judicial penalty, was clearly a more favourable one for the appearance of such a work that warmly supported the Monarchy. The Cornwallis name was thus firmly attached to the Royalist cause in the midst of a Civil War, and this, as we shall see, reflected the stance taken up by Sir Charles's nephew, Frederick.

Nor was this all that Sir Charles wrote on Henry. There is, amongst a collection of early Suffolk Tracts from Brome (or Broom), "A Relation of the Carriage of the Marriages that should have been made between the Prince of England and the Infanta Major and also after with the younger Infanta of Spain. Written to Lord Digby." We have already gathered the opinion of the Prince about such a projected marriage and here we have the source of one possible influence on his views. Sir Charles was clearly not happy urging either of these courses and having been at the heart of affairs in Spain he would seem to have been entitled to an opinion that would be heard.

Following the death of Prince Henry, however, such opinions were not exactly favoured by his monarch. As one commentator on the period has put it:

"This Prince was nearer to taking action than many thought. He lent fire to the King, his father, in the affairs of Germany and aspired to be the head of the confederation of Protestant Princes" and it is not by chance that we see the Elector Palatine and Henry's sister, Elizabeth, "sail away in the beautiful ship which had been built for Prince Henry. But this was a movement with which James was only half-heartedly in favour, and which, after Henry's death, he abandoned for a policy of neutrality with Spain, abandoning also Elizabeth and her husband." (F.Yates, *Shakespeare's Last Plays*, p. 59) It can be seen that Sir Charles's views had not exactly coincided with those of his Sovereign.

Later in 1612 Sir Charles applied unsuccessfully for the post of Master of the Wards but on 11 September 1613 he was sent to Ireland as one of four Crown Commissioners to investigate grievances there. It was not to be the only time that a Cornwallis would have such a task in that land but in reporting that the Irish did not seem to have any real ground for complaint Sir Charles and his partners obviously had somewhat different views from the Charles who went there some two hundred years later.

Matters now took a somewhat less happy turn. Sir Charles was suspected of having had a hand in fanning Parliamentary opposition to the Crown, whilst not even being a member of that body. In June 1614 we find him writing to the King from the Tower of London where he is held in custody. He voices his distress at having caused His Majesty any displeasure but claims that it was only an unfortunate accident that had prevented him becoming an M.P. The speech which seems to have been the source of the trouble had, he claims, been wrongly presented by Dr. Sharp and Mr. Hoskins who were M.P.s and was, in fact, intended to support the motion before the House urging supply of the King's wants. He did, however, believe that the best course for achieving His Majesty's goal was by preventing the increase of Papist influence that resulted from the suppression of his hitherto faithful ministers, by withdrawing the proposal of a French marriage for Prince Charles, and by ensuring that at least as many Englishmen as Scotsmen should fill the posts about His Majesty's person. It can be seen that Sir Charles must have touched a few raw, and royal, nerves.

Within the month he is writing again from the Tower declaring that he is sincerely penitent for his faults and imploring forgiveness in consideration of his innocency of intention and his long and faithful services. He acknowledges that as a servant of the Crown he should not have entered upon such matters without the King's leave but insists that his remarks about the number of Scots retainers could not be due to jealousy since he is closely attached to several of that nation. He had, it may be recalled, a Scots Peer as a brother-in-law. Moreover he can instance his having sold his own domestic plate in Spain in order to succour distressed Scots there. He nonetheless believed that it was more likely that the King would get more assistance from Parliament if no more Scots were employed at Court than at the present time.

He thus rested his case hopefully with the King but was in fact detained at His

Majesty's pleasure for another whole year before being released along with Sharp and Hoskins. He had learnt a very hard lesson in his sixties and Lord Carew, writing later that year to Sir Thomas Roe who had been Queen Elizabeth's first ambassador to India, as well as a personal friend of Prince Henry, remarked that Sir Charles was now free but 'will no more burn his fingers with Parliament (sic) business'. Sir Charles was too wise not to benefit from the experience and he now sought to re-establish himself and his position in Norfolk.

In 1614 he had received a small bequest in the will of Sir Nathaniel Bacon of Stiffkey and on his return from the Tower he sought further additions to his income from the manor at Beeston by performing local Crown duties. He apparently resumed his post of Collector of Privy Seals accounts in both Norwich and the County though in 1617 he was called upon to explain why sums due to the Crown that had been levied in 1611 had been entirely held by him for 5 years 'in his own hand'. His explanation must have been satisfactory because he was retained as a Royal servant and appears on a panel of Norfolk gentry in 1620 enquiring into local cases referred to them by the Privy Council.

By November 1624 Sir Charles had made real progress for he is now addressed as Deputy Lieutenant for Norfolk by Mr. Conway, Clerk to the Privy Council. He is thanked for obtaining a local pension on behalf of a Sergeant Pictoe, an experienced soldier who was a skilful instructor in the use of arms, but is further requested to try and secure expenses for Pictoe so that he could attend training meetings. It is clear that Sir Charles was still making new efforts and in 1625 Conway was writing to Sir Horace Vere of the Royal Household with a recommendation from 'Steenie', King James's favourite, the Duke of Buckingham, that Sir Charles be granted some further advancement. Whether this was to have been a step into the Peerage, a more lucrative post in royal service or a government office is not known. Whatever might have been considered is not mentioned in the State Papers.

Sir Charles died at Harborne in Staffordshire on 21 December 1629 but was buried in the church of St. Giles-in-the-Fields, London. His widow, Dorothy, was granted administration of his will on 1 January, 1630. A year later we learn by a royal writ issued at Cannock, Staffordshire, that this manor (also called Harborne and Smethwick) had been in the joint possession of Sir Charles and Sir Thomas Cornwallys (sic), his nephew, both of whom were now deceased. The said manor, worth £8 p.a., was leased from the Crown and in 1629 Dame Dorothy was also granted the sole original right to hold this property from the King until her only son, Charles, was of age. On 1 November 1617, however, there had been an indenture which allowed a 100 years' lease to be held by a Dame Katherine Cornwallis who was then the widow of Sir Charles's eldest son, William, and after her the occupancy of the house was to pass in due course to another Charles, Catherine's son, who was to be its tenant and to reside there.

It is at this juncture that we must take up the story of the Charles Cornwallis, Esq., mentioned above who was the only son of Sir Charles's marriage with Dorothy Jegon (née Vaughan), his third wife. He was born c.1619 and after being educated locally in Norfolk he married in June 1640. His bride was Edith, the daughter of John Newce of Rock,

Worcestershire, and co-heir with her brother John. The children of the marriage were one son, Francis, and 2 daughters whose names have not yet been discovered. We will look at the continuance of this line when we have completed their father's story.

By marriage Charles acquired the Rock estate though he and his wife lived chiefly in London in the house formerly occupied by Sir Charles.

As Sir Charles and his wife Edith's families were supporters of the Royalist cause he was appointed by Parliament in 1648 to the Worcestershire Committee for assessment and also held local office under the Commonwealth. At the Restoration he was given a post at Court and petitioned jointly with Sir Henry Bennet for the office of Postmaster General. Though he was unsuccessful in this application he obtained a post in Customs and £2,000 from the Crown's 'secret service' fund.

At a by-election in 1662 Charles was returned as M.P. for Eye and became a moderately active member of the Cavalier Parliament, being appointed to 55 committees of which 25 were dealing with estate bills. Although he had had no formal legal training he was apparently much in demand as a trustee. One especial and, on the face of it, surprising example of his involvement in these estate matters is his initial and persistent support for a bill concerning John Coplestone, the Cromwellian sheriff of Devon. This man's part in the suppression of Penruddock's rising must have left him many enemies and even though on the second introduction of the bill Cornwallis was instructed to carry it to the Lords it was still rejected there.

In 1663 subpoenas against himself, Sir Thomas Fanshawe and Sir Ralph Bankes were laid by the Papist Sir George Wakeham, who was later the Queen's physician, but these were parried by their Parliamentary privilege. Another notable Roman Catholic however, Sir Kenelm Digby, had obtained Charles as a security for an £8,000 mortgage and on the former's death he named Cornwallis as his executor. Greatly to the indignation of the Digby heir the Leicestershire and Rutland estates were temporarily conveyed to his father's creditors until their accounts had been settled. Even when the Digby family made their most strenuous attempts to recover their properties in 1670 Cornwallis managed to avoid any court involvement and on 25 February 1671 he was again granted all immunity from their claims upon him and does not seem to have suffered any material loss. His loss of their esteem was another matter.

Meanwhile, in 1665 he had been appointed Commissioner for Oyer and Terminer in the Norfolk circuit and the overseer of recusants in Suffolk. His parish church in London was St. Giles-in-the-Field and although he never seems to have served on the Vestry there he was in 1672 added to a Parliamentary committee considering the burden of the poor in this parish whilst by 1674 he was serving on a group that was inquiring into the condition of Ireland. One wonders if a descendant of his ever read their findings when he was closely involved in that country's affairs?

He died on 28 August 1675 and was buried at St. Giles nine days later. He had well established the Cornwallis name in the Lower House but as far as his branch of the line's presence was concerned it was not until 1722 that his great-grandson was to represent Cardigan there.

Charles's son, Francis, is recorded as having been admitted to Corpus Christi College in 1657 after which he was ordained in Norwich Cathedral and by 1685 had become the Rector of Abermarlais in Carmarthenshire. It is from there and in that year that his eldest son, Thomas Cornwallis, went up to Trinity College, Oxford and matriculated on 24 November 1685 aged 18. Thomas inherited property through his father's marriage and married Emma, daughter of Sir Job Charlton, 1st Baronet, M.P. for Ludford, Herefordshire. There was only one son born in 1693 and he was sent briefly to Eton and thence to Lincoln's Inn for his initial education.

By the time that he matriculated on 19 April 1711 at University College, Oxford, his parents had obviously also inherited the house at Ludford and it was there that Francis lived until he married Jane, the only daughter and heiress of Sir Sackville Crowe, 2nd Baronet of Laugharne, Carmarthenshire who had died in 1703. It was thus as resident of the property at Laugharne that he was put up for the Constituency of Cardiganshire by Lewis Pryse, M.P., with the support of William Powell of Nanteos the joint leaders of the local Tories. He served there as M.P. from 1722 to 1727 and thereafter for the Cardigan Boroughs until his death on 19 August 1728 and he was buried at Laugharne on 4 September.

He was a member of the society of Sea Serjeants, a reputedly Jacobite organization in South Wales and his obituary described him as 'hospitable obliging and benificent; a lover of virtue without ostentation, and of mirth without vice'. He died without issue and with his passing yet another branch of the Cornwallis family ceased.

It is now to the somewhat complicated but interesting branches of the rest of Sir Charles Cornwallis's family that we must turn.

As was mentioned in the previous chapter Sir Charles and his first wife, Elizabeth Fincham, had two sons, William and Thomas. William who is usually referred to as 'the Younger' to distinguish him from his uncle, was born in 1578/9 and in due time married Catherine, the daughter of Sir Philip Parker of Alwarton and Catherine Goodwin, the latter being the daughter of Sir John Goodwin of Winchendon, Buckinghamshire. We have already met the ancient family of the Parkers whose seat was at Erwarton in Suffolk and it may be recalled that it was William's grandfather, Sir Thomas Cornwallis, who completed the Brome estate holdings by purchasing the 'Erwarton' manor that the Parkers had held there. From the Parkers, on the maternal side, descended the Percevals, Earls of Egmont. From William's marriage came the 6 sons and 5 daughters already recorded. (See previous chapter)

If we have already noticed intimations of literary skill in William's last aunt, Dame Jane Cornwallis, and his father, Sir Charles, we now discover in Sir William the younger a member of the family whose writings are still the proud possession of some of England's leading libraries. As was stated in a letter from Ipswich to the Gentleman's Magazine for

1826, "Sir William was a learned and ingenious man, as is fully apparent from his Essays on several subjects, in which he has displayed, with much wit and judgement, the chief characters of life." For works that had already been around for 225 years that was no little praise.

Nor is that the opinion only of the 19th century. An American scholar, Don Cameron Allen, introduced a complete 1946 edition of Sir William's Essays with these words:

"It is not wholly unreasonable to call Sir William Cornwallis the first English essayist although this name is usually bestowed upon Francis Bacon because of (his work) published in 1597." Yet Bacon's influence on the essay before 1625 is slight, whereas Cornwallis was well-regarded by his contemporaries, as the regular reprintings of his works suggests . . .". Bacon's claim is that of complete originality. Though Cornwallis did not imitate Montaigne overmuch he was led to produce his essays by reading Florio's translation of that Frenchman's 'Essais' "But what he wrote in 1600 is a more finished essay than Bacon was to achieve before 1612." (Allen, p. x)

As in the case of his French 'mentor' Sir William allowed his thoughts wide rein as a glance at the topics of his Essays reveals. He writes 'Of Estimation and Reputation', 'Of Silence and Secrecie', 'Of Trappes for Fame' and 'The instruments of a Statesman' but he also has more personal pieces regarding 'Lady Hastings, Dudley and the rest' or his aunt 'Mistress Withypole' of Ipswich.

Moreover one set of these Essays has an intriguing frontispiece showing two hatted gentlemen facing each ofhter with pens in their hands. A long tradition has held that the two figures shown here were in fact Sir William and his father, Sir Charles. Cameron asserts that this is an absurd view since by the time this edition was published both characters were long since dead and could not have thus sat for their likenesses. Yet both men have a striking similarity and whilst one has the plain collar of an Elizabethan the other has a ruff of the Jacobean style. That the author had much for which to thank his father will soon be evident and both men, if such be the case, were persistent in their reading and writing. Even if this picture is only an emblematic representation of the essayist's art the idea that this skill transcended the generations can be grasped.

Happily we now know something more about Sir William than is found in the brief sketch in the *D.N.B.* William himself wrote of his parents,

I owe them voluntarily that which the lawes of God and of Nature exact of all men. I do it without Hypocrisie or Feare; yet should they loose their wealth or their lives, I would neither teare my hair nor melt into womanish exclamations . . .". This perhaps 'restrained' attitude was qualified in another essay by his admission that he had parents who were "more careful of my mynd than of my bodie". Of his education we are still uncertain, however, though Sir Thomas Overbury once noted that on a trip to Edinburgh he had met Sir William 'who knew him in Queen's Colledge at Oxford'. A search among the record of the students there produces no contemporary Cornwallis name though it is a fact that in 1597, which was in the period when Overbury was at Oxford, we see that there was a

Cornwallis, but not named, matriculating at Trinity College, Cambridge.

Cameron is of the opinion that since no clear evidence of a university education is forthcoming and William was then the potential successor of his uncle, who was still without an heir, the boy was probably reared by tutors in the squirearchical fashion. This does seem to be borne out by the fact that 'Like all (such) men of his age he knew enough about some of the Latin classics to misquote them from memory' but he does not seem to have learnt any Greek and even when he reads Montaigne we have seen that it was in an English translation.

He certainly knew some Spanish but since his father was the ambassador in that country this is not surprising. His knowledge of Italian was even better and we know that he not only read Guicciardini and Machiavelli in the original but was amongst the first Englishmen to read and applaud the great epic of Tasso. To confirm the 'country gentleman' type of upbringing, however, he tells us in his essay 'Youth' that

"I was bound then to 'Arthur of Brittaine' and things of that price, for my knowledge was not able to traffick with any thing more rich. 'Stowe's Chronicle' was the highest . . . My exercises & recreations or rather (as I then used them) occupations, I find worth somewhat. I would not loose my knowledge of Hawkes and running Horses for any thing." There was also one commentator on his life who reported that 'he was attracted by every trivial book or pamphlet that came in his way; of these he carried numbers with him to the privy, and tore them to pieces before he rose from his seat'. (Grainger) Perhaps one ought not to wonder why this latter action was necessary.

He was again like his uncle in being overly extravagant and this was not helped by his having eleven children of whom eight survived him. The image of him as the well-to-do occupant of a house at Highgate who once commissioned Ben Jonson to write an entertainment for the visit of King James and his Queen is a far from true reflection of his frequent meagre purse and rather disordered economies. His father had provided him at his marriage, as suggested earlier, with an income of £200 a year derived from the Manor of Grimston Hall with Marston in the parish of Trimley St. Martin, Suffolk, and the Manor and advowson of St. Mary Newbourne. Yet two years later he was having to sell this property to satisfy his creditors. Not that he ever seems to have given way to utter sadness and despair and his children he never regretted. Even in an essay entitled '0 Sorrow', composed when real penury seemed to face the family, he writes:

"The most acceptable blessing that ever I had was a sonne, in whose time of growing meete to see the world, I examined often how to fitte myself for his approach."

As has already been inferred he attached himself to the Devereux faction and, once more following in the steps of his namesake, joined Essex on his last and ill-fated expedition to Ireland. His stay 'at the Bay of Armes', as he put it, was a short one but again like his uncle he was knighted in 1602 in the course of this service. Thereafter he seems to have begun to adopt a life of sustained reading and writing and his father even wrote to the Earl of Salisbury commenting that 'he had at last begun to love a frugal life as he had once loved a prodigal one'. Indeed in the very first of the 'Essays' he records how "in the end I found my selfe; I and my soule undertooke to guide me into a more wholesome aire. I dare not say she hath kept promise really . . . yet in part she hath; her motions, my own memory, and bookes have done something." He even addressed a poem to John Donne, later Dean of St. Paul's, at this time:

> What tyme thou meanst to offir Idillnes
> Come to my den for heer she always stayes;
> If then for change of howers you seem careles
> Agree with me to lose them at the playes.

Due to their similar religious backgrounds, with evident Catholic family influences, the two men were drawn to each other in London and shared an interest in writing what were called 'Paradoxes'. Donne had composed his by 1600 and we know that William had written some that appear in Sir Stephen Powle's Commonplace Book.

During the years immediately after 1600 this member of the Cornwallis family strove to make some place for himself in public life and it was during his discharge of some minor commission that he had met Overbury in Edinburgh in 1602. In 1604 he held the now 'familiar', or rather' family' seat as M.P. for Orford and it was during this tenure that he made a speech in favour of the Union with Scotland which was later to appear in print. It was a fair-sized pamphlet entitled 'The Miraculous and Happie Union' and in the light of more recent developments in this field it is interesting to read what were some of this member's opinions nearly 400 years ago. "If they tell you of the poverty of Scotland, examine whether our wealth shall not come from the addition of their Kingdom, for at once we receive from them the stopping of our unnecessary wars, and the use of traffick." Or again,

"Now let us see the trial of reason, this hand (sic) is happily come within the circle of one Diadem, not by Conquest nor by weakness, nor for protection, but are drawn together by the vertue of an united blood, and made one man's Kingdom by the happy coniunction of the Royal blood of both nations." Or yet again,

"But it may be it will be answered, let their industries be spent upon their own soyle (sic) and so shall ours and we will crave nothing from them. Who seeth not in this answer either a wilful or ignorant folly? That forgetting their nearness, the danger of their mislikes, the gap for seditions and plotters to get entrance, we reckon them as a people that concern us not. No, no, they must have a hand in our business, our peace is theirs, our flourishing theirs, our success of all kinds theirs . . .".

One correspondent of John Donne's obviously held very different views for his criticism was scathing: "If he were not a kind friend of yours I would express that wonder which I have in my heart, how he keeps himself from the Coat with long sleeves. It is incredible to think, if it were not true, that such simplicity of conceit could not be joyned in him, with so impudent utterance."

The Coat referred to was of course a straitjacket for madmen so one is tempted to infer that such language could only have issued from an irate Scot. At least Sir William's opinions could be understood.

When his father became a resident abroad Sir William was employed in conveying despatches between Spain to England. His work at least secured the good opinion of the Earls of Salisbury, Southampton and Northampton as well as of Sir Henry Wotton. Indeed the latter speaks of 'the honest love which hath long beene betweene Sir William the younger and myselfe'. Even so the situation of this particular Cornwallis family during these years, 1605 to 1610, was financially precarious and letters from the Earls to Sir Charles reveal that relief for his son's distressed state was urgently and frequently required. There is even evidence that Sir William the Elder was seeking to secure some of his brother's property at this stage and at one point the Younger had to wield his pen to defend his father's good name and his interests. The father responded, as we discover in a letter to Wotton when the latter reported that for over 8 months he had had no response from the son. Sir Charles writes:

"My good Lo(rd): I thank yow much for soe good a testimony of your love to myne unthrifty and unfortunate sonne. Hee hath spent mee in yt Court above 50001. And now haveinge geven him 200li a year more where-with to live, he turnes his backe to his fortunes. Of all sorts of people I most dispaire of those of his sorte, that are Philosophers in their wordes and fooles in their workes. To God Almightie his mercifull and gracious providence I must leave him."

Old Sir Charles could also certainly turn a phrase and in 1606 and 1610 Providence at least provided new editions of the Essays though the new pieces which were added here were entitled: 'Of Adversity'; 'Of Fortune and her Children'; and 'Of the Admirable Abilities of the Mind'. One might remark that the headings say it all.

There are two other curious works which are ascribed to Sir William although Don Allen is doubtful whether the second was really his unaided work. The first was 'An Encomium of Julian the Apostate' and the other, 'The Encomium of Richard ye Third'. The latter, at least in one version, has a preface entitled 'To his worthey frende Mr John Donne'. His purpose in so writing is clearly stated:

"Receve then as a marke of my love, my Charitye, of this defamed Prince, whose life lately readinge, I found ill rather by supposition than asurednes . . . yet coulde I not suffer soe maney vertues (wherwith his Enemies coulde not denye him to be adorned) to be dusked, and drowned by vices.. .for the doeinge wherof the olde Proverbe will deffende me De absentibus et mortuis nil nisi Bonum . . .".

The question whether this is wholly Sir William's composition leads us into much more than simply the solution of a literary conundrum. We know that Sir Thomas More was attached to the household of Cardinal Morton, the life-long enemy of Richard III, and received a tract on the King written by his patron. This unduly bitter account was the basis for More's 'History of King Richard', a much more balanced piece, and the original copy of this latter, in turn, eventually came to William Roper who had married Sir Thomas More's eldest daughter. When we learn not only that Sir William's family was living in Holborn in 1604, for one of their children was then baptized in the Parish Church, but that the Ropers had also in that year leased a house there from the Earl of Southampton, one of whose aunts, Katherine, had married a Cornwallis, the possibility of Sir William having seen the earlier manuscript becomes quite likely. Nor is that all. In the Powle commonplace book already mentioned there are copies of letters from Sir William to 'cousin Roper' and it is significant that Donne, to whom the work is directed, had married Anne More, a relative of the great Sir Thomas. It is thus now generally agreed that whilst there may have been some influence on the 'Encomium' by the work of Sir Thomas More, and a few further 'amendments' when it came into the hands of Sir Henry Neville, Secretary to the Privy Council, this defence of monarchy was yet largely the work of Sir William Cornwallis. That it should not have appeared until the rule of the Tudors, King Richard's opponents, was over and the effects of the Essex plot of 1600 had faded, only heightens the significance of the composition when it at last appeared in 1616. Though it is not necessary to reproduce much of the work here it was with surprising perception that the author wrote the following in the light of what was soon to occur in England:

"Therfore the removinge sutch occasions of Civill warres in a well governd Commonwealth is moste proffitable, moste Comendable, being noe Cruelty but pittey, a Jelousie of theire Subiectes, and a regarde of theire owne safeties . . .".

Sir William was not to enjoy seeing the publication of this work for in 1613 it was spread abroad that he was already dead. The fact that he did not in fact die until 1 July 1614 suggests that he suffered a long and debilitating illness. Though his name was to be longer remembered than that of many others of his family he sadly had little of worldly goods to bequeath to his widow and dependants. As we noted previously Sir Charles granted a jointure in Harborne to Dame Catherine and subsequently sought an allowance for her from Sir Julius Caesar, the Treasurer of the Royal Household. She was not therefore compelled to depend on her husband's philosophic outpourings alone though happily his works were still being reprinted in 1632. She was eventually interred in the north aisle of the church at Erwarton where a brass plate records that 'Here lyeth ye body of Katherine Lady Cornwaleys . . . wife to Sr William Cornwaleys ye younger, Kt., by whom she had 6 sonnes and 5 daughters (all then named) . . . Shee lived 58 yeares and dyed ye 30th of January, A.D.1636'.

Before we turn to what can presently be ascertained about their off-spring who survived childhood we must return to Sir Willam's brother, another Thomas, because he, being even less well-documented or notable, can so easily be overlooked and yet it is his marriage and child that take the Cornwallis name into an area of the country more normally linked with the Cornwalls, the other descendants of Earl Richard.

Thomas was probably the unnamed Cornwallis who matriculated from Trinity College, Cambridge in 1597 but he certainy married Ann, daughter of Samuel Bevercott of Ordsall near Scrooby, Lincolnshire. Ann was either the sister, or a close relative, of another Samuel who was the local postmaster before William Brewster who became the leader of the first Pilgrim Fathers colony in New England.

The couple had a son, Bevercotes Cornwallis, who was baptized at St. Margaret's, Lincoln on 28 June 1620, then educated locally and duly admitted at Corpus Christi, College, Cambridge in 1636. He was then entered at Gray's Inn a year later and presumably practised law until his death in 1673. So far there is no indication that he either married or had any children.

Reverting to the family of Sir William the younger the information which we have so far is as follows. Charles, the eldest, was probably tutored by his own father for like his next brother, Thomas, he does not appear in any of the University lists. Though he was the heir there was not that much for him to inherit though in due time the property at Harborne that had been leased to his mother, Dame Katherine, was to become his.

As was also noted in the last chapter Frances, the eldest daughter, married Thomas Paston, and was eventually buried at Burnham Thorpe in November 1675. She was then in her 72nd year.

Thomas Cornwallis, Sir William's second son, married Penelope, daughter of John Wiseman, Esq., of Tyrrell's Hall, Essex, and the Middle Temple, and she bore him 10 children as named earlier. They lived latterly in a hall near Burnham Thorpe, Norfolk, though she was buried at Erwarton in November, 1693, being 57. That, however, is only a small part of what was a much more fascinating story.

As a second son Thomas clearly had to make his own way in the world and not least when his father had strictly limited means. Born in 1603, when the family lived in Holborn and his father was to become an M.P., Thomas probably went to a local school and at the age of 11, when his father died, continued some education near the family's new home at Harborne. He may then have been apprenticed as a clerk in some merchant's house for he was later to display his skills in that direction. Yet it was to military service that he also at some point turned, being single and ambitious for status. His efforts at last bore fruit when, aged 32, we find him commanding an expedition in a North American countryside with names like Choptank, Nanticoke, Wicomico and Pocomoke. Here, in a land already peopled with pirates, smugglers and privateers, the first naval fight on inland waters of any of the original American States occurred at the mouth of the Pocomoke in 1635. Two Calvert vessels, under Thomas's command, captured a ship belonging to William Clayborne, a Virginian trader. He was acting illegally in the Chesapeake district of Maryland and it was in this latter Province that Thomas Cornwallis settled. He thus became the first of the family to make his mark on this continent but he was certainly not to be the last.

In 1637 Cecil, 2nd Lord Baltimore gave an instruction that there should be a meeting of the Colony's legislative body and that the Governor, Leonard Calvert, Lord Baltimore's younger brother, should there present for acceptance the code of laws sent out from England. When, in January 1638 and with only a few members in attendance, the Governor and Secretary, Lowger, tried to force assent to these laws after only one reading it was Thomas Cornwallis who objected and moved that there be should be an adjournment. This was agreed and the legislature met again a month later.

It was now determined that all such suggested laws must be read three times and that each occasion was to be on a separate day. Unhappy with the independence displayed by the members the Governor proposed a further adjournment but Cornwallis, who is described in a contemporary pamphlet as 'that noble, right valiant and politic soldier', again opposed the proposal, stating that "they could not spend their time in any business better than this for the country's good." The decision was confirmed.

In February the following year the legislature met again and this time enacted the English law that stated "that Holy Church shall have and enjoy all her rights, liberties and franchises wholly and without blemish". That Church, of course, was the Church of England.

Matters now proceeded equably until September 1642 when a new order was received by the Governor from Lord Baltimore requiring further reorganization of government practice. In the Assembly Cornwallis was now designated as Councillor but he absolutely refused to undertake that office if he was required to take an oath on the same basis as that on which oaths were taken in the last commission.

During the following spring Leonard Calvert sailed for England and Giles Brent became the acting Governor. He commissioned Cornwallis to lead an expedition against the Susquehannah Indians and a record in Maryland of the day called 'Nova Albion' tells us that leading 53 'raw and tired Marylanders' Cornwallis faced 250 Indians, defeated them and killed 29. His men only suffered superficial wounds.

Thomas had in 1638 declared his intention of erecting 'A house toe put my head in, of sawn Timber framed, a story and a half hygh with a seller and Chimnies of brick toe Encourage others toe follow my Example for hithertoe wee Live in Cottages'. He had visited England in 1640 and on his return in December 1641 he obviously had more substantial funds at his disposal. He now erected his dwelling and it was called 'Cornwallis Cross' whilst today it is known as Cross Manor.

We have seen that he was a prominent figure in the Legislature that resumed in March 1642 and in 1643 an order was issued to the Colonial Surveyor "to lay out for Capt. Cornwaleys 4000 acres of land in any part of the Patowmack (sic) river upward of Port Tobacco creek."

When the civil war between the King and Parliament began Thomas Cornwallis was living in more ease and elegance than anyone else in Maryland. As he put it: "By God's blessing upon my endeavours I have acquired a settled & comfortable subsistence having a fine dwelling house furnished with plate, linen hangings, bedding, brass, pewter and all manner of household stuff worth at least a thousand pounds, with twenty servants, at least a hundred breed cattle, a great stock of swine and goats, some sheep and horses, a new pinnace about twenty tons, well-rigged and fitted besides a new shallop and other small boats."

Thomas was obviously emulating his earlier namesakes who had founded the estate at Brome and he was certainly outstripping his father's and elder brother's 'fortunes'. Yet even this was not the end of the story.

Appointing Cuthbert Fenwick his agent Thomas, who had now been named Lieutenant Governor, sailed again for England in April 1644. There he found his cousin, Sir Frederick Cornwallis, to be a close friend of King Charles I and also met Leonard Calvert who was not to return to Maryland until the following September. Back in that colony a Captain, Richard Ingle, commanding the ship 'Reformation', had been commissioned by Parliament to cruise in the waters of the Chesapeake and seek out 'malignants' which was the name given to supporters of the Crown. In discharging this duty Ingle appeared near St. Inigoe's creek where there was an uprising in favour of Parliament in which all the servants of Cornwallis participated, saving only some negroes and the new agent, a tailor named Richard Hervey Fenwick.

These latter persons were taken on board Ingle's ship and a landing party, led by Thomas Sturman, his son Thomas and William Hardwick, took possession of the Cornwallis house, burned its fences, killed the pigs, took the cattle, wrenched the locks from the doors and caused damage to the amount of two or three thousand pounds. When Ingle returned to England with a Jesuit, Father White, Cornwallis instituted a claim for damages against him.

For 8 years Cornwallis attended to business in London but in 1652 he returned to Maryland which was now controlled by supporters of the Parliamentary cause and laid a further claim for compensation for the injury done to his property during the Ingle period. In a memorial placed before the Maryland Assembly Cornwallis did not mince his words:

"It is well known, I have, at great cost and charges, from the first planting of this Province and for the space of 28 years, been one of the greatest propagators and increasers thereof, by the yearly transportation of servants, whereof divers have been of very good rank and quality towards whom and the rest I have always been careful to discharge a good conscience, in the true performance of my promise and obligations, that I was never taxed with any breach thereof, though it is also well known and I do truly aver it, that the charge of so great a family, as I have always maintained, was never defrayed by their labor."

He duly set about building once more and this time proposed a new home on the point of the Potomac, above Potopaco. A contract was made on 23 November 1652, with Cornelius Canada (probably Kennedy), brickmaker, and a former servant of Governor Green, to deliver 36,000 sound, well-burned bricks before a certain day in June 1653 and another 24,000 before the 24 June 1654. He was clearly intent on raising a substantial residence.

A house is still present on this site today and is still called 'Resurrection Manor'. The outline mark of bricks on the sides of the present structure plainly show how it changed its shape with a third stage in which the old gambrel roof type was made into a gable roof with dormers. The old garden is one of the most interesting in the State and was quite obviously laid out at the time that Thomas was granted his main plot of land. The once box bushes are now 'box trees and measure almost 50 feet in circumference.

There are two traditions as to the name of the oldest property. One story is that before the first Marylanders came to settle here a party of Virginian explorers were murdered by local Indians on the shore of St. Inigoe's Creek. A second party found and buried their remains and erected a cross over the spot and it was this cross that was found by Thomas Cornwallis.

The other but less likely story is that which appears in the novel, 'Rob of the Bowl' by John P. Kennedy in which he described how "one Cornwalys, while hunting, accidentally emptied a charge into the breast of his dearest friend. This Cornwalys went afar and made his fortune but the vision of his friend stayed with him. He returned to Maryland a wealthy man, went to a remote spot on St. Luke's Creek, near St. Inigo, and built a great cross of lasting locust wood on the spot where his friend had died. He then also erected a hermitage where he lived as a recluse and eventually died." The name of the second house was easy. What came after the Cross in the Gospels, said its owner, was the Resurrection. Let that be the name of the house that followed.

When this second house was completed Thomas once more set off across the Atlantic and before his return in 1657 he had contracted the marriage with Penelope Wiseman who was then only 21 years of age. The husband, we may recall, was 54. In 1658 we note that the couple were living in the new Maryland home but early in 1659 they were again on their way to England and this time neither of them ever returned. It was to be a century and more before that part of the American continent once again became acquainted with the name Cornwallis.

Thomas's affairs in Maryland were now entrusted to an attorney and he became simply 'a merchant of London' in what was no mean family tradition. He built another house near Burnham Thorpe in Norfolk, calling it 'Maryland Point', and here 'the prudent Commissioner' or 'best and wisest of Maryland's founders' eventually retired. He died there aged 72, leaving his widow of 40 to manage their family.

Before we come to Thomas's children, however, it will be as well if we complete the story of his two younger brothers, the younger of whom was born in, or just after, the year their father died. Whether or no the older brother contributed to the cost of their education we cannot be certain but they were both admitted as scholars at Emmanuel College, Cambridge. One whose name is not given, but may well have been the third son, was admitted a Fellow-commoner at Easter 1626 and the youngest, Philip, became a pensioner in June 1631, attained his B.A. in 1634, his M.A. in 1638 and in September 1644 was made Deacon in Norwich Cathedral. In August 1646 he was ordained priest by the Bishop of Lincoln and having already been presented to the living of St. Peter, Burnham Thorpe by his grandfather, Sir Philip Parker, in 1643 he was now also admitted to the living of All

Saints, Little Ellingham, Norfolk. He held the two in plurality but only for a brief period as by 1647 he had resigned from that cure. He remained at Burnham and it was there that he not only presided over his sister's burial but was himself interred. A brass plate records that he died on 30 December 1688.

Of merchant Thomas's children not many survived as the triple recurrence of the name Penelope suggests. William, the elder son, was born in 1659 but died aged 5 in 1664, and his younger brother called John also died young. Frances, their eldest sister, married the Rev Samuel Richardson but on 24 January, 1684, she too was buried by her uncle, Philip, at Burnham Thorpe.

It was the second son, Thomas, who was to perpetuate this line. Born on 19 April 1662 his elementary education was at Charterhouse which he entered in October 1672. In December 1677 he was admitted to Peterhouse Cambridge taking his B.A. on 20 January 1681. He was made deacon by the Bishop of Ely in the chapel of St. John's College, Cambridge and whilst serving his title seems to have sailed to Cadiz, staying in Spain until his return to Bristol in January 1684. In July 1685 he gained his M.A. and was duly ordained priest in Norwich Cathedral at the canonical age of 24 on 30 May 1686. He was then instituted the next day to the Rectory of Erwarton and by April of the following year was also appointed as Chaplain to the Rt. Hon. Edward Rich, 6th Earl of Warwick and 3rd Earl of Hoiland. In June he received the additional living of Bradley Parva in Suffolk and at this point he married Mary, the daughter of Mr. Robert Cock of Wherstead. In 1724 he also became Rector of Helmley. From this union there came 7 sons and 4 daughters, most of whom sadly died young, but whose details are listed below.

On a flat stone in the north aisle of Erwarton church this worthy cleric and his wife are commemorated in a long Latin inscription. We are told that for 45 years he had tenure of this parish as a dedicated, holy and faithful pastor and died, aged 70, on 11 July 1731. Here too lay his wife, 'a most generous and prudent lady with whom he had the most loving partnership for 44 years' and of their numerous progeny only 2, William and Anne (later Gaillard), were still alive at the time of their mother's death. Mary was laid to rest, worn out by many 'labours' (sic), on 29 March 1742, aged 76. The stone's message concludes, "Go forth, O Reader, and seek to emulate".

Philip, the eldest son, was born on 10 August 1688, and in 1716 married Elizabeth, the widow of William Pelham, of Bures (or Bewers) in Suffolk. Philip was a surgeon, an alderman of Harwich and himself the father of three children, Mary, Anne and Catherine. Sadly he died on 29 June 1729 at the age of 41, just 2 days before the birth of his last daughter. His wife had to bring up the 3 girls though she did not die till 11 May 1788.

Mary, the eldest daughter, married James Hatley, Esq. in 1747, and was buried beside him in the churchyard of St. Nicholas, Ipswich. From their table monument we learn that she died on 22 May 1796, outliving her husband who was buried in August 1787 at the age of 66. He came of an ancient family in Bedfordshire which later moved to Hunton, near Linton, Kent. The couple are described as having been 'eminent examples of conjugal love' and certainly their life together had been tested for buried with them were their son, Philip, who had died at the age of 14 in 1771 and their daughter, Isabella, who died in February 1784, aged 29. Mary's mother, Elizabeth Pelham, and Mary's sister, Catherine Cornwallis, were also buried here and they predeceased her respectively in May 1788 aged 74, and in July 1794, aged 65. Mary's other sister, Anne, married the Revd. Cuthbert Douthwaite, Rector of St. Mary Stoke, Ipswich. He died on 29 December 1781, and Anne outlived him until 31 January 1791. For the sake of greater clarity and to show the full extent of the branch that issued from the Revd Thomas and Mary (née Cock) Cornwallis the following chart is provided:

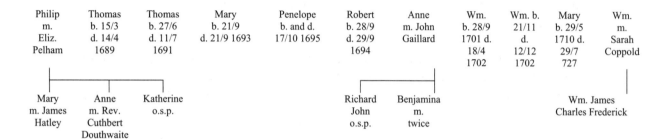

The seventh of Thomas and Mary's children, Anne, was born on 3 December 1696 and duly married John Gaillard, Gentleman of London on 15 April 1723. He died 3 December 1747 and was interred in the chancel of St. Stephen's, Ipswich. The flat stone above his grave states that he was aged 65. The couple had two children, a son Richard John born in October 1726 and a daughter, Benjamina, born in September 1732. She married twice: her first husband being the Revd Peter Hingeston, Rector of Capel St. Mary and Little Wenham, Suffolk, and the second, the Revd William Gee, Rector of St. Stephen, Ipswich as well as Vicar of Wherstead and Bentley, both just south of the town. It may be remembered that this lady's great-grandmother, Mary Cock, came from a family in Wherstead. Benjamina died on 27 March 1794 and was interred with her second husband under a tablemonument in St. Stephen's churchyard.

William, the last of the children, was born on 12 September 1708. He went up to Catharine Hall, Cambridge, taking his B.A. in 1729 and his M.A. in 1741. His presentation in 1732 to the Rectory of Great Wenham, just to the west of Ipswich, and in 1738 to that of Chelmondiston, close to Erwarton, would suggest that the Parker influence was still at work. In 1763 he was licensed as the perpetual curate of St. Margaret's in Ipswich and though that was where he died on 18 November 1780 he was actually interred in the chancel of the church at Chelmondiston. A tablet close to that spot records that there also lie the remains of his wife, Sarah Cobbol(d), who died on 20 October 1793, aged 79. She had borne him four sons.

William, the eldest, was baptized on 25 March 1751 and duly went up to Merton College, Oxford, where he obtained his M.A. in April 1774 and was later elected a Fellow. In 1778 he was presented by his college to the Rectory of Elham, Kent and in the same year his relative, the Hon. Frederick Cornwallis, Archbishop of Canterbury, offered him the parish of Wittersham in the same county. He married a Mary Harris in 1778, and she bore him two daughters, Sarah and Caroline Frances. The former married Mr. James Trimmer in 1802 and then sadly died in April 1803 having just given birth to their only child, James Cornwallis Trimmer. The boy was to die at the age of 12 in 1815.

Mary Cornwallis, the boy's grandmother, has left us a singular work that is still available at libraries such as those of the Bodleian, of Cambridge University and Lambeth Palace. It is a 4 volume work entitled 'Observations Critical, Explanatory and Practical on the Canonical Scriptures' which was published in 1817 and it is prefaced by a personal letter which is addressed to her grandson. Though a fuller commentary on her work deserves to be included in this story we must content ourselves here with some passages from that letter.

"My dear James", she wrote, "Your dear Mother, whose strong and well-cultivated mind seized with avidity whatever could inform the understanding and improve the heart . . . attentively perused all the observations which are here composed before she quitted the paternal roof.

"The ways of Providence are inscrutable, though ever wise and just:

– not quite a year had elapsed from the commencement of an union which promised more than the usual portion of felicity, when this beloved child, who never from her birth caused me a sigh but when she suffered, brought you into the world; and after a month of sufferings resigned her pure soul into the hands of Him who gave it; yet not before she had received the sacrament at the hands of her sorrowing father, imparted to you her solemn benediction, and given to me this extensive charge:- 'Mother, watch over my child for good.'. . .

"This work, already begun, of course assumed new interest, and you became its principal object. My prayers are daily offered that it may prove instrumental to establish in your mind sound principles, and to guide your steps in safety and innocence through the intricate and slippery paths of life . . . Much of this work has been composed on the bed of pain and sickness, and under continual interruption from domestic or parochial calls, the neglect of which would be culpable, though my time were devoted to this profitable object. (Yet) as the state of my health renders it extremely probable that I shall be no more, long before this is put into your hands . . . you will find, I trust, my dear James, sentiments which flow from a heart deeply concerned for your interest (and from) one who has the light of truth continually before her eyes."

Whether the boy ever did have these pages placed in his hands we do not know but the grandmother did in fact outlive him and was able to see her own gifts as an author reproduced in her other daughter, Caroline Frances Cornwallis.

This girl's talents were revealed at an early age. By the time she was 7 years old she began to produce several histories, poems, essays and commentaries and appears to have made a vow when 15 'to forsake all the follies of the age'. From 1810, aged 24, she devoted herself to a wide-ranging pursuit of further knowledge even though she suffered frequently from ill heath and was also assiduous in her home duties. She learnt Hebrew and German as well as the usual Latin and Greek and the range of her other studies were soon revealed in more permanent form.

In 1826 Sismondi, an Italian author, lent her his house at Pescia in Tuscany, even though she had refused his offer of marriage, and there she not only studied Tuscan criminal procedure and the social life of provincial Italy but revelled in the 'wild nature of her surroundings' and 'enjoyed life for the first time for many years'.

In December 1827, on the death of her father, she returned for a time to Kent, principally in order to settle his affairs and remove her and his belongings to a new home, but by 1829 she was back in Italy. Here she settled down to writing the first of a series of essays on Classical and Philosophical themes and entitled "Small books on Great Subjects". They began to be published in 1842, were issued anonymously, but were widely read in both England and America. Though more details can easily be found in any reputable library it is worth mentioning here that among the issues dealt with were Geology, Chemistry and the philosophy of the Ragged Schools. In 1853, indeed, now being 67 years old, she shared the prize of £200 then offered by Lady Byron for the best essay on the topic of 'Juvenile Delinqency'. She was also an ardent advocate for the higher education of women and the removal of the many legal disabilities under which her sex suffered. She would doubtless have been delighted to learn about one of her ancestor's efforts on behalf of women prisoners in Newgate 500 years previously.

Caroline died at Lidwells in Kent on 8 January 1858 after many years of continuing illness but she retained her vigour of mind to the end. She was able to see many of her hopes realized in the improvement of laws relating to women and the establishment of industrial and naval schools. In appearance Miss Cornwallis was large-featured, tall and thin. The continuance of her memory, if not of her line, was assured by not only the repeated reprinting of her books but by her Letters that appeared in 1864. As one contemporary critic wrote: 'They are truly remarkable for their thoughtfulness, variety and grasp of subject as well as a delightful play of humour.'

Her father, William's next brother, was Frederick. He was baptized on 19 February 1753 and joined the Army at an early age under the patronage of his kinsman, the Marquess Cornwallis. He rose to the ranks of Major and then Lieutenant Colonel in the 33rd Regiment of Foot and served for many years in India. In 1797 he retired from the Service and married Harriott (sic), the daughter of the Revd William Fonnereau, of Christ Church, again in Ipswich. Early in the new century Frederick became a Portman of that Borough and served as such for several years before his death on 12 May 1811. He left no issue and was buried in a vault adjoining the chancel of the church of St. Margaret where his father had been curate. Family links, it will be seen, were always quite closely maintained.

The third brother was James who was baptized on 4 December 1754. He grew up destined for the Navy, assisted and watched over by his relation, Admiral William

Cornwallis. He rose to the rank of Post Captain but died at the early age of 43 on 31 July 1798.

Charles, the youngest son, was also a student at Merton College, Oxford where he took his B.A. degree. In 1768 he was licensed to the curacy at St. Margaret's, Ipswich though he resigned this living in 1804 and in 1807 received from the Crown the Rectory of South Cove, Suffolk. In 1826 this clergyman became the sole male descendant bearing the family name who remained as a resident in the County. A subsequent obituary might perhaps help us to close the story of this branch of the family by recalling the connections that eventually led to this unwed incumbent.

"His descent on the paternal side was, as has been already shown, most honourable. But on the maternal side it was still more so, as his ancestors were nearly allied to the last reigning sovereign of the most illustrious line of Tudor. He was the great-grandson of Sir William Cornwallis the younger, the uncle of the first Lord Cornwallis, by Dame Catherine, his wife, the daughter of Sir Philip Parker of Erwarton, from whom, on the maternal side, are descended the present Earls of Egmont. Sir Philip's father, Sir Henry, Son of Edward Parker, Lord Morley, was married, secondly, to Dame Elizabeth, the daughter and sole heir of Sir Philip Calthorpe of Erwarton, whose wife was Amata Boleyn, aunt of Queen Anne Boleyn, the mother of Queen Elizabeth." It is to the paternal line of such a distinguished ancestry that we shall return in the next chapter.

Before we do that however it has to be recalled that there were other branches of the family that descended at this time from the brothers of Sir Thomas of Brome. I refer especially to the family of Henry since that of Richard was more fully indicated in chapter 5 p.68. Whilst we should not dwell on them at too great length there are references to some of these Cornwallises in the 17th century that are puzzling unless we have uncovered their descent.

Henry Cornwallis, it may be remembered, had married into the notable Catholic family of Rokewood at Euston but following the death of this wife Anne and service in the cause of Queen Mary he withdrew to Norfolk, married another devout Catholic wife, Anne Calibut, of whom he had at least two sons, called Richard and Henry, and a daughter. He lived first in the Chapelfield House, Norwich, which his father had used as a Town House during his period as Sheriff. In 1589, however, the title to the property passed, for a consideration, to Henry's nephew, Sir Charles, and Henry acquired Coxford Priory, north of Norwich, and lived there at Westwick in virtual seclusion as a quiet country gentleman until he died in 1598, reconciled to the Catholic Church. His unmarried son by Anne Rokewood, Thomas Henry Cornwallis, was executor of his will.

Richard, the first son by Anne Calibut, became a Catholic priest, as was described in an earlier chapter, but Henry, who is recorded in *Alumni Cantabrigiensis* as being born at Ranworth in 1593, was first educated at the school in North Walsham, close to Westwick, and then admitted as a pensioner at Caius College, Cambridge, in July 1609. He matriculated the same year and was registered as a Scholar in 1611. He continued to live in Norfolk, though where exactly is not presently known but circa 1620 he had a son also called Henry who went to Corpus Christi College, Cambridge as a Pensioner in 1669, taking his B.A. in 1673. Any traces of the family's Catholic links must by now have disappeared for this son appears to have taken Anglican Orders.

In April 1673 Henry Cornwallis was made a Deacon in Norwich Cathedral. He became Vicar of Chrishall, near Royston, in Essex from 1678 and Rector of Teston, Kent from 1682 to 1710 when he died. Teston lies just over three miles from Linton, to the west of Maidstone.

This Henry was a member of that interesting clutch of Cornwallis authors of which we have already had some samples. He began not only to write but also to be published for soon after his ordination there appeared a 'Country Curate's Advice to his Parishioners", a work in two parts. Some indication of his manner and purpose can be gathered from the following extract:

> " For vulgar Heads small Manuals I Compile,
> In homely Language, and familiar stile.
> Thus on my Books I'm forced to Sup and Dine,
> The Needy Author, props up the Divine.
> Howe'er, if my Designs so far are Blest,
> As to Convert ONE Soul among the rest . .
> With chearfulness I shall my Task renew:
> Heav'n gained a Greater Purchase than Peru."

In 1704 another sample of this clergyman's efforts appeared on London's bookstalls,
"Sabbati Christiani Vindiciae
or
The Strict Observation of the Lord's Day Recommended."

It was for sale at 3d a copy or 20s for a 100 and doubtless the author's City merchant ancestors would have approved his industry even if they might have wondered to what level one of their ancestors, and him a priest, was thus reduced.

It was, however, only another of his works composed between 1694 and 1709 a list of which is kept in the British Library and the full content of which can be obtained without undue trouble. Yet we cannot move on from the Revd Henry Cornwallis's publications without mentioning two others that have their peculiar interest. The first is an address with the intriguing title of "Set on the Great Pot" and which is described as "A Sermon upon Hospitality Preached at a late Visitation at Tunbridge Kent." It will be borne in mind that he was an incumbent in that county. The title comes from the text chosen, 2 Kings 4 v. 38:

> "And he said to his Servants, Set on the great Pot, and seethe
> Pottage for the Sons of the Prophets."

What is further intriguing is that in the printed version there is a formal dedication to an Alderman Vin of Norwich which suggests that Henry was not unmindful of his family's roots. Equally, he could well have been aware not only of a previous Alderman Vintner in his ancestry but also the fact that one of his relatives, Richard's son, Thomas, was at this very period seeking from the Vintners in London the right to control Innkeepers in one part of the City. His dedication therefore has a quite remarkable ring:

"Sir,
Innkeepers give these Words of our Saviour for their Motto, 'You were an Hungry and I gave you Meat; you were Thirsty and I gave you Drink': but seeing our Saviour meaneth not of those that Sell, but give away their Viaticum, it more properly belongs to you, whose House is a general Inn for all Persons both Poor and Rich; the first you Treat out of Charity the last out of Courtesy. Now that God may reward your Hospitality both in this World and that which is to come is the Prayer of your
Most Humble Servant,
H. Cornwallis."

By any standards that is a gracious, urbane and well-considered utterance and we also have from the outset of the address that follows a sense that Henry knew what he was about:

"I am now to Preach to a mixed Congregation, made up of Clergymen and Laymen . . . To you my Brethren of the Clergy that are this day come to honour me with your Company, I preach up Hospitality, not only from the example of Elisha but from the Word of God, which both commands and commends it to us.

To you of the Laity that are come with good and honest Hearts to hear my Doctrine, I preach up Justice, that you should be so just in paying your Tythes, that you may be hospitably and Charitably received at your Ministers Houses: for if you withdraw their dues, how can they perform their Duty: if you shut your Hands, how can they inlarge their Tables and be given to Hospitality . . ."

If this extract seems surprisingly down to earth it must be remembered that this sermon was delivered at a Visitation when such matters as parochial duties of all kinds were reviewed. Were one to record more of the address it would be seen that it has some very telling spiritual and moral lessons to impart.

The same can be said for the other publication to which attention needs to be drawn. This was a wedding sermon delivered in Suffolk in 1706 and entitled 'The Bridal Bush'. In the general preface for the 'Christian Reader' Henry asked that 'you do not read it with Levity of Mind, or Vanity of Thoughts, nor think of it a light jocular Thing, but believe it a Matter of Duty and the Neglect of it a great Sin'. His earnestness throughout is very evident but what gives this particular publication special family interest is the private 'Notice' that also precedes the text. This is addressed "To the Vertuous Lady, Madam Cornwaleys of Winkfield in Suffolk, Widow of John Cornwaleys, Esq." Since we know that it was the second John Cornwallis of the 'Cretingham' line (see p.72 above) who inherited and dwelt in the property at Winkfield (now Wingfield) and it was he who died there on 4 December 1698. He is buried beneath an armorial slab in between the choir stalls and and on it is written:

"Here lyeth the body of John Cornwalleys, JP., Deputy Lieut. and High Sheriff of this County who departed this life . . . in the 70th year of his life."

Alongside this gravestone is that of his sister Margaret which also bears the Cornwallis arms. The inscription here tells us that she was "the wife of John Stanhaw of Pulham Market, Gent. and 4th daughter of John Cornwallis, Esq. and departed this life June ye 12: 1704" The husband mentioned here was not the one given in the earlier tree so it would appear that she had married twice.

We can therefore now discern that it was clearly this John Cornwallis's second wife, Frances (née Edgar), to whom Henry's words were addressed. What is striking is the fact that Henry Cornwallis is still very aware of his family connections even though his family line and that of this widow's former husband had diverged into two counties three generations previously. That the Cornwallis tie, at whatever remove, was a strong one is thus underlined. The tie, indeed, was so close that the preacher could reveal his awareness of what kind of marriage this had been.

"Sister", he wrote,
You were several years Wife to my Brother, and I never heard you were Reconcil'd to him all the while you Lived with him, yet were you I believe as Loving a Pair as any in the County: I can easily Solve the Riddle; You Loved him so well, that You never gave him an Occasion to **fall out** with You; and where there is no **falling out**, there needs no **Reconciliation**.
May all Wives write after your Copy; and may the great God, the Author of **Marriage**, Reward Your **Temporal Love** to Your Husband upon Earth, with his Eternal Joys in Heaven, is the Prayer of
                                                                    H. C."

Only true members of a family can really speak to each other like that.

It is appropriate that, as mention is made of the widow Cornwaleys of Winkfield, we close this chapter with some further information about the 'Cretingham' branch to which she was allied. An initial 'tree' was shown earlier (Chap. 5 p.70) but we can now add some further leaves to its branches.

Richard, the son of Sir Thomas at Brome, was buried at Shotley whilst his wife, Elizabeth, was buried at St. Andrew's, Cretingham on 6 September 1603. A note attached to the appropriate page in the parish register records a note from the Vicar in 1834, a Revd R. B. Exton, that when the chancel was disturbed to create a vault for 'the vulgar family of Chenery of Eye the remains of the (Cornwallis) family were indecently and impiously exhumed . . . and among the relics the skull of this Lady, buried 223 years, having the hair entire, of great length and nicely braided on the crown, was taken up, and the hair divided among numerous by-standers. A portion of it was given to me (and) is in my possession.'

We can also record that the John Cornwallis who married Elizabeth Wythe had been enrolled as a Commoner of Corpus Christi, Cambridge, at Easter 1647, was admitted at Gray's Inn later that same year and began his married life in the Manor of Ashfield which lies close by both Earl Soham and Cretingham. His surviving son by that marriage, another John, became a Pensioner of Jesus College, Cambridge, in April 1669 and was later admitted to Lincoln's Inn. This John married Grace, daughter of Thomas Bishop, of Hesteley Hall, Thorndon which is next to Rishangles, the manor from which his grandmother came. The family home is now firmly established as being at Wingfield and that is why, as was said above, John's father was buried there. It is another interesting example of historical linkage that the body of this John Cornwallis was laid to rest close by the remains of the De la Poles with whom John's ancestors had also had close relations.

Because Wingfield was to be his inheritance after 1698 the Manor of Cretingham (or more properly Kettlebars) was granted first to his wife Grace for her lifetime and then to Margaret (or Mary), his daughter. the wife of John Rabitt of Bramfield Hall. She held it until her death, aged 53, on March 4, 1718 which is marked by a Bramfield church floor slab near the Coke tomb which has at its head the impaled emblems of 3 rabbit's heads and the Cornwallis choughs.

Another stone, between the choir stalls, provides us with a fuller picture of this family into which Mary Cornwallis married. It reads:

"Under this stone lyeth the body of John Rabett, Gent. (eldest son of Reginald Rabett, late of this Parish, Gent. dec'd and of Mary his wife, eldest daughter of John Hayne, late of Islington, County of Middlesex, Esq.,) who by Mary, his wife, one of ye daughters of John Cornwallis late of Wingfield &c had 6 children now living, Reginald, George, Mary, Frances, Elizabeth and Prudence, which said John Rabett changed this life for immortality the 25th day of September A.D.1702, Aetate suae 39° 'Disce Mori'."

It was to the eldest son, Reginald, that the Manor of Cretingham passed on his mother's death and it would have no doubt delighted his maternal grandfather to see that Reginald also was High Sheriff of Suffolk in 1737 as was his heir in 1778. It was this man's eldest son who was to marry Mary, sister of General Sir Edward Kerrison, who bought the Manor and park of Brome. As this branch ceased the Cornwallises might be said to have left their patrimony to a goodly heritage.

CHAPTER 7

The Tree that brought forth Peers

We left off at that part of the main family story where Sir William Cornwallis's will was described and Dame Jane, his 27 year old widow, was left to manage many of his estates, care for her stepchildren and bring up Frederick, their only son. The task was such as would have tested the abilities of any landed proprietor and it might well have seemed that such a young woman would find the burden too onerous to bear. Yet in Dame Jane we encounter a person of peculiar character and talents.

We have noted that she was born into a family that had already made its mark in Tudor society, not to mention the Court. Her grandfather, as we noted, had been an Ambassador and a Gentleman of the Privy Chamber, her brother was knighted in 1610 and her sister, Frances, took for her second husband no less a nobleman than Robert Radcliffe, 5th Earl of Sussex. Even her nephew, Hercules Meautys, was to be the Crown's choice as Governor of the island of Guernsey whilst another relative, Sir Thomas, became a Clerk of His Majesty's Privy Council in 1634. Yet Jane did not have to rely on her kinsfolk for either assistance or status. She was a person of quality in her own right. Happily we possess a volume of her incoming private correspondence between the years 1613 and 1644 and anyone who devotes the time to read these 300 pages will soon uncover some of the principal traits of her character.

Whilst always ready to receive advice from those she respected she was not easily swayed from making up her own mind and holding to what she decided. Accustomed to sharing or seeking the company and support of those in places of influence she was sensible of her own position in Society and did not always comply with the wishes or designs of those who might, with reason, consider themselves her betters. She had, following Sir William's death, clearly attracted, and was aware of, the affectionate attentions of a number of suitors but one senses that she never allowed her heart finally to rule her head. Above all she was a firm but understanding mother towards her child and in due course she was to reveal the same qualities towards the children of her second marriage as well as towards Frederick's wife and their children. What is abundantly clear is that before committing herself finally to a second husband and a new 'parent' for her son she took great care to ensure that she was making the best available choice. The outcome was to prove the wisdom of her decision.

It would be tedious to burden our present narrative unduly with over many quotations from Dame Jane's letters but if someone were ever to add to this work attention could usefully be given to further samples of her correspondence. However, some reference to her work is essential as there are passages in these letters which give us an overview of some of the events that occupied the middle years of her life and show her from the particular viewpoint of some of her closest acquaintances.

What is evident from the start of the collection is that the Bacon family were already eager to see a match with one of their sons. Anne, Lady Bacon writes in October 1613, "The absence of my Nathaniel doth brede in me the more continuall remembrance of hym and I know you is lodged in the principall part of his hart." The letter also reveals that Lady Cornwaleys (sic) was staying at Charing Cross in the house of her aunt by marriage, the widow of Richard Cooke of Gidding (sometimes Giddy or Gidea) Hall in Essex. This is interesting in itself because we saw in the last chapter how other Cornwallis members married into the same family. In 1614 we note that Dame Jane had lodgings in the Strand but in 1619 she was being invited by Lucy Countess of Bedford to stay with her until 'she have proper accommodation for her familie', whilst in 1622 the destination for her mail is still 'Lady Cornewalleys lodgings over against Yorke House, at the sign of the Stirrop'. York House, it will be recalled, had been a Bacon residence, but in 1622 it was the new home of the Duke of Buckingham, great nephew of Lady Bedford. The Lady "was responsible with Lord Pembroke for introducing George Villiers to the Court, hoping that the handsome young man would catch the eye of the King and undermine the influence of Robert Carr". (Georgiana Blakiston, *Woburn and the Russells*, p. 48)

Lucy, Countess of Bedford, was a constant correspondent and close friend of Dame Jane and it is through her that the latter was kept both informed of, and even offered entrée to, the major events and personages at Court. G.P.V. Askrigg in his most detailed account of the first English Stuart court tells us that from the very arrival of Queen Anne, wife of James I," the vivacious and beautiful Lucy Russell, Countess of Bedford, was destined to become Anne's closest friend." (*Jacobean Pageant*, p. 23)

The Queen "had fallen in love with the Harington family and Lucy was chosen before others to be her Lady of the Privy Chamber and became her principal favourite until death ended the friendship sixteen years later . . .". (Blakiston, p. 44)

It is therefore not surprising to read in several letters that Lady Bedford could not attend upon Dame Jane, or come to visit her in Brome, because she was required at either Whitehall or Greenwich, which latter was the Queen's special residence. When we learn that the Queen was in her latter years crippled with a form of gout and in some agony it is even less surprising that she should require the company of her most favoured ladies.

"The restless energy that compelled Lucy Bedford to move from one to another of the half-dozen houses of which she was mistress, also drove her pen, but her breathless, affectionate letters to Lady Cornwallis are written to amuse a person settled in the country, who having been a member of Lady Bedford's household, was acquainted with Court personages but perhaps took scant notice of poets . . .". (Blakiston, p. 47)

What certainly comes through the letters is the clear indication that Dame Jane had determined to stay at Brome during these early years of her son's life so that not only should Frederick be reared in what was eventually to be his own property but that she, Jane, could exercise her own undoubted talents as a landowner and manager in her own right. She fully recognized the past and present importance of the Bacon family into which she married on 1 May 1614 and the union was not just one of true hearts. Their first child, Anne, was born in 1615 and a boy, Nicholas, in 1617 and the couple at first passed most of their time at Brome with only occasional visits to Culford. Certainly the picture that is formed of these children living a happy, peaceful life with their fair-haired, caring mother and their studious botanist and artistic father, is a captivating one.

Nonetheless one discerns in much of the ensuing correspondence that despite the strong bond of attachment between the Lord of Culford and the Lady of Brome they still had their separate paths to pursue. In 1619, for example, Nathaniel was summoned by his father to be on hand when King James, accompanied by both Prince Charles and the Duke of Buckingham, came to dinner at Culford. Sir Nicholas, moreover, being now a widower, appreciated having 'his dear Nath' at his side to assist him in the management of what after all was meant to become the son's estate. A letter from Nathaniel of February 1623 provides a flavour of how matters stood.

"Sweet Harte,
. . . I am now at Redgrave wher I haue bin (ij nights excepted) euer sins my retourne, & wher I begin to grow very restless . . . Our childeren ar well; & little Nick hath cast his cote, and seemeth metamorphosed into a grasshopper. Jane (a third child) is a very modest mayden & is wholely taken upp with trauailinge by her self and wil be ready to runn at yr comand when you retourne. Thus, with my best love & prayers I leaue, resting alwaies & onely Yours, . . .".

This particular letter is addressed to 'his best respected friend the Lady Cornewallys' at her London lodging. Another, a year later, similarly addressed to Brome reveals another aspect of their relationship:

"If the childe be very sick, I pray do not hasten your cominge hither for yor presence may better be spared her than ther . . . with my continuall prayers for you and yors, Yor most affectionate, Nath. Bacon."

It is quite clear that still at this stage, when Frederick was just into his teens, Dame Jane both retained her first married name and kept her first son close by her side. As one writer has said, "She lavished on him intense affection and always jealously guarded his rights."

Before we look at how matters developed from this stage onwards it is perhaps proper that we should look in some more detail at the Bacon family into which the Cornwallis heir's mother had married.

The Bacon name first became one of consequence when the three sons of Robert, a yeoman of Drinkstone in Suffolk, established their reputations in the City of London. Thomas Bacon, the eldest son, became a member of the Salters' Company and thence an M.P. for London; James, the youngest, became a Fishmonger and then served as Alderman and Sheriff in 1568/9; whilst Nicholas, the middle boy, was intended by his parents to wear clerical garb.

Entered in the Abbey school at Bury St. Edmunds, where there was a substantial library with 2000 volumes, when Cambridge University could then only boast 300, Nicholas was prepared for entry to Benet College, Cambridge which he achieved with a Bible scholarship in 1523. We had occasion earlier in our story to comment on the influence of the 'iconoclastic and intellectually vibrant Cambridge of the 1520s' on Cornwallis students and Nicholas Bacon was equally affected. With no less a person than Matthew Parker, the later Archbishop of Canterbury, as one of his fellow students, it is no surprise to learn that Nicholas became and always remained a firm adherent of the Anglican communion. Convinced as he ever was in his religious beliefs it was not to the ordained ministry that he eventually turned. His entry to Gray's Inn in 1532 determined that henceforth he was to be a well-versed and highly respected lawyer.

As we have also seen in the case of the Cornwallis sons a passage through Gray's Inn was a sine qua non for those who sought public, and especially royal, service. The biographer of Sir Nicholas Bacon has indeed described this and other Inns of Law as "the foremost finishing schools of England where gentlemen's sons might acquire something of the etiquette and social graces" which would be required in both legal and regal courts. That Nicholas acquired more than nice manners during his stay there is revealed by the fact that whilst William Cecil took 7 years and Thomas Cromwell took 10 to move from 'utter' barrister to 'ancient', Nicholas Bacon only took 4. He was a marked man and it is no coincidence that one of his father's friends was called Francis Walsingham. By 1538 he was on the Royal Court's payroll whilst in 1540 he was one of the Officers appointed by Henry VIII to welcome Anne of Cleves as she approached London.

Yet it was his work in the Court of Augmentations, his influence in the care and direction of Royal Wards and the additional or moonlighting tasks requested of him by the Crown that not merely established him as a professional public figure but provided him with the fortune that befitted his station. The son of the 'sheep reeve of the Abbot of Bury' had by 1558 become Lord Keeper to Her Majesty Elizabeth I.

Of still more importance for our present story is the record of what happened in the personal and family life of this successful lawyer. In 1540 he married Jane Ferneley, whose hand he received from her father, William, in their family parish church of West Creeting, Suffolk. Apart from providing him with three sons and three daughters she helped him to establish his first country seat at Redgrave – which explains the mention of this property by his grandson, Nathaniel, above. In addition she brought connections with the commercial elite of East Anglia whose support was to be essential to her husband in many of his future projects.

Redgrave was but the beginning of what now was a carefully directed plan for acquiring real estate. Within a dozen years he had possession of land around Redgrave in Botesdale, Rickinghall, Hinderclay, Wortham, Mellis St. John, Walsham-le-Willows and Blackburn Hundred, some of which properties actually lay alongside manors owned by the Cornwallis family. Whilst at some dozen miles distant, but closer to where Sir Nicholas was born, he had his sheepfolds at Ingham and the manor of Talbots in Timworth. (See also map below)

REDGRAVE

WORTHAM   [OAKLEY]

HINDERCLAY

BOTESDALE   [BROME]

MELLIS

RICKINGHALL

[EYE]

WALSHAM-
LE-WILLOWS

Sir Nicholas mostly let out these properties on profitable terms and relied on his bailiffs to administer the rents and he was not even able to reside at Redgrave until 1554 when the house had been completed there. This was of 2 storeys with attics and was formed with 3 sides of an open court facing south. It had a hall, a minstrels' gallery, 2 parlours, a school chamber and other rooms for the preparation and storage of food. It did not have much accommodation for visitors, was generally lacking in ornamentation and had no strolling gallery. Yet Redgrave meant a great deal to its first owner for here he could at least entertain William Cecil in 1557 or Archbishop Parker two years later and to both, I am sure, he would have revealed what was an unusual and ingenious system of running water throughout the house. In due time, as he built more grandly elsewhere, this house was to become the property of his eldest son, Nicholas, who in turn was the father-in-law of Dame Jane Cornwallis.

Before we can close the story of this 'founding father' of the Bacon line we need to be aware of his second marriage to Anne, daughter of Anthony Cooke of Gidea Hall. This is the lady who wrote to Dame Jane about her stepson's decided affections. She was, by unanimous report, a very accomplished and formidable character. She must have been to contemplate the responsibility of taking on the six Bacon children, all under 12, who had been left motherless by 1552. Yet she was admirably fitted for the task of being Sir Nicholas's partner.

Brought up in the surroundings of Prince Edward's (the later Edward VI's) household and educated by their father and such family friends as John Cheke and Roger Ascham (both royal tutors) she and her sisters were as well trained as any other women in England, and Anne was the brightest of them all. She was fluent in several languages and was adjudged the foremost Latin translator of her century. She was well versed in theological matters and even before she became Bacon's wife at the age of 25 she had translated into English the sermons of a one-time Catholic monk, now a Reformed pastor, Bernardino Occhino. In 1564 she was to produce the much acclaimed English translation of Bishop

Jewel's 'Apologia Ecclesiae Anglicanae' and by the 1570s she had begun to shelter in the family home a succession of outspoken Puritan and Presbyterian dissidents. She was some lady.

Moreover marriage with her meant that Bacon now had a striking circle of relations. His brothers-in-law included the Queen's Secretary, William Cecil, the ambassador Sir Thomas Hoby, the diplomat Sir Henry Killigrew, the fashionable London Goldsmith Sir Ralph Rowlett and, after Hoby's death, John, Lord Russell, son of the second Earl of Bedford – hence another link with Lucy, Lady Bedford.

This was the highly competent mother not only of her acquired family but of those known as her sons by this marriage, Anthony and Francis. Her own letters make clear her ability to cope. When Nathaniel, her second stepson, married Anne, the ill-trained and illegitimate daughter of Sir Thomas Gresham, it was to Anne Bacon that the new wife was sent for her proper 'finishing'. It was also to Anne that Matthew Parker appealed for help in smoothing over troubled waters when he realised how he had upset Sir Nicholas by some heavy criticism of the latter's religious views. In these as in so many other ways Anne fitted comfortably into Sir Nicholas's developing life style and circle.

A major mark of this latter stage of their life together comes with the building of Gorhambury, just outside St. Alban's. "Within a day's ride from London, near to Cecil's still uncompleted Theobalds and Bedford's Chenies, and much closer to the centre of Bacon's interests than Redgrave, Gorhambury provided the ambiance of a country gentleman's estate which the Lord Keeper's official London residence at York House could not." (Robert Titler, *Nicholas Bacon*, p. 66)

This house which was to be forever associated with his 'son', Francis, Lord Verulam, was obviously built with the interior more in mind than the exterior. There were over 30 rooms around 2 courtyards, a chapel with cloisters running underneath a library, and a gallery of 120 feet in length constructed especially for the Queen's visit of 1577. Nor did any of these spaces include the actual living quarters of the family and their guests or servants. "Taken as a whole, the grand manner in which Gorhambury was built placed it just below the rank of Theobalds, Longleat and Kirby, all of which were completed a few years later, and on an entirely different scale from the homes of the prosperous merchants and lesser gentry typified by Redgrave." (Titler, op. cit., p. 67)

Lest it be thought, however, that the elevation of Gorhambury's towers took Bacon out of the reach of more local Suffolk affairs it is necessary to point out that his interest in and concern for both the East Anglian counties never abated. In 1563 he was helping the town fathers of Ipswich to unravel the complications of a charitable bequest, and 3 years later he was so helpful in another matter that they made him a full Burgess 'without oath taken'. It is no surprise therefore that in 1572 Nicholas Bacon Junior, the future father-in-law of Dame Jane Cornwallis, was helped considerably by the leading citizens of Ipswich in his election as First Knight of the Shire.

Even when Sir Nicholas had moved to Gorhambury he continued to supervise the changes to Redgrave which he gave to this son Nicholas, and when he purchased the manor of Stiffkey, Norfolk, for his son, Nathaniel, he carefully oversaw the building there of a fine house in which he, as Lord Keeper, never once spent a night.

Sir Nicholas's interest in East Anglia is further reflected in the marriage arrangements for most of his children. For his eldest boy and namesake he set his sights on Anne, the daughter of Sir Edmund Buttes who was himself the son of Henry VIII's physician, and the couple were married in 1561. The Buttes were closely linked to the Bures of Acton, Suffolk, and Anne's uncle, Sir William Buttes, was reckoned to be one of the most powerful men in the county until he died in 1583. Nicholas's other brothers and sisters made connections that are revealed on the 'Fearneley' family tree attached. Interestingly, neither of the sons belonging to Anne Bacon married or had offspring.

It was into this family that Dame Jane married in 1614, much to the surprise of her brother, Thomas Meautys, as a letter from him shows. Yet it was on the basis of equal partnership that the marriage was conducted. Dame Jane was clearly determined to preserve her own, and especially her first son's, independence. He was a Cornwallis – indeed the principal heir of the line – and whatever the feelings of Nathaniel Bacon for his wife it is clear that he had agreed to respect and preserve the status of Frederick as more than merely a Bacon stepson. It is to him therefore that we now turn our attention.

Of Frederick's childhood there are surprisingly few indications though we know that he was educated at home under his mother's caring eye. In 1619 Mary, Countess of Bath, whose brief 'marriage was mentioned earlier, writes to reassure her sister-in-law that any linen or plate that she wishes to borrow is at her disposal and she concludes,

"I praye remember mee to my brother Bacon and prety Frede; and so I will take my leve. My syster (Elizabeth Kytson of Hengrave) desyrs to be remembred to you and my brother, not forgettyng my littill nevewe,

Your unfortunate lovyng syster, Mary Bathon."

The reference to further plate and linen having been required no doubt relates to a recent visit to Brome by the Countess of Bedford which lasted from 'Tuesday att night, and staying with you all Wensday; but on Thursday you must give me leave to retorne homewards'. A note in the correspondence refers to an old household expenses book which showed that during the week of that quite brief stay 10 different kinds of bird were consumed, including 12 larks and 6 herons, and the charges amounted to £11.18s.6d, being double the normal bill. Such would have been one social event in Frederick's early life.

Frederick was educated by private tutors until 1623 and was still very much in the company of his mother as we see in yet another letter from her husband.

"I haue not yett receued any letter from you this week by reason of my beinge now at Broome with our children . . . onely I commend, by any occasion offered, my harty prayers for yor health with Fred's . . .".

Mother and son were now at Lady Cooke's house by Charing Cross since Frederick, in his fourteenth year, was to be introduced to the household of Charles (later Charles II), then Prince of Wales. It is more than likely that this introduction was made possible by his uncle, Sir Charles Cornwallis, who was a trusted courtier, though Lucy Bedford may also have been of help.

The next year King James had died and that his mother was eager to promote her son's career appears in a letter from Lady Russell:

"I have written as effectually as I could to my Lo. Chamberlain, who, I thinke, if it be in his power, will do what you desier. What the King's resolucion is yett for his owne and his father's servants, he hath not declared farder than the whight staves, which are to remain as they wear, but for the greene cloth, and other inferior officers both of the household and chamber, itt is thought he will imploye his owne and dismiss his father's . . .".

This was the last major service that Lady Bedford could do for her friend because after suffering for some time with acute attacks of gout she died in 1627, her influence meanwhile having passed with the arrival of a new Queen.

Frederick was to be one of those retained in Charles's service and such attendance was to form most of the pattern for the next two decades. In 1624 his first task was to accompany the Prince of Wales when he journeyed to Spain in search of a bride. He was thus early drawn to the attention of King Charles and as he entered his 21st year he might well anticipate a promising future. Certainly that was the earnest hope of his mother.

Thomas Meautys, who had now assumed his Privy Council office and was closely associated with Court circles, was ready to play the part vacated by Lady Bedford in seeking royal favour for Dame Jane and her son. He reported that a few months previously he had spoken up for a baronetcy for Frederick when he had heard that 'Sir Robert Crane, young Wingfield, Dru Drury's nephew and others from Suffolk were laboring for that dignity.' On 17 May the patent for Frederick was issued and he was placed as the first of those so honoured. In 1630 he was knighted.

It is at this point, however, that Dame Jane's correspondence begins to reveal some sadder notes. Writing again in July .1627 Thomas Meautys tells his sister:

"As soon as (Elizabeth, the Queene of Bohemia) saw me come into the roome where hir Majtie was, her second words was, "How dooth my Lady Cornwallis?" I gave her your present, and told her that I had left you with a hart charged with griefe for the death of your husband, but with a minde full of will and reddynes to doe her Majesty service . . .". This attachment to Elizabeth, Queen of Bohemia, is hardly surprising in view of the fact that the latter's upbringing had been entrusted by King James to the Harington family, "a distinction that annoyed the Catholics, cost Lord Harington a fortune, and probably hastened his end for he died on his way home from Heidelberg . . . and when the Winter Queen took refuge in Holland it was (Lucy) Bedford who communicated to Elizabeth the changes and shades of political opinion in England". (Blakiston, p. 49) Elizabeth's golden opinions of Lady Bedford no doubt continued in regard to Lucy's correspondent, Dame Jane, and since by 1627 Lucy's influence had begun to wane and an attack of smallpox caused her to withdraw from society the Queen's dependence on others grew.

In April and May 1628 Edmund Bacon, Sir Nicholas's younger brother and Dame Jane's brother-in-law, wrote from Redgrave eager to settle the inventory of his father's estate and in reply to this letter we have one of the very few copies of Dame Jane's compositions.

"Brother,
I received your letter with your unkind token (a subpoena from the Exchequer Barons) which I think I did not deserve, I haveing been as forward, if not forwarder, to a peaceable end than anybody els; but since you have made choice of this way to walk in, I will go along with you upon as faire and friendly tearmes as you will, and rest,
Your very loveing sister . ."

Thus spoke the lady of business in a world of men.

There was however another matter on which the correspondence was to record a saddened note. From 1629 onwards Dame Jane was obviously matchmaking and several letters between her and Dorothy Randolph ('your most true harted cosin') reveal that she has been sizing up possible wives for her eldest son. One such letter reads:

"My most honoured Lady,
. . . However, there is one Lord whose daughters are so much commended that I would keep an option open – it is Lord Bridgwater. Sir Henry St. George is he who propounded it . . . and thinkes he (the Lord) will give 6000 pounds. One girl could be right . . .".

Like most parents in similar circumstances and bearing very much in mind the costliness of serving at Court, managing his future estates, raising a family and establishing a noble line for the future Dame Jane was not insensible of the endowment that any suitable marriage for her son ought to embrace. That she would have totally overlooked matters of the heart in such an engagement is hard to believe but having managed her son's life, career and properties for the last 20 years it was not untoward for her to expect that she should have a major say about so important a step. That is not what happened.

It was at the end of 1630 that Frederick married his first wife, Elizabeth, the daughter of Sir John Ashburnham of Sussex. Not only was this an alliance with an ancient and distinguished line but John (or 'Jack') Ashburnham, his new brother-in-law, was a Groom of the Royal Bedchamber and a special favourite of the monarch. Moreover Elizabeth herself was a Lady-in-Waiting and a Maid of Honour to Queen Henrietta Maria. Yet though the new bride seems from all accounts to have been an excellent and very amiable person she was somewhat poorly endowed and this fact, allied with the failure of

Frederick even to consult his mother about his choice, produced a rift in their relations that looked like being deep and lasting.

On 1 January 1631 Frederick wrote a letter of apology:

"My deare Mother,
    When I consider in what a contradictorie waie I have gone to your Ladp's commands and my one (own) ingagments, I cannot but bee extremly troubbled at my one misfortune, in that it appears to you (and I confesse it may verie well appeare so) that I am the worst of children to the best of mothers; yet I beseech your Ladp . . . would be pleased to forgive this last act of mine, it being done by the commands of the King and the Queene, whoo had appointed the time at my last being in the countrie, it not being in my power to alter it, espetially at that time both of them being pleased to express there favour so farr as to give us a £1000 for ievells and £2000 in monie, all of which with our selves we shall bee readie to cast down at your Ladp's feet . . . I beseech you doe not cast of and lose your childe, who neither can nor will bee happie without your Ladp's favor, and whoo with that regained will ever strive and I hope shall prove to bee as great a comfort as heether tow (hitherto) hee hath proved otherwise; this is the onelie act which hath manifested mee to bee as you please to tearm it your unnaturall childe."

His invitation to allow his wife and himself to collect Her Ladyship at Brome or Newmarket and entertain her was obviously ignored for two days later Elizabeth, the wife, is writing:

"Madam,
    Both dutie and desire dooth, by the asshurans that your soon hath euer gifen me of your Ladp's goodnes and loue to him, giue me confidens by these (lines) to beg your blessing and his pardon who thinks himself most unhappy in your Ladp's displesure . . . therfor, I beseech your Ladp, let vs not any loungger suffer the want of that which will make vs so infinitly happy . . .". She too repeats the invitation to collect her.

This appeal also having not the slightest effect Elizabeth wrote once more with a most surprising suggestion:

" . . . but while you are plesed to stand at this distans, I feare my husband will not do that which his hart most desirs, for he does asshure himself that affection you ons had to him is clear gon, and that it is hopeles for him to seek your love. I hope by your goodness thes doughts (doubts) shall bee taken away; and if the King's and Queene's promis to yourselfe, of doing that for us as soon as they can, will bee any satisfaction to your Ladp, I will procure them to you . . .".

Elizabeth was as good as her word and the very next letters in the collection are indeed from Their Royal Highnesses 'To our Trustie and Welbeloved Lady Bacon' and sealed with the royal arms. The crucial parts of these unusual missives are as follows: first from King Charles:

". . . wee were pleased to honour yor sonne's marriage both with our royall presence and by admittinge the ceremonie to be done in a place where none have accesse but such as the Kinge purposeth to honor . . . . We hereby will you to attend us at Newmarkett, whither wee purpose speedily to repaire, and where you shall understand our further pleasure and grace towards yorselfe and yor son . . . January 4th."

And from Newmarket Henrietta Maria adds her own pertinent remarks:

"Having taken into our particular care and contemplation the good of your sonne, Sir Frederick, in regard of his matching with one who serves us in a place of such nearnes, wee cannot but be very soary to understand that you are displeased with him for doing that wherby he hath made himself so pleasing and acceptable to us . . . but at our intercession vouchsafe to look upon him with the eye of a mother; assuring yourself that . . . your sonne could not have taken a better course, eyther for his owne advancement or for your satisfaction . . . And so much you may beleeve from the mouth of this bearere, one of the gentlemen ushers of our privie chamber, until you heare it from our own, which, if you do not frustrat the King's expectation, may be before wee go from hence . . . Jany. 24th". There cannot be many private families that have two such communications.

And it worked. "There followed the meeting at Newmarket, Dame Jane riding over accompanied by her maid and probably Mr Morse (her agent) and her younger son Nicholas. The young King, elegant and striking in his appearance, must surely have been moved by the sight of this slim, good looking young widow who made her deep obeisance to him. And she, Dame Jane, how could she refuse the request of the King himself? In later years, when grim tragedy ended Charles's life, how often must she have pictured her meeting with him here at Newmarket, and his kindly concern for her son." (Gertrude Storey, *People and Places*, p. 129)

A week after that visit there was yet another letter from the Queen:

"Wee are so sensible of the respect that you have shewed to our request, in receyving again your sonne into your favor . . . If wee can prevaile but this much further with you, that you will extend the same kindnes towards your daughter in law, and so receive them both into your motherly care, you shall put such an obligation upon us as wee shall never forget, but remember upon all occasions wherein our favour can be of any use to you . . .".

To round off the reconciliations Susan, Countess of Denbigh, the daughter of Sir George Villiers and sister to the favoured Duke of Buckingham, added her note,

"Though I have not the honour to be acquainted with you, yet I must give you thankes for this favour that you bestow uppon my deare cosen in entertaining her for your daughter, in whome, before it be longe, I know you will thinke yourselfe happy . . . and if there be any thoughts remaine in your mind of the disobedience of your sonne, I beseech you to blotte it out . . . and what is in my power shall not be wanting to do him service; and to yourself there lives none that shall be more affectionately yours . . .".

By mid-February Elizabeth Lady Cornwallis is thanking Dame Jane for lending Sir Frederick and herself her coach for a visit to Brome, though her words were chosen carefully, "thanks for the noble welcom and favor which, for my gratious mistrise's sake, at this time your Ladp gave me. But, Madam, I hope the next time will bee for your sonne and my owne; in confidens whereof I will ever bee,

Yr Ladp's most affectionate daughter to comande, E. Cornwalleis" In November of that year there is a letter from Sir Frederick to

"My deare Mother" which is clearly a reply to one from Dame Jane. "In obedience to your Ladp's commands I take the libertie to tell you that my wife and my selve, with all we have, are very well, thanks be to God, and a great deale the better since we heard of your good health . . (and he adds) I humbly thanke you, sweet Maddam, for the monie you weare pleased to send me by Mr. Morse (her Ladyship's steward)."

This addendum is important because it begins to reveal that whilst Dame Jane was in some measure willing to promote good relations she was less ready to release into her son's hands more of the resources which he no doubt now expected and required. There is a hint of how this dependence still spoilt the family link in a letter written by Dorothy Randolph three months later.

"Sins I writ this letter my Lady Cornwalies (sic) came to me, but not Sir Fredrick; for he plaies least in sight for feare, I think that, I should tell him his owne, but I am like to doe it the more, next time I see him, I tould his Lady the manner of his carage at Brome, and that it was his own fault he came away upon noe better termes." (My italics)

Frederick's career at court progressed and he became Gentleman Usher of the Privy Chamber in 1633 and was to hold this office until 1645, when he was granted the post of Treasurer in the Household of the Prince, continuing in that office when Charles II became King after his father's execution. He accompanied Lord Arundel on his mission to Bohemia in 1633 and from the Continent he writes to his mother more regularly, even asking her blessing on his newborn son, Charles.

At this point in the correspondence it may be of interest to note that following the death of Sir Nicholas, his father, Nathaniel, in 1624 was "drawn out of his serenely quiet life in the country, and called to London, where he was created a Knight of the Bath in honour of the Coronation of Charles I: thus Jane, Lady Cornwallis, became Lady Jane Bacon, Lady of the Manor of Culford, and she walked in the coronation procession with her husband, Sir Nathaniel." (Storey, *op. cit.*, p. 123)

This change of title was also more appropriate because following the death in 1627 of her second husband Dame Jane was much more frequently in residence at Culford which was hers by the Bacon bequest. Though we shall have ample opportunity shortly to follow the course of the Cornwallis descendants residing at Culford it might be as well to record here the manner in which the property came into the hands of their predecessors.

Culford lies about 4½ miles to the north of the market town of Bury St. Edmunds, in that part of Suffolk called the Blackbourne Hundred. It is mentioned in the Domesday Book as 'Culeforda' (or Cula's Ford) but the first mention of a particular local landowner is in a 14th century copy of an Anglo-Saxon charter in which a Thurketel Dreing granted this manor to the Abbey of Bury St. Edmunis. By the 12th century evidence suggests that there was already a church attached to the manor and in February 1281 King Edward I was a visitor here, following that up in 1290 with a stay of 2 weeks after the death of Queen Eleanor. It is likely that the visit was because of the friendship between the King and the then Knight tenant of the Abbey.

There is a full list of the clergy serving the parish from Roger de Saxham, incumbent in 1319, to Joseph Balkley in 1524, and as a result of a tax imposed for the war against Francis I in the latter year we learn that the only persons of any substance locally were the Longes, Wynters, Rumbelows and Feltwells. But far more important is the fact that the Lords of the Manor were now members of the Coote family. They owned the manor of Easthall (once Syffrewast) in Culford from 1429, having come from Blo (or Blow) Norton in Norfolk just north of Redgrave. At the dissolution of the monasteries in 1541 this family, being *in situ*, purchased the larger manor of Culford Hall from the Crown and when Christopher Coote died in 1563 the manor passed to his son Richard and thence in 1580 to the next heir Nicholas.

Yet there was another claimant to this property. In 1540, as we noted earlier, Sir Nicholas Bacon, Lord Keeper of the Seal, had purchased the adjacent manor of Ingham and there is an entry in the State Papers indicating that at the same time Culford was granted to Sir Nicholas for a Fee of no less than £4,881.15s, thus permitting him, if he so wished, to 'alienate or transfer the manor to his father, Robert Bacon'. He, it may be recalled, lived at Drinkstone, just the other side of Bury. Here were the grounds for some future disagreement in law.

By 1553 Keeper Nicholas Bacon had also acquired the adjacent manor of Timworth and on his death both manors passed to his son, also Sir Nicholas, the father of Nathaniel, second husband of Dame Jane. In 1586 a renewed effort was made by the Bacons to obtain their rightful' possession of the Culford Fee and at last they were successful. The Cootes withdrew and Culford Hall, together with the neighbouring manors, began to form the Culford estate. Sir Nicholas Senior at once started to build a new manor house which became the home of his son and grandson.

Sir Nicholas Junior added one special feature to this property which already had its many windows looking out over the surrounding quiet acres. This was the creation of the 'great pond' that was created by making a canal of the stream that flowed through the village and forming a dam within the house's bounds near the Church. It was this pond which was enlarged in 1791 by J. H. Repton to form the lake that exists to this day.

It was here that Dame Jane Bacon at last took up her own residence and she made her own contribution to the features of the place. She erected a memorial to her husband's memory which is now on the north wall of the porch of Culford Church, showing a bust of

Sir Nathaniel, which, according to a letter written to Dame Jane by her brother-in-law, Sir Edmund Bacon, is a very good likeness: there is an artist's palette and brushes at each corner of the tablet reminding us of his skill as a painter." (Storey, op. cit., p. 124) Sadly, in the October of the same year that Nathaniel died their third child, Jane, aged 3, was also buried at Culford.

Yet Dame Jane was not alone, for from various letters in the mid-30s it is clear that she was now the active grandmother not only of Frederick and Elizabeth's children but also of Hercules, the son of Anne Meautys. A letter from 'Eliza' Lady Cornwallis at Whitehall in 1639 gives us a picture of what was happening:

"Deere Mother,
     I humbly thanke you for your kind letter and desire of my company, which, truly, Madam, is very pleasinge to me, and I shulde be very glad to see prattling Frede (her second-born) and all the rest of my good frends at cheerly Culford, if I coulde; but alas, Madam, I feare I shall not this somere . . . But, Madam, though I see not our babes, yet my comfort is that within 2 months I shall have the happiness of seeing her that, under God, is the preserver of our babes . . . I am sorry silly Harriote (the fourth child, Henrietta Maria) is still so great a wagler (one who walks unsteadily) for now I shall feare her not out growing it; but God's will be done: and for Frede, I think the best is your opinion of not letting him use them (his legs) till it shall please God to give him more strength . . .".

In 1639 and 1640 Sir Frederick was with the army in the North as Lieutenant of Horse in the Captain General's troop and Regiment and during his absence Lady Cornwallis, who was almost continually in attendance on the Queen, lived in the parish of St. Margaret's, Westminster. More locally Sir Frederick was named to the Suffolk Commission for piracy in 1627, was appointed Steward of the Honour of Eye from 1639, retaining that office until 1649. He represented this royal borough in both the Parliaments of 1640 and in the latter he was made a member of the Committee on the Star Chamber, having himself been a suitor in the latter Court in 1635. He was also noted as having argued against the disbanding of the army in Ireland because of the 'enemy in our bosome'. As one who also voted against the attainder of Stafford and who, having gone abroad 'entertaineth and sendeth over Officers from Holland to England against the Parliament', he was deprived of his rights as an M.P. in September 1642. Thereafter he was totally identified with the Royalists.

It was at this stage that letters inform us of the uncertain health of Dame Jane. Sir Frederick writes:

"Madam, I heare by my sister, whome I have had time but just to see and also by my wife's letters, that your Ladp is inclinable to a dropsie. I need not tell you how dangerous that disease is, if not timely prevented; but, Madam, give me leave to desire you most humbly, if not for your own sake, yet for your children's sake, nay even for God's sake, that you will be pleased to come up to this towne and ask the advise of our phisitians here, who say that the waters at Tunbridge are extreme good for your condition . . .". He closes by saying that the King's affairs are in such disorder that he is unable to get away at the present. Lady Cramond, the re-married mother of Elizabeth Cornwallis, also offers advice for Dame Jane's condition and closes with the moving words:

"for I do beleeue there are few ladies in England whose death would be so great losse as yours would be to your children and grandchildren." Happily Dame Jane did take advice and physic and duly recovered.

Mention by Sir Frederick of 'his sister', or half-sister, Anne, prompts a mention of her marriage meanwhile to the much older Sir Thomas Meautys who had been of help to Frederick at Court. The bride was only 25 when she became wife to this older husband but at least she was able to live in comfort because her noble relation, Francis Bacon, had bequeathed Gorhambury to her husband. She bore him one daughter, Jane, who was baptized at Culford in October 1641 though sadly dying when only 10.

In April 1643, having been with the King at Oxford, Sir Frederick brought a Message from Charles I to both Houses of Parliament which was enclosed in a letter from Lord Falkland. Albeit in possession of a pass permitting him to return to Oxford on May 11 he was imprisoned for a week. By June he had clearly returned to the City of Spires because we have mention of where he and his servants were lodging and of his attending the Parliament summoned to Oxford at that time. We also know of a letter from the King to Prince Rupert in October stating that Sir Frederick appeared to have misunderstood the King's directions to Sir Lewis Dye regarding the plan for Newport Pagnell.

Sir Frederick's wife, who had been such a devoted Lady of the Queen's Bedchamber, died in January 1644 and was buried in Christ Church Cathedral. She had borne him 3 sons and a daughter but the youngest son, George, died in childhood and her husband was thus left with Charles, aged 11, Henrietta Maria, aged 10, and Frederick who was 8. Happily the children were still being cared for at Culford but by April Sir Frederick had certainly moved house to All Saints parish, Oxford, and thenceforth he was still very busily employed on the King's business.

In that same month he attended the Queen to Avebury and Bath on her way to the south-west and probably as a member of the King's Lifeguard of Horse he rescued Henry, Lord Wilmot during the engagement of Cropredy Bridge in June. In July he was assessed at £1000 but made plea on the Exeter Articles that being a servant of the King he could not raise all that was due since his royal service required him at that time to be on service in the North and moreover the major part of his estates were in jointure to his mother, with the remainder mortgaged.

In such a situation it is not surprising that he sought another mother for his children as well as a partner who might have her own portion. Early in 1645 he married another Elizabeth, daughter of Sir Henry Crofts of Little Saxham, Suffolk close by Culford, and it is likely that as she was also one of the Queen's Ladies-in-Waiting it is in that circle that Sir Frederick would have met her. Though the lady seems to have welcomed the match her father did not and when the couple married the inheritance of the wife was halved and she brought with her only £2000. That this sum was still a welcome addition there seems little doubt but supporting the Crown was, as for so many others, a costly act of loyalty. Serving again in the West country Sir Frederick was struck down with illness at Exeter and remained there until the surrender in April 1646. He came to London, took the Negative Oath, and sought to resume his role as a landed gentleman but this must have been short-lived as both he and his new wife are known to have been together in France in April 1646. Both of them are described by the then current title of 'Delinquents' but at least they were the happy parents of a daughter named Jane born in October 1647. She in due course married William Duncomb (or Dunscombe) of Battlesden in Bedfordshire but they had no children.

Meanwhile Sir Frederick's eldest son, Charles, seems to have received some kind of private education whilst Frederick, the second son, who had attended Culford School, is registered as having been admitted a pensioner at Christ's, Cambridge in June 1653 and at Lincoln's Inn in November 1656. Of Charles's marriage and prospects we shall speak a little later but Frederick was to marry an Anne Barber of whom he had 3 daughters – Jane, Anne and Catherine. Of these only Jane survived childhood but she, like her namesake aunt, also married a Dunscombe, one Anthony, the Governor of Scarborough Castle, in May 1682. Her aunt Harriet (or Henrietta) Maria Cornwallis, never married.

Following the execution of his father in 1649 Charles II and his close companions withdrew to Jersey and Sir Frederick is recorded as having been amongst them. His stay abroad was still not permanent, however, for in June 1651 he was fined a further £100 and threatened with more demands unless he paid his assessment of a year's income from his estates. If he was again, as one writer says, 'obliged by the violence of his creditors to withdraw himself into parts beyond the seas' (see Copinger iii, p. 238), this was not for too long as he was arrested in England in 1655 for assisting the escape of royalist agents and in 1659 he contrived to attend the funeral of Dame Jane, his mother, at Culford.

She had attained her late 70s and had lived a full, if not altogether exciting, life. She had been a careful manager of the estates and properties of two families even through the Civil War and she had seen her grandchildren and great-grandchildren baptized but also buried.

She had known the friendship of a King and had had lands bequeathed to her from his Queen and yet she had not been able to enjoy the company of her eldest son, or of his wives, because he was so often abroad on royal service. What she could do was to leave a mark for later generations to appreciate and this she did by ordering her tomb and very carefully arranging her final will and testament.

To execute her tomb she chose the same stonemason, Thomas Stanton of Holborn, who had created the bust of Nathaniel Bacon. The agreement regarding the work was quite explicit:

" . . . before the 1st of August, 1658, to well and artificially make, cut and carve, according to the best skill of a stonecutter, alle in whit and blacke marble, and toucht fine policht, to be of the height of tenn foote fromme toppe to bottom and in breadth seaven foote . . .".

The charge was to be £300 and since she only commissioned this work in August 1657 one might say that she had a fine sense of timing.

The tomb, or 'devout monument' as she called it, is there to this day and is now considered to be amongst the finest work that Stanton ever produced. She is shown seated in a chair holding her granddaughter, Anna Grimston, on her knee. (This child was the daughter of Sir Harbottle Grimston, 2nd Baronet, who married Anne Meautys when she became a widow. He had also bought Gorhambury from her husband whenever he died. In terms of family relationships it should be recalled that John Cornwaleys of Cretingham had also married into the Grimstons.)

By Dame Jane's right side stand her own daughter, Jane, who died aged 3, and Jane Meautys who died aged 10. On her left stood Anne, Frederick and Nathaniel Cornwallis who all died in infancy. In the presence of this amazing work, which she had had the intense satisfaction of seeing before she was buried in front of it, Mr. Martin Norridge, the Vicar of Culford, preached the funeral sermon that she had expressly desired.

It was not the only requirement laid down in her will.

She made provision there for another monument to her first husband, his first wife and herself with all their children, in the chancel of the church at Ockley (now Oakley) and another plain stone 'costing no more than £100, for William Cornewallis, great-grandfather of her first husband', to both of which items we have earlier referred.

As far as her own funeral was concerned she asked that there be 'no pomp or solemne funerall early in the morning and not in the Night' but that all those attending, including her doctor, her servants and her Executors, should be provided with 'Blackes (clothing) for mourninges according to their severall degrees . . .'.

She then dispensed gifts to the local poor, ranging from £14 for those in Brome and Ockley to £4 to those in Osmondiston alias Scole. Her directions about how these were to be dispensed show her perception, for the sums were to be given by the 'advice of the minister and chief inhabitants of the same parishes . . . Soe that it may be noe hinderance to their weekly or monthly collection to be made according to the statute for I intend to relieve the poor and not to spare the purses of the rich.'

Culford Hall was to be held in trust for Nicholas Bacon her son, who, after being educated at Cambridge, had sought to follow one of the professions but without success and was, like his older half-brother, constantly in financial straits and in his late teens was imprisoned for a debt of £600. He was knighted in 1637, became an M.P. for Ipswich, and duly married a lady called Elizabeth. Of very modest and retiring personality he died without issue in 1660 and his effigy was added to his mother's tomb. He appears lying full length at his mother's feet, with his head resting on his right hand and with the other he holds a book. Sadly he did not have the time to enjoy the coach and coachhorses, together with several other heirlooms that his mother specially itemized but his widow at least received a legacy of £100.

Sir Frederick was noted as having already received £13,000 in settlement of debts incurred but he was still granted a large annuity from the Culford estate, an annual sum of £500 from other manors and, when due provision had been made for the 'education' of any remaining children of whichever generation, there was still a substantial residue, including the ancestral home at Brome, which was left to Sir Frederick. In the event the early death of Sir Nicholas without an heir meant that the whole Culford inheritance reverted to the Cornwallis line. It meant that when Sir Frederick returned home with the monarch at the Restoration his financial difficulties were over and his prospects were encouraging.

For him to be able to assume the Lordship of the quiet house at Brome, where the white roses planted by his stepfather were now in bloom, must have been a great comfort, no less than his being reunited with his wife and their now 14 year old daughter. The remaining 2 years of his life gave him ample cause for thanksgiving as he was rightly rewarded for the faithful service which he had rendered to the Crown.

Though it could be said that whilst he may have deserted Parliament he had never actually taken up arms against it he was, as a known Cavalier debarred from seeking an open seat in the Long Parliament of 1660. On 30 May he was re-instated as Treasurer to the King's Household and on 6 July he became a Privy Counsellor. He was recommended as a court-candidate for a by-election at Haverford West but on being restored as a Justice of the Peace for Suffolk and being made a Freeman of Ipswich the electors there supported him and he became their M.P. in the autumn.

In September he was given a seat on the Commission appointed to order the arrangements for the Coronation of Charles II and in the honours that followed the King created him Baron Cornwallis, of Eye. Thus by 20 April 1661 the family had once more been restored to yet another link with the patrimony of their prestigious forebear, Richard, Earl of Cornwall, who had also been Lord of Eye.

The first Lord Cornwallis merited a mention by Samuel Pepys even if that well-known diarist spoke of Frederick from such knowledge as he had as a 'bold, profane talking man'. Lloyd in his Memoirs gives us a fuller and more balanced view of him.

"A Man of so chearful a spirit, that no sorrow came near his heart; and of so resolved a mind, that no fear came into his thoughts; so perfect a Master of Courtly and becoming Raillery, that he could do more with one word in Jest, than others could do with whole Harangues in Earnest; a well-spoken man, competently keen in modern Languages, of a comely and goodly Personage."

Perhaps Pepys wasn't really listening to the real man. What seems certain is that despite the disruption of the Civil War or even, in no little measure, because of it Frederick Lord Cornwallis had achieved a great deal. He had eventually inherited

Frederick, 1st Lord Cornwallis

The private collection of Lord Braybrooke, on display at Audley End House, Essex
© ENGLISH HERITAGE PHOTOGRAPHIC LIBRARY

137

BROME HALL. 1630.

properties in Suffolk, Norfolk and Yorkshire and with the acquisition of Culford from the Bacons he was able to leave a very appropriate property to those who would subsequently assume the family's noble title. When he died of apoplexy on 7 January 1662 he had certainly planted a tree with a branch that bore peers.

As we have already indicated Frederick Lord Cornwallis had established a firm succession. His eldest son Charles, 2nd Lord Cornwallis, was, as has been mentioned, educated at Culford and by a private tutor, befitting his station whilst Dame Jane herself was no mean scholar and exemplar.

He appears to have grown into a most reliable man with his grandmother naming him as one of her executors. The repeated references to him in her will certainly suggest that he was the one in whom she placed her greatest trust. Sir Henry Crofts of West Stow Hall, whose daughter Elizabeth became Charles's stepmother, also appointed him as an executor, and in his will devised the sale of his manor and advowson of Saxham upon him and Sir Thomas Cullum as trustees. All this reveals the close and friendly connections between the two families. Elizabeth Lady Cornwallis was buried at St. Martin-in-the-Fields in December 1667.

Charles married Margaret, the daughter of Sir Thomas Playsted of Arlington, Sussex. He must have been about 19 at the time as his eldest boy, Frederick, was born in July 1652. Then came Nathaniel and Anne but sadly all these 3 had died within 2 years and they are depicted on the left of Dame Jane Bacon on the tomb which she prepared for herself in Culford Church. Another 8 children were produced before their mother died in March, 1669 but Ann and Elizabeth did not outlast infancy and only six survived her. She also was buried in the church at Culford and there is a memorial on the south wall of the porch in her memory.

Charles, who was to become the 3rd Lord, was born on 28 December 1655, and his only sister, not surprisingly called Henrietta Maria, followed in October 1657. Dame Jane left her £600 and she lived a fairly quiet life as a family dependant, first at Culford and then Fornham All Saints where she was eventually buried in October 1707.

Of the rest of the boys we know merely that Frederick joined the Army and in due time, and no doubt with Royal approval, became the commander of an independent company in Jersey. It will be recalled that King Charles had resided in that island prior to the Restoration and a secure military base there was part of his strategy.

William, born 31 March 1661 at Stanhowe and a colleger at Eton, was then admitted a fellow-commoner of Corpus Christi College, Cambridge, in April 1676 under the tutorship of a Mr. Lane, and matriculated in 1677.

James died as an infant and of George there is so far no more information than that like his two elder brothers he died unmarried. Thomas, the sixth son, however, was a person of such note as to merit a place in our *Dictionary of National Biography*.

Born in Suffolk on 31 July 1663 he joined his elder brother William at Cambridge under the same tutor and it is thought that it was due to the latter's inspiration that Thomas produced some very creditable Latin poetry which bears his name. These pieces appeared in the collection entitled 'Epithalamium ab Academia Cantabrigiensi decantatum' which was produced in 1677 on the occasion of the marriage of the Princess Mary with the Prince of Orange.

Thomas apparently left Cambridge without a degree and obtained a commission in the Guards and some years later succeeded his brother Frederick in the Channel Island command. In 1709 a system of parliamentary lotteries was introduced and it is Thomas who is credited with first proposing the project. The scheme envisaged 150,000 tickets being sold at £10 each and the principal of the resulting sum was to be sunk and 9% allowed on it during the next 32 years. 3,750 of the tickets gave prizes ranging from £1000 to £5 per annum and the rest were blanks but even the blanks gave a return of 14 shillings per annum for the 32 years. The scheme proved very popular and was the foundation of all subsequent state lotteries. Such a lottery was set on foot every year until 1824.

Thomas Cornwallis was annually appointed the Commissioner of Lotteries until the year of his death which occurred on 29 December 1731. He had been twice married: to Jane, widow of Colonel Vernon, and then to Anne, daughter of Sir Hugh Owen and widow of John Barlow of Laurenny, Pembroke.

Though it had become customary at this time for the eldest son to be returned M.P. for Eye it could not be so in the case of this Charles until after the general election at the Restoration and for the years 1660-1662. He became Captain of the Militia Horse for Suffolk in 1660 as well as a Commissioner for the County assessment, acquiring a similar post for Middlesex in 1661.

In Parliament he was at first regarded as reliable rather than active, making no recorded speeches but serving on a committee of privileges, two others of less importance and being a teller in five divisions. A Court supporter, having been made a Gentleman of the Privy Chamber in 1660 and a Knight of the Bath and Surveyor of the Customs the following year, he was a teller for the vote on the grant of a second moiety of the excise to the King for life.

After being re-elected in 1661 he became a much more active member and was appointed to 39 committees, including the prestigious committee on security, and acted as teller on at least three occasions. His career in the Commons was cut short by the death of his father at the end of the Christmas recess, 1662 and we then find him engaged in more local service as a J.P. for Suffolk from 1662, an Alderman of Thetford from 1669 and Steward of the Honour of Eye from 1671. All these posts he held until he died on 13 April 1673, aged 41.

It was as a County J.P. that the 2nd Lord was involved in the trial at Bury St. Edmunds of the "Lowestoft Witches", two poor women named Amy Derry and Rose

Elizabeth, 3rd Lady Cornwallis

Charles and Henry, as boys

The private collection of Lord Braybrooke, on display at Audley End House, Essex
© ENGLISH HERITAGE PHOTOGRAPHIC LIBRARY

Cullender. One account of the trial states that "Several gentlemen were dissatisfied with the evidence, upon which, an experiment to see whether the afflicted children recognized blindfold Amy Derry's touch, having failed, Lord Cornwallis, Sir Edmund Bacon, a great-nephew of the Sir Nicholas who built Culford Hall, Sergeant Keeling and others openly declared that they did believe the whole transaction of this business a mere imposture. But a dissenting minister's arguments and those of the learned Dr. Brown prevailed. Judge Hall summed up and the prisoners were condemned to be hanged". Even Lord Cornwallis's protests could not save these poor wretches and doubtless he felt as moved by the condition of these female prisoners as his London ancestor had felt 300 years previously. To have heard his table talk with Sir Edmund later as they dined at Culford would have been interesting.

Lord Cornwallis must have been a quiet, retiring man, albeit he entertained King Charles at Culford in 1668 and was duly made a Privy Counsellor. Though little more is known about him there is enough to show that he was sensible of his heritage and was respected both at Court and in his Suffolk localities and we happen to have a narrative that concerns his final days.

Lord Cornwallis was by now suffering from 'a debility of his stomach, attended with a swelling in his legs'. A physician, Mr. Easton, was recommended to him by a City friend and after a first consultation Mr. Easton was asked to come on 10 April 1673 to administer a well-tried Posset drink that would effect a vomit and bring relief. By 10 o'clock the medicine was not working and a further dose was taken.

By 3 p.m. His Lordship had had sufficient ease to be ready to enjoy his dinner and he took 'mutton-broth, pretty freely, and two ribs of a neck of mutton boyl'd, and drank heartily several times'. He then felt so well that at 5 Mr. Easton took his leave, only to return on the Friday to be told that His Lordship was resting but was very well. He promised to come on the Monday.

After a visit to Kensington and having dined on Frumety and hot, buttered Salmon at the home of a friend, Sir J.D. (not named), on Saturday evening Lord Cornwallis began to shiver and showed all the signs of an Ague, which turned to a very violent burning sensation and sweating by Sunday morning. Mr. Easton came soon after 12 and after questioning his patient suggested a 'Stomachick Cordial'. A Court doctor who was also present forbade this and insisted on giving his Lordship a Cardum Posset-drink. This latter, he insisted, was necessary to remove the Antimony poison which Mr. Easton had earlier prescribed. A discussion ensued about the alternative potions proposed but in the end Mr. Easton withdrew, saying that the other must do as he pleased. The narrative concludes:

"About 3 o'clock (i.e. about an hour after Mr. Easton's departure) there was (as Mr. Easton is informed) ligatures made upon his Lordship's arms and thighs. About 5 o'clock there was a vein opened and (as is reported) eleven ounces of blood taken. Within a quarter, or half an hour after, his Lordship departed (this life)."

After his death in the parish of St. Dunstan-in-the-East he was buried by his wife's side and beneath the memorial slab which he had already placed there. It takes the form of a long double tablet, the right side recording the death of the Margaret Lady Cornwallis, with the names of the six children who survived her as well as the five she lost. It was evidently intended that the left-hand panel should record the death and attributes of her husband but after his death, at the early age of 41, his sons and daughters appear to have made no attempt to complete the task. Lack of resources may well have been the reason.

The next Lord of the Manor, Charles, 3rd son and 3rd Lord Cornwallis, was 18 when he took over from his father. Baptized on 28 December 1655 he was evidently a Christmas baby and it is recorded that Dame Jane saw to it that Doctor Buckenham, her own physician, was brought in to the great log fire in the hall and made very welcome when he brought news of the birth of another son.

This child, destined to survive and become the heir, was far from being the steady, respected character that his father had been. Whilst in his teens and serving in the King's Troop of Horse Guards he fell in love with Elizabeth, the daughter of Sir Stephen Fox, a very rich and very shrewd man who subsequently became the Paymaster-General and had much to do with the building of the Royal Hospital, Chelsea. The marriage took place on 27 December 1673, whilst the couple were still only eighteen, but when the bridegroom had succeeded to his father's title. They were married with much pomp in Westminster Abbey. That it was an important social event is hardly surprising since the bride's father was now Treasurer to King Charles II's household and such was the favour that both these families enjoyed that the King and Queen and many of the Court circle were present. Sir Stephen, says the diarist, John Evelyn, "gave her £12,000, and restored that intangled family besides".

The union produced four sons, Charles, William, James and John and though the family would henceforth regard Culford as their main home it is interesting that the baptism of Charles, the heir, in 1675 is not recorded there. This in itself may be indicative of the fact that for some time after the marriage Culford saw little of its new Master.

The 3rd Lord was a gambler, a spendthrift and a lover of life at Court.

The appeal of country life weighed very little with him. In fact he lent Culford Hall for a time to the Duke of York who was later to become James II. In 1674, for example, in a list for Suffolk relating to the hated 'Hearth Tax', the Hall is described as having 29 chimneys, is listed under the name 'Duke of York' but classed as 'empty'. That the Duke did at some stage occupy the premises is proved by a letter of 21 March 1675, from Sir Robert Carr to Charles, which states:

'The Duke has gone to Culford, I have sent his letter after him.'

The fitful use of the hail by the Royal Duke may be explained by realizing that he would have found it useful when the King stayed at Euston Hall after the racing at

Newmarket, or to occupy occasionally when there was hunting in Thetford Chase. Yet such events were infrequent.

There is one such occasion however when Culford was the scene of a Royal scandal. Charles II was visiting his friend and equerry, Edward Proger, of West Stow Hall. Having ridden over to see Charles and his ducal tenant there ensued a great deal of drinking and merriment. As the day was a Sunday one of the party preached a mock sermon to amuse the King and the Rector, the Revd Martin Norridge, one of Lady Bacon's appointees, was brought in to give some semblance to the scene. Hearing that he had a very presentable 21 year old daughter, Elizabeth, he was instructed to bring her along also and in due course the girl and the King were left alone. No one knows what then happened save that afterwards the girl was so panic-stricken that she took her own life by jumping from a window of the Hall. She was certainly buried on 23 May 1674. It could well be that it was in connection with such an event that the Hall stood empty for a time, there being too much local gossip and ill feeling for it to be an fitting place for the King's relations and friends to assemble.

It could of course be that the son, Charles, was baptized at Brome since it was there that Elizabeth was to bring up him and the boys that followed whilst her husband was living his somewhat dissipated life in London. Gramont in his *Memoirs* is hardly complimentary:

"He was a young spendthrift, was very extravagant, loved gaming, lost as much as anyone would trust him, but was not quite so ready at paying." An event indeed was soon to take place that would confirm the Elizabeth, Lady Cornwallis in the rightness of her choice.

Following a drunken brawl near Whitehall in 1676 Lord Cornwallis was charged with the murder of a boy-soldier called Robert Clarke. He and a friend named Gerrard had become involved in an argument with some young soldiers in Whitehall and during the angry encounter Gerrard threw the boy Clarke (or Clerk) to the ground, killing him instantly. Both men were accused of murder but his Lordship was tried separately by his peers in the Court of the Lord High Steward.

It was notable as being one of the last cases to be held in this manner and by 1686 this Court had fallen into abeyance. The features of it which made it unique were that unlike a trial in Parliament the peers present were only allowed to judge as to the facts and the High Steward, in this case Lord Finch, Lord High Chancellor, was alone able to judge on matters of law. Although the King and Queen were usually present in specially allocated boxes the central Chair of State was occupied by the Lord High Steward and the peer on trial found himself raised above the attendant law officers in the pit of the Court and facing the Steward directly. From the outset it was this important officer of State who addressed the prisoner. The Lord High Steward's words on this occasion were such as to strike any normal person, not excluding a noble Lord, with a sense of awe. A brief extract will suffice "My Lord Cornwallis,

The violation of the King's Peace, in the chief Sanctuary of it, his own Royal Palace, and in so high a manner, as by the death of one of his Subjects, is a matter that must be accounted for . . .

"It is indeed a dreadful thing to fall into the hands of Justice, where the Law is its Rule, and a severe and inflexible measure both of Life and Death. But yet it ought to be some comfort to your Lordship that you are now to be tried by my Lords your Peers, and that now you see the Scales of Justice are held by such Noble hands you may be confident that they will put into them all the Grains of allowance, either Justice or Honour will bear . . .".

The case was duly tried with Serjeant Maynard, as the King's Counsel, strongly pleading the cause of a 'Child slain without any provocation in the world . . . with Oaths that a Christian would blush at . . . the Obscenity that they used . . . but who of the murder is the question though it is manifest that this Noble Lord was concerned in it . . . (so that) if it be a murder in Mr. Gerrard this Noble Lord is as guilty as if his hand had been as much upon him (the soldier).'

The uncertainty as to the exact nature of the crime being raised their Lordships were invited to give their verdict and thereupon all declared him not guilty of murder though 6 of them declared him guilty of manslaughter.

The Lord High Steward called the Prisoner to the Bar, the Deputy Lieutenant of the Tower held the edge of the Axe towards him as the judgment of acquittal was given, whereupon the Lord High Steward took the white Staff offered by the kneeling Usher of the Black Rod and snapped it in two above his head to signify the end of the Assembly. Gerrard, at his trial, pleaded the King's Pardon and was also discharged, afterwards, according to custom, presenting gloves to all the judges of the King's Bench.

The following year not only did the couple's second son, William, die but the young Lady Cornwallis herself never recovered from her last pregnancy. She actually died at Tunbridge Wells on 28 February 1681 but was buried, still only 25 years old, on 5 March in the little church at Brome, and in a lasting token of remembrance Sir Stephen Fox built the row of almshouses that stand opposite the Church to this day. He was later also to rebuild the church at Culford.

These three events appear to have brought Lord Cornwallis to his senses and he seems to have retired for a time to pursue more rural pursuits followed by quieter royal services during the reign of James II. On 6 May 1688 he married again, being thereafter by all accounts in the special favour of King William, following the Glorious Revolution of that year. This time his bride, who was four years his senior, was Lady Anne Scott, the Duchess of Buccleuch and from 1685 the widow of James, Duke of Monmouth and Buccleuch. The marriage, which took place at St. Martin-in-the-Fields, was not as surprising as might at first appear as some introduction to her previous life makes clear.

The experiences which Anne had previously undergone did not conduce to make her the most transparent of characters. Married in 1663 at the age of 12 to King Charles's illegitimate son she was early introduced to all the arts and dissimulations of the Restoration Court. In 1667 we read of her productions, including Dryden's 'The Indian Emperor', before the King and Queen and the comment of no less a person than Samuel Pepys that none of the women could act at all except Anne and Mistress Cornwallis, who were both very good. This at least indicates that the Duchess and Lord Cornwallis were already acquainted and Maurice Lee, Junior in his book, *The Heiresses of Buccleuch* states that Charles was a man she knew well.

Added to such talents there were also other qualities of survival in such circles and the most quoted description of Anne is that of the essayist, John Evelyn. Having dined with her and Monmouth at Lord Arlington's in 1673 he described her as 'certainly one of the wisest and craftiest of her sex; she has much wits. Whilst not unflattering it was hardly an enthusiastic appraisal, but that it was near the truth is confirmed by the opinion of Henry Sidney that whilst she was 'very assuming and witty she hath little sincerity'.

If her tribulations as the young wife of a clearly discontented and eventually rebellious Royal offspring were not enough she had also to recognize from 1680 that her husband had fallen genuinely in love with Lady Henrietta Wentworth, an attractive 20 year old. This was a love affair that was passionate and lasting with Monmouth regarding Henrietta as his real wife and going to his death on the scaffold with her name on his lips. Henrietta had shared his troubles and his exile and she died of a broken heart just 9 months later, in April 1686.

Anne was, perhaps not surprisingly, hardly a warm person yet at the time of Monmouth's execution Evelyn again described her as 'a virtuous and excellent lady'. Certainly she had to accommodate to a new way of living. She was no longer royalty and had to leave her Whitehall apartments. She could not know whether her Buccleuch estates would be restored to her but happily King James allowed friendship to prevail and not only these lands but also whatever plate and jewels Monmouth had left behind in Holland were to be restored. In May 1686 he even instructed the Scottish Privy Council to set aside any further enquiry into the Duchess's affairs in view of her 'exemplary loyalty, unblameable deportment and constant duty'. Thus she kept the barony of Hawick and an annual pension of £4000 but even King William, in 1688, refused her request for the Monmouth title and gave it to the Mordaunts. It had previously been created in February 1626 for The Hon. Robert Carey, 4th Son of Henry, 1st Lord Hunsdon whose son Henry, 2nd Earl, died 13 June 1661 leaving no male borne.

By Charles Cornwallis and in a marriage that lasted 10 years she was to have 3 children, the Hon. George Scott Cornwallis, the Hon. Anne and the Hon. Isabella. The first two of these children died young and were buried in Westminster Abbey. Whilst it is proper to mention these children of the union it has not to be forgotten that there were 4 Cornwallis boys in their teens and the new Lady Cornwallis had 4 children of her own still alive including her eldest son who was unmarried. Whilst the 3rd Lord had begun to withdraw from his previous gaming habits and companions he still had some extravagant tastes and his new partner was unlikely to provide the curb he still needed. Under her direction Culford once again came to life and assumed its position as another centre of Cornwallis family life. In a 'Book of Accounts: 1689-1692' we find items such as the following:

Paid for repairs at Culford Hall 1689/92	£781	13s	8d
Charges re Brome Hall and Culford Gardens 1689	485	19	1
Paid charges of Brickmaking	191	16	0
To Jim Rust for Charcoal 1689	19	10	0
Spent on meat at Brome and Culford	152	0	0

It is evident that the repairs needed at Culford were considerable and it is also interesting to see how the gardens that had been one of the Bacon delights were now being laid out afresh in splendour.

There is also an entry concerning £1 10s paid to a Mr. Ross as one year's salary for being both sexton and mole-catcher during 1688 and this shows that moles were as much a trouble then as they have since remained. Another entry of £320 19s 1d as an Annuity to Madam Henrietta Cornwallis reminds us that though this lady, the Lord's sister, had obviously used up the £600 bequest made to her by Dame Jane Bacon but, being unmarried, relied on her older brother for maintenance until she was buried in 1707 in a tomb at the east end of Fornham church.

Whilst this care of the Cornwallis property and payments is commendable the truth is that there were money troubles in plenty. Within a year of their marriage the couple found themselves £30,000 in debt. "It was an uphill struggle. Matters came to a head in 1694, when there was so little cash and Anne's credit was so bad, that she had difficulty paying for her (first) son's wedding . . . There was a tearful scene; Fox (her husband's father-in-law), with the Earl of Melville's cooperation, at last persuaded her that she would have to economise." (Melville was her estate manager for the Scottish properties) (M. Lee, Junior, pp. 120f)

That the family fame or its finances were hardly in a healthy state probably accounts for the fact that James Cornwallis does not appear on any University list though John went up to University College, Oxford in 1694 at the tender age of 14 and then seems to have transferred to the Middle Temple within a year. Whatever their careers may have been they, like their sister, died unmarried.

The fresh boost to the Culford property did however reflect in the character of Charles. He now seems to have taken an active part in public life and in 1689 he was even made Lord Lieutenant of Suffolk. This was followed in 1691 with his being called to serve on the Privy Council and becoming First Lord of the Admiralty in 1692 and 1693 as well as being appointed to the post of High Steward of Ipswich. These latter appointments may account for the greater food bills in 1692/3 since there would clearly have had to be much more entertaining. Culford was once again taking on the splendid appearance and position that it had enjoyed in Elizabethan days under Sir Nicholas Bacon.

Yet the dissipation of his earlier days had its effect. At the age of 42, on 29 April 1698, Charles died of a fever and was laid to rest near his first wife at Brome on 6 May. As one writer says, "His peaceful demise was in sharp contrast to what might so easily have been the noisy end on a silken rope at Tyburn." Yet with his departure there was some chance that the sedate life of the family in the 18th century could begin though that had first to cope with the remaining years of the Duchess.

Following the 3rd Lord's death all Anne's "accumulated resentment at the self-made upstart who had been dictating her financial behaviour burst out. Fox, as part of the arrangements for the funeral, which he paid for, set up a coat of arms which quartered that of Cornwallis with those of his daughter and Anne. Anne was furious and had it pulled down, and the offending escutcheon of Fox's daughter removed, to the accompaniment of violent and pejorative language about (Elizabeth) and her son, the new Lord Cornwallis. Anne was, wrote Fox, wholly governed by 'rage, passion and self-interest' . . . she added injury to insult by ordering that Fox should not receive another penny from her estates, even though she owed him £1,500 . . . Whatever Anne's motives, her treatment of a man who had been involved in her affairs for over thirty years and had repeatedly bailed her out of financial difficulty was both mean and shabby." (M. Lee, Junior, p. 121)

What is most relevant to our story is the assertion by Sir Stephen that Anna laid hands on her Cornwallis husband's jewels and plate as well as the arrears of his pension so that the new Lord was left with nothing that was movable save the sheep and cattle on the Culford estate or as Fox put it, with 'neither spoon nor napkin'. Fox did not cease to pester Anna for her money and they were still arguing in 1710.

In 1701 Anne decided to go to Scotland since there she could behave as a royal personage, which she could no longer do in England. As head of her family there she knew it was time to repair her neglect of her tenantry. So she settled in Dalkeith and set about rebuilding that family property and of course on a lavish scale. The house was redone in marble, including the adorning of her bedroom with carving by Grinling Gibbons. The rebuilding took the better part of a decade and in the process it ceased to be called a castle and became a 'Palace' which is how it is still referred to in the guidebooks.

"Anne was royalty. She styled herself 'Mighty Princess' in some of her charters to the town. Her cousin, Margaret Montgomery, dining with her, remarked that Anna was served on bended knee. She as Anna's relative, was allowed to sit; everyone else stood." (M. Lee, Junior, p. 122)

As she entered her fifties Anne became increasingly suspicious of what she thought were encroachments on her possessions. She sued the heirs of her uncle and step-father, Rothes, for 'looting her estate', and in 1704 she quarrelled bitterly with Lord Melville. As her sister's husband he had been immensely useful to her for over 20 years and in 1700 he had even suffered personal injury when saving her Charter chest from destruction by fire. No matter: he was accused of mishandling her money and the lawsuit she brought was not settled until 1711, some years after Melville's death.

Four years after the death of the Duke of Hamilton and without any by your leave from the monarch she transferred the title to her eldest son. Neither Cornwallis nor Anne's son and heir (George Scott who predeceased her) ever became Duke of Buccleuch. She remained Duchess to the very end and the end was a long time in coming.

"Anne outlived her eldest son, her daughter-in-law, even her grandson's wife . . . For all of her 'Scotch heart' – she disapproved of what she called 'this unlucky Union' of 1707 – Anne preferred London . . . She quickly became very friendly with the new Princess of Wales, Caroline of Ansbach, that very clever lady who, like Anne, was married to a king's son notorious, like his father, for his infidelities. 'The Princess loved her mightily', wrote Lady Cowper in 1716, 'She had all the life and fire of youth and it was marvellous to see that the many afflictions she had suffered had not touched her wit and good nature, but at upwards of three score she had both in their full perfection.' Her finances recovered and she added to the family property, most notably the lordship of Melrose, which she purchased from the Earl of Haddington . . . She dined out on stories about the king (Charles II) and the virago Castlemaine and pretty, witty Nell – though never Prince Perkin (Monmouth) – till her death in London in February 1732 just before her 81st birthday . . . Her body was transported from London to Scotland, where it lies in the family vault in St. Nicholas' Church on the High Street of Dalkeith. There is no mention of Monmouth on the plate on her coffin." (M. Lee, Junior, p. 123)

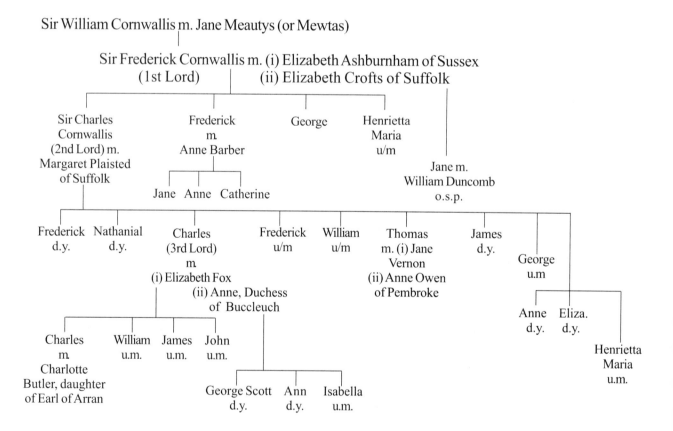

CHAPTER 8

Reaching the Top of the Tree

Compared with the eventful lives of the Cornwallises in the preceding century the pattern of life at Culford in the 18th century was quiet and domesticated. Mr. Martin Norridge, who had been Rector for close on 38 years, died peacefully, unlike his daughter, in 1684 and was buried in Culford Church. A slate slab on the chancel steps marks his body's resting place. When the 4th Lord Cornwallis assumed the title the Rector was the Revd James Davies (1688-1709).

Charles, the new Lord of Culford was born in 1675 and after the closer care of his somewhat 'reformed' father and a private tutor at Culford he became a soldier as so many of his ancestors had been. He is known to have served in campaigns in Flanders but in 1695, as had now become customary with the eldest sons, he was able to obtain the 'family' seat in Parliament as the Member for Eye until he succeeded to his father's title in 1698.

In this year he was appointed Lord Lieutenant and Keeper of the Rolls for Suffolk and on 6 June the following year he married Lady Charlotte Butler, the only daughter and heir of Richard, Earl of Arran, at St. Martin-in-the-Fields. The father-in-law was the third of four sons of the Duke of Ormonde.

By this marriage there was thus restored a link with the Butler/Ormonde family that had first been created by Richard, Earl of Cornwall, in the 13th century. As if to confirm this renewed bond after 5 centuries a legal agreement, drawn up by the 4th Lord in 1700, granted Eye Hall and Castle and the site of the Priory, all properties once held by Earl Richard, to a trust of which James Butler, Duke of Ormonde and Sir Stephen Fox were the principals.

The new Lord Cornwallis now served his county and country faithfully and well for in addition to being Lord Lieutenant of Suffolk he was the Recorder of Eye, and was made a LL.D. of Cambridge University, in October 1717. He was made Joint Postmaster General from 1715-1721, a Privy Counsellor from November 1721 and was then also Paymaster General of the Forces until his death. A description of him in Macky's *Characters* suggests that he acquired his mother's graces and his father's experience: "A gentleman of sweet disposition, a great lover of the Constitution, and well esteemed in his native county of Suffolk; inclining to a fat and fair complexion."

He and his lady produced 12 children – 9 sons and 3 daughters, of whom only 2 were actually baptized at the church in Culford. One was the Hon. Stephen Cornwallis on 1 January 1703, and the other the Hon. Charlotte Cornwallis who lived only from November 1704 until 22 April 1705.

Of the eldest surviving son, again named Charles, a great deal more will be said in due course but as we turn to the other children of the 4th Lord we note that some of them were to become persons of real consequence.

The second son, Captain James Cornwallis R.N., was born 16 September, 1701 and having entered as a Midshipman in his early teens had become a Lieutenant by 1720 and was commanding the fire-ship *Griffin*. Two years later he was returned by his elder brother, Lord Cornwallis, as one of the M.Ps for the borough of Eye though there is no evidence of his having been involved in any committee work in the House.

He was however a sailor of some distinction who died "May ye 27, 1727 in Copenhagen Roads in ye 26th year of his age beloved by all who had ye Honr to know him". He never married.

Stephen, the next brother, born 23 December 1703, was educated at Eton but then at 16 joined the army, becoming an Ensign in the 2nd Foot Guards. By 1723 he was a Captain of Dragoons but then returned to the Infantry and by 1725 was a Lieutenant Colonel of the 34th Foot. Subsequently he was Colonel of the 11th Foot (1738) eventually rising to the rank of Major-General in 1743. In 1727 on the death of his older brother; James, he began to share the Eye constituency with his next younger brother, John, and that partnership lasted through the next three Parliaments until Stephen died. He married a Mrs. Pearson in August 1732 but died in May 1743 without having any children.

John, the fourth son, born on 23 December 1706, similarly joined the Army after being at Eton until his 17th year. This son was less interested in making this his main career though it enabled him to serve from 1731 to 1737 as Equerry to Frederick, Prince of Wales. In the meanwhile he was elected at the age of 21 to serve as one of the M.Ps for Eye and shortly after taking his seat he married Sarah, the daughter of the Revd Hugh Dale. They had four children, John, Sarah, Charlotte and Mary but only Sarah reached adulthood and she married the Revd Walter Earle.

John was an active Member of Parliament making his name particularly as an opponent of the repeal of the Septennial Act in 1734. He is noted as speaking on many occasions but when the Prince of Wales supported the Opposition in 1737 John gave up his post as Equerry 'because the pension he had from the King was more than the salary from his place and he feared that if he continued in the one (as a Court official) the other would be stopped'. With a family to rear that was no slight consideration.

During the last days of Walpole's Administration, in 1728, things took a more serious turn. John is said to have been 'decoyed away' to vote with the Opposition for Pulteney's proposal that there should be a secret committee to inquire into the conduct of the war with Spain. When Walpole turned this otherwise routine motion into a vote of confidence in himself the whole security of the Government was at stake and those who so threatened it were regarded with scorn. When you recall that Walpole's sister, Dorothy, was married to Lord Cornwallis's father-in-law it is hardly surprising that the very next day John was 'shown the door' by his eldest brother and was not renominated for Eye when the next General election came in 1747. That is why his partnership with Stephen would have ended in any case for though John was put down for the Eye seat on the 2nd Lord Egmont's list of persons he was not successful and he did not stand again. He resumed private life on his Royal pension and died 9 June 1768. His experience shows that whilst the system of patronage in Parliamentary elections might often be geared to family or party interests marriage alliances were even stronger than mere blood ties in managing government.

Richard, the 5th son, was born in 1708, was educated at Eton and at the age of 18 made a Cornet and then a Lieutenant (1736) in Wade's Horse, the Regiment which later became the 3rd King's Dragoon Guards. During his time as a serving officer he was also given the Court post of Gentleman Usher and later Daily Waiter to Queen Caroline. He obviously gave satisfactory service because he was promoted in 1727 to be Personal Equerry to her son, the Duke of Cumberland. He never married and had died by 1741, aged 33.

The next sons, the twins, Edward and Frederick, were born at 14, Leicester Square, London, in what one writer calls 'a fine house and retinue', on 22 February 1713. With them we come to members of the family whose careers are very much more fully recorded and do indeed begin to reach the top of the national tree.

Edward began his life in much the same way as Richard save that along with his twin brother he was appointed a royal page at the age of 12 so that for 2 years they attended the Royal Family at Windsor and Hampton Court. At the age of 14 Edward went to Eton for the next 4 years before joining the Army and being gazetted 4 May 1731, as an Ensign in the 47th Foot, then stationed at Canterbury. He next performed garrison duty near London and was promoted to the ranks of Lieutenant in 1734 and Captain 3 years later on being transferred to the 20th Foot, later the Lancashire Fusiliers, that was to win fame in the 1759 Battle of Minden.

From 1738 to 1743 Edward was employed by Whitehall in a diplomatic capacity and especially between the Hague and London, but in 1744 he was gazetted as Major and joined the personal staff of the Duke of Cumberland, perhaps in succession to his elder brother, Richard, who had recently died. In the same year, and certainly replacing his brother Stephen, he also became one of the M.Ps for Eye, speaking for the Government on a vote for extraordinary charges in respect of foreign troops in British pay.

Yet Edward was a serving soldier and in 1745 he was present with his regiment at the ill-fated battle of Fontenoy. When the Dutch and Austrian troops broke before the French who were under the command of Marshal Saxe it was the 18,000 British troops who covered the retreat in what is still regarded as a masterly achievement. Amongst the 2000 British dead was Colonel Craig of Edward's Regiment and along with him died 8 other officers and 385 men. It meant that Edward was effectively in command for most of the engagement. On their return to England the glorious record of Marlborough's days was considered to have been obliterated by the gross incompetence of Cumberland and the Army was the butt of public rage.

For Edward Cornwallis however it was a time of Royal favour and he received his first Court appointment as a Groom of the Bedchamber to George II, as well as being gazetted Lieutenant Colonel of the 20th Regiment. He was shortly to be stationed in Edinburgh and Stirling at just the time that there was to be the Stuart uprising of the '45.

Thanked as he and other commanders were for the successes of the battles at Prestonpans and Culloden an onset of ill-health and some consequent lack of proper supervision led to threats of mutiny in his Regiment and Cornwallis felt compelled to resign and return to his Court duties. He was replaced by a slightly built son of Kent called Major James Wolfe who, by his tact and skill, brought the troops back to a proper state of discipline. It was Wolfe's handling of this situation which led directly to his being appointed to the command of all the military operations in America and not least to his victory and early death on the Plains of Abraham at Quebec.

It was also at this point in the life of the 20th Regiment that the attachment of Edward Cornwallis to Freemasonry reveals itself. He was not the first of the family to join the Craft that had been newly re-established under the Grand Lodge of 1717 but he is certainly the first notable member to do so. The first recorded Cornwallis member was Richard, Edward's older brother, who is shown as belonging to the Lodge that first met at the Nag's Head, Mr. Faulkner's house, London from 1723. By 1725, when 'The Hon. Mr. Cornwallis' is noted as a member, the house is shown as belonging to a Mr. Glover and by 1730 it was in the hands of a Huguenot emigré, Mr. LeBlon.

It would thus seem that not only was Richard influential in preparing the way for Edward at Court but he very probably introduced his sibling to Freemasonry around 1734 when Edward became of full age and was in the London area. There does not appear to be any evidence that Edward joined the same lodge as Richard's but the Craft was already beginning to grow in the Army and warrants from Ireland were already being issued to Regimental units. It was just such a step that Edward was involved in when Lord George Sackville had succeeded Wolfe as Colonel of the 20th.

On the 27 December 1748 the Lodge of the Regiment was authorized and, as stated in the Centenary History, those named in the warrant as the first Worshipful Master and Wardens were Colonel Sackville, Colonel Edward Cornwallis and Captain Milburne. There can be no question of course that the Founders named in the warrant were Masons of some experience. The Lodge after 1760 became known as the Minden Lodge No. 63 and it was not the only lodge that Edward Cornwallis would help to found.

It was through his proximity to the Throne that in early 1749 Edward was entrusted with the novel task of establishing afresh the colony of Nova Scotia, which could protect British sovereignty and interests from the French on the extreme east of the Canadian territories. This was not the first time that such a project had been conceived. We know that as early as the reign of James I it had been hoped to create such a colony but lack of sufficient finance eventually prevented such a plan from being properly implemented. There was a token capital at Annapolis Royal, which name implies the Stuart design, but there was much more that had to be done to cement British influence firmly.

The need to create a well-established British presence between Louisburg and Boston had long been requested by the locals and not least by the fishing communities who were constantly harassed by the French who in their turn did not wish to see their lucrative monopoly in the trade endangered.

In order to devote all his energies and abilities to the post of Captain-General and Governor of Nova Scotia Edward resigned his seat in the House of Commons. He was 36 years old and is currently described as "of slender build, somewhat over middle height, an aristocrat to his finger tips, conscious of his dignity and inclined to be cool and ceremonious except when his 'great temper' took charge of him, but possessing a pleasant voice, fine eyes and a winning expression".

It was late in May that he headed the expedition of settlers, mostly ex-sailors and soldiers from the Marlborough wars, with a grant from Parliament of £40,000 and the bestowal on the Governor of unlimited powers in the new territory. Crossing the Atlantic in the sloop-of-war *Sphinx*, Cornwallis and his suite arrived in Chebucto harbour on 21 June 1749 followed a week later by 13 transports and 2400 colonists of whom 1500 were men. For Cornwallis there was much at stake. If he was successful in his enterprise he could expect further reward but if not then he would probably be facing the end of his public career and total obscurity.

The first step was to establish the new seat of government on the spruce-clad shores of Chebucto Bay. This proved to be a far from easy undertaking. The settlers were largely those accustomed to the rough and tumble of life in camp, barrack rooms or the crowded decks of men-of-war and whilst there were conspicuous exceptions the majority of those whom Edward and his closest advisers had to manage were a hard lot who now had to survive the harsh climate of this northern outpost.

Added to that there was the opposition of the local Indian tribes, there were difficulties about the regular provision of the funds from England and some of the merchants were quite ready to trade with the French. The new city was named Halifax, in honour of the Lord President of the Board of Trade and Plantations, George Montagu, 2nd Earl of Halifax, but the rude encampment of tents and log-houses was more like a temporary armed outpost in enemy country. It was hard in those first days to conceive that what was being begun was to become the nub of the great Cunard seagoing enterprise, the location of a great University or a cradle of Canadian literature. The firm foundation of Halifax and thence all Nova Scotia was a prime factor in the determining of Britain's permanent sovereignty in British North America.

The Hon. Edward Cornwallis's executive ability, patience and kindness were the principal ingredients in inaugurating this achievement and despite his comparative youthfulness he earned the commemorative bronze statue which stands in a central position in the great square in front of Halifax's Nova Scotia Hotel. His sturdy figure, dressed in contemporary gentleman's attire, was positioned with his face towards the Atlantic and his native homeland.

Yet it would be unfair to Edward to ignore the others without whom he would not have achieved so much in those three years of his Governorship. In his suite was a friend and companion, Captain Richard Bulkeley, who came from a crack regiment of Dragoons and had already accompanied Edward on other occasions. He had with him his own domestic household, consisting of a valet, groom and butler, 3 horses and a whole range of travelling luxuries. As both an aide-de-camp and an administrator his help was invaluable and when Edward returned to England Bulkeley was to remain and become the much admired leader of official and social life in the colony. His long career closed there in 1800 after a most useful life, the last survivor of the original expedition.

Yet it was in Freemasonry that Edward and Richard also shared a common interest and in Nova Scotia the Fraternity was already in being. Two writers on early Canadian Freemasonry refer to a stone marked with a square and compasses discovered on .the shores of the Annapolis basin and bearing a carved date, 1606. It was very possibly the remains of the grave of an operative mason who came with De Moats and Champlain and it had disappeared by the 1960s. What is more certain is that among the New Englanders who came north from Boston after 1713 there were men who were undoubtedly speculative Freemasons (See M.M. Johnson, *The Beginnings of Freemasonry in America*, pp. 195-201).

It is also a fact that it was at Annapolis that the first Masonic lodge in Canada was duly constituted in 1738 and its principal founder was a military administrator of the 40th Foot called Major Erasmus James Philipps. He had come out in 1720 as a nephew of the then largely absentee Governor, Colonel Richard Philipps, and through his association with other officials of the colony who were Masons he had become a Master Mason by 1737. 20 years later he was nominated Provincial Grand Master for Nova Scotia and, it was in this capacity that he started what was only the sixth regular lodge in North America. A memorial to him was erected in St. Paul's cemetery, Halifax, in the.bicentennial year, 1938.

In 1750, just a year after the landing in Chebucto Bay, there was a meeting of several settlers who were Freemasons at what was called Government House. It was declared that it was desirable to have a lodge there and the Governor agreed to give the desired lead. The petitioners were referred to Major Philipps and on 19 July the warrant arrived. That same evening the Lodge was opened with Edward in the chair and a number of naval officers, the most distinguished of whom was Alexander, 7th Lord Colville, were initiated. Other residents, including Richard Bulkeley, then became joining members and the latter

156

eventually became the Grand Master.

The historian of local Freemasonry, the Hon. William Ross, tells us that the Governor appointed a Deputy to occupy the Chair of the Lodge whenever he was absent and that when eventually he returned to England he was succeeded by another soldier, Colonel Charles Lawrence, who was also a later Governor Ross gives us two vignettes of lodge practice in Edward's time: that on the first anniversary of the Lodge's founding, being St. John the Baptist's Day, 'the brethren resolved to celebrate the festival with the usual pomp by walking in procession to St. Paul's Church to hear prayers and an address'. Subsequently they heard that Frederick, Prince of Wales, the father of George III and also a Freemason. had died and they again gathered in the newly completed Parish Church to hold a service of respect and remembrance. Since this was attended almost wholly by brethren and their ladies it has been deemed the first Masonic service to be held in Canada. The lodge has continued until the present and is now known as St. Andrew's Lodge, No.1, once described as 'the oldest lodge in the British Empire overseas'.

Bulkeley was not Edward's only close colleague. There was a Captain Gates who was especially adept in establishing the defences of the new town and arranging the proper disposal of both the population and their stores. He too was a member of the new lodge and, leaving Halifax in 1754, was to continue his masonic and military career in New York, becoming in due course the better known General Gates of the Revolution. His family's link with Edward's nephew, the first Marquess, will be dealt with later.

In 1752 Edward was suffering from persistent and acute rheumatism and the effects of constant dispute with the Department in London. One of his last letters makes all things plain:

"Did your lordships consider the distress and disappointment I have met with and struggled through, I flatter myself you would rather pity and cherish than censure and discomfort me; and that you will intercede with his majesty *sic* to allow of my resignation of government and grant me liberty to return home . . ."

In October 1752 he was at last given permission to return to Britain and in January 1753, on the death of Sir Peter Warren, M.P. for Westminster Cornwallis was chosen for the vacant seat. In the same year he married Elizabeth Townshend, daughter of Charles, the 2nd Viscount Townshend. There were no children of this union.

In October, 1753, Edward was appointed Lieutenant Colonel of the 24th Regiment (later the South Wales Borderers) and in 1755 he served with them in Minorca. It was here that he underwent the most unfortunate episode in his career.

France was at this time preparing to attack Minorca and reduce the threat from Port Mahon, which the British considered as of only second importance to Gibraltar. Yet the British Government again failed to provide the funds or resources to enable the military base of Fort St. Philip to be garrisoned adequately. However, when the French threat seemed likely to succeed a fleet with additional troops was sent under the command of

Admiral John Byng, the son of an earlier Admiral who had been raised to the peerage as Viscount Torrington. Yet the son was of lesser capacity than his father and with little active experience and this was made worse by his reputation as a brutal disciplinarian.

Cornwallis, with Colonels Lord Effingham and James Stuart, embarked some of their troops on 1 November 1756, and set off for Minorca. The 3 soldiers and the Admiral sailed on the flagship *Intrepid* and no doubt enjoyed each other's company as they were all members of a rather select and 'fast' London set called 'The Corinthians'. In view of what was about to happen it is sad to say that at least 2 of them were also active and well-known Freemasons.

Through Byng's incompetence and a delay in leaving Gibraltar due to the Governor there, it was 18 January before the fleet reached Minorca. Blakeney, the besieged commander of Fort St. Philip, was first relieved by Byng's arrival and then amazed to find that the Admiral made no attempt to communicate and liaise with him. A French fleet appeared briefly and withdrew.

On its reappearance Byng gave such a confused signal for engagement that there was no concerted action, some of his ships collided and others were suddenly told to hold fire. Rear Admiral West, Byng's second in command, did attack the enemy line with some success but having no support from other vessels had to withdraw. The French fleet sailed away and was never pursued. Next day Byng decided to return to Gibraltar leaving Blakeney and his garrison to a further hopeless 5 weeks of resistance. They were eventually granted an honourable capitulation and Britain lost Minorca for ever.

The fury in England, especially after hearing the French naval account of the events, was enormous. Edward shared the odium of being in that Council of War which agreed to a retreat and, along with his fellow commanders, was subjected to grave physical threats on their arrival in Plymouth. Effigies of the Admiral and the three Colonels were burned in many towns and a board of enquiry was set up under General Ligonier.

Fortunately for Edward the influence of powerful friends led to a favourable outcome to the long and tedious court-martial. Though the three military men were finally exonerated, as having been restricted by their presence on board ship, they were for many months the subject of public ridicule and caricature. Byng was sentenced to death and was shot. His courage at the end was apparent to all and it therefore seems ridiculous to reveal that what apparently curbed his willingness to engage the enemy had been a desire to protect the collection of rare china which he had in his cabin.

That Edward Cornwallis was not abandoned by his friends in Government is clear because shortly after Byng's execution in March 1757 he was promoted to the rank of Major General whilst on service in Ireland, and in October 1760 became Lieutenant General and Colonel of the 24th Foot. Less than 18 months later, on 18 March 1762, he was appointed Governor and Commander-in-Chief of Gibraltar, a post that he not too willingly accepted since it was well-known as being the most unhealthy station in Europe with bad water supply and drainage always rendering it open to black vomit, smallpox and yellow fever. His wife's reaction can well be imagined. Indeed it was bad health that led to their temporary return to England on 14 June 1765.

They were to resume residence a few months later and it was during this last period of his life that he again took the lead in founding another Lodge there, No. 426 on the register of the Grand Lodge of England and in the 24th Regiment of Foot. What is a little puzzling is that in the records of the Grand Lodge there is a dated letter from the Master of this Lodge, Peter Margarett, to the Grand Secretary, stating that having information from Bro. Dunckerley, that their warrant is ready they are ready to pay the £4.10s required. The names of the members are therein attached but the name of the Hon. Edward Cornwallis is not listed and one wonders if in fact he was the Consecrating Officer and therefore was attached to the Lodge in an honorary capacity. At least it shows that Edward's attachment to the Craft persisted to the end. For despite many requests for, and refusals of, appointments elsewhere it was in Gibraltar that he died and was buried in January 1776. He was in his 64th year and his services closed with the grim record of the War Office – "D.D." – discharged dead.

We must now turn to his twin brother, Frederick. He attended Culford school before also being sent to Eton, where one observer of the time reports that he and his brother 'were so alike that it was difficult to know them asunder'. Whilst there he had amongst his friends Charles Pratt, who was created Lord Chancellor Camden in 1766, and also Dr. Sneyd-Davies, a scholar and poet whom he early appointed as Bishop's Chaplain at Lichfield. It was whilst at Eton that he first suffered what was to be a lasting deformity of his right hand.

Frederick then proceeded to Christ's College, Cambridge as a pensioner in February 1732, qualifying for his B.A. degree in 1736 and becoming a Fellow in 1738. Cole, who was quoted above, also relates how 'he was my contemporary at the University where no one was more beloved, or bore a better character, than he did all the time of his residence therein; during which, towards the latter end of it, he had the misfortune to have a stroke of the palsy, which took away altogether any sense in his already damaged right hand, and obliged him to write with his left, which he did very expeditiously; and I have often had the honour to play cards with him, when it was wonderful to see how dextrously he would shuffle and play them." It is also likely that it was this disability which prevented Frederick from pursuing the military career which he too desired. It seems clear also to anyone carefully examining his portrait by Dance that this may be the reason why he was desirous of being painted with his left side to the artist.

Frederick's principal tutor at Cambridge was Dr. Edmund Law, a somewhat provocative divine of the time, whom his pupil was later to make Archdeacon of Stafford before his subsequent promotion to the Bishopric of Carlisle in 1769. Frederick, however, was made a Deacon at Norwich Cathedral in 1739 and ordained priest there a year later, after which he was presented by his brother, the 5th Lord, to the rectory of Chelmondiston, Suffolk (1740). He subsequently held this living with that of Tivetshall (or Titteshall) St. Mary, Norfolk in 1742. He must have continued as a Fellow of Christ's, employing curates in the parishes because in 1744 he attained his Doctorate of Divinity at

Oxford. It was already evident that he was marked out for preferment.

In 1746 he was appointed a Canon of Windsor by patent dated 21 May and became a Chaplain-in-Ordinary to the King as well as being collated on 14 January 1747 to the Prebend of Leighton Ecclesia in Lincoln Cathedral. It might be recalled that one of the first Cornwaleys priests also held a prebend there. It was at this stage that in writing to the Duke of Newcastle about these appointments Archbishop Herring said of him: "By the character Dr. Cornwallis bears one has nothing more to wish but that his health may equal the goodness of his heart and understanding.

After four years' service in attendance on the Royal Family Frederick's noble brother seems to have been at work again on his behalf. The see of Lichfield and Coventry was offered in January 1750 and following his consecration in February the new Bishop wrote to Newcastle as follows:

"I want words to express how much I am obliged to your Grace for the fresh instance of your regard and kindness to me. I shall endeavour to please our friends in this diocese and to promote His Majesty's interest in these parts . . . I am sure my brother will always remember that his obligation is solely to your Grace for this Bishopric.
It is always wise to acknowledge the source of one's preferment.

Reaching his ancient but landlocked diocese was a trial in itself. It took 3 days to get down from London to Staffordshire and 6 years later he was still remarking on the parlous state of the roads. In 1758 it even took him 4 days to reach Westminster because one of his 6 horses – 'poor Squeaker' – dropped dead in his harness at Dunstable Hill. "Having a seventh horse", remarks the Bishop," it retarded us but a little." One can well imagine how heavily the episcopal coach of even an unmarried prelate was laden. Incidentally the letter in which this information is given also presents greetings from the Dowager Lady Cornwallis and one wonders whether in fact the Bishop's widowed mother was perhaps acting as the Lady of the House until he eventually married.

The Bishop of Lichfield and Coventry's home at this juncture was not actually at the Palace in the Close at Lichfield but at Eccleshall Castle, near Stafford. The reason for this apparent anomaly was that just under a hundred years previously the Bishop, Thomas Wood, had been a more than usual absentee prelate who lived in Middlesex. The official house in Lichfield was grossly neglected and eventually the Archbishop of Canterbury suspended the Bishop. His successor had to be housed somewhere and though, as a punishment, Wood had to repair the Palace at Lichfield at his own expense it was some time before it was ready for occupation. In Frederick's time it was handsome, spacious and well-appointed but as the Bishops had become used to living at Eccleshall the Lichfield property was leased to suitable tenants. It continued to be so rented out until 1868.

Around this time (1759) we are given a revealing snapshot of how sleepy life in the diocese could be. Writing to Sneyd-Davies who now had a living in Worcestershire the Bishop says, "We have been endeavouring to establish a County Hospital but I fear it will not do. There is money enough subscribed but there is a supineness and inactivity towards the executive part of it that must frustrate it." On second thoughts he might not have found things today all that different.

If Frederick thought the state of his diocese was soporific he was not alone in that opinion. Samuel Johnson, a son of Lichfield and an exact contemporary, gave 'the field of the dead' as his considered derivation of the city's name. Others have since differed from this opinion but even they can only offer 'marshland' or 'the settlement by the gray woods', both of which confirm a similar impression.

The city itself was little more than a mile or so square and Johnson's father as Sheriff of the County of Stafford could easily ride the bounds within a day. These were but narrow lanes between green hedgerows and old pathways eroded into ditches. In both city and diocese one really was in the heart of rural England.

Even more pronounced was the contrast of the life of the Cathedral Close from that of the neighbouring residents. In 1781 the Close was still made up of 43 houses compared with the city's 722. It was entirely exempt from civil jurisdiction, having its own magistrates and constables, its own local bye-laws and even water supply. "There was a smell of Latin, Hebrew and Greek in the Close. Many of the clergy had travelled and some spoke French, Italian and even German, in addition to keeping Latin a live language on their tongues. The Close community tended to look down on the City because the ecclesiastical families were in general of a higher social rank than the City folk . . . [Yet] though this cleavage existed the relationship was friendly and some families were at home in both sets . . .

"Although the Close did some repairing and a little building within its narrow bounds it interested itself chiefly in music, writing and theorizing . . . [Its] religion was so undeviating as to be stolid. The mysticism of the Quakers and the rising vigour of the Methodists were repulsed by a wall of religious conservatism. If any of the clergy had spiritual natures it was not they who held the highest preferments . .

"The hubbub of trade was replaced by the rhythm of chimes floating over the countryside, the chant of ritual and the music of men's singing voices . . .[here] strode the sombre clergy in black kneebreeches, black wool stockings, voluminous robes, full-bottomed wigs, and round, low-crowned, broad-brimmed felt hats. Hoop-skirted ladies in bright silks strolled along the shaded Dean's Walk [and] children dressed like little men and women played in the gardens . . . (*Dr. Johnson's Lichfield*: pp. 22f)

Samuel Johnson and David Garrick both made the transition from City to Close because they were 'adopted' by the tenant of the Palace, a Mr. Gilbert Walmesley, Registrar of the Ecclesiastical Court of the Cathedral. Being a bachelor he made his home a centre of social life, especially helping the more promising youngsters of the town.

It should not be imagined, however, that whilst the Bishop lived at some remove he was not involved in regular service of the diocese. In the local Record Office are

Frederick's 'Day Books' which record his official activities as Bishop and it is worth noting that no such record was kept by his two predecessors from 1717 to 1749. A close examination reveals that throughout his occupancy of the see he was engaged in ordaining, licensing or instituting clergy every quarter. It is true that these were usually carried out in his chapel at Eccleshall, in the Grosvenor Chapel in London or privately wherever he might happen to be but at least he was personally involved and through such encounters and, for some, their presentations in the parish he must have become very familiar with every part of what was then a very large portion of the Midlands. The names Cholmondeley, Montgomery, Fitzherbert, Bagot, Wombwell, Cavendish and Clowes, to mention but a few, are enough to show that in several cases he was dealing with family acquaintances.

Speaking of family acquaintances it was towards the end of his time at Lichfield, on 8 February 1759, that he married Caroline, eldest daughter of William Townshend, third son of Charles, 2nd Viscount Townshend. Writing again to his schoolfriend, Sneyd-Davies, some of whose relations lived in the lovely manor of Belmont in North Staffordshire, he says:

"I return you many thanks for your kind congratulations upon my marriage; I shall be much mistaken, indeed, if it should not greatly advance my future comfort and happiness in life."

The new wife was certainly from a great family and this marriage would ensure that even if the Bishop was already 'accepted' in the highest circles of society he would now be sure of retaining his place there. She was known as 'a reigning beauty and the toast of her day' but of this marriage there was sadly no issue and Caroline Cornwallis was to survive her husband for 28 years until September 1811.

By September 1759 Frederick had been at the same post for almost a decade and whether it was on his own initiative or possibly with the additional prompting of his new partner he wrote thus to the Duke of Newcastle:

"The Bishop of Worcester is very ill. I hope your Grace will pardon my troubling you with this, barely to mention without importuning that a removal to that see would be most agreeable to your Grace's most obliged and most humble servant, Fred. Lich. and Cov."

Whatever may have been the attractions of moving to but a neighbouring rural diocese, and the fact that his close friend, Sneyd-Davies, was at Kingsland, which lay within it, can only have been one of them, he was not to have what he sought. The Duke replied a week later that he had to give that see to the Bishop of Gloucester, a rebuff that gave rise to one of Frederick's rare bursts of anger and led him to speak openly of the 'loss he had sustained'. Nonetheless, despite his disappointment, when the Duke fell out with the new Prime Minister, the Earl of Bute, and resigned it was remarked by Horace Walpole "that after crowding his rooms for forty years together there was but one that had the decency to take leave of him at his parting levee. That one was Cornwallis."

162

In 1765 a vacancy in the see of Salisbury seemed imminent. Newcastle was now embarrassed by his wife, Henrietta, having in an unguarded moment promised this see to John Hume, the Bishop of Oxford. In a letter to Archbishop Secker, however, Newcastle affirms that 'with the utmost respect to the Bishop of Oxford the Bishop of Lichfield has much superior pretensions to it' and he followed this up with another letter in the same direction suggesting that the 2nd Earl Cornwallis's friendship with William Pitt the Elder (who was now Prime Minister) would surely make the latter tend to serve the Earl's uncle. Again it was not to be. The Archbishop returned from an audience with the new king, George III, and Hume went to Salisbury, Lowth to Oxford and Cornwallis to the Deanery of St. Paul's.

What transpired at the episcopal breakfast table when the news broke we have no need to imagine for we have yet another letter from Newcastle to Archbishop Secker.

"The person wished for by the University of Cambridge (of which Newcastle happened to be Chancellor) and intended by me as the next Bishop of Ely was the Bishop of Lichfield and though the bishop and his whole Family have broke off all correspondence with me, that does not alter my opinion of his general merit . . ." The Archbishop, after consulting with Lord Chatham wrote:

"I cannot entertain the least doubt of his being fixed upon." He was wrong. Having held a Canonry of St. Paul's Cathedral since 1760 Frederick finally accepted the Deanery there from 28 November 1766.

Yet he was not pleased and one feels with some justification. His letter on the subject, when Newcastle wrote congratulating the Bishop on his appointment, was for once lacking in tact and reveals his state of mind.

"You say you are much rejoiced at my having accepted the Deanery of S. Paul's. For what reason I know not. As to myself I have no joy in it, I am not fond of expedients. Had the recommendation to it come from your Grace by way of atonement I shd [sic] have rejected the Deanery. After the hard treatment I had met with I could not with honour have accepted it. It is by no means a preferment either agreeable or suitable to me. It would have been kind of your Grace not to have kept me so long in suspense with regard to the Bishopric of Salisbury. Had you told me it was a real promise, it wd at least have mitigated the severity of the disappointment. You say it is the only instance, but seven years ago you gave Worcester to the Bishop of Gloucester. Surely, my Lord, the disregard then shewed to me may be allow'd to have given just cause of some dissatisfaction, at least not only to me but to my Family and Friends. It certainly did. You begged forgiveness: it was immediately granted, and the hardship forgotten. The late unfortunate circumstance brought it back to my mind."

Alfred Rowden, K.C., quoting this letter in his work, "The Primates of the Four Georges" (pp. 321f) suggests that these sentiments reflect badly on one who was to be an Archbishop. I can only say that in the frankness of their admission and the temperance of their tone they reflect credit on one who had, after all, been surprisingly ill-used.

It was in 1768 that owing to the unexpected death of Archbishop Secker Frederick was chosen by the Crown to succeed to the Primacy and to be consecrated to the See of Canterbury. It seems likely that this preferment was due to the influence of the 3rd Duke of Grafton who was a personal friend of the Bishop and his nephew, the 2nd Earl Cornwallis. Whilst there are those who can point a finger at the Duke as one who had a flawed domestic relationship there are equally others who speak of his being a nobleman with a high sense of duty, at least as far as service to his country was concerned. What is more he had a strange interest in religious matters. He was throughout unorthodox, rejecting the degree of LL.D. at Cambridge because he could not subscribe to the Thirty-nine Articles and becoming a professed Unitarian during his retirement. That it was this nobleman, currently Prime Minister, who finally made the choice is confirmed by another letter to Frederick from Newcastle: ". . . acquaint the Duke of Grafton how much I approve the measure. I don't mean to take any merit to myself, for I have none."

To this Frederick made his own suitable reply:

"I must own I feel myself very unequal to so high a station, and wish I could have declined it with propriety, but found I could not as things were circumstanced. All that can now be done is to exert my utmost endeavours to answer in some degree the favourable expectations my friends have entertained of me."

The appointment was certainly not anticipated and Mr. Charles Godwyn, a learned Fellow of Balliol and of episcopal descent, after expressing his approval of some of Archbishop Secker's works, wrote:

"What learned works are we to expect from his successor? He himself is a person quite unexpected."

Despite his Doctorate the new Primate would himself have acknowledged that he was not as learned as many of those who had held the office before him but he was a much respected pastor and came to be highly regarded by his diocese. Hasted, the historian of Kent, wrote of him from Canterbury,

"The archbishop gives great satisfaction to everybody here: his affability and courteous behaviour are much taken notice of, as very different from his predecessors.
Dr. Ducarel, the Lambeth Palace librarian, was also soon writing to Bishop Lyttelton of Carlisle:

"He is, I think, the first Etonian who has attained to that high honour. [Ducarel also came from that school.] I paid my respects to him last night [10 August 1768] and he has been graciously pleased to continue me librarian at Lambeth and received me with the greatest civility and friendship." Does one detect a sense of the unexpected?

Certainly from the instant that he entered its walls, the new Archbishop began to make his mark on the Palace. His predecessor had lived a quiet, cloistered and somewhat serene life but Frederick Cornwallis brought into the place a very different atmosphere.

164

Archbishop Cornwallis

The private collection of Lord Braybrooke, on display at Audley End House, Essex
© ENGLISH HERITAGE PHOTOGRAPHIC LIBRARY

CULFORD HALL. 1612.

He was after all from a noble family much acquainted with the Royal Court and there was a standard of living to which he was accustomed.

Within a year he had improved the palace with two handsome additional rooms, whilst in the dining hall he changed the seating arrangements. The previous and long-standing practice had been for the Private Chaplains to be seated with the chief domestics or to be provided for on special occasions with a separate dining table. Such a procedure was abolished and these clergy always sat at the same table with His Grace. Though his personal tastes were moderate his hospitality was princely, especially on public days, it being normally the custom for the Archbishop of Canterbury, when resident at Lambeth, to provide a public food table once a week when Parliament was in session. However the grateful recognition of such generosity provided by the Archbishop was somewhat offset by the offence caused in some circles by the equally generous but much more rowdy social gatherings or 'routs' which were organized by the Archbishop's wife – not only on weekdays but even on a number of Sunday afternoons and evenings.

The background to this matter is important. "In the reign of George I an effort had been made by Archbishop Wake to check the fashion for masked balls or masquerades, which enjoyed royal favour but tended, as vigilant critics believed, to a growing slackness of morals . . ." A note still at Lambeth recording the Bishops' meeting on the matter 'desired my Lord Townshend [Caroline Cornwallis's grandfather] to request his Majtie to forbid the Masquerades intended to be held at the beginning of ye year'. The memorial did not produce the desired effect and apart from a hiccough when the Lisbon earthquake disaster of 1755 brought even English people up with a start the masques recommenced even though Archbishop Cornwallis himself was urged to remonstrate against their misuse. Horace Walpole wrote of the latter event:

"That knave, the Bishop of London, persuaded that good soul the Archbishop to object, but happily the age prefers silly follies to serious ones and dominoes comme de raison carry it against lawn sleeves" The sting of this satire was not far to seek. Mrs Cornwallis was heralded in the journals of the day as a leader of fashion whose entertainments eclipsed all others in magnificence. It was now made clear why the new occupants of Lambeth had wanted to add 'very noble apartments', a new drawing and retiring room to the Palace.

It is certainly a matter of record that on one occasion the Archbishop was constrained to receive a visit from the formidable Selina, Countess of Huntingdon, whose Connexion of Evangelical chapels had already become a force in the land. She was not only related by marriage with both the Cornwallis and Townshend families but she was on this occasion attended by the Lord Townshend, Caroline's cousin. She berated the Archbishop for his wife's behaviour and thought it most unbecoming that the very fount of the State Church should have become such a place of offence to many in the nation. The Archbishop's response was resolute and lively, expressing dislike of 'Methodists and hypocrites', and it is true that he was gravely offended by this interference.

Sadly the crusading Countess also sought and received a royal audience at Kew which lasted an hour and resulted in a letter subsequently being sent by His Majesty to his Archbishop.

"My good Lord Prelate," the missive ran, "I could not delay giving you the notification of grief and concern with which my breast was affected, at receiving authentic information that routs have made their way into your palace . . . I must signify to you my sentiments on this subject, which hold these levities and vain dissipations as utterly inexpedient, if not unlawful, to pass in a residence for many centuries devoted to divine studies, religious retirement, and the extensive exercise of charity and benevolence . . . From the dissatisfaction with which you must perceive I behold these improprieties I trust you will suppress them immediately so that I may not have occasion . . . to interpose in a different manner . . . your gracious friend, G.R."

Whilst it is true that his wife's social activities were somewhat curtailed and especially as far as Sundays were concerned, the Archbishop was not willing to be browbeaten completely. What could not have been known by guests or outsiders was that Caroline Cornwallis had a strong and inexplicable fondness for the Lambeth Palace Library which she is said to have visited and read in almost daily. That this was neither a transient interest nor one done for effect is shown by the continuing bequests that she made even after her husband's death. Frederick also added significantly to the library's contents. He had responded as Bishop of Lichfield to the then Archbishop's request for copies of diocesan records to be lodged at Lambeth and Dr. Ducarel's project in 1778 of listing all the Bible editions between 1626 and 1776 was published in 250 copies entirely at this Primate's personal expense.

At this very time he also gave support to Beilby Porteus, the Bishop of Chester in his efforts to have Good Friday better observed. This was met by a cry of 'No Popery' and for many weeks the Presbyterian newspapers were full of abuse of Archbishop Cornwallis and his family. One paper complained of the shutting up of the city shops on Good Friday as "a sanctified hypocritical triumph over both reason and Scripture – the civil and religious right of Englishmen – which could not but be highly acceptable to tyrant and hypocrite of every denomination, especially at Court."

This was not the only problem that faced the Archbishop in his London home. On 6 June 1780, some 4 to 500 No-Popery rioters, believing that the Archbishop was a favourer of Roman Catholics by his support of recent legislation, came to the gateway of Lambeth, knocked noisily and repeatedly on it, paraded for many hours around the walls and when they could not gain entry swore to return. Thus alarmed, the Archbishop, his wife and close attendants were persuaded to lodge elsewhere and at last found a refuge at Lord Hillsborough's house at Westerham where they stayed until the disturbances were over. A detachment of 100 Guards under a Colonel Deacon was first installed at Lambeth, placing sentinels on the tower and parapets as well as clearing the roads approaching the Palace. They were later replaced by a detachment of 2 to 300 militia, with their families, who kept strict garrison duty, the officers being housed in the best apartments and entertained by the Chaplains, at His Grace's expense. The men on duty, again with wives and children, attended chapel each morning and evening and were given their food in the great hall. Not surprisingly their provisions were so good and plentiful that when, by 11 August, all possible danger had ceased, they departed from their comfortable quarters with great concern. It is also recorded that their behaviour throughout seems to have been exemplary.

That the Archbishop discharged his many episcopal duties with as much diligence as any of his contemporaries is shown by excerpts from the *Gentleman's Magazine* of the time. He held visitations of his clergy at Sittingbourne, Canterbury, Ashford and Dover, confirmed candidates at those places as well as Ramsgate, Sandwich, Hythe, Romney, Cranbrook and Maidstone. This, it should be recalled, was done without the help of more modern roads, transport and even adequate accommodation.

The same magazine reports that whilst visiting Dover Frederick and his wife stayed at the London Tavern. They were much alarmed at midnight by the door of their room being burst open by a drunken English squire who had just arrived from France and who insisted on taking possession of their apartment. The couple apparently gave way 'for peace sake, though next morning when, being sober, the squire offered to make any submission, His Grace would not see him."

Speaking of accommodation it is worth recording that it was Frederick who oversaw and approved the disposal of the ancient Archbishop's Palace at Croydon. The somewhat monastic style building had been shamefully neglected in Secker's time as being unhealthy and uncomfortable. Accordingly it was sold in 1780 to an Abraham Pitcher and the Archbishop bought a farm site at Park Hill, Croydon, to provide for an alternative residence. He died before it could be built and it was not until 1808 that Charles Manners Sutton in his Primacy secured the grounds at Addington and erected another Palace there.

Though Frederick never produced a learned book he contributed verses to the University collections on the occasion of the marriages first of the Prince of Orange (1733) and then of Frederick, Prince of Wales, (1736) and caused a very curious collection of old printed tracts and pamphlets from the reign of Henry VII to that of Queen Anne to be bound in 60 volumes and lodged at Lambeth.

We have some of his sermons in published form. Two extracts from these latter will give an indication of their style and substance. The first was given at the Yearly Meeting of 'Children educated in Charity Schools in and about the Cities of London and Westminster' in 1762.

"These are the good and salutary Ends proposed by that excellent Work of Charity I am now recommending, and well worthy it is of your Assistance and Encouragement. – For the proper Education of Youth is a Point of the utmost Moment to the Happiness of a State. – The tender Mind is susceptible of good or bad Impressions, and may either be enlisted, by Care and Attention, in the cause of Virtue, or engaged by Neglect and Idleness in a Course of Vice. And whoever imagines that the Superior Parts of Mankind are uninterested in, and unconnected with, the inferior Parts of Society, adopts an Opinion utterly inconsistent with the Institutions of the wisest Politicians, and is either ignorant of the Nature of Community, or regardless of the Good of it – For the good Condition of a

Nation depends principally on the Dispositions of the Poor; and where the Poor are virtuous and industrious, there the Rich have a security for the Blessings vouchsafed unto them; and may quietly enjoy either what they have procured for themselves, or have received from others."

The other is part of his Sermon preached before the 'Rt. Hon. the Lords Spiritual and Temporal in Parliament assembled in the Abbey Church Westminster':

"Whatever System of Politicks we may have adopted; whatever our Opinions may be in relation to the Rights of the Governor, and the Subject; however inclin'd we may be to advance the Privileges of the one, and to lessen the Power, and object to the Claims of the other, yet as long as we have the common Sentiments of Compassion, (the brightest and most amiable Part of human Nature) we shall be strongly dispos'd to look with Pity upon the unfortunate sufferer."

As he advanced in years Cornwallis felt the infirmities of old age. In the February of 1783 he was confined to his rooms by a gouty complaint in one of his legs. On 14 March he was fit enough again to attend the House of Lords, where he had certainly been a regular member and on the Sunday, 16th, he attended worship in Lambeth Chapel and seemed well in the evening. He relapsed however on the Monday and died on the evening of Wednesday, 19 March.

He was buried beneath the altar in Lambeth Parish Church, alongside Bishop Thomas Thirlby, whose body was found entire, 'including a cap of silk adorned with point lace – but which had lost its black colour - on the head'. The funeral service was conducted by Bishop Porteus of Chester and Dr. Vyse, the Rector of Lambeth, with Dr. Lort, another of Frederick's chaplains. A monument was later erected on the south side of the chancel. He died a rich man and not having made a will, at least during his time at Lambeth, his widow became the principal beneficiary. Sadly it has not been possible so far to discover how or where she spent the remainder of her days.

Of the other junior members of the family there is also sadly little to tell. William, the 8th son, was, like his next brother, educated at Eton but beyond the fact that he died unmarried nothing further has so far come to light. Henry, the 9th boy, born in September 1740, became an Ensign in the 1st Foot Guards at the age of 15 and a Captain three years later. Whilst still under age he was elected M.P. for Eye but he never took his seat because he died whilst on active service in Germany. The fact that he was made an M.P. under age does rather suggest that his immediately elder brother may also have died before he was 21. Of the girls Charlotte and Elizabeth died as infants and Mary died as a teenager in 1756.

The senior member of the family, Charles, 5th Lord Cornwallis was baptized in March 1701 in the parish of St. Martin-in-the-Fields. After being educated at home with a tutor he was admitted as a nobleman at Clare College, Cambridge on 9 November 1717, and left there, albeit without a degree, to study for the law in the Inns of Court. Though he was active in the affairs of his day he did not represent Eye in the House of Commons, as was now customary for Cornwallis sons, but this was probably due to the fact that being about 21 when his father died he went straight to the House of Lords. On 19 August 1721 he had become a Groom of the Bedchamber to George I and on 28 November 1722, he married Elizabeth, the eldest daughter of Charles, 2nd Viscount Townshend, of Raynham Norfolk, a connection of no little importance. Since his brothers, Edward and Frederick, also married Townshend daughters it may be as well to say something about this family connection.

Horatio Townshend was born in 1630, the second son of the prominent Norfolk landowner, Sir Roger Townshend. When his elder brother died in 1648 Horatio inherited the family estate as 3rd Baronet and shortly afterwards married Mary, sole heir of Sir Edward Lewkenor of Denham, Suffolk. Their marriage lasted until her death in 1673 but was childless and in addition to that disappointment Horatio was facing a constant and growing drain on his finances. The completion of the country house at Raynham started by his father, finding partners and dowries for 3 of his 4 sisters, and the costs of maintaining a county as well as a national profile, plus some lavishness in personal expenditure, meant that the Townshend purse was running down.

It is true that he was elevated to the peerage in 1661, as Baron Townshend, of Lynn Regis, and three years later was given a royal grant worth £2000, but though he was made Lord Lieutenant of Norfolk at the same time and even sought a regular place in government he never really established his claims and by 1676 he lost the Lord Lieutenancy and had turned his disgruntled back on Whitehall.

Meanwhile, in 1673, he married again. His wife, who was only 20 years of age, was Mary, daughter of Sir Joseph Ashe of Twickenham and before her death in 1685 she bore him three sons. The responsibility of fatherhood spurred him to restore his financial affairs to a more solvent state and though his health became steadily worse he could at least concentrate on his domestic and estate affairs. He died in December 1687 2 years after his 2nd wife.

The fatherless son, 12 year old Charles Townshend, at least inherited a bright future. "Thanks to honest estate management in his minority, based on lines his father had established, he took over a thriving Landed estate when he came of age. The deaths of the first generation of Norfolk Tories and Whigs . . . left something of a political vacuum in the county, into which Charles Townsend (sic) slipped with little opposition." (James M. Rosenheim, *The Townshends of Raynham*, W.U.P. 1989, p. 7)

He became Lord Lieutenant of Norfolk in 1701 and by his marriage in 1698 to Elizabeth Pelham he not only received a dowry of £30,000 but gained the assistance of her politically influential father, Thomas Pelham (later 1st Baron Pelham) of Laughton in Sussex. Undeterred by any need to seek remunerative government favour "he rose in stature both locally and nationally (and through) the perspicacity and willingness to work which the son displayed in the capital (he achieved) before long the kind of reward his father never attained." (*Rosenheim*, op. cit., p. 7)

In 1706 he was named one of the Commissioners to negotiate the Union with Scotland; in 1707 he became a Privy Councillor and 2 years later he was ambassador plenipotentiary in diplomatic negotiations with the Dutch. By 1714 he was Secretary of State and though from 1717-1720 he was not in office the following 15 years saw him on royal visits to Hanover, attending at Court and prominent in both City and Parliamentary life. He received the Garter and could have had an Earldom. Yet he too suffered personal loss.

After some 13 years of apparently close and affectionate marriage, Elizabeth Townshend died in 1711, predeceased by three of the nine children she had borne in that time. Two years later he married Dorothy, the sister of his long time political partner, Sir Robert Walpole, another Norfolk landowner, and their marriage also lasted about 13 years, during which Dorothy lost four of the 11 children she bore, with yet another dying shortly after herself. Not long after Dorothy died, in May 1730, "public loss was added to private ones as Townshend, losing influence with George II, submitted his resignation . . . All the same, when he departed he left office with honour and voluntarily, perhaps worn down with ill health as much as anything." (Rosenheim, p. 8) He was to enjoy 8 more years of retirement at Raynham.

Such was the family with which the Cornwallises were in one generation thrice allied. Charles, 2nd Viscount, two of whose daughters became Cornwallis wives is known to have been a considerate and affectionate father, and "as they matured they received more-than-adequate provision from their father in the form of education, appropriate marriage partners and assistance in their careers". Though both Sir Horace Mann and the Earl of Chesterfield voiced doubts about the provision made by the Viscount such judgement "fails to consider that providing in any fashion whatsoever for the 11 of his children who attained adulthood was in itself an accomplishment; it will be seen that Townshend's provisions, while not extravagant, were ample." (Rosenheim, pp. 119f) Some of the Cornwallis fathers would have claimed no less.

Elizabeth, the only surviving daughter by his first marriage, was married by 1722 and whilst we do not know the size of her dowry we can assume that it was not unduly large since her eldest brother, the family heir, was to be married only 6 months later. Expense would have been keenly watched at a time when the Viscount was making his way in the world and there were 4 other boys to be started on careers.

Returning to the 5th Lord Cornwallis's family it was only on 31 December 1738 that the first boy, Charles, was born 'at his Lordship's House in Grosvenor Square, London', and he was rapidly followed by Henry in 1740; James born 'at His Lordship's house in Dover Street, London 25 February 1743; and William in February 1744. Charles, James and William all became persons who rendered substantial public service but Henry (or Harry) died when he was only twenty-one.

As the places of birth indicate the family spent a good deal of time in London with Culford as their country home. From 1722 until 1740 the 5th Lord was Chief Justice in Eyre, South of the Trent, and on relinquishing that office he was made Constable of the

Charles, 1st Earl Cornwallis

The private collection of Lord Braybrooke, on display at Audley End House, Essex
© ENGLISH HERITAGE PHOTOGRAPHIC LIBRARY

Monument of Charles, 1st Earl Cornwallis

© ENGLISH HERITAGE PHOTOGRAPHIC LIBRARY

174

Tower and Lord Lieutenant of the Tower Hamlets until his death. In 1753, when he was created Earl Cornwallis with the attendant title of Viscount Brome in the County of Suffolk, it might reasonably have been thought that the family tree had at last reached its greatest height.

Whilst it is true that His Lordship saw his own and the family's future as dependent on the connections that could only be fully pursued in London it is not true that he neglected the Culford estate. In 1742 he had the park surveyed and redesigned by the landscape gardener, Thomas Wright, whose plan can still be examined in the Record Office at Bury St. Edmunds. Noted for his love of lime trees it may have been Wright who introduced this feature to Culford and who provided for generations to follow the intoxicating fragrance that surrounded those who sat or walked on the South Front during early summer evenings.

For this was the age of George II, an age of elegant manners and picturesque costume, when the members of the House and their neighbours from all the great houses and halls around would pass their time in amassing wild flowers, sharing in 'strawberry gatherings', observing the deer or idly chatting and gossiping beneath the trees on the lawns. Dressed like the porcelain figures which they avidly bought the women were like Dresden or Meissen shepherdesses in delicate silks whilst the men wore flowered waistcoats and richly embroidered jackets. In the evenings their meals would be followed by cards and music, or dancing in the gentle glow given off from candelabra and sconces. It was into this world and this setting that the 6th Lord, 2nd Earl and later 1st Marquess Cornwallis, his generation and his family were now to make their impressive entrance.

CHAPTER 9

Life in the Tree Tops

The Hall and estate at Culford which was the home of the 1st Earl and his young children did not differ greatly from the property which had come into the possession of the family through Dame Jane Bacon. The lake was still the same size as when Sir Nicholas Bacon dug 'the greate pond' in 1624 and the house and its immediate surroundings were much the same as in Dame Jane's day. The park had been replanned with new stables and a laundry block built by the 1st Earl whilst the Church was somewhat re-built, largely as a result of the generous help given by Sir Stephen Fox. There was little difference then to be seen overall. Even by 1784 the view described by François de la Rochefoucauld when visiting Culford was such as would have been recognized by many of the house's previous occupiers:

"The house is just like a great square lantarn, for the four fronts are so similar that the first time we were there we didn't know which side contained the entrance. The number of windows is immense. The house was built in the time of Queen Elizabeth, altogether in the Gothic taste".

Yet all this was to change. Whilst serving abroad in the spring of 1789 the 2nd Earl asked his brother James and his cousin, Charles Townshend, later 1st Baron Bayning, to organize and supervise considerable alterations to the house. By February 1790 a letter from Townshend gives a detailed description of the Hall before any improvements were made and the following brief extracts give some impression of why changes were desirable. He wrote:

"The Terrace prevented Carriages from coming close to the Porch . . . From the Drawing Room you went into the Eating Room, which was low with three awkward windows, and two of them to the west, the worst aspect for an Eating Room . . . There were two few Bedchambers upon the second floor and the Passage leading to them was dark . . . I must not omit to mention the open Court in the middle of the House, which, by letting in the weather, had a very bad effect upon the whole House, making it cold and damp." One might properly wonder how any of the previous Lords and their ladies could have stood living there at all.

The work of improvement was entrusted to James Wyatt, the Surveyor of the Royal

Works and one of the foremost architects of the time. The plans submitted by this gentleman were acceptable but considering his many other assignments it is not surprising that he only visited the site once and then soon appointed a Clerk of Works in his stead. The latter, however, was not properly advised or guided and was therefore soon dispensed with by Townshend.

The work of carrying out the Wyatt plans was now committed to an unnamed craftsman who had been employed on Townshend's own house at Horningham in Norfolk. The man had also assisted Wyatt in constructing the Pantheon in London's Oxford Street and this confirms that the glass dome that was added at Culford was part of the original Wyatt plan.

The changes which now took place included easier access for coaches to enable them to draw up at the door, by erecting a long portico that became even more grand when eight Ionic columns were added in 1828. There was to be much greater access of light to the inner rooms, with the Eating and Drawing Rooms now lit from the south, and the central court glazed over with a dome and including the 'Great' and 'Little' staircases. The Library was to be on the west side, 'a proper aspect for a bookroom' and even the kitchens were given most careful attention. These were raised from the cellars, moved to the south so as to be of best use to the rooms that they most served and yet also shaded and partly camouflaged with hornbeams so to preserve the Hall's overall appearance.

Much of the actual labour was carried out by the firm of de Carle, stonemasons of Honey Hill, Bury St. Edmunds, and what was almost certainly a final account in March 1794 shows a sum of £2014.8s.7½d. The Earl wrote to his brother, "I am convinced I shall find the house at Culford just what I would wish and that I shall like it infinitely better than a *more magnificent* building . . .' My emphasis is to suggest that perhaps ideas of a lesser Blenheim that may first have occupied the thoughts of this national soldier and diplomat were tempered by the facts of a certain degree of economy as well as his absences in a life of much travelling. But more of this latter anon.

To complete this facet of the Hall story we might note that in 1807 the main entrance was moved from the south to the north front of the house and it was George Wyatt who designed a semi-circular portico that would have stood in the centre of the present Inner Hall. It was demolished during the Cadogan ownership after 1894.

At the same time that the Hall was being reordered another plan was being made for the Park. In November 1790 the 2nd Earl initiated changes to the plantations when he wrote: 'I wish you would be so kind as to order James Cooper [the Estate Steward] to make what plantations you think proper for if I do not approve them I can cut them down on my return.' It was not until the alterations to the Mansion had been made by 1794 that serious and planned work in the Park was undertaken after Humphrey Repton had begun to be employed. Repton was a native of Bury St. Edmunds and a past Scholar of King Edward VI Grammar School there and his suggestions for the lake and canal were still being implemented in 1795. His basic principles were 'to enhance the natural beauty and hide the defects of the landscape; to give the appearance of expanse and freedom by masking the boundaries of the property; and to cancel any evidence of 'art', so that the landscape appeared 'natural' and uninfluenced by man'. Since the Hall had very little by way of natural eminence Repton planned to have the water features flowing at the lowest level possible and so he rearranged the existing lake contours and as a result had to provide a bridge to allow the normal park entrance from Fornham Lodge to continue to be used. It was always said that this was constructed from the iron provided by several cannon captured by the Marquess's troops in India and certainly the dates would fit. What has only recently been learnt is that this construction may now claim to be the first iron bridge in the land albeit of less impressive dimensions than the hitherto famed erection at Ironbridge in Shropshire. Repton also suggested moving the kitchen garden from the south to the east side so as to improve the landscape view from the Hall and the de Cane account books show that there was work on new hot houses, heating pits, garden steps, a well-head, a 58 gallon stone trough and new Garden House.

Yet the owner of the Culford estate had more to manage than what was immediately on view. As was stated in an earlier part of our story the Bacons had purchased the additional manors of Ingham and Timworth and the Lords Cornwallis pursued a common policy of enclosure from 1714. Extant deeds between 1735 and 1754 relating to land and buildings in Timworth show that there was a gradual purchase of both freehold and copyhold land whilst also reserving to the family all the common rights that also went with each purchase.

In the mid-1760s the Revd Nicholas Wakeham of Culford made a series of detailed sketch maps of all the glebe land in the 3 local parishes but by 1793 all such land had disappeared and by the Spring of 1798 the 2nd Earl was ready to proceed to the enclosure of the entire parish of Timworth. A similar process took place in regard to Ingham and Wordwell and on 23 April 1798 the old road from Timworth to Fornham Green was legally closed and a new connecting road from the Turnpike to Timworth Green was opened instead. It should be recorded that in exchange for these transfers of glebe land there was not only a comparable grant of other property but new or improved clergy houses were provided at Ingham, West Stow and Timworth.

It only remains to mention the village at Culford which was close to the Hall. This brought some revealing comments from Repton.

". . . village hovels often obtrude on the dignity of a Mansion, and in many cases have been sacrificed without mercy to the necessary parade of solitary pomp. It is hardly possible for a Noble family to reside at a shooting seat without the aid of more labourers than it is convenient to lodge under the same roof, and Benevolence will surely commiserate those who are frequently obliged to walk many miles after a hard day's labours to reach their miserable homes . . . It is on this principle I am of the opinion there is no impropriety in showing that a house has offices provided they hold a subordinate place in the composition. In several cases where it has been impossible to conceal a village by plantation I have advised neatness of repair whereby it should become a part of the improved scenery by giving each hovel some simple design of ornament . . ."

General Lord Cornwallis

Jemima Tullekens, wife of 1st Marquess Cornwallis

Earl Cornwallis had already decided not to embark the village and writing again to his brother, James, from India, he assured him that "no person shall ever persuade me to demolish it". Repton's plan was to avoid the village by making a new wooded curved drive from the bridge in the village street and passing through the Laundry Meadow and roughly along the line of Butcher's Road. This was not in fact carried out but in 1804 permission was obtained to divert the highway along its present route so that 'through traffic' was carried round the Park. It was after his time that more drastic changes in the street and houses were made.

In July 1768 however Culford village still clustered round the Church and its inhabitants came out of their cottages to welcome the next Lord Cornwallis, the 2nd Earl, when he brought home his bride. She was Jemima Tullekens, the 21 year old daughter of Colonel James Jones, of the 3rd Foot Guards, and his wife, Mary, whose grandfather had been a Dutch General, Willem Tullekens. Jemima was also the sister of Arnoldus Jones who was duly to change his name to Skelton on inheriting property at Brenthwaite in what was then called Cumberland. How the couple had first met is not known but it was probably through one of Cornwallis's army Guards friends. What was surprising was that whilst occasionally a member of the aristocracy might marry someone of the middle-class it was normally because the latter was able to contribute a substantial fortune – and this was certainly not the case with Jemima. When her father died in 1758 and his house and goods were sold by auction they raised the very modest amount of £2,805.9s.6d. The only conclusion to be reached is that Charles married Jemima for love. What is certain is that Jemima was devoted to her husband.

The couple had been married at St. George's, Hanover Square, on 14 July and the location for this fashionable wedding was highly fitting for a bridegroom who was by now an Aide-de-Camp to George III and a Groom of the Bedchamber to His Majesty. His Lordship was 29 years of age and the periods that the couple were to spend together at Culford were very happy and enjoyable ones though the sad-looking, if beautiful, young wife conveys the sense of grief that she always felt when Charles' military duties took him away from home.

The 2nd Earl may well have acquired his fascination with soldiering from hearing about the exploits of his uncle Edward in faraway campaigns and he was certainly well prepared to follow in his uncle's footsteps. Though educated at Eton, which he warned his own son was not an altogether easy experience, he then turned down the chance of a University course so as to travel and acquire practical military skill elsewhere. As the Military Academy at Sandhurst only opened a year after Charles died it is no surprise to see him having a formal audience with the King of Sardinia and his family before being enrolled in the Military School at Turin. He then spent time with German and Swiss military figures which only stimulated his desire for active service, and after a brief period in Prince Ferdinand's forces he was gazetted as an Ensign in the Grenadier Guards at 17 and was an Aide-de-Camp to the Marquis of Granby in Germany 2 years later. At 23 he had become Lieutenant Colonel of the 12th Foot, having fought at the battle of Minden and commanding troops at Kirch Donkern whilst also being the 'family' M.P. for Eye from 1760 to 1762.

It was during the Rockingham ministry that he became Lord of the Royal Bedchamber for a year and in addition to his post as an Aide-de-Camp to the King he was at the time of his marriage also Chief Justice in Eyre, South of the Trent, and Colonel of the 33rd Foot. He was to retain this latter position until he died. At 29 he was thus a most experienced and reliant servant of the Crown but more will be said of his own family and further career when we have looked at what happened to his sisters.

The first child of the 1st Earl was another Elizabeth who may have been born in London (1 September 1723) but was brought to Culford to be baptized on 1 October. She was to marry in 1753 a Bowen Southwell, Esq. the son of Colonel William and Lucy Southwell and thereby a cousin of the 2nd Lord Southwell, a Suffolk peer. The young man took his first name from his mother's family for she was the younger daughter and co-heiress of William Bowen of Ballyadam, Queens County, in Ireland. On his father's side he was descended from Sir Thomas Southwell of Castle Mattress who was created a baronet by Charles II and buried at Rathkeale in County Limerick. Unlike the other branch of the Southwell family with which the Cornwallises had been linked by marriage in Tudor times Sir Thomas, his son Richard and his grandson, Thomas, the 1st Baron Southwell, were firm Protestants and it was the constancy of the last named, even when taken prisoner by supporters of James II, that impressed King William and led to his being honoured with both rank and offices between 1690 and his death in 1717. He had married Meliora, eldest daughter of Thomas, then Baron Coningsby, of Clanbrassil, County Armagh, and later Earl of Coningsby, and was succeeded by his eldest son, Thomas, as 2nd Baron.

Thomas's brother William had shared in many of his early exploits and distinguished himself by his courage and leadership. These qualities were amply displayed in the military career that followed and Charles, 2nd Earl Cornwallis would have been well aware of his bravery in Spain under Marlborough, as a result of which Colonel Southwell was made temporary Governor of Monjuich in Catalonia. A year later he sold his Regiment to Colonel Harrison for 5000 guineas and withdrew to his seat in Ireland, becoming the M.P. for Baltimore until his death in 1719. Bowen's mother died in 1733 and the young Guards officer came to know his prospective brother-in-law in the Service.

Charlotte, the 1st Earl Cornwallis's next daughter, born in 1724 was both attractive and strong but like her sisters had but a modest dowry and could not therefore expect to make a 'brilliant' match. She did not in fact marry until she was 29 and then, to the disappointment and with the disagreement of her parents, fell in love with the Revd Mr. Spencer Madan. At first the couple agreed neither to meet nor to correspond but coming across each other accidentally when she was looking after an uncle their love was renewed and Charlotte at last obtained her father's assent but never that of her mother. After their father's death Charlotte was to become even more dependent for help and guidance on her brother Charles and though he found her wheedling an irritation he still did all he could to help the Madans financially.

Charlotte's husband was the second son of Colonel Martin Madan and Judith, the daughter of Judge Spencer Cowper, and thereby the aunt of the poet, William Cowper.

Spencer Madan was born in 1729, attended Westminster School from 1742 and in 1746 entered Trinity College, Cambridge. In 1749 he graduated with a B.A. as Third Wrangler, was an M.A. in 1753 and took the Doctor of Divinity degree in 1756. He was at first intended for the Bar like his elder brother Martin, but influenced by Martin's dramatic conversion and example he decided, prior to taking his M.A., to seek Holy Orders. He was elected to a College Fellowship but after a short residence he accepted two livings in Lincolnshire, as Vicar of Haxhay and Rector of West Halton, close to the Humber.

Thereafter his career developed steadily upwards. In 1761 he was appointed a Chaplain in Ordinary to the King, a position which would certainly have brought him into contact with the 2nd Earl Cornwallis as they both attended at Court. It cannot have been this connection which led to Madan's marriage with Lady Charlotte Cornwallis since this took place in 1757 and it seems more likely to have been both the military connection of Colonel Madan with either of the Earls and the clergy link with Archbishop Frederick and Bishop James.

From 1770 to 1794 Spencer Madan was a Prebendary of Peterborough Cathedral as well as being the Rector of Castor in Northamptonshire. In 1776 he was also granted the 'sinecure' of Ashley Rectory in Berkshire. During these years he and his wife had three children: Spencer in 1758, William Charles in 1760 and a daughter also called Charlotte.

Spencer Junior followed his father as a King's Scholar at Westminster and was elected to Trinity, Cambridge in 1776. The genes of his notable relative, the poet of Olney, had already revealed themselves in his grandmother and his uncle Martin who were both authors and poets but this young man gained the Sir William Browne medal for Latin epigram at Cambridge in 1778 and his poem 'The Call of the Gentiles' secured the prestigious Seatonian Prize in 1782. As a preparatory exercise for ordination he produced a translation of the Latin work of Grotius's 'The Truth of Christianity' which subsequently ran to three editions. After a curacy in Wrotham, Kent, he became first Rector of Bradley Magna in Suffolk and was then presented by his uncle, Bishop James Cornwallis to the prebend and vicarage of Tachbrook in Warwickshire. In 1787 he was given the living of St. Philip's, Birmingham and a year later he succeeded his father as Chaplain in Ordinary to the King.

The uncle's influence was not over for in 1790 he became a Canon Residentiary of Lichfield with appointments as Chancellor of the Diocese of Peterborough in 1794 and the post of Prebendary to follow. These latter preferments are easily explained for whilst the son was making his way in the Church his father was also honoured. In 1792 Spencer Senior was promoted to the See of Bristol as Bishop and in 1794 he was further translated to Peterborough where he remained until his death, aged 84, on 8 November 1813. His tomb there bears the following lines:

> "In sacred sleep the pious Bishop lies:
> Say not 'in death' - a good man never dies."

He was a man of austere habits who to the end of his life rose very early to light his own fire and study the Scriptures in Hebrew and Greek before the day's duties began. It is reported that when starting his final round of confirmations and visitations he remarked, "I would prefer that I die in the discharge of my duty than that I should live a little longer by reason of neglecting it." Such was the husband whom Lady Charlotte Cornwallis married and with whom she shared the delights of music and scholarship until 1794 when she also died though not before seeing her husband honoured with the See of Bristol. That is why she was buried, aged 68, in the Abbey Church at Bath.

Their second son, William, also chose the Army as his career and after having been chosen as an Aide-de-Camp to the Marquess during his time in India went on to become a Colonel, like his grandfather. The daughter, Charlotte, became a most charming young lady and in Squerryes Court near Westerham, Kent, there can be found a delightful portrait of her in a corner of the main living room. Why she should appear there is because two years after the death of her mother the Bishop married again and his bride on this occasion was Mary Vyse, daughter of William Vyse of Lichfield and the sister of William, the Archdeacon of Coventry. Charlotte's stepmother had no children of this marriage but she proved to be a true friend and parent. She and Charlotte no doubt spent many happy hours visiting one of the family homes connected with the Vyse family – Squerryes Court – and so honoured was that family to have this Cornwallis connection that on the upstairs landing there was placed a noble bust of Charlotte's uncle, the 1st Marquis. It is still there.

Charles's next sister, the Honourable Louisa Cornwallis, lived but a short time and was buried 4 January 1725, and this, sadly, was also the case with another child, Lucy, who was born 13 October, 1727, but died 4 days later. In the West Porch of Culford Church there is a slab that commemorates her interment. It thus becomes clear that whatever the benefits and surroundings which the nobility enjoyed the danger of childbirth in that age was no respecter of persons.

Happily the next daughter, Mary, baptized on 6 June 1736, survived infancy and was still at home and unmarried when she was 33. It was then that a Bedfordshire widower came into her life and within a year they were married. His name was Samuel Whitbread.

"Bedfordshire", says Roger Fulford, the biographer of Whitbread's son, "is certainly not an arresting county for the headlong sightseer, since it is neither distinguished by dramatic scenery, nor studded with antique architectural fragments." Yet Bedfordshire was far from unknown to the Cornwallises and several of Mary's family predecessors originated from that area. Like Suffolk it is still largely agricultural and in the words of an early 20th century devotee of the county: "it's all deuced pleasant". Mary's ancestor, Dame Jane Cornwallis (or Bacon), would have associated the area with her close friend, Lady Russell, Duchess of Bedford, and mention of the Russells serves to underline the fact that if there was one feature that Bedfordshire lacked it was its complement of noble families. Still, says Roger Fulford, "if the clay soil and clear air of Bedfordshire proved fatal to the feudal aristocracy, it combined to produce a sterner breed of famous sons [like] John Bunyan and John Howard – the prison reformer . . . Among them was Samuel Whitbread, father of the subject of this biography." (p. 3)

Apprenticed at 16 to a London brewer called John Wightman, for the huge fee of £300 Samuel Senior completed his indenture by opening up a small brewery on his own account with two partners. It was in Old Street in the City. Setting up at just the right moment when home-brewing was on the decline, and a whole new breed of hefty men in the London markets needed porter and stout, the elder Samuel soon made what Horace Walpole rudely called 'his insolent wealth'.

If his business success was phenomenal he was less successful with his family plans. In his thirties he married a Harriet Hayton whose lawyer father owned property in Ivinghoe and through whom Samuel became linked to the Duncombe family. It was into this family that two earlier Cornwallis girls had also married and it may thus have been this link that led to a present acqaintance with the Whitbreads.

In the Whitbread home at The Barns, Cardington, two girls were first born and then a son, also called Samuel, in 1764. Sadly the children's mother died only 6 weeks later, too late to enjoy the new Bedwell House, near Hatfield, which Samuel Senior had arranged to be their future family home. Still standing in 1967 the property testified "to the well-lined pockets and to the stylish, up-to-date taste in country house life which influenced the family that bought it". (p. 5)

Though he also had a home in Westminster it was to Bedwell house that Samuel Senior would drive most summer evenings and one of his daughters has recalled the house of those days:

"its pointed roof, old staircase and window, old yew and fir trees hanging over it as you drove in at the gate, through a double avenue of oak, on a summer evening it had a most captivating charm". (p. 6)

It was such an experience that Mary Cornwallis was to enjoy because 5 years after his bereavement Samuel asked for Mary's hand in marriage and she accepted. To have as his wife a niece of the Archbishop of Canterbury and a sister of such public figures as her brothers, Charles a Marquess and James a Bishop, might be thought to have given Samuel ground for new social pretentions but we find him writing to his first wife's brother as follows:

'It is both my wish and intention to keep up the connection that has subsisted between our families . . . Lady Mary is particularly desirous it may be continued, and I will answer for her behaving in all respects accordingly.' Samuel was also, it has to be remembered, a friend of William Pitt and Samuel Johnson.

Sadly the new wife was to have little chance of acting as her new husband wished for she died in giving birth to a daughter, Mary Elizabeth, in December 1770. She had been married just a year. The daughter was in due course to marry into the Grey family and become the great-grandmother of Viscount Grey of Fallodon.

Lady Mary's death by no means ended the links between her new family and the Cornwallises though the twice motherless children were largely brought up by their grandmother, Mrs. Hayton, and her unmarried daughter. Elizabeth, Lady Cornwallis, the 1st Earl's widow's influence is seen in the choice of Eton as a school for Samuel Junior with the College Register describing the boy as her grandson'. Even though Samuel Senior had relinquished his iron regime of upbringing enough to encourage foreign travel for the boy from the age of nine it was Samuel Junior's time at Eton from the age of 11 that gave him a sense of liberation. It was there that he eventually made friends with Charles Grey, the future Prime Minister, William Lambton, father of the celebrated Lord Durham and Richard Wellesley, a noted future Governor-General of India. It was the first of these friendships that led to both his and his youngest sister's marriage with the Greys.

Meanwhile the 1st Earl's sons were becoming men and taking up their careers. The eldest, Charles, whom we have already briefly met, was to become a figure of national and lasting fame and is still probably the one member of the family whose name and exploits are most widely known. As he would have been the first to acknowledge he came of a distinguished line and the many talents which he displayed were what we might now describe as the expression of long inherited genes. Nevertheless, it is not simply the possession of inherited abilities which makes any man or woman. It is the exercise and application of them that counts and Charles Cornwallis, 2nd Earl and 1st Marquess, was to reveal a healthy appetite for engaging in life.

His career following his marriage can be generally divided into four parts – his participation in the War for American Independence, his work as Master of the Ordnance, his engagement as Viceroy of Ireland and his double stint as Governor and Commander-in-Chief of British India. For those who might wish to pursue the full story of these years certain books will be mentioned in what follows but I shall attempt, albeit all too briefly, to cover all the most salient issues and events in what was by any standards a very important life.

It is quite obvious from what has just been said that the Marquess was a man of considerable ability, strong principles and an immense sense of service, to his King, his family and his country. What has not been touched on thus far, however, is the effect that these qualities had on those nearest and dearest to him, his wife and two children.

Mention has already been made of the sadness Countess Jemima displayed when her husband's military duties caused them to be separated. This might appear strange in the case of a Colonel's daughter but strange or not she was always deeply affected by each such occasion, especially after the birth of her two children, Mary in 1770 and Charles, Viscount Brome, in 1774.

Before his son was two years old the American war had broken out and the 2nd Earl was given command of a Division. Jemima was so upset by the prospect of what might ensue following this going overseas that she even prevailed upon his uncle, the Archbishop of Canterbury, to persuade George III to allow Lord Cornwallis to return home and relinquish his command. His Grace was successful in his pleading but

Cornwallis, as a professional soldier, was unwilling to comply with his wife's wishes and did not come home until January 1778 after an absence of almost 2 years. Even then it was only on official leave of absence and in April his sorrowing wife and children accompanied him to Portsmouth as he left for another tour of duty across the Atlantic.

Jemima bade him farewell and returned to Culford. The park there was beautiful with the trees opening up in their soft green and the new families of birds occupying their branches. Yet the nightingale's song on summer nights only heightened the sense of sadness that the lonely wife felt and even with the love and affection of her growing children she found no consolation. Her grief, not lightened by the news of the conflict and terrain in which her husband was engaged, gradually assumed dangerous proportions and she became seriously ill.

Towards the end of 1778 her doctors and household attendants realized that her condition was becoming dangerous and this time, on receiving word of how she was, Lord Cornwallis set sail immediately, arriving home at the end of January 1779. But he was too late. Nothing could be done to save his wife and she died on 14 February.

Lady Cornwallis's personal maid later made clear that she died of a broken heart and had requested that a thorn tree be planted as a sign of the sorrow which had killed her. The inscription on her coffin reads:

"Jemima, Countess Cornwallis, died February 13th, 1779, aged 31½ years." A thorn tree still grows near the Cornwallis vault on the north side of the Church, expressive not only of Countess Jemima's sorrow but of her husband's anguish at losing her so soon.

It is when you know this side of the 2nd Earl's personal story that you the better understand some of the more commonly known facts of his military and diplomatic career. You appreciate for instance his disappearances from the battlefields of the eastern States of America when his continuing presence there might have seemed most profitable. One understands better why he never remarried despite the obvious needs of his daughter and heir but one can also appreciate the evident sympathy and understanding that Lord Cornwallis was to demonstrate in his dealings with Catholics in Ireland and the children of Tippoo Sultan in India. His frequent letters to his own children certainly deserve an edition of their own.

One such letter that may give a flavour of the rest was written in February 1787 when he had arrived in Bengal, having been made a Knight of the Most Noble Order of the Garter. His son was 13 and at Eton:

"My dearest Charles,
        The intelligence packet arrived here on the 11th of this month and to my great joy brought me your letter of the 14th of June . . . I am a Knight and no Knight, for my Stars, Garters and Ribbons are all lost in Arabia and some wild Arab is now making a figure with 'Honi soit qui mal y pense' round his knee. I hope you have got enough French to construe that, but I own it is not a very easy sentence. If I continue to hear good

accounts of you, I shall not cry after my stars and garters.

Your most affectionate father,   C."

The Marquess would have heard from his younger brother, the Bishop, who had agreed to be a guardian to the boy as well as of the Estate. For the moment, however, the father and his children were again separated by the War in America. The most recent commentary on the conflict, William Seymour's "The Price of Folly", 1995, offers some perceptive judgements on Cornwallis's contribution whilst Franklin and Mary Wickwire, in the first of their two closely researched studies on Charles's career, "Cornwallis and the War of Independence", make his position regarding this seminal event very clear. Anyone wanting to get a balanced picture of Cornwallis's involvement from 1776 until the handover at Yorktown in 1781 could not do better than refer to these two accounts.

Two things need to be said by way of preliminary comment. The first is that, contrary to general opinion, the idea of independence for the American colonies did not suddenly erupt with the famous Boston Tea Party. Anyone who takes the trouble to read Theodore Draper's book, "A Struggle for Power", (1996) will be left in no doubt that the seeds of separation from Britain or a real measure of self-government were being planted during the whole half century before there was any open conflict. As early as 1723 a British agent was reporting the views of many of those American colonists amongst whom he moved:

"such as, His Majesty has no business in this country, he is our nominal King, but has not one foot of ground among us, neither he nor his deputys or Governours [*sic*] have anything to do here, the Country is ours, not his . . .Yet still H.M. shall be heartily prayed for by us, as our titular King, but we ourselves must have the uncontrollable power, to act despotically as we please [for] the true state of this country has never yet been known to H.M. or his Ministers, but all huddled upon secrecy and juggle . . . what wonder then his Governour is called blockhead, and has dead dogs and cats throwen into his coach." (p. 59)

In 1733 the Marquis d'Argenson, Louis XV's Secretary of State for foreign affairs, left a remarkable collection of 'Pensées' and amongst them appear these words:

"Another great event is being prepared on this globe . . . I say that one fine morning you will see these dominions (in North America)separate themselves from England, rise and set up an independent republic, as Holland did with respect to Spain. These English colonists already refuse to obey; they have their own will . . . One day when they are driven to the extreme, their limit overreached, will they not be able to say, Why should we be dominated by England from Europe? Let us be our own masters and work only for ourselves." (pp. 78f)

Nor was this all. There were, in Britain itself, loyal and highly respected Members of Parliament and the nobility, to mention no others, who had growing and informed sympathy for what it was that the colonists might be feeling and seeking. Of relevance to our present story is the fact that the 2nd Earl Cornwallis was one of that particular group of people. This is how the Wickwires have described the situation:

"Although Cornwallis was not politically active to the point of seeking office, he foresaw the disaster that must come . . . He voted with the Rockingham 'whigs' against the Stamp Act in 1765 [but he] did not follow the Rockinghamites blindly, however. When in 1766 the British Government voted to repeal the Stamp Act, that retreat was associated with the Declaratory Act, a bill which proudly asserted Britain's right to legislate for the colonies 'in all cases whatsoever'. Lord Cornwallis was one of the tiny minority of 5 peers who voted against the Declaratory Act. During the recurring crises that followed, he sympathized with colonial grievances." (*War of Independence*: p. 41)

What might seem even more surprising is that in 1765 the 2nd Earl, "a sober and dignified man, a staunch supporter of society and the established order", might have been seen walking the streets with John Wilkes, whose very name seemed to epitomize public uproar and radical outcry. "But politics breeds strange bedfellows, and that tête-à-tête with Wilkes was a measure of the Earl's support for his party's views. His support brought him material reward" as we have already noted at the time of his marriage, but "despite the offices they helped him to obtain he did not follow them into opposition when the Rockingham ministry broke up in August, 1766." (*op. cit.*, pp. 44f)

He turned instead to Pitt administration and just because of his honesty and openness as a person, not characteristics best calculated to fit him for intense political manoeuvrering, he went on receiving favours from the Government. He became Vice-Treasurer of Ireland, was a Privy Councillor in 1770 and Constable of the Tower of London in 1771. The Wickwires here interpolate a very interesting passage

"Why he continued in the King's grace despite his opposition to government policy is something of a mystery. The only explanation seems to be the obvious one that the King liked him better than other Whigs. Probably George III liked Cornwallis for his domestic virtues . . . That the King saw so few men of that type around his court must have made the 2nd Earl yet more attractive to him." The fact of his ancestry, however, cannot have escaped the royal notice.

What was the supreme irony was now effected. In September 1775 this aristocrat was appointed a Major General of the army in North America and five months later raised to the rank of Lieutenant General. The man who at the dictates of his conscience had opposed the King's colonial policies was now compelled, by his duty to King and Country and by his military rank, to lead the King's troops in the endeavour to re-establish royal authority over the colonies." (*op. cit.*, p. 46)

So for the next six years the British Army across the Atlantic received Cornwallis's almost wholly undivided attention. It was indeed this 'attention' which most endeared Lt. General Cornwallis to his men and made him one of their most popular commanders. What struck them above all was his attempt to be a professional, his attention to their welfare through good administration and his evident determination to share in carrying through whatever plan or tactic had been decided. As the Wickwires say:

"The Earl's sense of discipline, justice and compassion made him more than Howe or

Clinton a part of the British Army in America . . . He could not write plays, as Burgoyne did, nor organise the festive revelries that entertained Howe in Philadelphia nor spend idle hours with a mistress as Clinton did in New York. He lived and marched and suffered with the army. He campaigned through the Carolinas on the same simple food as his men. Like them he went for a period with barely enough clothes to cover his body. Like them at one point he sickened and almost died. He never asked of his soldiers anything he was not prepared to do himself, from facing bullets to facing starvation." (p. 78)

It is when you recognize that he was this kind of soldier and leader that you also understand something of the anxiety and concern that was felt by his wife back home. The letters she received, the reports that circulated and the comments of those who came home on leave must have made her realize what trials and tribulations her beloved husband was undergoing. The more she loved him the more she must have suffered.

What was probably his greatest and most recurring tribulation was the plain fact that he was not ultimately in charge of the American operation. He had realized when he made his offer of service to the Secretary for the Americas, Lord George Germain, that he would initially be under another's overall command, whether it be Carleton's in Canada or that of Howe in the Eastern Provinces. That is why he specifically asked to be assigned to the Cape Fear River expedition where he would at least be in temporary sole charge until he had linked up with the main body of the army. It was not to be. Howe had already dispatched Clinton to the area whilst Cornwallis was on the high seas and therefore when he landed he was, at best, third in command in this highly important venture. "A friend of both Cornwallis and Clinton, Brigadier General William Phillips, reported the Earl as 'very happy to think he shall serve under an old friend and a man he has so good an opinion of'.

Neither Phillipps, Clinton nor Cornwallis could foresee that the campaign would end in a fiasco, bringing neither glory nor honour to the generals involved and that the stress of war in America would reduce the cordiality between Cornwallis and Clinton to mutual dislike." (p. 81)

The Battle of Long Island that followed helped to restore both the confidence and the hopes of these two commanders though they both kept their counsel as to the unwillingness of Howe to push home his victory in what would have been an almost knock-out blow for Washington. It was now that Cornwallis was summoned home by Germain at the insistence of his uncle, the Archbishop, and on behalf of a very distressed wife. During his stay in London he was actually summoned to testify at a Parliamentary Committee but he was adamant that his participation in one part of the operation prevented him from making any overall judgement. "He never revealed what he actually thought of Howe's conduct on that day. Unlike Clinton, Howe had at least led the British to victory" (p. 90)

In the autumn after his return to New York Cornwallis was given the opportunity he craved. Driven from their positions on the Hudson River the Americans began a withdrawal across New Jersey to the southwest. Whilst Howe consolidated his gains along the river he entrusted Cornwallis with the pursuit of the retreating enemy. It was undertaken vigorously and with such skill that General Greene's rearguard scrambled out of Newark as the British vanguard arrived.

Marching his men 20 miles a day over appalling tracks it was all the more galling to arrive on the Raritan River and find that New Brunswick was deserted. "His men were worn and hungry. They had been so intent on pursuit that they had not even taken the time to bake their flour into bread. Even had they been able to march farther that day, the artillery and baggage horses would have been too fatigued to move. Furthermore the Americans had torn down the only bridge over the river.

So Cornwallis stopped. His orders permitted him to give up at this point and he did have a bridge to repair. Yet even he subsequently admitted that "had I seen that I could have struck a material stroke by moving forward, I certainly should have taken it upon me to have done it." (p. 92)

What is singular, and not only in his own case, is what appears from time to time a singular reluctance to press the advantage against the enemy to a conclusion. The Wickwires, considering not only the events at Trenton and Princeton, but also his behaviour when at last he was in virtual sole command of the southern force in the Carolinas, put it thus:

"He displayed the same contradictory qualities – extraordinary energy, superb leadership and brilliant tactics, coupled soon after with foolish blunders, and an amazing insensitivity to those critical moments, great and small, which demand immediate and decisive action . . . Indeed, he was never dull on the battlefield and he was often brilliant. But in a prolonged endeavour it almost seemed sometimes as though he lacked the mental staying power, a form of patience – it was as if he grew bored or inattentive . . . Not until a decade later in India did he seem willing and able to devote his entire attention . . . and in India he won." (pp. 88f.)

It has of course to be realized that his next immediate return to England was to witness the death of his wife. That cannot have been an easy experience and the recognition, when he again sailed away from England's shores, that he was leaving 2 orphaned children must have exercised him greatly. When those concerns were allied to an increasing antipathy to his new chief, General Clinton, and also a recognition, however little voiced, that amongst those who were his opponents there were those, like Washington himself, who shared the high ideals and fraternal concerns of the Masonic Craft, it can be imagined why, from time to time, there might have been lapses from that all-out military application that marked commanders like Nelson or Napoleon.

It is thus, says Seymour, that in 1781 the Carolinas were lost and "the blame must be attributed almost entirely to Cornwallis. Cowpens was a disaster which Cornwallis regarded as a personal affront and he was determined to avenge it and speedily . . . The decision at the end to forsake [South Carolina, against Clinton's orders] and march north can be understood, but not condoned." (pp. 207f)

Hence we come to the closing act of the campaign. "Back in 1780 Clinton had put forward to Germain a plan . . . that showed the strategic advantages of an operation against the Delaware neck, that piece of land bordered by the Chesapeake and Delaware Bays. Later his thoughts were to combine this with a strike north up the Delaware against Philadelphia in conjunction with troops moving down from New York. This had received approval in London, but the extra 4000 troops required for it were not readily forthcoming . . ." (p. 209) What Clinton did not know until too late was that Cornwallis was already on his way north to what they both then regarded as a strategic centre at Yorktown. As Cornwallis, however, had not secured his rear at Charlestown and in South Carolina there was a real danger that unless there was an injection of new troops attacking Washington's forces from the north and/or coming as a relief force by sea, it was more than likely that Cornwallis would be isolated and destroyed. That in effect was what happened.

From early July until mid-October Cornwallis prepared for, considered breaking out of, and finally endured, the siege of Yorktown by a much larger American and French force. Yet it was not until Cornwallis had not a single gun left firing that he made the decision to surrender. "At 10 a.m. on 17 October [1781] – four years to the day since Burgoyne had surrendered at Saratoga – he sent a note to Washington under a flag of truce requesting a cessation of hostilities, to which Washington agreed . . . It was indeed a clamant disaster and until recent times the largest and most lamentable surrender a British army had endured. It was also virtually the end of the war. Ironically, on the same day that Cornwallis asked for terms, Clinton at last set sail with 7000 troops aboard a convoy of 25 ships of the line . . . It is entirely possible that had he been able to muster his force in time to reach the Chesapeake on 11 October, the day he had given Cornwallis, the outcome at Yorktown might have been very different" (p. 225)

When on the afternoon of 19 October the British redcoats marched out to ground their arms in the field appointed Cornwallis pleaded illness and remained in his quarters. "Perhaps", say the Wickwires, "the illness was psychological rather than physical. Certainly he, as an English peer, had suffered a grand humiliation. On the 27th he received George Washington formally at his headquarters [and] gave the usual parole as a prisoner not to talk or to act against the United States . . . On November 4 he was on board the *Cochrane* and sailing to meet Clinton in New York . . . What would the King and Parliament say when he returned to England?" (pp. 387f)

In the event, and though he suffered a further indignity of seeing their ship bound for England boarded by French privateers, his reception back home was nothing like so troublesome as he might have anticipated. George III declared that 'he did not lay anything at the charge of Lord Cornwallis' which from someone who had desperately wanted to retain the American colonies was indeed surprising. Nor would the King hear of the Earl's surrendering his needed income as Constable of the Tower. He even enjoyed the support of both political parties since "the North government had blamed Clinton for doing nothing and had encouraged Cornwallis to his Virginia venture, while the opposition had blamed the North government for not giving the Earl sufficient support". (p. 7, Wickwire, *Imperial Years*)

Yet the choice of a suitable employment still eluded him. He first turned down the Ordnance and Ireland, and was temporarily but hectically involved in the Board of Land and Sea Officers as well as promoting his younger brother William as M.P. for Eye. He even found a personal visit which he proposed to the Prussian military reviews turned into an exercise in government diplomacy. It was an interesting lesson for what was to come later. Meanwhile he had some domestic issues to face.

If Charles, Viscount Brome, had been managing to come to terms with his father's absences and his mother's early death this does not seem to have been the case with Mary, his older sister. Though she sometimes went to visit her great-aunt Caroline, the Archbishop of Canterbury's widow, she often spent much time on her own at Culford. On 14 December 1785 a notice appeared in the 'Bury and Norwich Post':

"A few days since was married Capt. Singleton, of the Guards, to Lady Mary Cornwallis, daughter of the Rt. Hon. Earl Cornwallis of Culford near this town."

This union was not with the approval of the bride's father and Mary had run away to Gretna Green to be married whilst still only in her 17th year. It would appear that lacking physical affection in two areas where she might have expected it she sought it in the nearest sphere available. Her husband was Mark Singleton, an officer in the Guards, and a stepson of Sydenham Fowkes, the owner of West Stow Hall near Culford. This gentleman recognized that he should have prevented the marriage and though the boy was a second son he agreed to make a decent settlement and clear the young man's debts.

Faced with this fait accompli Lord Cornwallis "eventually reconciled himself to the inevitable and settled on Mary stock worth £400 a year". (Wickwire, p. 17) He also gave them a home in the Hall and allowed them to occupy it when he again left England's shores in 1786. However, when in 1789 he thought he could plan for his return to England from India after his tour of duty he wrote to his brother James:

"I leave it to your discretion, either to confine yourself to the repair, or to make alterations to Culford House, [but] at all events I wish it not to be inhabited next year and will give £200 to the Singletons for the hire of a house for that time . . ." It can be guessed that all was still not exactly 'at ease' in that direction.

Indeed "Cornwallis never forgot the elopement and never fully forgave Captain Singleton. In his will he left £10,000 in bank annuities. Interest on these dividends, the will stipulated, should go solely to Lady Mary 'exclusive of the said Mark Singleton and any future husband'. On her death the stock would revert to her children according to her wishes. During her life she could use it, if she chose, to forward their careers." (Wickwire, *Imperial Years*, p. 17)

In February 1786 the Prime Minister, Pitt, now pressed him to accept the appointment of Governor-General in India. Cornwallis, who had done his homework, was granted the terms he desired and having made further arrangements for his family in England and the 'family' of officers who would accompany him he set out to meet the beckoning East.

193

After a unusually swift passage for those days – from 6 May 1786 to 24 August – Lord Cornwallis landed at Madras and after a few weeks of adjusting himself to both the weather and the work that lay ahead of him he transferred to the seat of government in Calcutta. It was a mixed blessing for him to know that he was stepping into the shoes of two predecessors whose reputations required but little effort to surpass. Warren Hastings had gone home in 1784 under the shadow of impeachment and his successor, the large and bluff Sir John Macpherson, was described by Cornwallis as "certainly the most contemptible and the most contemned Governor that ever pretended to govern." What the Earl soon discovered gave ample support to such a judgement.

"Macpherson's system of jobbing and peculation, his duplicity and low intrigues, had sunk the national character for sincerity and honour. Cornwallis's main task throughout his term was to reinstate British reputation." (Thompson and Garratt, *Rise and Fulfilment of British Rule in India*, 1935, p. 171)

As but one example of what had been going on the Nawab of Oudh explained to his important visitor why he had got into serious arrears with the heavy tribute that had been imposed upon him, why his land was so desolate and how he could not plan his state economy because of the uncertain demands that might at any time be made on him by the previous European adventurers. When in particular Cornwallis asked why there had been no payment for the Corps of troops granted for his use the Nawab revealed that the whole transaction had been a pretence and General Sloper and his army colleague, now back in England, had simply divided up the amount allowed to them by the East India Company Board but had made no attempt to produce the troops it was supposed to provide. Cornwallis was so appalled at what he heard and saw that he at once reduced the Nawab's tribute by a third, removed the exemption on all Company trading in the Nawab's domains, stopped camp bazaar practices that again reduced the Nawab's income and forbade any Resident or other servant of the Company to interfere in the internal affairs of the Oudh government. The effect on the economy was not noticeable immediately but the impression made on the new Governor General's subordinates certainly was.

To enable Cornwallis to act like this Pitt had pushed his India Act through Parliament giving the holder of his office enlarged powers, especially over inferior Presidencies, even though in the present case the Earl's rank set him apart from any truckling to others. As one of his contemporaries put it:

"Here was no broken fortune needing to be mended: here was no avarice having to be gratified: here was no beggarly mushroom kindred wanting to be provided for: no crew of hungry followers gaping to be gorged."

Cornwallis's "military experience and talent, whilst not exceptional, were respectable and generally respected. He was indifferent alike to pecuniary gain and adulation, a man of sturdy courage and honesty exceptional in any century, and in his own almost a portent." (*op. cit.*, p. 171) In that situation there was a great deal to be said for government by the right kind of aristocrat.

Here then was a new kind of Governor-General who, instead of pouncing on any pretext to raise demands, listened courteously to reason and when convinced by facts responded with elementary justice. On finding the Nawab of Bengal 'as poor as a rat' he returned the congratulatory gifts which this ruler had made on hearing that George III had recovered from mental derangement, the gifts made to himself and those to everyone else from whatever quarter they came.

To deal with a succession of such problems he established the first bases for the later renowned Indian Civil Service. The Benares Resident was told that he must be content with a salary of Rs.5000 a month (or about £25,000 a year in modern sterling value), the Indian employees' salaries were all raised so as to remove the temptations of bribery, and new procedures and standards of behaviour were made known and then strictly enforced.

Nor was the tackling of local holders of office his only difficulty. The Prince of Wales (later George IV) "importuned the Governor General with monotonous regularity (but increasing diffidence and humility) to look after this or that young gentleman, in no single instance with success. In 1789 he pressed . . . that 'young Treves' should be given the chief criminal judgeship at Benares 'which is now held by a Black named Ali Cann'. Cornwallis pointed out that Ali Ibrahim Khan, the 'Black' in question, was 'a man of great talent and universally respected whereas young Treves was at the very bottom of the list of the Company servants. Yet whilst he thus began to improve the civil administration he encountered a harder task in the military quarter. It is true that he made some headway with the sepoy establishment and could claim that "I have abolished their dancing about in various forms to jig tunes, and have substituted marching to time so that a brigade of our sepoys would easily make anybody Emperor of Hindostan". On the other hand "the contemptible trash of which the Company's European force is composed, makes me shudder". The Duke of York fully understood:

"As for the accounts which You give of the State of the European Troops in the Service of the Company, it grieves me, though it does not in the least astonish me. It is totally impossible that they be otherwise than the riff-raff of London Streets got together by the Crimps (or pressmen) and the Gleanings of the different Gaols. The Officers are, in general, young men who have ruined themselves and are obliged to fly their Country or very low people who are set out to make their fortunes . . ." Was he too aware of the recent career of Warren Hastings?

Yet whatever the calibre of his men Cornwallis had quickly and seriously to give his attention to the politics that confronted him. Denys Forrest in his book "Tiger of Mysore" (1970) helpfully explains the task he had in dealing with Tipu Sultan. Indeed, despite the formidable problems which we have just indicated, one of his very first acts was to get down on paper the issues likely to set him on a collision course with that ruler. He had much to consider. Tipu was so ingrained a liar that he could not even see that sometimes the truth might be to his advantage. He was keeping British captives in defiance of the Treaty of Mangalore and he had already had some circumcised into Islam, trained some boys as janissaries and their sisters as dancing girls.

By 27 September 1786, a mere month after his disembarkation, Cornwallis had written an admirable Minute summarizing the whole situation. While confident that the offer of troops to the Marathas, Tipu's present opponents, by his immediate predecessors, "proceeded from the warmest anxiety for the public good I am equally clear that if so executed it would (a) amount to a breach of Article 1 of the Treaty, whereby both sides undertook not to help, directly or indirectly, the enemies of each other; (b) contravene the solemn injuction in Pitt's India Act against warlike commitments to the country powers." (Forrest, p. 113f)

In view of what has already been said about the state of his forces there was more than keeping to the strict letter of a treaty in what was at first Cornwallis's clear policy of 'keeping out of scrapes. 3 years later, however, and with Tipu having routed the Marathas and swept across a great swathe of southeastern India Cornwallis was beginning to have other thoughts. He wrote to Henry Dundas at the Board of Control on 5 December 1789:

"I cannot for my part believe that Tippoo [*sic*] has any intention of breaking with us but if he should resolve to do it he would be very unwise if he did not begin, as his father had done, by over-running the Carnatic and ruining our resources."

Cornwallis was not a man who sought 'military laurels in Hindoostan' or feared the risk of 'being beat by some nabob' but when at last Tipu launched his attack on Travancore the Governor-General must have greeted the news with a sense of release. Once he took command against this nabob in person there was no fumbling, no irresolution. There was also no quick fix. In training and organization immense steps had been made but transporting guns and supplies, not to mention the coordination of troops from the various principalities that were allies, across the whole of the sub-continent and throughout a whole year was an immense undertaking. Nor was his opponent lacking in skill and resource. It is therefore hardly surprising that the final battle was not waged until January 1792 when Tipu was caught and defeated at his capital, Seringapatam.

The terms of the Treaty of that name were severe but they were to ensure that open war disappeared for the next seven years. Tipu was compelled to cede half the territories he had acquired, to pay an indemnity of about £8 million and to hand over two of his sons as hostages. Cornwallis assured those negotiating for Tipu that 'as he had only one son himself he experienced the affection of a parent in more than an ordinary degree but even that child could not be received by him with greater tenderness than would Tipu's'.

When he offered to allow the choice of two of the three eldest he was given some curious reasons for the choices made. The eldest, Fath Haidar, the latter name being that of Tipu's father, was said to be obnoxious to his father, being illegitimate, and that is why his father was averse to losing him [*sic*]; Abdul Khaliq was about 8 and owing to a disease from infancy was not fit to be moved from the women's apartments – but on being produced was found to be about 10, well-bred, intelligent and quite healthy; whilst Muiz-ud-din, just a few months younger than the last brother, was said to be the favourite and chosen heir and his being handed over was the best proof of Tipu's sincerity. This choice moreover would enable the future ruler to become acquainted with the principal

Beechey full length of Charles, 1st Marquess Cornwallis

The private collection of Lord Braybrooke, on display at Audley End House, Essex
© ENGLISH HERITAGE PHOTOGRAPHIC LIBRARY

Lord Cornwallis receiving as hostages the sons of Tippoo Sahib

circa 1750   MATHER BROWN   1831

personages of the country. Forrest tells us that this too was a bogus offer as the real heir was a boy called Muid-ud-din whose existence was concealed so that one with a similar name could be substituted. The reception of the second and third boys named above has of course been the subject of many descriptions in both prose and paint. Forrest even tells us that it was Mather Brown's portrayal of the scene which now hangs in the Oriental Club, London, which led to his thinking of Tipu Sultan as a subject for a biography.

The handover of the boys was certainly a piece of oriental theatre. Led by 7 standard bearers carrying green flags and 100 pikemen with silver inlaid spears the princes each arrived on an elephant fitted with a silver howdah. A battalion of Bengal Sepoys formed the guard of honour and as the boys dismounted at Cornwallis's tent he took them by the hand to their appointed seats.

"These children , said their spokesman, "were this morning the sons of my master, the Sultan, but now they must look up to your Lordship as their father." The tall, rubicund and well-proportioned English peer responded with words that brought obvious relief to the children. In their long white muslin gowns, with rows of large pearls around their necks and further jewels in their turbans, they created an engaging sight and their bearing and obvious intelligence made a lasting impression.

Having each received a gold watch from their 'new father' the boys once more climbed back on to their mounts and returned to their father's camp. It was next day after the Earl and his staff had been ushered into Tipu's fine chintz tent, had admired the bearing of the Mysorean Guards and had seen a sword presented to Cornwallis and firearms to the boys, that the real transfer of the boys took place. Sadly their stay was to be much longer than anyone could have predicted for it was May 1794 before all the articles of the surrender treaty had been fulfilled. In the carrying out of every detail of that agreement Lord Cornwallis was as scrupulous as he was in the maintaining of his own people's laws.

When he found for instance that the Madras Government provided no stretchers for their native wounded but just pitched them into rough blankets he immediately blazed out at such false and cruel economy and changed the practice. Equally when a court martial leniently handled a surgeon who had neglected his wounded, or an officer who had thrashed an Indian to whom he owed money, "he scarified them with a rigour never to be forgotten. For nothing more infuriated him than assaults committed by Europeans on people of the country." (T. and G. p. 178)

In the time that remained to him "Cornwallis was deeply engaged upon those legal and land revenue reforms with which his name is almost as much associated as with the Seringapatam campaign – though not always so happily." Moreover his longed for return to England did not take place until October 1793 since the news had broken that France was at war with England and it was necessary to attack Pondicherry. It was thus at Madras that Cornwallis placed himself to control any such campaign but before he had to become so engaged it was from there that he boarded the ship *Swallow* for his return home.

On 23 February 1794 he stepped ashore in Tor Bay and with bitterly cold fingers announced to Dundas that his term of office was over and that when he left Madras 'our affairs in India were in the most prosperous state'. "It had indeed been a great Governor-Generalship. Though he may have been misguided in some points of policy, such as his famous 'Perpetual Settlement' of the land revenues of Bengal, he had set a standard of justice, disinterested government and rigid personal integrity from which there was no going back." (Forrest, p. 201) Cornwallis certainly hoped that for him there was no going back.

His return home was a happy one. He made a brief visit to Suffolk and then took up lodgings in New Burlington Street. It was there on 5 April 1794 that the Lord Mayor of London conferred on him the Freedom of the City and from there escorted him by coach to a banquet at the Guildhall. Honoured by the Crown with a Marquesate he was also granted £10,000 and a pension of £5000 a year for 20 years by the East India Company in return for forgoing the gratuity of £47,244 which the Company owed him. He also distributed his campaign prize-money of £6,148 amongst his troops. He brought some of his cannon to Culford but his greatest delight was once more to be reunited with his children and share again in their lives.

The local newspaper for 12 February 1794 commented:

"Few circumstances have ever given more general satisfaction to the inhabitants of this county than the safe arrival of Marquis Cornwallis after so long an absence; his private virtues are so well known to almost all ranks in this neighbourhood . . . The Marquis is now at his brother's house in Wimpole Street, Cavendish Square, where he arrived on Saturday morning. The news of the noble Marquis's arrival was most welcomely received on Thursday last at Eye where it was celebrated by the firing of guns, ringing of bells, etc. and in the evening the corporation and freemen were respectively entertained at the Town Hall and the White Lion."

Almost a month later there was further news of the family:

"Monday evening Marquis Cornwallis, accompanied by Lord Brome, Mark Singleton, Esq., and Lady Singleton, arrived at Mr. Edward's at Chesterfield Inn [Bury], at which place they slept the night, and yesterday morning set out for Culford Hall, near this town, where the Marquis and his family arrived yesterday to dinner, and we have great pleasure in saying, in a much better state of health than the public has reason to apprehend from recent accounts given in some newspapers."

The Marquess had certainly had his fill of being out of England and hoped now to be able to live the life of a country gentleman. During his time in India, and through the good offices of his brother, James, he had bought the estate of Little Saxham, possibly with the intention of eventually living there, but on reaching England and seeing the beauty of Culford he decided against this and was able to exchange Saxham for West Stow. This was in the year 1795, a very hot summer, as a further letter to Ross indicates:

"Culford, 20 September.

The same dry and hot weather still persecutes us and is equally hostile for shooting and to the turnips, and there never was a year so universally bad for partridges . . ."

In 1799 Lord Cornwallis further enlarged his estate by purchasing Wordwell from Lord Bristol for the hefty sum of £33,000, thus enlarging his lands to 11,000 acres. His years of service to his country were bringing him and his family wealth as well as distinction.

Yet the Marquess still had to find some worthwhile occupation. As a professional soldier his natural desire was for active service and being on good terms with The Duke of York, the Commander-in-Chief, he was quite prepared to be posted to a command under his direction. When a position on the Continent was at last approved it was soon obvious that more was involved than mere soldiering. The Marquess's skills as a diplomatist were also to be exercised and it did not take long for him to realize the confused and impossible situations in which he might find himself.

Within a month he had been given leave to return to London to explain the situation as between Prussia and Austria. That accomplished, Pitt still sought to employ this now experienced peer in an appropriate role. He dared to suggest that Cornwallis might be put in command of the Imperial troops but when it emerged that this could mean that in battle The Duke of York might have to acknowledge the Marquess as his superior officer the former excellent relations between the two men began to turn sour. Even when the whole project was shelved Cornwallis thought it only proper to write a long letter to the Duke trying to explain his own passive role in what had been intended.

At last, in February 1795, a further reorganization of his Cabinet by Pitt meant that the Marquess was appointed Master-General of the Ordnance. Since the Commander-in-Chief was not included in the new Cabinet's composition it meant that as the only professional soldier present Lord Cornwallis became the Government's chief military adviser. "There was", say the Wickwires, "need of advice. The British army was a confused and inefficient organization with various overlapping jurisdictions. Too many people had too much independent authority . . . so plainly, at the time Cornwallis joined the Cabinet Britain's military establishment needed overhauling and streamlining." (*Imperial Years*, pp. 190f.)

Compared with what he had had to oversee in India this task, even if it meant trying to make some reforms in the Army, must have seemed a comparatively minor one. Yet with less power and responsibility came more time for relaxation. He needed to unwind occasionally, to spend time with his family, grow his crops and shoot wildfowl. He leased a house in London but spent half his time in Suffolk.

Not that the job was, or was regarded by him as, a sinecure. He at once wore two hats. In his military capacity he commanded the Royal Regiment of Artillery, the Royal Corps of Engineers, the Royal Military Artificers and the Royal Corps of Artillery Drivers newly formed by his predecessor, the 3rd Duke of Richmond.

As a civilian controller he managed the Ordnance department with its factories that supplemented private suppliers, the erection of essential fortifications, especially at this time of threatened invasion by Napoleon, the provision of topographical surveys and the management of the buildings and cadets at Woolwich Academy. It was a responsible and extensive remit and Cornwallis undertook it with his usual gifts of common sense, dedication and energy. Whilst we cannot look in detail at what he achieved there were three areas in which he specially left his mark.

The most evident concerned the coastal defences. "He began a regular practice of consultation with the Chief Engineer, continued the triangulation surveys begun by Richmond, and travelled all about England to inspect the defences. Though the expected invasion never came (thanks to the Navy), Cornwallis tried his best to make sure that England would be prepared to hurl the French back if they landed." (p. 195)

Whilst he was not able to standardize the small arms supplies as he would have wished he was able to start bringing some direction into the establishment of an effective and adaptable artillery force. His objective was "that the Army should not scatter guns about, but form artillery into brigades under experienced officers. That way a force could concentrate massive firepower on specified positions. The future Duke of Wellington would do precisely that in the Peninsular campaign". (p. 200)

It was in the running of the Academy at Woolwich, however, and in the care he took of its personnel, that he made one of his most important contributions. He improved the skills and remuneration of the instructors, exercised more impartiality and discretion in the choice of candidates as cadets, even introducing a scholarship scheme for some of less favoured social standing, but made the standards to be achieved more exacting with dismissal for those who continued to slack or under-achieve. He also began a scheme of training for boys from age fifteen who might eventually be of value to John Company.

Overall, in the 3 years that he held the post, he truly made his presence felt. He prevented a mutiny at Woolwich, he significantly raised the salaries of crucial secretarial staff, he improved pensions especially for widows and orphans and in the case of a certain Mrs. Caddy he was even ready to break the rules out of sheer compassion. When he was again on the receiving end of the ordnance supplies he could be assured that the service was better than when he took it over.

In the meantime and following his years at Eton Charles, Viscount Brome, had gone on to St. John's College, Cambridge in 1791 and hence had graduated by the time his father came home. On attaining his 21st birthday he received his M.A. and was also appointed to the seat in Parliament for Eye, the town which so many of his family predecessors had represented. He was to retain this seat until 1802 when he became M.P. for Suffolk and this he held until in 1805 he took his seat in the Lords. His reputation throughout this period was that of a very likeable and kindly man who was "as much beloved as he was respected" and who was "held in great and deserved estimation".

On 17 April 1797, he married Louisa, the 5th daughter of Alexander, 4th Duke of Gordon, and brought his bride to live at Culford. His father, having already been disappointed at the manner of his eldest child's marrying, is said to have looked somewhat askance at his son's possible union with a family whose notoriety was disturbing. The loose morals of the Gordon parents were not exactly consonant with the standards which the Marquess set for himself and his heir. It is therefore revealing to discover in Brian Master's book, "The Dukes", a passage concerning the Viscount Brome's marriage which suggests that it was not entirely straightforward:

"Jane, Duchess of Gordon, who married three of her daughters to drunken dukes, married the fourth to the heir of Lord Cornwallis, but not without some difficulty. Cornwallis objected to the match because there was said to be madness in the Gordons. The Duchess re-assured him: 'I understand you object to my daughter marrying your son on account of the insanity in the Gordon family: now I can solemnly assure you that there is not a single drop of Gordon blood in her veins'." (p. 21) Whether this 'doubtful' assurance or his son's insistence carried the day the wedding clearly took place and in due course the daughter-in-law seems to have won her way into the Marquis's heart as also did her children, all girls.

Not that it happened all at once for in August 1797 the effect of house parties of elegant young men and women, patched and powdered, dancing by night and filling the house with hilarious chatter by day, seems to have irritated the weary warrior and he wrote to his friend, Major General Ross:

". . . The comfort of the country which I proposed to myself has suffered considerable abatement by the house having been completely full of young ladies in the highest spirits since Tuesday last. Thank God the Cadogans leave us tomorrow and the Townshends on Tuesday next . . ." One of those young ladies was Lady Emily Cadogan, then 19 years old, who was in time to become the great-aunt of the 5th Earl Cadogan who ultimately bought Culford Hall for that family.

It may not therefore be surprising that when Pitt, the Prime Minister, urged Cornwallis to go to Ireland as Viceroy and Commander-in-Chief, rather than India again for which he had already been sworn in, the opportunity to escape from a 'disturbed' country retreat was more readily accepted. Yet the disturbance in Suffolk was as nothing to that which awaited the Marquis in Dublin and its hinterland.

In Thomas Packenham's book "The Year of Liberty", first published in 1969, the story of the potentially explosive Great Irish Rebellion of 1798 is told in fascinating detail. Not least in that chain of events is the arrival and impact of this new Viceroy:

"In Dublin it rained. The extraordinary weather of the last seven weeks seemed to have broken at last, as the state procession of Privy Councillors, gentlemen ushers, axe bearers and the rest followed Lord Camden to the quayside. Otherwise nothing marred his send-off in the vice-regal yacht *Dorset* . . . The new Viceroy, Lord Cornwallis, had slipped into Dublin two days earlier, by the ordinary packet boat . . . At 59 he was now in indifferent health, and looked older than he was . . . Still, to Pitt and his party in Britain he seemed uniquely qualified, both as a soldier and a statesman, to bring peace to Ireland."

It is clear that Cornwallis was soon aware of what he had taken on. He wrote home, "The life of a Lord Lieutenant of Ireland comes up to my idea of perfect misery" and yet he was a man with a powerful sense of duty. Moreover he was never one who craved 'official magnificence' and he at once left the Castle in order to camp out in the smaller and more private Viceregal lodge in Phoenix Park. An account of his austere daily regime has come down to us from one of his officers.

Having breakfasted early he withdrew to work with his secretary and continued to do business and to write till 2 or 3 o'clock when he got on horseback and rode till six. After dinner he spent time chatting with his close colleagues or visitors and retired about eleven. What struck those who had most to do with him was that he was as unpretentious in manner as in his plain style of living but, says Pakenham, "perhaps this was the effect of his always having felt himself superior".

Cornwallis's policy had been agreed before he left England. It was to prevent any French invasion of Ireland, to impose needed discipline on the local army and to compel the surrender of the rebels. What was an irritant to some of his Irish officials was that he was known to have some sympathy with Catholics but the new Viceroy had a simple, soldierly attitude to such people – he completely ignored them. His recorded judgment sent to Pitt after just one week in the country might almost be a replay of what could still be said more than 200 years later. He wrote:

"The violence of our friends and their folly in making it a religious war, added to the ferocity of our troops who delight in murder, most powerfully counteract all plans of conciliation.

Having made a careful assessment of the situation Cornwallis began to act and "some fresh air began to blow down the dusty corridors of the Castle". He announced that he was determined to stamp out indiscriminate floggings and hangings by yeomen and magistrates, and such punishments could only be administered after a properly formed court martial. He told his Generals to offer a pardon to the rank and file of the rebel forces if they handed in their arms and took an oath of allegiance to the Crown. When this did not obtain the results he expected he even issued a general amnesty whereby the Leaders of the rebels would be spared their lives but were exiled abroad. This hardly served to endear him to the main figures amongst the Loyalists but when the Chancellor, Lord Glare, gave up his own previous opposition to concessions for Catholics and supported the new Viceroy the tide began to turn and the Marquess began to make headway. Glare had seen that what was far worse than Catholic antipathy was the likelihood of that being turned into Jacobinism – the very root of the recent Revolution in France. With the Chancellor at his side Cornwallis could take steps to bring the still raging conflict to a conclusion.

This meant finding a way to end the guerilla war in Wicklow and Kildare for "nothing gave the Loyalists a better pretext for violence than the Government's inexplicable failure to cope with these elusive insurgents in the bogs barely 20 miles from Dublin." (Pakenham, p. 273)

It was at just this moment that the very forces that seemed to be such a threat failed to agree on a joint plan to link up with their colleagues in the Midland counties and thus fell prey to the pursuing troops. The general rising that had been expected on 23 May never happened and even the daring Edward Fitzgerald admitted that he felt betrayed. The emergence of the General Amnesty at this point also helped to lessen the tense atmosphere but as soon as people began to surrender and claim their pardons another two problems emerged. The gaols were full to overflowing and the brutality shown to the so-called leaders in some areas when they were discovered dispelled much of the trust in a new administration. Cornwallis was to hear of one High Sheriff who claimed that 'only by cutting off people's heads could they be made to talk' whilst another local Captain, when acting as a trial witness, revealed his own brand of evil humour:

W. We met 3 men with green cockades - one we shot, another we hanged and the third we flogged and made a guide of.
Q. Whom was it you made a guide of?
W. The one we neither shot nor hanged.

If Cornwallis was adamant that there should be no executions without a fair hearing he was nonetheless determined to show firmness in government. His policy began to pay off and by mid-August 1798 General John Moore, who was noted as never having to call one court martial, wrote to his chief:

"The good conduct of the troops who were kept from marauding (in the Wicklow area), made to pay for everything they got, and not permitted to molest the people, together with kind treatment and encouraging language from the officers, gradually brought the people back to their houses.

During this initial period Lord Brome and his wife had come over to spend time with the Marquess. A tour of the centre and south of the island was eased for the new Governor by this presence of his son, though Lady Brome stayed in Dublin in the company of Lady Castlereagh. It is worth recording here that in 1787 Lord Brome had received this message from his father:

"I have no wish for any honours but as they may offer the road for fame and reputation to you. I have no desire to increase my fortune but as it may tend to increase your happiness. It is for you I am toiling.

Certainly with Brome he could talk about the improvements at Culford, the construction of the new bridge, the state of the partridges and those local matters which were so dear to the hearts of eighteenth century aristocrats. It was perhaps that kind of gossip that helped the Marquis to bear the seamier side of Irish politics into which he was now having to delve. And there was the danger too. "On the evening of 11 August 1799 he decided to walk alone to the Castle from Phoenix Park. During his stroll, a man disguised as a sentry on duty, supposedly a United Irishman, shot at the Lord Lieutenant and then fled. Shortly after that incident Brome and his wife left, probably to the Marquess's mingled relief and regret." (Wickwire, *Imperial Years*, p. 244)

Yet if the environs of Dublin and the south-east and central areas of the island were under control again there remained one further threat – the possibility of a French landing in the south- or north-west. So the Marquis began a new disposition of his local and English troops in order to combat any such eventuality. He was none too soon for on 23 August Joseph Stack, the Anglican Bishop of Killala, was holding a dinner party for some of his clergy and 2 officers of the Carabineers. They talked of the naval ships that had sailed into their bay that afternoon and of the extra visitors they might have as a result of the invitation which had been extended to those naval officers by the Bishop's sons.

The guests were indeed coming to dinner but when they rode up to the Bishop's 'castle' it was a French General who led the party. They had come, he told his astonished host, "to liberate them from the English yoke". It was news that naturally sent a further shudder through the folk in Dublin.

Within 24 hours some of the English militia soldiers were embarking on barges at the harbour of the Grand Canal for the journey to Tullamore and they were only a part of the 7000 men who were mobilized to converge on the French. "The same day", says Pakenham, "the Viceroy and his suite rode out of the capital. Cornwallis was to lead the army in person – the first Viceroy for more than a century to take the field against a foreign enemy." (p. 297)

It is not possible to dwell at length on the details of this campaign save to say that before the Viceroy arrived in the Mayo area some of his subordinates had failed to await his larger force, as he had ordered, and had suffered a shameful defeat which is still known as the 'Races of Castlebar'. His first report to Pitt must therefore have given him some displeasure but it also determined him as to his next actions. The Irish troops could not be relied on and must be stationed elsewhere and the task of confronting the invaders must rest squarely on the shoulders of his Scottish and English regiments. Armed with 4 brigades under his own English Generals he wisely blocked the two possible routes south which the French troops under General Humbert might select.

His prudence was redeemed. When the route of the enemy towards Dublin was clear he not only created a well-nigh invincible shield in their path but was able to send General Lake to pursue the enemy from the rear. The encounter when it came lasted half an hour and the French commander wrote to the Directory in Paris,

"After having obtained the greatest successes and made the arms of the French Republic triumph during my stay in Ireland, I have at length been obliged to submit to a superior force of 30,000 men." (p. 326)

Apart from the detailed mopping up of French or rebel groups around Killala and

Catlebar Cornwallis had in 6 months achieved his military objectives but he also had a political goal. He now cast his mind to "the great point of ultimate settlement, as he called the Union. But he confessed he could not see the most distant encouragement . . . Full political rights could be given to Catholics without any risk of their abuse, as Catholic representatives would be *in a minority in the new imperial Parliament*." (p. 294)

This, in Cornwallis's opinion, was the only just and certainly most expedient outcome to be aimed at. "I certainly wish", he wrote, "that England would now make a union with the Irish nation instead of making it with a party in Ireland and although I agree with those who assert that the Catholics will not be immediately converted into good subjects, yet I am sanguine to hope . . . that we should get time to breathe, and at least check the rapid progress of discontent and disaffection." (p. 338)

It was not to be. Urged above all by John Foster, the Speaker of the Irish Parliament, Pitt drew up the terms of a new alliance with all mention of Catholic Emancipation expunged and though Cornwallis made yet one more attempt to sway the Prime Minister's decision he finally and most regretfully withdrew from the fray. Some words of his in a letter to a friend were sombrely correct and prophetic:

"You will hear much of a Union: God knows how it will turn out. Ireland cannot change for the worse, but unless religious animosities and the violence of Parties can be in some measure allayed, I do not think she can receive much benefit from *any plan of Government*." (p. 340)

Cornwallis can hardly be said to have been a man with ideas before his time as the time has still not come 200 years later. Even if he had been allowed more time to pursue his firm but even-handed treatment of all the Crown's subjects on Irish soil, even winning over Pitt to most of his views in the next 2 years, there was one insuperable hindrance. "The alliance was encouraged by George III who claimed, with perfect truth, that the idea of Catholic emancipation drove him mad. Pitt was forced to resign, and Foster's friend, Addington, took over. Pitt's partners in Ireland – Cornwallis, Castlereagh and Cooke – all resigned in sympathy." (p. 354)

Cornwallis was not allowed to relax, however, for he was soon sent to France to lead the negotiations for peace with Napoleon Bonaparte. One late 19th century writer commenting on this period of his life says "as Indian affairs were the subject of a brief discussion by Bonaparte they clearly needed the capacity of the ex-Governor-General for dealing with politicians who were as disingenuous and subtle as any Indian prince could be".

Great Britain's aims were clear – the restoration of certain colonies, the evacuation of the French from Egypt, the freedom of certain Italian states, and Malta restored to the Knights of St. John, together with the exchange of prisoners of war and settlement of their expenses for maintenance during captivity. Bonaparte is clearly seen as simply wanting a period of peace before again waging war.

Since the Government were all too aware of the public desire for an attempt to end the conflict Cornwallis's departure was made as elaborate as possible. He was provided with a town coach painted yellow, with arms, supporters and crest, including the emblem of the Order of the Garter and containing reclining cushions of silk and morocco. 12 horses with silver harness and reins, tassels and toppings decorated with silk buttons, were sent on ahead and though he only travelled with Lord Brome and a small staff; 16 servants and 3 King's messengers would eventually attend him at the journey's end.

He left Dover early on 3 November 1801 and was in Calais late that evening. He pushed on to Paris along roads specially repaired, met Talleyrand, whom he at once mistrusted, on arrival on the 7th and by the 10th had an interview with Napoleon himself, Lord Hawkesbury also being present. After hearing many compliments paid by the First Consul to England's Monarch and having himself remarked on his host's abilities as both a commander and a legislator, Cornwallis withdrew, was later treated to fireworks and illuminations and certainly appreciated the greetings he received as he drove through the Paris streets. What was a surprise was that thereafter, except for one half-hour on their own, Cornwallis dealt not with Napoleon but his brother Joseph. What was clear in the private interview was that when matters regarding India or the other side of the Atlantic came up Cornwallis was speaking from personal acquaintance and would give not an inch. "Vous êtes bien dur", was his host's response.

Amiens was the location for the formal discussions that had been agreed from the start. Supposedly Cornwallis had simply come for a brief stay to sign a document that the diplomats had already concluded. That was far from being the case and debate went on through December, January and February. As if to enliven the otherwise very serious atmosphere that surrounded the whole event we have a letter from Lord Brome who had accompanied his father. It was written to a family friend, General Hope.

Charles had been enjoying trips to see the local sights around Paris in the morning and dinners attended by up to 40 or 50 people in the evening. He described their 'dress as that of mountebanks, and their manners those of assassins'. His attendance at the Legislative Assembly led him to remark that 'No puppet show could be more ridiculous and a man who came in so oddly dressed that it was natural to imagine that he was going to exhibit on the tight rope' turned out to be Citizen Chaptal, the Minister of the Interior. The fact that he was a chemist who had set up some of the largest factories for beet-sugar production did not enhance his status in the eyes of the chief negotiator's heir.

Though Cornwallis grew increasingly morose at the lack of progress, especially after Brome had returned home, he was always most civil to all the local notabilities, giving large dinners for them twice a week as he had been used to doing in Calcutta. He also rode every day unless prevented by extreme bad weather or the swelling of his legs which had first been noticed during his time in Dublin.

Yet the physical pain he thus occasionally suffered was as nothing to the constant frustration he underwent during the apparently interminable negotiations. "What can be expected", he wrote, "from a nation naturally over-bearing and insolent, when all the powers of Europe are prostrating themselves at its feet and supplicating for forgiveness and future favour, except one little island, which by land at least is reduced to a strict and, at best, a very inconvenient defensive?. . . I could wish myself again in the backwoods of America, at two hundred miles distance from my supplies, or on the banks of the Cauvery without the means of either using or withdrawing my heavy artillery."

At last, however, peace was agreed and the Treaty of Amiens signed on 27 March 1802. The table on which the Declaration was signed is still preserved in the Hotel de Ville and at the end of the apartment used there is a full-length picture of the Plenipotentaries and their attendants. There is even a street called 'Rue Cornwallis'. Cornwallis is generally considered to have distinguished himself further in his role as a diplomat. On the occasion of the Bicentenary of the Signing of The Treaty in 2002, the present 3rd Lord was invited to the occasion by the City. He was flown from London to Paris, met there and driven to Amiens where he was their guest for four days, together with the present Napoleon and his cousin.

Following this assignment he returned once more to Culford, hoping at last to find the rest and peace that he had well earned. The days passed pleasantly enough as the life of a country gentleman then could. He delighted in the company of his son and his son's children, albeit all of them were girls, and he mentioned them often in his copious correspondence. He seemed particularly anxious when "little Louisa has the whooping cough". His letters included some to the most eminent men of his day and usually discuss politics or the connection of various members of his and his sibling's families with other noted personages. Like many of his forebears the Marquess was ever aware of the importance of these relationships and knew only too well how crucial they had been in bringing the family to the eminence which it now knew. In several letters the state of mind of his beloved monarch, George III, always referred to as 'a certain Person', is clearly of great concern, whilst close family matters were discussed with his brother, James, who shows throughout that he had the Marquis's best interests at heart.

Early in 1805, however, Charles was appointed Governor-General of India for the third time, to replace Wellesley, the Marquess Wellesley. The expansionist measures which the latter had undertaken were proving too costly for a nation that was once more facing all-out war with 'the little Corporal'. To reverse Mornington's policy required an equally strong Governor-General and the fact that Mornington's appointment had probably been due to the fact that he was a protégé of the Marquess's uncle, His Grace the Archbishop of Canterbury, may have suggested such a recall as a tactful way out of a difficulty. His return had been on the cards ever since he left the sub-continent for, as *The Oxford History of India* records, "Pitt regarded him as an infallible cure for all ills" (p. 604) and Marshman in his *History of India* states: "Lord Cornwallis was Mr. Pitt's invaluable refuge in every Indian difficulty." (p. 279) The Most Noble Lord, a form of address by the way which he never encouraged, viewed it somewhat differently, as a letter to his friend, Lt. General Ross, makes clear:

". . . Nothing could induce me to return to India but the firm persuasion that it was the earnest wish of the Government and of the respectable part of the Directors. It is a desperate act to embark for India at the age of sixty-six; prepared, however, as I am to forego all further comforts and gratifications in this world for the sake of my family, I cannot sacrifice my character and my honour."

He left in March 1805 only to find on his return to Calcutta that his noble predecessor had sought, without consultation, to enhance the dignity of the Governor-General by building a vast house that was modelled on Kedleston Hall, Derbyshire, including a breakfast room which was 114 feet long and other luxurious interior apartments. On welcoming George, Viscount Valentia, in 1803 Wellesley is reported as having remarked that he wished India 'to be ruled from a palace, not a counting house; with the ideas of a Prince, not with those of a retail dealer in muslins and indigo'.

General Cornwallis's reaction was somewhat different. "Like it? . . . Not at all. I shall never be able to find my way about the place without a guide, nor can I divest myself of the idea of being in a prison, for if I so much as show my head outside a door, a fellow with a musket and fixed bayonet presents himself before me."

Yet though "he acted like the old Cornwallis he did not look like him. The long passage and the enormous climatic change had wrecked his constitution. Hickey and everyone else who saw him were 'greatly shocked to see how ill his Lordship looked . . .'

"Yet the governor general refused to heed the symptoms. He would not let ill health deter him [and] soon conceived it his duty to visit the army posts up-country and proceeded there by boat . . . Though he had no specific complaint, he simply seemed to wilt away." (Wickwire, *Imperial Years*, p. 265)

He was equally disturbed to find that General Lake was the military commander and had learnt nothing from his Irish experiences. Shortly before he died at Ghazepore, near Benares, on 5 October 1805, the Marquess was still protesting about Lake's treatment of the natives. What is certain is that he was buried in accordance with his oft-repeated cry:

"Where the tree falls, let it lie." A mausoleum marks the spot. The notice in the *Bury and Norwich Post* for 5 February 1806, told of how the *Medusa* frigate arrived at Weymouth from Bengal with the intelligence and made the not surprising final comment:

"A Nobleman highly distinguished and respected in this his native county, and whose absence therefrom at such an advanced age (however laudable the motive) was much regretted in this neighbourhood, where, probably, he might have continued in the enjoyment of health and life to a period more distant than that in which it terminated . . ."

A week later the same newspaper reported on the solemnities to mark his passing: "The principal inhabitants and corporation of Eye appeared in deep mourning on Sunday se'nnight as a mark of respect for the late noble Marquis Cornwallis, and walked in procession to the Church where the organ played that solemn anthem, "The trumpet shall sound and the dead shall be raised", which was very impressively sung by Mr. J. Clouting, organist. The tradesmen of this town and his Lordship's tenantry in the neighbourhood

Bust of the first Marquess Cornwallis in Lord Braybrooke's Sitting Room

© ENGLISH HERITAGE PHOTOGRAPHIC LIBRARY

"Jane Cornwallis" by Pickersgill

The private collection of Lord Braybrooke, on display at Audley End House, Essex
© ENGLISH HERITAGE PHOTOGRAPHIC LIBRARY

also paid a tribute to his memory by appearing in mourning on Sunday last, when the parish church of Culford was hung with black. It is needless to say how much his Lordship's loss is lamented as a sincere friend, an excellent landlord, and a liberal benefactor to the poor in the vicinity of his hospitable mansions at Brome and Culford."

A monument was later erected to his memory in St. Paul's Cathedral, London and the original model for this by Charles Rossi can still be seen in the chapel at Audley End, near Saffron Walden. The model was presented by Lady Mary Singleton, the Marquess's daughter, to her niece, Jane, the eldest daughter of the 2nd Marquess, when she went to live there as the bride of Lord Braybrooke.

Yet such reminders of the 1st Marquess are not the only ones still extant. In a comprehensive survey of "British Sculpture and the Company Raj" we are treated to no less than 3 other monumental reminders of the part he played in creating British notions of sound government and beneficial rule. No other figure in that theatre surpassed him in such commemoration nor in the variety of the styles adopted to signal his achievements.

The most impressive of these is possibly the Victoria Memorial in Calcutta by John Bacon Junior. A commentator has suggested that the subject of the memorial "seems burdened by the allegorical figures of Prudence and Fortitude, the sizable [sic] but characterless females endemic to 18th century sculpture" but when a discerning eye sees that Cornwallis also holds a sword in his left hand and a sprig of acacia in his right it is clear that his lifelong attachment to the Masonic Fraternity was not overlooked by the sculptor. The fact that the statue is set on a plinth above three steps, before an arch with a prominent keystone that is between two pillars, seems to emphasize the arrangement.

The monument in Fort St. George, Madras, has the Marquess dressed in his peer's robes with coronet, coat of arms, and trophies piled up behind him. He stands on a drum pedestal on which the main relief displays the historic reception of the Tipu Sultan's children. "Commissioned by the citizens of Madras to memorialise Cornwallis's military achievements the statue was erected with much pomp on 15 May 1800 . . . After several moves, including a sojourn in the Connemara Public Library, the statue is now in the museum at the Fort." (*Raj*, p. 64)

This depiction of the incident at Seringapatam is the link with the Flaxman monument made for St. George's Church, Prince of Wales Island (Penang). There a helmeted figure of Britannia gently directs an Indian boy to raise his eyes to a medallion above that displays the General in profile. To the right of the pair is a representation of 'India' sitting on the ground with bowed head against a tell-tale palm frond. Whilst mentioning Penang it is perhaps not often realized how longstanding has been the connection of the name of Cornwallis with that part of our Asian 'empire'. A park, several streets and even a School still maintain the family name in what is now an almost forgotten part of the former British dominions.

"Cornwallis may perhaps be best described as a statesman on whom the Ministry of the day could always rely. His patriotism, his regard for discipline, his sense of duty to the State, were the qualities which attained their fullest development in Wellington" but were already amply indicated by him. Above all his life was one of almost uninterrupted devotion to the task in hand. It was so devoted that he died with his family name at its most illustrious thus far. He was not to know how his successors would develop but the distinctive story of how the Cornwallis line continued now awaits us.

CHAPTER 10

A New Spread of the Branches

Unhappily, as had been the case with many of his line, the 2nd Marquess's life was short and he died on 9 August 1823 in Old Burlington Street, in his 49th year. His widow, Louisa, Marchioness Cornwallis, survived him for 27 years dying herself aged 73 on 5 December 1850. Both were buried in Culford Church where 2 tablets on the west wall now appear to their memory. Two of their daughters, Louisa and Elizabeth, who died unmarried are also buried in the Cornwallis vault. The expiry of the Marquessate saw the end of the family line at Culford.

Jane, the eldest daughter of the 2nd Marquess married the 3rd Lord Braybrooke and two of the sons of this marriage fell in the Crimea, one at Balaclava and the other at Inkerman. The present Lord Braybrooke is the great-great-great-great grandson of the 1st Marquess.

Another descendant, Charles Cornwallis Ross, who also died in the Crimea, was the grandson of the 2nd Marquess by Lady Mary Ross, his 4th daughter. Lady Jemima, the 3rd daughter of the same peer, married the 3rd Earl of St. Germans and the eldest son of that marriage, Captain Edward Charles Cornwallis Eliot, was killed at Inkerman. The 4th and 5th Earls of St. Germans and the Hon. Charles Eliot were issue of the same marriage and the last named perpetuates that line.

In order to tell the full story of the main Cornwallis line it is first necessary to relate what happened to the 1st Marquess's brothers. Charles's immediate sibling was Henry who also elected to serve in the Army, reaching the rank of Captain in the 1st Foot Guards. Though he had just been elected M.P. for Eye, like so many other male members of his family, he died unmarried in Germany at the age of 19. The following extract from a letter written by his father to William, then a young naval lieutenant, explains the circumstances:

"I am very sorry that I must relate to you a misfortune that has befallen our family, which has given us all the most distressing affliction; your poor brother Harry, who was on his road, coming home from Germany, was seized with a violent fever, which occasioned his death. We believe it was contracted by the great fatigues he underwent the latter end of the campaign, and lying frequently out in the open air."

James, the third brother, was the scholar of the family and the next of the Cornwallis line to be a clergyman. Born in Dover Street, Piccadilly, London, on 25 February 1743 he was educated at Eton and Christ Church, Oxford where he graduated B.A. in June 1763. He was then elected a Fellow of Merton College and from there took his M.A. in 1769. He was entered as a member of the Temple and intended practising at the Bar but on the advice of his uncle, Archbishop Frederick, he altered his mind and took Holy Orders.

This career began with his being appointed Chaplain to his cousin, Lord Townshend, who was then Viceroy of Ireland, but in 1769 he was presented to the living of Ickham, Kent, which was in the Archbishop's gift. The neighbouring parish of Adisham was added to that benefice in the succeeding year. Nor was this all for at the close of 1770 he became a Prebendary of Westminster, Rector of Newington, Oxford and then of Wrotham in Kent. Not surprisingly he resigned the earlier livings though in 1771 he was again inducted to Ickham with which was joined the chapelry of Staple. It hardly needs stating that in regard to most of his parochial duties he was an absentee incumbent who doubtless employed local curates.

On 30 April 1771 he married Catherine, the daughter of Galfridus (or Godfrey) Mann, Esq. of Egerton, Boughton Malherbe and Linton, and M.P for Maidstone. More will be said about the Mann family in the next chapter. The ceremony took place in Lambeth Palace chapel and the couple were to have a daughter, Elizabeth, who lived from 1774 to 1813 but died unmarried, and two sons, James and Horace. Of James junior more must be said later but Horace, who was born in 1780, only reached his 19th year and was also unmarried.

In view of the new family connection it is hardly surprising that in 1773 their father duly resigned the Ickham living and was inducted as the Rector of Boughton Malherbe through his uncle's patronage, but also doubtless as a result of his father-in-law's influence. If this is where they now resided it was not to be for long as in 1775 James gave up his Westminster post and became Dean of Canterbury, at which time the University of Oxford also conferred upon him the honorary degree of D.C.L. . The family were to live in Salisbury for the next 6 years but on 16 September 1781 James was consecrated Bishop of Lichfield and Coventry and relinquished his several Kentish parishes.

A picture of life in Lichfield at the time that Frederick Cornwallis was Bishop was given in the previous account of that prelate's life but some features that developed during James's episcopate may be of interest. One of these was the rapid growth of 'box clubs'.

"These precursors of savings banks and insurance companies were of financial help to the poor . . . and one of the occasions which Dr. Johnson enjoyed in Lichfield was the annual walk of the Ladies Amiable Society . . The members made a pretty picture, dressed in white or light colours with ribbons and gay bonnets, carrying wands topped with nosegays. The sunshine, the flowers, the pealing church bells, the music of drums and flutes and the children capering alongside, made it a joyous occasion. Clergymen, the society physician and other important men of the town led the procession." It was frequently to the Cathedral to hear a sermon that the procession from the Guildhall made its way.

Another annual event was the use of celebrations to commemorate the Court Leet on Whit Monday. In a book describing the town during Bishop Cornwallis's time we read that "the business of the day commenced about 8 o'clock in the morning, when the constables, attended by men wearing their colours of distinction, with drums beating and preceded by morrice dancers [sic] with the maid Marian, tabor and pipe, etc. conducted the bailiffs and sheriff and other city officers to the bower in Greenhill where they were received with a salute from the men at arms . . . Greenhill was on these occasions crowded with shows, booths and stalls and the day was looked upon as a festival for the City and neighbourhood. About 9 o'clock in the evening the whole of the traditional 'trade' posies being collected a procession was formed to conduct them to what was called 'the christening' . . . and being arrived at the door of St. Mary's church an address was given by the Town Clerk, recommending a peaceable demeanour and watchful attendance to their duty; and a volley being fired over the posies, the business of the day ended."

Among the City's institutions one anciently connected with the Bishop was St. John's Hospital where the poor men who were housed there each received by the Bishop's grant 2 loads of wood from the forest of Cannock. The Bishop was the patron of the house and should others not fulfil their duty of nominating the inmates then the last choice fell to his Lordship. Sadly we read that whilst a visitation was made in 1752 by Bishop Frederick Cornwallis his nephew had not fulfilled that task when the inmates book was compiled around 1800. Whether he did so later is not known.

Bishop James served this diocese for the rest of his life though in 1791, on the translation of Bishop Douglas of Carlisle to the see of Salisbury, his successor left vacant the Deanery at Windsor and this post was also conferred on Bishop Cornwallis. Three years later, on 22 February 1794, he was to exchange that Deanery for the one at Durham.

Of his official and important duties at Windsor there is appropriate notice but it is perhaps surprising to find that he was also more than just a figurehead in the post at Durham. In September 1794 we are told that the Dean and Chapter met and 'Agreed that Mr. James Wyatt, the then most fashionable architect in the country, (and, we may recall, the redesigner of the Hall at Culford) be wrote to, to come down to inspect the repairs to the Cathedral, and to give a Plan of the future Repairs and Improvements.' Mr. Wyatt duly appeared in 1795 and made recommendations. The most serious of these concerned the Galilee Chapel which had been constructed on a distinctive outcrop of rock by order of Bishop Hugh de Puiset in the latter 12th century. To some purists in earlier times the mixture of Norman and Early English styles seemed unworthy of the rest of the Cathedral and Wyatt now proposed that the whole Chapel should be removed. This was not, however, as has been sometimes suggested, simply so that a carriage drive round the Church could be constructed, but so that the great West Door could again be opened. In its place there was to be a new outer porch by moving the recently re-cased Nicholson north porch to that position.

Whether the effective decisions of the Chapter about the West end of the Cathedral had been taken since the Dean's last annual period of residence there the fact is that when he arrived in the summer of 1796 to take up his annual duties he found to his horror that the Chapel roof had already been stripped of its lead so that the demolition of its walls might be begun. A commentator in 1833 then takes up the story:

"The Dean, to his infinite credit, put an instant stop to this barbarous proceeding. "I saved the Galilee", was his lordship's frequent boast to the writer of these pages many years ago; and the writer of these pages as frequently pledged himself to record a fact for which posterity will reverence the name of Dean Cornwallis." (p. 75) What is certain is that the singularity of the Galilee Chapel's architecture is now one of its most appreciated features.

Yet his life story was to assume one further dimension. As we already know his nephew, the 2nd Marquess, died in 1823 without a male heir and whilst the rank of Marquessate ceased the earldom passed to James as 4th Earl. The Bishop was then in his 80th year and was to last only until 20 January 1824. He died at Richmond, Surrey and was buried in Lichfield Cathedral where he had reigned for over 42 years.

"Another relative who caused the 2nd Earl concern was. . . Horace, a son of James. While in Ireland as Lord Lieutenant, Charles Cornwallis had to deal with the vagaries of this nephew. Horace had told his father that he wanted to wed a Dublin girl but he promised not to marry without the Bishop's consent. Lord Cornwallis, however, discovered that his nephew planned to run off with the young lady and convey her to Scotland. His Lordship at once took steps to prevent this scandal but had to keep his nephew 'close prisoner' until he could send him back to his father 'under the care of 2 messengers'. "He is a weak, idle Boy", Charles observed," and will always, I am afraid, be a trifling character"." (Wickwire, p. 38)

Meanwhile William, the 2nd Marquess's fourth brother, born on February 25, 1744, went to Harrow at the age of 9 but by his 12th year joined the Navy and was to make in it a long and distinguished career. Through the labour of a singular character called George Cornwallis-West, using letters and papers found in the attics of William's later home, we have a fairly complete story, 'The Life and Letters of Sir William Cornwallis' first published in 1928. Those who want to pursue that story in detail can there do so but it is not enough for us to dismiss this interesting member of the family quite so easily. His adventures include some events of particular relevance to the full story of his parents and siblings.

His father wrote to him in June 1761 when he was 17:

"I am very sensible it must be more expensive to you now that you are a Lieutenant. I am very willing to allow what is necessary to you, and would by no means have you live worse than your brother officers. I suppose you will not be able to do with less than a hundred a year . . . By this time William had crossed the Atlantic, roamed the Mediterranean and had had his first baptism of French fire.

The Right Revd. William Cornwallis, Bishop of Lichfield

William, Admiral Cornwallis

His <u>mother</u>, Elizabeth, Countess Cornwallis, was also a regular correspondent with William and from the many letters that have survived we can see how carefully she sought, even as a <u>Dowager</u>, to leave no stone unturned in order to further her <u>son's</u> progress. She writes, August 1763;

"Lord Halifax . . . gave me an absolute promise he will make you a Post Captain . . . yet there are none of my friends in town, so I can get no secret intelligence how things go on", though she sensibly adds,

"I hope you have the sense and prudence enough to consider your whole future happiness consists in getting an established character of a good officer and a sober man. You will then rise by your own merit which is ten thousand times more satisfactory than the doing it by the assistance of friends . . ."

That William was not without friends is seen when, writing on the incident in which William's ship was badly damaged, his <u>mother</u> says:

"Oct. 19th . . . I was so fortunate not to hear of the accident that befell you till I had it from your brother, who had a great deal of company at Culford and was informed by Admiral Keppel . . . Molly (her daughter, Lady Mary Cornwallis) then wrote from Culford to me."

In 1763, on the verge of his 20th birthday, William began the first of several periods in the West Indies. Healthy and vigorous as the young Lieutenant was it is hardly surprising that, like many other Servicemen, he formed some attachments during these many months abroad. (See tree attached)

Happily escaping shipwreck he was back in England by 1765 and was promoted to Post-Captain under the new Government. Cornwallis-West comments: "To be a Post-Captain at 21 was quick-work, even at that period of British naval history, and so far as men who made a name for themselves in their profession, only equalled by Nelson and Barrington."

By the time he was back in the West Indies for a year from 1771 he had gained immensely in experience in the Mediterranean and in the harsh seas of the North Atlantic and in 1773 he even went on half-pay as a lull in war with the French reduced the need for active service. Yet it was only a lull and in 1775 William was making a long and memorable trip via West Africa to his now familiar Caribbean haunts.

The rumblings of the American War of Independence now affected him and in 1777 Cornwallis was involved in the attempt by the fleet to sail up the Chesapeake, effect a landing in Maryland and thus make possible the capture of Philadelphia, General Washington's capital. It meant that William was becoming acquainted with territory that his military and noble brother was also coming to know well. The exploits of both brothers in the same area meant that the name Cornwallis was often mentioned, and not least because one of the vessels used in these operations also bore the family name.

The Cornwallis Jamaican Genealogy

The Hon. William Cornwallis, R.N.
(fathered the following children)

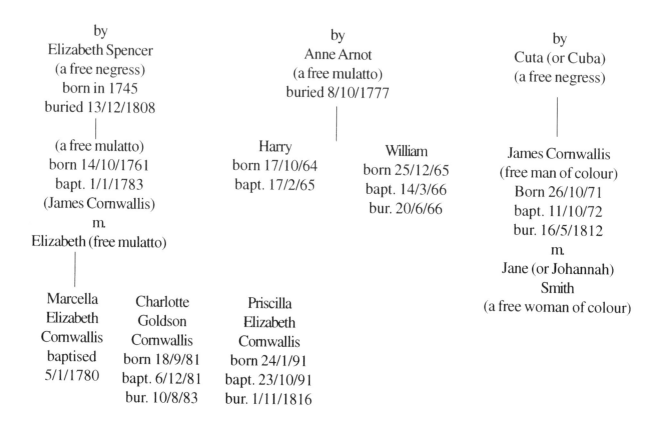

by
Elizabeth Spencer
(a free negress)
born in 1745
buried 13/12/1808

(a free mulatto)
born 14/10/1761
bapt. 1/1/1783
(James Cornwallis)
m.
Elizabeth (free mulatto)

by
Anne Arnot
(a free mulatto)
buried 8/10/1777

Harry
born 17/10/64
bapt. 17/2/65

William
born 25/12/65
bapt. 14/3/66
bur. 20/6/66

by
Cuta (or Cuba)
(a free negress)

James Cornwallis
(free man of colour)
Born 26/10/71
bapt. 11/10/72
bur. 16/5/1812
m.
Jane (or Johannah)
Smith
(a free woman of colour)

Marcella
Elizabeth
Cornwallis
baptised
5/1/1780

Charlotte
Goldson
Cornwallis
born 18/9/81
bapt. 6/12/81
bur. 10/8/83

Priscilla
Elizabeth
Cornwallis
born 24/1/91
bapt. 23/10/91
bur. 1/11/1816

(The I.G.I. records of Port Royal also show
Mary Anne Cornwallis Rose, a negro slave, 3/9/1821
Sarah Cornwallis, a negro slave, bapt. 30/12/1821
Frances Arnot, slave, bur. 17/1/1822)

Yet William was sufficiently exhausted to be ordered home on sick leave in 1778 and it was whilst waiting for his next ship that his sister-in-law, Jemima Countess Cornwallis, wrote to him from Esher:

"I do not know how to wish you, out or detained; all I know is that these are frightful times in all respects . . I am really so bilious as to think that our army in America, fleets everywhere, possessions in the West Indies, &c, &c. will be frittered away and destroyed in about another twelve months . . I assure you I do not think a female ought to talk politics, but when it comes to husband, friends, &c, one must feel and it will out."

There spoke a very distressed wife and mother who wrote again a fortnight later: "I am as yellow as an orange, feel very ill, (but) Hope to get away to Bath on Saturday." She was indeed far from well and, as was recorded earlier, occasioned the return of the Marquess from America but only to witness her death a few days after his arrival home. He wrote to William:

"I am now returning to America, not with views of conquest and ambition, (for) nothing brilliant can be expected in that quarter; but I find this country quite unsupportable to me. I must shift the scene . . I most heartily wish you all possible success, and that you may have an opportunity of acquiring great honour and some money. I don't think it impossible that we may meet in the West Indies, as I have signified my willingness to go thither . ."

His brother's wish seems to have begun to come true for William distinguished himself in the battle for Grenada when in command of *The Lion* and commendations of his bravery came from the Archbishop and Lady Mornington, Lord Longford and Admiral Keppel, to name but a few. Yet if this was commendation that he valued there was further praise that he appreciated even more keenly a year later.

Admiral Sir Peter Parker commended him warmly to the Admiralty for his action at Mobile but then, being despatched to England with a large convoy, it was in William's ship, the *Lion*, that Captain Nelson himself chose to sail. The two men had become acquainted in Jamaica and it was only Nelson's death that ended their lasting friendship. The latter's gratitude on arriving home was recalled in a letter sent from HMS *Victory* on 30 December 1804,

"My Dear Friend,
    I always feel happy in hearing from you, for I shall never forget that to you probably I owe my life, and I feel that I imbibed from you certain sentiments that have greatly assisted me in my Naval career – That we could always beat a Frenchman if we fought him long enough . . ."

Commendation from such a quarter was valued above any other. It was incidentally in that same letter that Nelson expressed his first intention regarding the vital part that Cornwallis should play in the 1805 event, but we shall come to that in due course.

Meanwhile two further engagements in the Caribbean led to the following address to the crew in his new ship, *Canada*.

"Captain Cornwallis takes this opportunity of expressing his thorough sense of the Spirited behaviour of the Officers, Seamen and Marines in both Actions, at St. Christophe (i.e. St. Kitts) and on the 12th of April last . . . and he assures them that it will always give him particular pleasure to meet an enemy whilst he has the honour to command those Brave men." (*op. cit.*, p. 131)

The happy outcome of these engagements formed the substance of what was to be the last letter he now received from his ailing mother. She at least had the pleasure of writing:

"The Bishop of Lichfield [his brother] was at the levee the Friday after the news came. His Majesty made your praise the subject of his conversation to him . . ." (p. 132)

Yet much as William must have cherished this missive he was probably even more excited by the prospect that opened up in the next letter from his eldest brother. The latter wrote in strict confidence to say that he was destined for the post of Governor-General and Commander-in-Chief in India and therefore hoped that he might be able to appoint William to the principal naval command there. One can imagine the Captain's expectations. Yet it was not to be. The Admiralty were apparently insistent on someone with the rank of Admiral being in that position, though William was assured that if he came out East he would still have been given an honourable post. Even that was to be denied him for by the end of 1782, and after having come home with a further convoy, he was placed on half-pay as an unemployed officer. Though mightily disappointed it was not to last too long. By late 1783 he was in command of the Royal Yacht, *Queen Charlotte*.

It is during the next 6 years that William enjoys a comparative ease. He had been elected M.P. for the Eye constituency since 1763 but in 1784 he was made M.P. for Portsmouth where he shared the seat with Sir Harry Fetherstonhaugh "whose only indirect connection with the Navy was the fact that he is supposed to be the first man who led Emma, Lady Hamilton, from the path of virtue." (*op. cit.*, p. 141)

At last, in 1788, Cornwallis was offered and accepted the appointment as Commodore and Commander-in-Chief of His Majesty's Squadron in the East Indies. No sooner was the post announced than he received an application for service from a half-pay Captain who was newly married and living in Norfolk. It was his friend, Horatio Nelson. Having presumed that Nelson would not appreciate being stationed so far away when newly-wed Cornwallis apologized for not having mentioned his name in the first batch of appointments but promised that should any further ships be required Nelson's name would be given one. Though obviously somewhat piqued Nelson still wrote with fervour that "my wish has been (for I may now say a series of years) to serve under you [so] always recollect that I can leave my humble and peaceful cottage" should occasion arise. He signed himself, "your rural friend".

Certainly William was soon left in no doubt that service on the India station had its benefits for before his departure his brother was writing,

"With the utmost propriety of living my savings are vastly beyond my expectations, and by the 1st of January 1800 will exceed £90,000." (*op. cit.*, p. 147)

It was early in that fateful European year, 1789, that Commodore Cornwallis finally sailed from his native shore and 7 months later touched down at Madras. His arrival there was marked by two letters from the Governor-General thus showing all present that the land and sea forces were now firmly in the hands of the Cornwallis brothers. That there would be a happy cooperation in both strategy and purpose seemed assured. Certainly William was as determined as his older brother to see that the administration of such local matters as fell under his sway would be efficiently discharged. It is at this point that Cornwallis-West inserts an interesting passage.

Having pointed out that the amounts agreed to be paid by the East India Company for the maintenance of forces in India were decided in advance the terms of their contract then state that "as this amount was not actually expended in the upkeep of each regiment, any surplus was to be collected from one William Burke, who was the Deputy-Paymaster-General in India, and paid to the Commodore, who was to apply it 'towards defraying the expense of purchasing such stores and provisions as the Squadron in your command may stand in need of, when the supplies sent from England, or furnished by the East India Company shall prove deficient . . .' One wonders", the biographer reflects, "whether the Governor and Court of the East India Company realized that they were paying more to the Home Government per each regiment than was the actual cost of its upkeep." (*op. cit.*, p. 151)

These considerations were not uppermost in the new Commodore's mind. His concern was to put the arrangements for supplying his Squadron on a sound commercial and effectively operational basis. By 1790 he was writing to Sir Charles Middleton (the later Lord Barham) at the Admiralty:

"By what I now see the Less we have to do with the Company's people the better. I have appointed my present secretary to be Store-keeper, as somebody must keep the accounts. And I will take all the care I can, but it is not easy to stop abuses which have gone on for so many years, and where so many have an interest in Their continuance." (*op. cit.*, p. 157)

Sir Charles, having been in his identical situation, was less than sanguine about any lasting improvements being made but the Prime Minister (William Pitt the Younger) and Admiral Hood were eager to encourage him. The former wrote:

"I cannot conclude without expressing to you the full sense entertained here of the great zeal and attention with which you have applied yourself to correct, in all transactions on behalf of the Government, those abuses which had been too prevalent in India." Hood wrote in similar vein. (p. 160)

If accounting was one concern the other was the irritation caused by the activities of both the local French commanders and a few of his own British subordinates. The renowned globe-trotter and diarist, William Hickey, now portrayed William in a disparaging light, comparing him unfavourably with his older brother, describing him as of rough disposition and of a temper more suited to the folk of the Andaman Islands which are "inhabited by a race of anthrophagi or cannibals [and] being utterly incapable of civilization". That William equally disliked Hickey is obvious.

It was true that in manner Cornwallis could be bluff and peremptory, as was so often the attitude required with those amongst whom he spent almost all his time and on whose obedience to his orders the success of his activities so much depended. As it was the record seems to show that only 3 of his Captains needed to be severely dealt with and of these only one, Captain Schomberg, had to be sent home in disgrace. It is not without significance that Admiral Hood wrote to him again at this time mentioning that "You will likewise hear of the Bounty armed ship being run away by a part of her crew, under the direction of a Mr. Christian. Probably you may think it right to send one of your frigates to Otaheite [Tahiti] to endeavour to recover her . . ." Had he done so we know that the journey would have proved fruitless.

We learnt earlier of the campaign waged by the Earl against the forces of Tipu Sultan but it is worth noting here that William's share in that expedition was to ensure that the French naval force was not able to supplement the Tipu's army with reserves or supplies which the French might try to land. Having therefore detached some of his ships to shadow the French along the Coromandel coast Cornwallis took the rest of his Squadron to Prince of Wales island in the Malay peninsula where trouble was brewing with one of the local potentates. The traditional appearance of British men of war in such a situation seems to have speedily helped matters to be settled and it is not without note that to this day there are in that island (now called Penang) certain roads and a park that bear the family name.

On his return to Madras the Commodore was engaged in a lively correspondence with Sir Richard Strachan regarding the need to transport bullion in H.M. ships. William was at first most reluctant to engage in such an enterprise but when the shipping agents paid him over 3000 rupees in freight charges he was forced to ask his superior officer what to do with the money. His brother's reply was admirably brief, "Bank it".

What is of further and more lasting interest during the correspondence on this subject is the first mention of a certain Lieutenant Whitby who was then in command of H.M. Sloop 'Dispatch'. From the start of their acquaintance the Commodore took a strong liking to this officer, many years his junior. He was to be first his Flag-Lieutenant and then his Flag-Captain and as we shall note they were almost inseparable until Captain Whitby's death in 1806.

Though war with Spain had now been avoided it became increasingly clear that trouble with France was brewing as the King there was deposed and subsequently beheaded. This trouble was reflected in incidents that now took place in William's area of operations and the successful management of which brought him further commendation. Yet this was by no means his only occupation. Both the Home and Indian Governments were eager that he should involve himself in surveys of the coasts and islands south or east of the Bay of Bengal and it can now be said that the work he carried out led to the foundation of what were to become several of the Empire's valuable colonies. As one example of this work we note that from 1790 letters are sent to him from a new harbour created in the Andaman Islands and named Port Cornwallis. In order to carry out this work he had even been given permission to purchase a schooner with a more shallow draught and this was also commanded by his friend, Whitby.

It was only in the summer of 1793 that the news of increased naval activity back in Home waters began to reach the Indian sub-continent because on 1 February England had declared war on her neighbour across the Channel. By now the Commodore had been promoted to Rear-Admiral and had also been given the nickname 'Billy Go-Tight' by his seamen in view of his practice of hardly ever touching wine or spirits whilst serving in the Tropics. His term of command in those waters was now to end and by April 1794 he had landed in England. His passage home had taken 6 months.

After a suitable period of leave, during which he regretted missing the battle of the 'Glorious First of June', he was again promoted, this time as a Vice-Admiral of the Blue and started on what was to be for the rest of his naval career commitment to service with the Channel Fleet. That he distinguished himself in that service is proved by the many expressions of praise for his tactical exploits from his superiors and of which the words of Lord Romney are an example:

"No Fleet deserved more the thanks of their Country than that you had the Honour to command; knowing this I only did my duty in giving Ministers an opportunity (which they very readily took hold of) of pointing out to Europe another occasion where the Abilities, Judgement and determined Bravery of our Naval Officers and Seamen rose superior to all difficulties."

His being made an Admiral of the Red in June 1795 was yet another mark of the esteem in which he was held but there was also the appearance of a ballad that bears the title which Conwallis was given after 1804 – *Billy Blue*. The Biography gives us the whole text but two verses will provide a taste of the whole:

> It was just at break o' day
> We were cruising in the Bay,
> With Billy Blue int' Sovren in the van
> When the French Fleet bound for Brest
> From Belleisle came heading west –
> 'Twas so, my lads, the saucy game began
> Billy Blue, here's to you, Billy Blue . . .

Aye, Billy Blue: here's to him, with 3 x 3
To the honour of his nae upon the sea.
"He upheld Old England's credit", said the country
in its pride
"Cornwallis's Retreat",
Great Xenophon's great feat
In its spirit we may claim to set beside,
Billy Blue, here's to you, Billy Blue . . .

Despite all the plaudits, which he received at this time, there was one occasion in 1796 when he must have wondered what kind of a future faced him. He was in fact brought before a Court Martial, which was presided over by no less a person than Lord Hood. The principal charges related to what seemed to be disobedience of his orders from the Admiralty when he was in charge of a convoy bound for the West Indies. Being naturally concerned for his good name he presented a long and detailed defence of his actions during the voyage and after due consideration he was totally acquitted. It was an anxious time, as he freely admitted, and there was a sense of relief when, shortly after the verdict he was ordered 'to strike his flag and come ashore', for what were to be 4 years of honourable retirement from active duty.

He began these in a small house at Aldwick, near Chichester where he could indulge his love of horses and his curricle. He was also doubtless delighted to know that his protégé, Captain Whitby, was being looked after by Nelson who was shortly to announce his success at the Battle of the Nile. Yet William's stay at Aldwick was cut short when 4 months later he moved further west to his new estate at Newlands, then a farm and land which he had purchased from Sir John d'Oyley. He lived temporarily in a 2-roomed wooden hut or bungalow whilst the farmhouse was being prepared for him, but however modest might seem his circumstances he was certainly not lacking in contacts who kept him fully up to date with events which closely concerned him. He learnt, for example, of his successor, Lord St. Vincent's problems with the Channel Fleet, he was kept informed by the Marquess, now Lord-Lieutenant of Ireland, of the problems that needed attention there and members of the Government kept him posted about events in Europe. A rest, however, was what he needed even though, as he remarked, "Whenever people see a man walk lame, they immediately cry out that is gout. For my part, I am pretty indifferent about these matters. If a man of 62 can go quietly off the stage without pain, he has no right to be dissatisfied . . ."

As he entered a fifth year of inactivity he began to find even his hobbies and new household irksome but in *The Times* for 23 February 1801 there appeared the announcement of his reappointment as Commander-in-Chief of the Channel Fleet. The threat of Napoleon's invasion of Great Britain was now a reality and the containment of Bonaparte's naval forces required close attention from the North Sea to the coasts of Brittany. It was not only the French who needed supervision, however, as there was a brief but serious outbreak of mutiny amongst the men at Berehaven, some of whom had not seen their families or homes for 9 years. The mutiny was put down, with one of the ringleaders declaring before his execution that British sailors should take note that

228

attempts at mutiny were always likely to fail for "Sailors", he said, "never did, nor ever would stick to each other on such an occasion." (*op. cit.*, p. 382)

The Admiral's engagement was not a long one this time for within a year a Peace Treaty, not a little due to the work of his older brother, had been signed at Amiens and on 1 April a general demobilization was ordered. On 28 April, 1802, he was back in Newlands though the house was no longer just the old thatched farmhouse. During his last absence a servant had left a naked light untended and whilst the local congregation were at worship next morning they saw one whole wing of the residence burnt to the ground. William's library and a collection of Indian artefacts were all destroyed. When the Admiral came up his drive he saw the new additions to the home he had left.

During the next year he was joined there by not only his protégé, Captain Whitby, but the Captain's new bride, Theresa Symonds, who was only 19. She was the daughter of a friend and shipmate of both Cornwallis and St. Vincent whilst her brother, later Admiral Sir William Symonds, became one of the foremost naval designers ever employed at the Admiralty. The lady was both cultured and beautiful, spoke 3 languages and was also a talented painter. The Admiral became extremely attached to her and treated both her and her husband as his children. The new Gothic-style edifice which was now developed and extended as their home was superintended entirely by Mrs. Whitby who also designed the lay-out of the gardens and plantations. The need for her to do this was because the Peace recently declared was once again breached by Napoleon and led to her husband and the Admiral again being called up for active service. At the age of only 21 she had been vested with the latter's power of attorney and was wholly in charge of all his private affairs.

What is not perhaps generally known is that it was due to Admiral Cornwallis that Nelson was soon able to hoist his flag again in H.M.S. *Victory*. This vessel was originally designated by the Lords of the Admiralty as part of Cornwallis's fleet though it could be disposed of as he desired if it was surplus to his requirements. It was thus that he transferred it to Nelson who wrote:

"The Victory joined me last night, having been, via Malta, 7 weeks from Gibraltar. I can only say to you thanks for not taking the Victory from me; it was like yourself and very unlike many others which you and I know . . .
(signed) Nelson and Bronte".

Now began that cat and mouse period as the British and French commanders sought to outwit each other. What is of more than usual interest is the content of a letter received by Cornwallis in 1803 stating that a "Mr. Fulton, an American resident in Paris, has constructed a Vessel in which he has gone down to the bottom of the Water, and has remained there-under for the space of 7 hours, at one time – that he has navigated the said Vessel, under the Water, at the rate of two Miles and a half per Hour; that the said submarine vessel is uncommonly manageable; and . . . that the Ships and Vessels in the port of London are liable to be destroyed with ease . . ." Though it was in fact never used it clearly gave food for thought and Mr. Fulton also followed up this invention with the first steamship and a Star Torpedo.

In February 1804 the Admiral was compelled by bad weather to make for the safety of Torbay. No sooner had he arrived there than he wished his crews to realize that this was to be but a brief stay which would end as soon as the storms in the Channel subsided. He accordingly hoisted the Blue Peter and thereafter acquired the title mentioned above, Billy Blue.

His responsibility was clear. It was in his hands to prevent the French naval forces on the Atlantic seaboard taking to sea so that they could effect the landing of an armed force on either the English mainland or on the southern and western coats of Ireland. So concerned were the Government as to the efficacy of this policy that when Cornwallis had a 3 weeks' shore leave whilst his flagship underwent a refit Lord Melville, aged 61, took a post-chaise from London to Newlands in order to discuss the situation in person with the Admiral. His anxiety to see Cornwallis back on station was apparently quite evident. Lord Melville need not have worried for it was to be the succeeding year which proved crucial for Britain. Meanwhile, despite political manoeuvres to replace Cornwallis with St. Vincent the Admiral retained his command and, recovering from another bout of illness, set out for what was to be his last important phase of service.

On 7 July 1805, he joined his ships off Brest. Having been picked up near Lymington he had boarded the sloop, *Ranger*, bound for Spithead where he raised his flag on board the *Ville de Paris*, a captured French man o'war. The next few months were to be the most eventful of his career for he was to be called on to make decisions which were vital for the safety of his country, and it does not take much imagination to guess what were his feelings as he once more trod the quarterdeck of his flagship.

The French were again active everywhere and it was clear that a move on a big scale was being contemplated. Was he, he wondered, to have at last the chance of meeting and then beating the French with a force adequate for the occasion? Certainly, capable and gallant as he was, his heart pined for an opportunity that had so far been denied him.

The naval situation as he now resumed his command was as follows: *Ganteaume*, with 21 sail, was blockaded in Brest by 19 English battleships; *Allemand* had 5 line of battle ships in Rochefort and he was being blockaded by Rear Admiral Stirling. *Gourdon* and a Spanish Admiral were in Ferrol where they were being watched by Calder with 9 sail of the line and still further south Collingwood was watching the Spanish Fleet under Gravina in Cadiz.

It was known that Nelson had hotly pursued Villeneuve to the West Indies but on 8 July the Admiralty became aware that Villeneuve was hastening back to European waters and was making for the Bay of Biscay and not the Mediterranean. The problem to be solved was how to destroy the Toulon (or Villeneuve's) fleet before it could reunite with the blockaded squadrons.

Lord Barham at the Admiralty had authorized any manoeuvre to effect that purpose and Cornwallis was able to inform the Admiralty by 11 July that as instructed he was standing some 30 to 40 leagues westward with 7 three-deckers and 3 eighty-gun ships plus 10 other vessels, and would do so for up to 10 days. He was patrolling on a course about 100 miles long. He soon came to a strong conviction that Brest was not the French Fleet's destination and on returning to the Brest station he was overheard by his ship's Captain to say that he now wished he were Calder.

How right he was. 2 days previously Calder had encountered and fought with Villeneuve, and Nelson, who had made for the Straits of Gibraltar, now turned north and proposed to join the Channel Fleet. He wrote to his colleague Cornwallis:

"My dear Friend,
    The enemy's fleet from the West Indies being certainly gone into some port in the Bay, I am proceeding to the northward with 11 sail of the line . . . I shall only hope, after all my long pursuits of my enemy, that I may arrive at the moment they are meeting you, for my very wretched state of health will force me to get on shore for a little while. I am ever, my dear friend,
                          your most faithful and attached,
                          NELSON AND BRONTË."

What Cornwallis had now been told by the Admiralty was that Nelson must be sent home in the *Victory* as soon as the two sailors met. Cornwallis knew the precarious nature of his friend's health and almost before the last gun had sounded to salute Nelson's arrival the latter was packed off as instructions directed. Nelson nonetheless sent a boat to Cornwallis with the following words:

". . . wished much to have taken you by the hand. I am sure you have felt for me. "Bellisle" wants going to port; the others are perfect. I send you their state: I send you a case of Noyau, a jar of tamarinds and a jar of ginger. I am but very so and so, and very indifferent this forenoon. May every success attend you . . ."

Whilst Calder's action had significantly diminished the Villeneuve force it had required Stirling's help and as a result Allemand's ships had escaped from Rochefort. However, even if this force joined with Villeneuve's and sought to storm the Channel route in order to support Napoleon's barges preparing for the invasion of England Cornwallis still felt strong enough to deny them that option.

But what if they joined up and went for the Mediterranean where English sea-power was now almost nil? Without hesitating Cornwallis acted. He sent Calder with 18 of the line to Ferrol and commanded him 'to prevent the enemy sailing again or to intercept them if they attempted it'. Whilst it is always pointless to conjecture what may have happened in other circumstances one thing now seems clear. If this 61 year old Admiral had not acted with promptness it is difficult to see how the battle of Trafalgar could have been fought 2 months later. Certainly Lord Barham at the Admiralty was to follow up this decisive action by signalling:

"We have at this moment received yours, you have entered completely into my views."

The only variation made to Cornwallis's plan was to order that Sir Charles Cotton become Commander of the detached squadron and within days that order too was rescinded and Nelson was again to be back on the scene, battered though he was.

Meanwhile Cornwallis sent his two fastest frigates, *Iris* and *Naïad*, ahead of Calder to watch Villeneuve in Ferrol. It was these ships that discovered where the main French force was at anchor. *Naïad* went south to warn Collingwood whilst *Iris* came to Ushant to alert the Commander-in-Chief. Ireland and the Channel were now obviously safe from attack and the whole scene began to assume its final shape. Cornwallis's last order to Calder was:

"Go in pursuit of the enemy instead of just patrolling Ferrol."

There only remained the irritation value of Allemand's escaped squadron when a combined East and West Indies merchant fleet, worth 10 million pounds sterling even in those days, was expected in the area. Cornwallis was asked 'to contrive to spare 5 vessels to cruise in the chops of the Channel for 10 days to preserve this convoy'. Having had a short but successful encounter with some of the Brest ships that tried to leave port Cornwallis was not afraid to diminish his force further.

Indeed, when in late September news came that Allemand was about 100 leagues south-west of the Scillies, Cornwallis's captain wrote:

"To be flouted in so impudent a manner in the heart of his own station was more than old 'Billy-go-tight' could endure. The Admiral, when he sees or scents the enemy, rises up like the sun from behind the clouds – all dull and inky vapours vanish. He boldly determined once more to leave Brest open and do himself what his detachment had failed to achieve."

Allemand's ships were not destroyed but Cornwallis's venture drove them to make a dash for the Canaries, and as the Admiral resumed station outside Brest he could at least be reassured that he had denied the French this addition to the force at Cadiz. The pieces of the jigsaw were almost all in place. It needed only a letter from Collingwood dated 26 October to complete the picture:

"I have the very greatest pleasure to inform you that the combined [French] fleet was engaged by the British squadron on Monday, 21st, off Trafalgar and totally defeated . . . Sorry I am to tell you that the noble Commander-in-Chief fell in the action; but he will live in the memories of all who knew him as long as they have being."

Cornwallis felt the death of Nelson keenly. "The Admiral grieves much", wrote Captain Whitby, "never a word of envy for his glorious victory, only a deep regret that they did not meet and speak in August when they might have bade farewell." He had nonetheless played his part in the "immortal memory".

It only remains to comment on the Admiral's own latter days. Some dissatisfaction at the way he and other senior commanders were treated after the decisive victory of 1805 led him, after his own replacement as Commander-in-Chief of the Channel Fleet, to offer his resignation. He was always sad that he had not been able to face the enemy in a major decisive engagement but he had done his duty faithfully in many other areas. Sadly his withdrawal from active service also coincided with the death of the Marquess in India and of his much loved Captain Whitby. The latter's widow, who had so competently carried on the whole management of the Newlands estate during the absence of her menfolk, now felt it right to leave Newlands with her 1 year old daughter and live with a sister at Wallington, near Fareham.

When the sister herself married a Mr. Tindal, who was in due time to become Lord Chief Justice of England, the Admiral, already experiencing loneliness, begged Mrs Whitby to return and share his remaining years. Of course people talked, and whilst today the two might have married, such a step was then thought unsuitable.

Not that anything like this seems to have occurred to them for the relationship was simply that of a 'father' and 'daughter' – a relationship always endorsed by William's brother, the Bishop. Indeed it was only after the Admiral's death, when he had made Mrs. Whitby his sole heiress, that some of his family became critical or even spiteful. Even they were outdone by Mrs. Whitby's own and her husband's family who became totally hostile so that even the 2nd Marquess remarked, "I cannot understand the cruel sentiments which Captain Whitby's family express . . . I find them most unnatural and uncalled for."

Whatever relatives might think the Admiral spent the last 12 years in the peaceful pursuits of his country life. It was, as might be expected from one so long used to the demands of the Service, a disciplined routine. Rising at 4 a.m. he rode his favourite pony for 2 hours and in all weathers, followed by a breakfast of green tea and thick unbuttered toast. A plain lunch at was taken at 1 and dinner at 6 with a bottle of port present whatever others of his frequent guests might take. Having had his fill of salt beef at sea he preferred mutton and a cold joint was always to be seen on the sideboard. He then took a cup of strong coffee, a game of bagatelle if there were no guests and so to bed.

Publicly he was known as a strong Churchman who did not take kindly to dissenters and as a benefactor towards the poor. He set up the second known day school for the villagers and was especially renowned for his interest in and care of all types of animals. He disliked fox hunting and hare coursing and seems to have held strong views on the peerage. Most of what we know about him in this period was recorded by Mrs. Whitby's daughter and she reports how one day she was poring over a book on the nobility. "Put that nonsense away", he said, "Don't you realize that half the men in that book are living on the reflected glory of their forebears? Honours are very well in their way, but remember this, 'Worth makes the man and want of it the fellow'."

In due time his own worth was recognized, being made a Vice Admiral and created

K.C.B. In 1816, when returning from a driving excursion, he had a stroke at Salisbury. He was never the same again and 3 years later he died peacefully with the 13 year old Miss Whitby's hand in his. That girl became Mrs. West and it was her son who took the name Cornwallis-West, hence the name of his son, the biographer. Yet if William's death marked the end of one branch another was to grow anew.

CHAPTER 11

The Tree Acquires New Stock

James, 4th Earl Cornwallis, had married Catherine, the daughter of Galfridus Mann, Esq., of Egerton and they had two sons, James and Horatio (or Horace). Horace, born on 27 March, 1780, was named after his mother's brother, Sir Horace Mann, Bt. After attending Eton he was admitted as a pensioner at St. John's College, Cambridge, and then became an Ensign in the 1st Foot Guards, serving with some concern, as we saw, in Ireland. He died 6 February 1799, still unmarried.

His elder brother, James, born on 20 September 1778 in Middlesex, inherited his father's title and property in 1824. He had been a pupil at Eton before being admitted a Fellow-commoner at St. John's College, Cambridge, on 12 April 1796, and was made an M.A. in 1798. Elected in the family tradition as M.P. for Eye from 1799 to 1806 and again in 1807, he also inherited the Linton estate from his uncle, Sir Horace Mann, in 1814. To understand the background to this step some details here about the Linton property and how it came to the Mann family are probably required.

Linton Park was the stately home and estate referred to by no less a person than Horace Walpole as that 'citadel of Kent with the Weald as its garden'. Certainly, as you approach from the south via Marden and Cross-at-Hand the sharp white house sits proudly on the side of the ridge facing you, looking over many acres that were once all its domain.

Having entered the estate by the main gate, on the road that connects West Farleigh and Leeds Castle, you have another experience. 2 gentle curves bring you to a fine, broad drive of rich loam over ragstone, flanked with mature trees, and the open crest of a ridge that seems to offer you nothing but empty space. Only as you reach the ridge itself is there revealed the entrance frontage of a 2 storeyed mansion with an ample forecourt and glorious flower bed facing the main porch. This is Linton House which represents the culmination of some 700 years of fairly varied history. Let us run over some of the pages of that record.

Linton was anciently written 'Lyllington' and in Latin 'Lilituna' and obviously had its origins in Anglo-Saxon times. The name means 'the farmstead of Lil's folk' and the original founder may not have been of great stature for 'Lyltlan' in Anglo-Saxon also means 'little Un'. The soil on the southern stretches of the ridge is stiff clay and it was here that the first parish was established. Though not separately mentioned in the Domesday Book the area of present day Linton was included in the entry there made for the Manor of East Farleigh. What is clear is that there was an early and simple Norman church made up of sanctuary, chancel and nave which was held by Earl Farleigh. It was rebuilt around 1280, and there are still Norman period materials in the chancel wall of the present parish church.

The first known name of the later estate was Capell's Court and it would seem that this was the centre piece of the large Kentish landholdings amassed by the de Capella family who were granted the present site in the reign of Henry III. This family, whose principal residence was at Ivechurch in Romney Marsh, also held lands at Boxley at the same period under a charter granted by King Henry to the Abbey there. This charter tells us that the Lord of Linton was a John de Capella and he was succeeded by Richard.

A dwelling has existed on the site of the present house from approximately the middle of the 13th century and it was therefore the influence and assistance of the Capell family which led to the new additions to the structure of the parish church. A private chapel and the south aisle of the nave were added in the reign of Edward III. The estate was to remain in the hands of Richard's descendants for most of the next 2 centuries but it was eventually sold to a Richard Baysden in the reign of Henry VI (1422-1471).

The next family to own the property was that of Mayne (or Mayney) from Biddenden and a fine memorial to Sir Anthony Mayney and his wife, Dame Briggat (Bridget) 'daughter unto William Tanfield of Cayten in Northamptonshire esquire' still exists. It is in the Cornwallis chapel and shows a man in armour and a lady in a ruff kneeling and facing each other. We are informed that they had two children, Anthony and Elizabeth, and that Sir Anthony lived 69 years 'and then (which fewe arrive att) made a most happye end'. His 'enteerly beloved wife' erected the monument in 1615 when she was 65. It was during their time, in 1560-1565, that the church was substantially rebuilt and this generous assistance was mentioned in the Visitation of Archbishop Parker in 1573. It is therefore in every way fitting that the new structure should be adorned with the Mayney monuments.

The son, another Sir Anthony, is also commemorated on the north aisle wall of Linton church by a hanging ornament of alabaster which portrays not only the knight but also his two wives. The monument is a distinctive one because at the top there is a little draped figure known as the faithful gardener. The story goes that the estate gardener was so stricken with grief at Sir Anthony's demise that he died very soon afterwards and those who erected the memorial could not leave him out. That the Mayneys cared for their tenantry is shown by the fact that in 1610 4 almshouses were built to house poor families.

The Mayneys owned the property for three generations – Walter succeeded in 1627 and Sir John in the late 1630s. Sir John was a staunch supporter of Charles I, who created him a Baronet in 1641 and knighted him. When the house that then stood there was attacked by Cromwellian soldiery Sir John is said to have put up a good fight by posting his servants and some friends at the windows during the day. However, when darkness fell one night the house was rushed and 3 servants were killed as well as many being taken prisoner. The first Mayney memorial was also severely damaged and the house taken over. Sir John was fined £1600 in 1648 and a further £1970 the following year.

After the Restoration Sir John was allowed to buy back the property but his support of the Crown cost him so much that he was in severely reduced circumstances and in order to provide for his heir as Baronet in 1676 the estate of Capells Court was sold to a Sir Francis Wittens (Wythens or Wythen). Some indication of the straits in which the Maneys found themselves is shown by the fact that Sir John's eldest son died in 1706 from 'actual want' and his younger brother was said to have committed suicide in 1694 for the same reason. Royalist support was bought at a price.

Sir Francis Wittens (or Wythers), the next occupier of the estate, was one of the Justices of the King's Bench. His occupation cannot have allowed much time for farming but his name will be for ever remembered by those worshipping in the parish church for he presented one of the present communion patens which is dated 1683. A Hanaper or standing cup that must often have been associated with it for communion was given by the Mayneys and is dated 1619. Following his death his only daughter, Catherine inherited and in 1710 she brought it with her when she married Sir Thomas Twysden, 4th Bt of East Peckham. Sadly their marriage had only lasted two years when Catherine became a widow though she soon married again. Her husband was now Brigadier General George Jocelyn, the 4th son of Sir Robert Jocelyn, 1st Bt of Hyde Hall, Hertfordshire. It was in 1724 that the Brigadier sold the property to an Edward Louisa Mann and it is at this point that we enter upon the story of what might be called the modern house and estate.

The Manns were a Suffolk family of whom an early mention is made in Sir Edward Bysshe's *Visitation of the County* in 1664-68. Edward Mann of Ipswich was described as the Comptroller of Customs there. This gentleman would have been acquainted with one of the leading families in Ipswich, the Withypoles, into which family Frances Cornwallis of Brome had married at the end of Elizabeth's reign. Her children and grandchildren would have been the contemporaries of Edward's family.

The purchase of the Capell's Court estate by Edward Mann was almost certainly done in the name, and on behalf, of his father, Robert Mann, for it is the latter who is recorded as being the initial owner from 1724. Robert was the son of a John Mann of Ipswich and London who, however, seems to have quickly used up the small estate which had belonged to the family for many years. John's children could only hope for prospects of improvement in their fortunes through the Walpole connection, which was established through their father's maternal grandmother. Such help did seem likely for we have evidence that Colonel Walpole, the father of the first 'Prime Minister', Sir Robert, used to stay with 'cousin Robert Mann, a linen draper in the Strand, when the Colonel was in London carrying out his duties as an M.P. in the 1690s.

The proof of patronage for Robert Mann appears in the account of an enquiry regarding possible corruption which Sir Robert had to face in 1712. It was alleged that he had placed two forage contracts for the army in Scotland on condition that the contractor kept a share of the profits – some £500 – for his sleeping partner. Robert Mann was the recipient of the sum. There was also another cheque made out to Sir Robert and this too was passed to Robert Mann. Though Sir Robert spent time in the Tower as a result of these findings he was soon back at the Treasury where a post was found for his relative.

The Robert Mann family grew up in Chelsea and there doubtless met their Walpole cousins. The Mann boys, like the Walpoles, went to Eton and Sir Robert Walpole's equally famous son, Horace, even had portraits of Horatio and Galfridus Mann, Robert's second and third sons, on the walls of his dining room at his Twickenham home. Indeed Galfridus was at one point Horace's secretary.

A further member of the Mann family is mentioned in a tablet in Linton Church recording that the fourth son died in 1755 at the age of 47, whilst the youngest, James, was a woollen draper of St. Martin-in-the-Fields and he died in 1764. The eldest daughter married Sir John Toriano, a London merchant and from that union there came a daughter who was the wife of the John Martin who founded Martin's Bank. Mary married a Mr. Benjamin Hatley Foote whilst Catherine was the wife of the Revd Francis Hender Foote, Rector of Boughton Malherbe and Linton for 22 years, both livings being in the gift of the Mann family.

In the county archives office at Maidstone there is the original 1724 document which records the purchase of 'a Capital Messuage called Caples [alias Linton] and Loddington Farm'. This shows that from this point onwards the name Linton was to replace the earlier title. This was confirmed when from 1730 onwards there appeared the replacement for the demolished Capells Court. The house which Robert Mann, the new county squire, built in its place was now named 'Linton Place'.

It was a 7 by 5 - bayed house, with 2 storeys to the north and 3 to the south. The ground floor plan consisted of a hall, with a similar room as a saloon to the south and rooms, 2 bays square, flanking them. The original building remains at the heart of the present structure although the original Georgian staircase has been removed. The width of the original house is now represented by the long room behind the entrance hall. The view from the south looking rooms embraced Marden, Staplehurst, Cranbrook, Tenterden and Headcorn until it terminated in the far distance some 30 miles away with the Sussex Downs. It is not surprising, knowing now the relationship of the Manns and the Walpoles that Horace Walpole gave it the description with which we began.

Robert Mann rebuilt the original almshouses in 1749 and increased the stipends of each family from 2 marks (13s 4d) to £1 whilst in the church he erected a vault in the chancel with a plain white marble slab. It was there that he was buried after his death on 12 March 1752 at the age of 73 and there too is the record of his wife, Eleanor, who predeceased him a year earlier when she was 74. His will, which covered 8 sheets of the register, left all his manors, with the exception of those in Kent, to his eldest son Edward Louisa [sic]. The Kent properties, some of which we shall note shortly in dealing with his younger brother, Galfridus, were left to Benjamin Hatley Foote and the Revd Francis Foote, the sons-in-law, as trustees for Edward's eventual use.

The new master at Linton was born on 17 June 1702. He was a colleger at Eton from 1716 to 1720 and was admitted to Clare College, Cambridge on 5 October 1721. He was to die unmarried on 16 December 1775 and there is a brown and white marble tablet in Linton church recording that event. At that point the bulk of his estates passed legally to his brother Horatio, better known as Sir Horace Mann, but he specifically bequeathed "all his messuages lands etc. at or near Heysham, Surrey, to a Mary Mann, whose story is told elsewhere in this family history. Before we turn to Sir Horace, however, we need to consider the significant contribution made to the family's well being by his younger brother, Galfridus.

Galfridus never owned the Linton estates but, being a draper like his father and having prospered as an Army clothier, it was his foresight and initiative which led to the steady accumulation of the Kent estates. By a 1750 deed the Earl of Chesterfield, of the famous 'Letters', assigned to Galfridus the Manor of Boughton Malherbe with the site of Boughton Place and the advowson of the Rectory appendant to the Manor, and all the rest of the Wotton estates in the county. These were:

> the heritable Manor of Bocton, alias Boughton Malherbe;
> the manors of Burscombe and Wardens, alias Egerton;
> of Southerdon, Colbridge and Marley, alias Marleigh;
> of Sturry, East Farborne, Holmill, alias Harrietsham and Fill.

The manors of Wisperhawke and Hampden in the parish of Headcorn were also conveyed to Galfridus by sale on behalf of the heir of Thomas Hennard. The fact that the church building at Boughton was an appendage of the manor explains why Galfridus's brother-in-law, Francis Foote, was Rector there from January 1751 to January 1773 and the Hon. James Cornwallis, who married Catharine, the 3rd daughter of Galfridus, was the next Rector from 1773 to 1779.

Galfridus had married a Sarah Gregory and when he died in 1756 he left 1 surviving son and 4 daughters. His eldest son, Edward, born in 1735 survived only to the age of 2 and his eldest daughter born in 1736 died in the following year. Of the daughters, Alice married John Althorpe, Sarah died unmarried, Eleanor Mary was the wife of Thomas Powys, later Lord Lilford, and it was thus through the Catherine already mentioned that the Mann estates eventually passed into Cornwallis hands.

Before that event, however, we note that in the will of Galfridus, which ran to 12 pages, all his manors, lands, etc. in Kent or elsewhere, except those in Warwickshire, were put in trust with Edward Louisa Mann and Benjamin Foote for the surviving boy, also called Horatio Mann. He was to have the lands for life and they were then entailed on his sons with any remainder going to his daughters or their heirs. If the estate descended through one of the daughters then his heir was to adopt the arms and name of Mann.

The exclusion of the Warwickshire estates showed wise management. These were to be sold and with the residue of his personal wealth were to provide £7,500 to be invested for each of his daughters when they were 21, with any residue to be laid out in purchasing land in Kent as near as possible to the estates he already possessed. These were to be used for the maintenance of his son prior to the age of 21.

Before we consider the contribution to Linton of this son, Horatio, a word should be said about the Sir Horace, Galfridus's older brother. R.W. Ketton-Cremer, the Norfolk historian, in his biography of Horace Walpole, says that Horace Mann was 33 years old in 1739 and though the *D.N.B.* gives his birth date as 1701 the fact that his elder brother was born in 1702 would suggest that this must be incorrect. The fact that he was at Eton in 1718 and was briefly a student at Clare Hall, Cambridge, about 1720 also fits in with Walpole's dating. He seems to have left the University early because of ill health and it is further said of him that when he left Clare he set off for Naples and *took his own coffin* with him. He was to be almost wholly resident in Italy for the rest of his life and though, as we have noted, he was the inheritor of the Linton properties from 1775 he never visited them or resided there and in 1779 he made over the ownership of Linton to his nephew Horatio, the son of Galfridus. It was this nephew and heir who was beside his uncle when he died in Florence, 6 November 1786 after 46 years of residence there. Sir Horace was, nevertheless, buried at Linton.

This next master of Linton, Horace Mann, had been born on 2 February 1744 and was educated at Charterhouse, which he was attending when he succeeded to his father's estates at the age of 12. He was later admitted a fellow commoner at Peterhouse, Cambridge in May 1760 and matriculated at Michaelmas 1761, becoming an M.A. in 1763.

Having been knighted in 1772, which is why it is easy to confuse him with his uncle in Italy, Sir Horace became M.P. for Maidstone from 1774-1784 and for Sandwich in 4 parliaments from 1790 to 1807. He was a well-known Kent landlord who had a real concern for the estates he possessed and was eager to improve the conditions which he inherited. This was particularly the case at Linton.

Until 1817 Coxheath stretched in a broad band from Boughton Monchelsea some 3 miles westward and 50 yards to the south of the present northern boundary of what is now called Linton Park. Until it was turned into a huge army camp it was one of the wildest places in the county and was notoriously unsafe to cross at night. The camp was situated to the east of the turnpike road (now the A229 from Maidstone to Hastings) and lay towards Boughton Monchelsea, except for the Wagon train and Artillery units which were sited on the west of the road.

Encamped here were 12,000 Hanoverian and Hessian troops and in 1778 a royal review of 15,000 troops was held here by George III whilst Linton Place was used as the residence of the Commander of the army. The last camp was in 1804, and in 1817, under the Enclosure Act, the greater part of the land was distributed to those who held grazing rights and some was sold to cover the cost of enclosure. As a result the boundary of Linton Place was extended some 50 yards to the north to the road which runs from West Farleigh to Boughton Cock (now the B2163) – a road which had been made by the troops through Coxheath. It may be recalled that it was at just this time that Sir Horace was at the height

Linton Park

Horace Mann

of his local and political influence.

But he was also a keen athlete and a cricketer with some original ideas. In 1800 he arranged a cricket match between two teams on horseback and had bats made to fit the height of the batsmen from the ground. Cricket had started as a 16th century village game but by the 18th century it became increasingly popular among the nobility and gentry and not least in Kent. It provided active exercise, was played in shoes and without pads, and offered an opportunity for gambling. Sir Horace would lead his team onto the field at his country seat at Bishopsbourne, near Canterbury, in matches where stakes were as high as 1000 guineas. He even brought an outstanding batsman from the Hambledon club and made him his Bailiff.

In the *Gentleman's Magazine* for July 1883 the Revd John Mitford selected the 3rd Duke of Dorset and Sir Horace Mann as the principal patrons of the game in Kent. They were not only patrons in that county for Nyren described them as keen friends and supporters of the game in Hampshire.

Sir Horace was certainly a character. In one match where Ring, who was Sir Horace's huntsman, was playing against a David Harris, the game was clearly in the latter's favour. Sir Horace was in the outfield cutting swathes among the daisies with his stick, a mannerism that always showed his agitation, whilst also cheering every run that his man made. When a new man was preparing to go in to bat Sir Horace went over to Ring and said, "Carry your bat through and make all the runs and I'll give you £10 a year for life." Ring was out for 60 runs and with only 4 to beat the last man in made them. Sir Horace kept his word.

He played twice for Kent in 1773 and his last recorded match was in 1782 when 6 from Hambledon played against 6 from Kent. Most notable of all, and not least in the light of the later Cornwallis connection, Sir Horace and the Duke were, with 35 gentlemen, those who made the attempt in 1787 to create a County Cricket Club. Lord Harris, in his history of the game in Kent, thought it was impossible from the start for the choice of Coxheath, 'a bleak, desolate, unpopulated spot without accommodation for the cricketers and onlookers' was unlikely to attract. Linton Park Cricket Club however persisted and its bicentenary was marked by the visit of an M.C.C. side in 1987.

Sir Horace had 3 daughters of whom the eldest, Lucy, married James Mann, the illegitimate son of her grand-uncle, Edward Louisa. By 1805 Sir Horace was in desperate need of money and sold most of his estates. Unable to dispose of his father's settled properties he allowed his son-in-law to purchase the tenure of Linton. James and Lucy had in fact been living there already for some years because 2 of their sons, Horatio and William Henry Galfridus, are shown in Alumni Cantabrigiensis as having been born there.

Sir Horace died on 2 April 1814 at Union Crescent, Margate, and with him the baronetcy became extinct. His obituary says it all:

"His life was rather dedicated to pleasure than business. Enjoying a good constitution

243

he was much attached to gymnastics, exercises, especially cricket, which as he advanced in life he relinquished for the more sedate amusement of whist."

On his death his father's settled estates passed to his nephew, James, the son of Bishop Cornwallis. Somewhat confusingly, but in accordance with the terms of the bequest, James took the name Mann by royal licence. What at least helps to distinguish him from the preceding James Mann who occupied the property was the fact that this James was also the 5th Earl Cornwallis.

He was born on 20 September 1778 and baptized on 18 October at St. James's Church, Westminster. Educated at Eton and St. John's College, Cambridge he obtained his M.A. in 1798. From 1799 to 1806 and from January to April 1807 he was a Tory M.P. for Eye, but he was subsequently to vote in the Lords for Catholic emancipation and supported Pitt in his abandonment of the Corn Laws. He remained a Peelite for the rest of his life.

He was married 3 times. First, on 18 December 1804 at her father's house in Savile Row, Westminster, to Maria Isabella Dickens, who died on 16 January 1823. He was married again on 22 January 1829 at St. George's, Hanover Square to Laura, daughter of William Hayes. She died childless on 3 August 1840 at Hill Street, Berkeley Square. His third wife was Julia, the fourth daughter of Thomas Bacon, and their wedding was by licence on 4 August 1842 at Croydon. She died at St. Leonard's-on-Sea aged 37 on 4 November 1847.

By another royal licence dated 16 September 1823 James was authorized to subscribe the name of Mann before all titles of honour and it may be recalled that the next year he inherited his father's title as 5th Earl Cornwallis. We also learnt earlier that the second Sir Horace Mann's daughter Lucy had married another James Mann and it was from this namesake that James Cornwallis/Mann had purchased Linton Place in 1820. With the advent of his peerage and a suitable property now in his hand the 5th Earl made large additions to the house from about 1825. A third storey and 2 storeyed wings of 4 bays were added, the south front was underpinned with a balustraded terrace and an arcaded basement and the gardens were rearranged. A large service court surrounded by the servants' quarters was placed to the north-east and now the whole was stuccoed and painted white, as it is today, with a tetrastyle Corinthian portico placed in the centre of the south front. The alterations were carried out by that most famous of 19th century London developers, Messrs. Cubitt of Gray's Inn Lane and William Cubitt was the architect. This, by the way, explains why much of the present Linton House resembles those terraces in Belgravia which the firm was also constructing at the same time. Cubitt only designed a few private houses and they are all of the 'Palladian' or 'Italianate' style.

The 5th Earl had 3 sons and a daughter by his first wife. The 2 eldest boys, Henry James Galfridus and Henry Horace, both died young but his third son was Charles James Cornwallis, afterwards Mann, who was styled Viscount Brome. He was born in 1813 and matriculated at New College, Oxford, on 10 September 1832. He died, unmarried, on 27 December 1835 at Linton and was buried there. The Earl thus died without male issue on

James, 5th Earl Cornwallis

Catherine, wife of 5th Earl

21 May 1852, also at Linton where he was buried and all his titles and honours with him. With his exit into the Cornwallis chapel of St. Nicholas, Linton, it seemed as if the Cornwallis line had ended.

The estate passed to his only surviving child, Lady Julia Cornwallis. She was the Earl's only child by his third wife and had been born on 2 July 1844. She married, 27 August 1862, William Archer Amherst, Viscount Holmesdale, who became 3rd Earl Amherst in 1886. It is singular to note that as her mother had brought the Bacon name back into the family so now she introduced the name of one who had been a close military partner of the 1st Marquess.

The interior of Linton Park was entirely redecorated by Lord and Lady Holmesdale. The walls and ceilings of the reception rooms and even Lady Holmesdale's boudoir were covered with elegant designs and colouring in the French gilt style in which medallions with scroll frames contained oil paintings by Morant. None of this remains. They also sought to make an impression outside and the avenue of Wellingtonias mentioned above are said to have been planted in 1866. The Orangery on the north side of the Pinetum actually carried Viscount Holmesdale's initial and coronet.

During the 18th century many country houses were set in parkland which was designed so that it came right up to the house itself and the availability of new ranges of plants in the following century encouraged their bedding where the occupants could see them. The disappearance of the tax on glass in the late 1840s meant that 'glass houses' began to be popular, as is famously shown by the erections created by Paxton at Chatsworth and then the Crystal Palace in Hyde Park.

Mention of Paxton reminds us that this was also the period of the Head Gardener. John Robson of Linton was one of this Victorian elite. It was he that devised the oval bedding area just below the terrace where the land swiftly falls away towards the south. He so arranged it that when the area was looked at from the windows of the house it seemed to be circular though it was in fact 90ft by 30ft. The bed was filled with a different design every year and in addition to providing these horticultural scenes outside Robson was also responsible for the supply of flowers for set pieces throughout the house and on the dining table.

John Robson was a man of firm opinions about what was suitable in his area of responsibility and on one occasion he had water fountains piped direct to the dining room from the kitchen below. He also oversaw the regular supply of vegetables to the kitchen every morning and the supply of seasonal fruit for dessert, strawberries in February, peaches at Easter and grapes all the year round. Pineapples seem to have been his finest achievement and Robson expected to cut about 150 a year. It was only the emergence of new market gardeners, now Garden Centres, and the new interest taken by house owners in their own gardening which led to the demise of these once important employees.

In addition to the extensive changes to the house and gardens the year 1860 saw a major reconstruction of Linton Parish Church. This was carried out by R.C. Hussey whilst the whole cost was borne by Ladies Louisa and Elizabeth Cornwallis, unmarried daughters of the 2nd Marquess. Hassey altered the chancel by removing the east central wall and window and also extended the nave by adding the north aisle and simply copying for the latter the existing 2-bayed south arcade. He pulled down the old, plain and rather crude tower and replaced it with the steeple and larger tower base which we see today. He replaced the clock which had been there since 1700 and also rehung the three oldest bells that were made by John Waylett in 1717.

Lady Julia died on 1 September 1883 and the estate devolved on the issue of Lady Jemima Isabella Wykeham-Martin, daughter of the 5th Earl by his first wife. She was the only child to have issue having married Charles Wykeham Martin of Leeds Castle, Kent and Chacombe Priory, Northamptonshire on 12 April 1828. She died on 17 December 1836 and at this point we ought to trace the background of the families from which would come the next owner of the Linton estate.

The earliest sure record of the Martin family is of a Clerk in Holy Orders who was born in 1574 and married Elizabeth Bird, the daughter of Dr. John Bird, Prebendary of Canterbury, whose wife had Dr. John May, Bishop of Carlisle, as her father. These clerical gentlemen must have been amongst the very first to avail themselves of the right to marriage allowed in Queen Elizabeth's reign.

It was not from this marriage that the Martin line we are concerned with descended but through Dr. John's second wife, Joan Boveken (or Buffkin) and their son, John. Through this John's first marriage to a person unnamed there was a son, also called John, and a grandson called Denny Martin. It is with this Denny Martin that we begin to see the link that would lead to a Cornwallis connection for he married, as his second bride, the Hon. Frances Fairfax, a daughter of the 5th Lord Fairfax of Cameron. This Lord Fairfax had been born at Bolton Percy, Yorkshire in 1657, matriculated at Magdalen College, Oxford on 10 November 1675 and then, like other members of his family, pursued both a parliamentary and military career. He was M.P. for Malton, North Yorkshire and in 1688 supported the invitation to William of Orange to take the throne of England. That allegiance was confirmed when, as a Lieutenant Colonel in the 3rd Regiment of Horse Guards, he was present at the Battle of the Boyne.

Some 3 years before William of Orange's arrival, Thomas 5th Lord Fairfax of Cameron, married Catherine, the daughter and heiress of Lady Colepeper of Leeds Castle, Kent and thus became not only the occasional occupant of that property but also Deputy Lieutenant for that county. Though all his children were in fact born at Leeds he himself lived chiefly in the house at Castlegate, York or at Denton Hall. It was only in 1710 that his mother-in-law, Margaret, Lady Colepeper, died and the Castle became their sole property. Though Lady Colepeper has left a reputation for being difficult it has to be recognized that it was entirely due to her that Leeds Castle remained in the family, and her descendants, by one line or another, were to reside there until 1926.

That the lady appreciated the Fairfax connection is shown by her approach to Constantine Huygens, one of William III's Dutch secretaries to request an English peerage

James, Viscount Brome, son of 5th Earl

Lady Julia Cornwallis

for her son-in-law. It was not granted. In her will, however, she also made provision for her grandson, the future 6th Lord Fairfax, by granting him her one-sixth part share in what was called the Virginia Proprietary. It was to prove very beneficial.

The Hon. Frances Fairfax mentioned above was the sixth of 8 children and apart from her brother, Thomas, the 6th Lord, and her eldest sister Margaret, she was the only other child to be married. Baptized at Bromfield Church on 19 November 1703 she married Denny Martin of Salts Place, Loose, in 1721. They had eight children and though, unusually for those days, they all reached maturity not one of them married.

It was her son, Thomas Bryan Martin, who also maintained the Fairfax link for when, after 1747, the 6th Lord finally decided to leave England and reside on his Virginia property it was this young man who was to become his uncle's constant companion and aide for the next 30 years. Leeds Castle from this juncture was left in the hands of Robert Fairfax, the 6th Lord's youngest brother who became the 7th Lord in 1789. His first wife, Martha Collins, died in 1743 and their only son, Thomas, in 1747. Because Robert had grandiose ideas for the renovation and extension of the Castle it was necessary that he should remarry and with a wealthy heiress. He found one in Dorothy Sarah, the child of Mawditsley Best of Park House, Boxley. The Bests, successful brewers of Chatham, had amassed a great fortune and the marriage of this girl to a future peer and the owner of Leeds Castle must have seemed for them a dream come true. The dream was short-lived for the couple married at Boxley Church on 15 July 1749 but by 21 May 1750 Dorothy was dead. Sadly also the wealth that had come to Robert Fairfax was not well managed and despite the generous settlement that came with his marriage his plans for the Castle and other ventures constantly outstripped his resources. Indeed, when in 1763 he at last responded to a plea from his designated heir, a second cousin, George William Fairfax, to come out to Virginia to mitigate the influence of Bryan Martin on the 6th Lord Robert had to resort to another mortgage on his property to find the money for the trip. During his absence the Castle was to be managed by the Revd Denny Martin junior, the Curate of Loose and the domestic chaplain at Leeds.

It was this unmarried clergyman who eventually turned out to be the most fortunate beneficiary of all. He was generously treated in the will of the 6th Lord Fairfax, who died in 1789, receiving a sum of nearly £50,000. A claim by Robert, now the 7th Lord Fairfax, (b. 1707) did allow him a life interest in the Virginia incomes but whatever money that produced was at once swallowed up by his current debts. The only requirement made with the legacy to Denny Martin was that his name was henceforth to include Fairfax and he was to add the Fairfax arms to his own.

The settlement turned Robert into an ill-mannered recluse who earned himself no good opinions. On 19 September 1790 the Hon. John Byng, afterwards 5th Viscount Torrington and a noted traveller and author, was observing the beauties of the Maidstone area. He wrote:

"Some few miles of good road, in a changing country, brought us to Leeds Park . . . It would be one of the first and most curious Places in this Kingdom. Col. Bertie was charmed with The Scenery, as everyone must be. For some time we sat beneath a Grove at an Hill Top, contemplating all these Beauties, and bemoaning our ill choice of Day (Sunday) or the Rudeness of Ld. F(airfax) in refusing us admission to the castle."

Almost 3 years later the said Lord died, and the *Gentleman's Magazine* for August 1793 reported that 'after living in the most extravagant profusion this last nobleman was buried in a manner more humble than the corpse of one of the meanest cultivators of his estate'. He also left whatever remained to him to his faithful nephew, the domestic Chaplain who doubtless read the burial service over him at Bromfield. The Revd Denny Martin was then 65 years old and he died 7 years later on 3 April 1800.

By the terms of his will this bachelor clergyman left his English manors of Loose, Brushing, Langley, Boughton Monchelsea and Maidstone equally between his 3 unmarried sisters, Frances, Sibylla and Anna Susannah and they also received a legacy of £4000 each. Since their other brother, Thomas Bryan Martin, also died in Virginia in 1798 and left each of his sisters an equal share in his plate, personal items and residual money which amounted in total to some £35000 they were extremely well provided for and this was to have a significant influence on the future of the family property. By Denny's will the Castle and its estate was left to his youngest brother, General Philip Martin, whose first act on taking up residence was to charge his sisters £100 per annum for the privilege of living in the ancestral home.

General Martin also ended 147 years of direct Colepeper influence over a large part of Virginia. The 6th Lord Fairfax had employed an up-and-coming attorney, Thomas Jefferson, to regulate his transactions there and had sent his cousin, George William Fairfax, on a field trip to survey exactly what was the state of the Virginia properties. This affable young man chose as his companion on that 1748 trip his 16 year old brother-in-law's brother, George Washington. Such were the close personal ties before the American revolt.

Though this Artillery General and his 3 maiden sisters had none of the financial restraints that dogged the later life of the 7th Lord Fairfax their mode of living seems to have been similar in at least one regard. An anonymous traveller in Kent in 1809 records that "We took a walk to see Leeds Castle which . . . is at present enjoyed by General Martin and two maiden sisters who mix but little with the world and, according to reports, these ladies are not without considerable singularities of disposition, among which is their positive Aversion that any Strangers should be admitted to see the inhabited or uninhabited parts of this magnificent and ancient Building which is situated in a Moat . . "

It will be noted from the above that only 2 sisters are mentioned because Frances had died in 1813, bequeathing her personal estate of £10000 to her 2 sisters and any remainder after their deaths to the General. Sibylla died in 1816 leaving £12000 in the same fashion and by 1817 Anna Susanna had also gone and their brother now received £35000. All the sisters were buried at Loose.

Even the General was now an extremely old man and without any direct nephews and nieces to consider the problem of to whom to leave his property and wealth became a serious issue. In the event he ignored any possible Colepeper or Fairfax relations and selected Fiennes Wykeham whose family had been in contact with him and his sisters since 1779. The gentleman selected was the great-grandson of the half-sister of the General's grandfather.

Fiennes Wykeham was a prominent solicitor in the Banbury area who lived at Chacombe Priory in the county of Northamptonshire. In his conversations with the General about the inheritance it was agreed that the final bequest of Anna Susanna was to be spent on the refurbishment of the Castle and that Fiennes Wykeham was to take the arms and name of Martin in addition to his own. David A.H. Cleggett in his comprehensive *History of Leeds Castle and its Families* makes the apt comment:

"It is ironic that the legacy of Bryan Martin, who detested the very name of Leeds castle, passed through his sisters to his brother Philip and was eventually used to render the castle into broadly what it remains to this day." (p. 154)

The name Wykeham-Martin which persists to the present began officially with the granting of the royal licence on 18 October 1821. The changeover was none too soon for General Philip Martin, R.A. died early in August 1824, aged 89, as the last direct heir of the Colepeper and Fairfax families. It was through his choice of an heir, however, that we return to the connection with the last of the previous Cornwallis line, the sole remaining child of the 5th Earl Cornwallis's first marriage, Jemima Isabella.

As we can see from the exquisite full-length portrait of this young lady still on display in Linton House the attraction she presented to the eldest son of Fiennes Wykeham-Martin was not simply one of good breeding and some substance of property. Charles was captivated by her and their marriage on 12 April 1828 was to prove a happy one. Jemima's father, however, was anxious about the match as he worried over the serious debts that had at that time been incurred by Charles's father. The latter's problems became acute when, on top of the failure of the Maidstone bank with which he dealt, he was required to purchase, rather than inherit, Chacombe Priory which he had occupied through his wife's grandfather, the noted Charles Fox. Together with over-expenditure on the castle at Leeds Fiennes and his wife, Eliza Bignell, the sister of a Banbury legal colleague, had even been compelled to economize by living for some time abroad.

The Earl Cornwallis therefore only allowed the marriage of his daughter to take place under strict conditions. Charles was to pledge that neither his personal income nor the generous marriage settlement made by the Earl were ever to be used to assist in settling the debts of Fiennes Wykeham-Martin. With that assurance the marriage went ahead and the couple entered wedlock.

To close this part of the story the newly-weds lived at Egerton House which was also provided by the Earl Cornwallis. Because of Fiennes Wykeham-Martin's urgent liabilities a sale took place at Leeds Castle in April 1830 under the direction of a Mr. James Christie. The dispersal of long cherished family items was exceedingly hard to bear and as Fiennes

Wykeham-Martin bitterly observed, "Even the window blinds were sold". It has to be said that whilst not directly meeting his father's debts Charles and his wife did buy many items that would enhance their own home and help retain links with the past of Leeds. The castle itself was to remain largely empty and forlorn for the next 15 years with much of the 17th century park timber being removed. At the end of his life Fiennes lived there in sparsely furnished rooms and in complete retirement, dying there on 14 September 1840. He was buried in the family vault at Bromfield and his estates passed to his eldest son.

At this point the marriage dowry which had sustained Charles and his wife in their first home could now be supplemented by the Hampshire properties that had been bought by Lord Colepeper and which, kept separate from Leeds, now became his. Yet Charles's life had already had its own sadness. Not only had his new brother-in-law, Viscount Brome 'of Linton', died in 1835 but Jemima herself died the following year in what had become their second home, Arreton Manor on the Isle of Wight. The couple had had 3 sons and a daughter, Philip, Fiennes, Cornwallis and Maria.

Philip Wykeham-Martin was born in 1829 and became M.P. for Rochester in 1856 where a fine portrait of him still hangs in the Guildhall. He married Elizabeth Ward and they had one son named Cornwallis Philip. Though Philip outlived his father, Charles, who died in October 1870 at Leeds, he too died suddenly on 31 May 1878 in the library of the House of Commons. His widow continued to occupy the castle until her death in 1893 when their son took up residence there.

Of the second son called Fiennes, as the one from whom the present Cornwallis line descends, more will be said in the next and final chapter.

The third brother, Cornwallis, entered the navy in 1846 at the age of 13 and following service in the Baltic and then Panama he was so ill that he was sent home. The morning after his arrival he met one of the Leeds house guests, Anne Rolls, fell in love at first sight and after marriage in 1861 settled at Purton in Wiltshire, though they later moved to Packwood Hall, Warwickshire.

Cornwallis Philip saw the castle through to the start of the 20th century but when he died in 1903 the trustees thought that there would be trouble meeting the death duties and so sought ways to dispose of the castle. Fairfax, the son of his second marriage, never lived there and on 13 March 1925 *The Times* carried an announcement that Leeds Castle would be let. It was the end of an age.

Leeds Castle

Toby, ridden in the Charge of the Light Brigade by Major Fiennes Wykeham-Martin

CHAPTER 12

The Tree That Still Remains

A brief mention was made of Fiennes Wykeham-Martin in the last chapter but this is the place where he rightly takes his proper and important place. He was, as has already been said, the second son of Charles and Jemima Wykeham Martin and service in the Army became his career. Fiennes married, on 29 July 1863, Harriet Elizabeth, the second daughter of John Thomas Mott of Barningham Hall, Norfolk and they had two sons and two daughters of whom more will be said shortly.

He was a popular officer with his men and something of a social celebrity in other parts of his life. At the Charge of the Light Brigade at Balaclava he was referred to as Cornet Martin in the official documents. A picture of Toby, his horse on that occasion, now hangs in what is one of the offices of Linton Park. Promoted in due course to the rank of Major in the 4th Hussars he was a man who was fond of outdoor sports and his portrait shows him dressed for a day's shooting. Indeed it was when he was out hunting one day that he was thrown from his horse, kicked in the head and from that injury a tumour developed which led to his death on 24 April 1867.

Through him two principal contributions were made to our story. The first was that by royal licence dated 15 October 1859 he resumed the surname of Cornwallis only and the blood line from that ancestry could once again be recognised by the old patronymic.

The other factor was that by the careful settlement arranged by the 5th Earl the inheritance of the Linton Park and other estates could not be granted to the eldest Wykeham Martin grandson, Philip, because he was likely to have the Leeds Castle property and the Earl, it will be remembered, did not want the Mann estates to be used in financing any Leeds expenses. The inheritance at Linton and elsewhere was thus vested in the second grandson of the Earl should the latter's only remaining child, Lady Julia, die without offspring. As this occurred after the death of Major Fiennes it was to his eldest son, Fiennes Stanley Wykeham Cornwallis, that the Mann estates were now transferred.

His mother, Harriet Elizabeth Cornwallis, remarried in July 1873 but on 20 January, 1884, when her second husband, the Revd Arthur Edward Robinson, Rector of Wootton, died, she applied for and obtained a royal licence enabling her and her eldest son to take the name Mann in lieu of Cornwallis and to bear the arms of Mann and Cornwallis quarterly. In the event her son preferred to retain the name Cornwallis though the arms of the family now displayed quarterly first and fourth Cornwallis and second and third Mann.

Born on 27 May 1864 he was educated at Eton and on 10 February 1886 married Mabel, eldest daughter of Oswald Peter Leigh of Belmont, Cheshire. The couple had 3 sons and 4 daughters. Before attending to some details of his career and family, however, it will be as well to review briefly the details of his brother and sisters.

Arthur Wykeham Cornwallis was born 24 April 1865, and was to live a long life, dying at last on 9 February 1952. He married Marcia Blanche Florence, the daughter of Robert Bower of Welham, Yorkshire, in 1890 and they had one daughter, Iris Beryl, who in turn married Captain Edward Henry Lee-Warner, OBE, of Denton House, Harleston, Norfolk. She died in 1975. The two sisters of Fiennes and Arthur were Helen Florence who died, unmarried, in September 1957, and Caroline Vere who died without marrying in November 1909.

It was the renewed Cornwallis line through Fiennes Stanley Wykeham which was clearly going to provide fresh life for the family tree and the father of this new branch provided ample evidence of his vigour and dedication as both a parent and a servant of the nation and his more local communities. The awards of CBE, TD, DL, JP alone speak for themselves but he was specifically Chairman of the Kent County Council, Lieutenant Colonel and Honorary Colonel commanding the West Kent Imperial yeomanry, Honorary Colonel of the Thames and Medway Heavy Brigade, Royal Artillery, (Territorial Army) whilst also becoming M.P. for Maidstone in 1888-95 and 1898-1900. It is scarcely surprising that in an age when it was still possible to recognize outstanding public service with a noble title, and in a line with such antecedents, he was created 1st Baron Cornwallis, of Linton in the County of Kent on 31 January 1927. Those who were to succeed him would do no less justice to the honour thus given expression.

The restoration of a Cornwallis to the peerage was not the only sign of recognition that marked the previous twelve months. In 1926 Right Worshipful Bro. Fiennes Stanley Wykeham Cornwallis was appointed Deputy Grand Master of the United Grand Lodge of Freemasons of England and Wales and thus confirmed in yet another avenue of service the type of dedication that he had shown elsewhere. It was not the first honour that he had received in the Craft for in 1901 he was appointed Junior Grand Warden of the United Grand Lodge of England but when in 1905 Lord Amherst resigned as Provincial Grand Master of Kent Colonel Fiennes Cornwallis, his nephew, was installed by him as his successor.

Not only did this appointment emphasize the place rightly earned by the Cornwallis family in their now native County but it renewed the Masonic line with the Fiennes family, one of whose sons, the Honorary William Thomas Eardley-Twistleton-Fiennes, later 15th Lord Saye and Sele, had been Provincial Grand Master in 1829. The new Provincial Grand Master was the direct descendant of the Revd Richard Wykeham of Chacombe, Northampton, whose mother was the sister and co-heir of Richard Fiennes, the 6th and last Viscount Saye and of Sele.

First Lord Cornwallis
(re-created 1927)

Mabel, 1st Lady Cornwallis

His tenure of this important office for 29 years during which he consecrated 60 lodges is still well remembered and the *History of the Kent Province* by E. Dudley Grasby has rightly preserved two of the carefully prepared addresses which he gave on such occasions. At the All Saints Lodge inauguration in 1932 he said this:

"You will meet almost within sight of one of our Kent Cathedrals . . . Our own stay on earth is short but the Church and Freemasonry, we feel assured, will be bulwarks of our national life for centuries to come . . ."

His service in this exalted rank in Kent was not the last of his Masonic appointments as the full length portrait in Freemasons' Hall, Great Queen Street, London confirms. Here he is shown, dressed in his robes of office as a peer of the realm and Pro Grand Master, or temporary replacement for a Grand Master who was a member of the Royal House. This position was to be a presage for one of his descendants though sadly this 1st Lord Cornwallis died before he could be installed. It was fitting that the one who spoke at his memorial service at Linton should be the Archbishop of Canterbury, Dr. Cosmo Gordon Lang. He spoke what many felt: "When you think of him as the Squire of Kent, remember that he was one who regarded his possessions and position like a kingship. He realised that the trust given to him was by the grace of God." The tablet to his memory bears the words: "In honour chivalrous, in duty valorous; in everything noble; to the heart's core clean."

It was in their home at Linton that Lord and Lady Cornwallis reared their family. It consisted of three sons and four daughters. The eldest son, Fiennes Wykeham Mann Cornwallis, was born on 21 August 1890 and after his time at Eton, he joined the 17th Lancers and served with them as the first World War broke out. Of the bravery which he clearly showed his awards of the Croix de Guerre and the Military Cross speak eloquently but his further service as a Captain after the War took him to Ireland where he was murdered on 15 May 1921. He had never married but in the now family tradition he was a member of the Douglas Lodge. This lodge was consecrated in 1877 and met in Maidstone. It was named after its first Master, Aretas Akers-Douglas, later Viscount Chilston.

As the Government of the day would not agree that Fiennes had been killed on active service full death duties had to be paid on the Linton estate which had been handed over and this destroyed any future for the property. His death left the eventual succession to the Linton title to Wykeham Stanley Cornwallis who was born on 14 March 1892. Like his older brother he was educated at Eton and then entered the Royal Military College at Sandhurst. Of his no less impressive career in national, county and local affairs much more will be said below. Here, however, we need to record that he was married twice, first, in 1917, to Cecily Etha Mary, the daughter of Sir James Heron Walker, 3rd Bt. of Sand Hutton, near York, and secondly, to Esmé Ethel Alice, the widow of Sir Robert James Milo Walker, the 4th Bt. and son of Sir James. The present 3rd Baron Lord Cornwallis was the son of the first marriage.

The third son of the 1st Baron was Oswald Wykeham Cornwallis who was born 16 March 1894 and educated at the Royal Naval Colleges of Osborne and Dartmouth. He married the Hon. Venetia Jane Digby on 5 December 1923, she being the third daughter of the 10th Baron Digby. He rose to the rank of Captain in the Royal Navy and was awarded the OBE in 1919.

His wife died in March 1956 and he in January 1974 but they left behind them two sons and a daughter. Michael Wykeham Cornwallis was their first child, born in November 1924. He entered the Navy after being at Eton and is now a Lt-Cdr, RN (ret.). He married Margaret Dorothy Cannon of Faversham, Kent who died on February 21, 2003, and there were two children, Richard Wykeham born in November 1959 and Diana Margaret, born in August 1957. Richard is married to Anastasia Sardjiati and lives in Indonesia where they have a son, Thomas Hugo Wykeham, and a daughter, Venetia Putri. His sister married David Casey of Alloway, Ayrshire and they have a son, Colin Wykeham, born in 1994. Michael married recently Gladys Cornwallis, no relation, and now lives in Sydney, Australia.

Captain the Hon. Oswald Cornwallis's second son, Charles Wykeham, was born on 22 September 1937 and died, unmarried, on 15 December, 1978. Michael's sister, Venetia Mabel, was born 8 November, 1928 and married in 1956 Lt-Cdr Geoffrey Arthur George Brooke, DSC, RN. They too have a family.

The 1st Baron's daughters all married and have left issue. Julia Dorothy became the wife of Capt. the Hon. Sir Archibald Douglas Cochrane, 2nd son of 1st Baron Cochrane of Cults, in 1926. She was a leading light in the Girl Guides ending up in the most senior position in that movement. She was accorded a CBE in 1952 as well as being made a CStJ. and died in June 1971.

Her husband served in the 1914/18 War and was trapped in the submarine nets in the Dardenelles. He, reportedly, had bets with the crew as to whether the next depth charge would blow them up, or blow the submarine nets away. Fortunately the latter happened. He and his brother officers were imprisoned in Turkey. They managed to escape, and walked their way to the Persian Gulf. He later became M.P. for Dumbarton for many years and was one of the last Governors of Burma. They had a son and a daughter.

Vere Mabel married Sir Samuel Strang Steel, Bt. on 3 August 1910 and died on 8 October, 1964. Sir Samuel was M.P. for Ashford, Chairman of the Forestry Commission in Scotland and they had four sons and one daughter. One son was killed in North Africa. The daughter died unmarried. The other three sons all had children. The present baronet, Sir Michael Strang Steel, lives in Philiphaugh in Selkirk, the family home.

The third sister, Yvonne, married Cdr. the Hon. Henry Mitford Amherst Cecil, OBE, RN. on 27 January, 1923, and the Commander's mother was a Vanderbilt. They had one son and two daughters. The son Rear Admiral Sir Nigel Cecil (Os to his friends) was the last Naval Commander in Simonstown and in Malta. On retiring from the Navy he became Governor of the Isle of Man.

Rt. Hon. Lord Cornwallis KCVO.KBE.MC.
1892 - 1982

Rt. Hon. Lord Cornwallis, OBE, DL

The last sister, Bridget Frances Kate, married Lt. Col. John Cecil Petherick, OBE, MC, of Porthpaean, St. Austell, on 4 July 1921 and they had one son and two daughters. They were always a very Conservative family. He was Chairman of Maidstone Constituency for years and his eldest daughter was Conservative Agent for Plymouth.

After Linton was sold they had a clock which was at the top of the stairs in their house. One of the daughters, when visiting, noticed that this was missing, but was told by her mother that she had had a good offer for it. The clock was later sold in London for £250,000 and turned out to be a gift from King William III and Queen Mary to one of our ancestors.

At the other end of the scale, they had a soda stream which broke down in the 1970s. The manufacturers were asked to service it and duly sent their man to do so. He went away saying that he had not got the right parts with him and would be back. Shortly after this the company wrote and offered to provide a new soda stream free of charge if they could have the old one for their museum. It was No. 2 in their sales register.

Returning to the new 2nd Baron of Cornwallis it has to be said that he entered upon his new and unexpected role with a measure of reluctance. He had intended to make the Army his career, becoming first a Subaltern in the Royal Scots Greys and serving with distinction in the First World War. He won the Military Cross in the Battle of Loos and was badly wounded in the Battle of the Aisne. Thereafter he held staff appointments with the 2nd Cavalry Division and the Cavalry Corps.

In 1919 he was appointed A.D.C. to Earl Haig at the H.Q. Home Forces, Whitehall and later took part in the formation of the British Legion. He then took up the post of Instructor at Sandhurst. He was captain of Kent cricket club from 1924 to 1926 and it was from there in 1926 that he acceded to his father's request that he should begin to take some part in public affairs. To indicate how long the feeling of some disappointment at his new prospects was, it is worth noting the inscription in a book that he was to give to the present holder of the title in 1960. The book was entitled "Spirit of Kent – Lord Cornwallis" and preserves in great detail the extensive and demanding life of County service that was that of this peer. The words to his son on the flyleaf are:

"To Fiennes from Father – A warning to avoid the antics of Public Life".

The truth is that whilst this might reveal his private feelings his public image was one of incessant interest, vigour and dedication. By 1935, being now 43, he was already a well-known Kent figure and the title which Pratt-Boorman gave him in this biography was one that he had already acquired.

This image and popularity derived from the start with his inclusion in the County cricket team, a move ordered by Lord Haig. He played for the County for 7 years, ending up as Captain. It was on a cricket ground that he was given the sad news of his elder brother's death in County Galway. He was playing for Kent against Hampshire at Southampton. His brother, Oswald, was keeping wicket for Hampshire in the same match. To complete this side of his interests he was in 1947 elected President of the M.C.C.

By 1920 he was a member of the Kent County Council representing Holhingbourne and in 1935, after being Vice-Chairman, he succeeded to the Chair. Shortly after this appointment he ended his connection with the Council as he now knew that other duties would fall upon him in his new role and, as he said and demonstrated all too clearly in much else he did, "This is a job which must be done full time or not at all."

Nothing perhaps so reflects the energy and dedication which he had given to that task than one of his last engagements in this sphere – on behalf of the unemployed of Kent. On 7 June 1935 at a meeting in the Town Hall, Maidstone, an appeal was launched for funds to remove the United Service Training Centre from Loose to Tenterden. Amongst many other fine speeches by the Bishop of Dover, The Minister of Health and Sir Wyndham Deedes, Capt. Cornwallis, as he still was, said, "Men are going to waste now who will be no good in the future unless somebody does something for them . . . by giving these men some form of training they will be able to find a job." The response was immediate and on December 11th the Centre was opened by the late Queen Elizabeth, Queen Mother.

Another event in that part of his life and one which linked the 18th century family with that of the 20th was the news which the family received of the setting up of a statue in Halifax to their ancestor, the Hon. Edward Cornwallis, first Governor of Nova Scotia. Though the statue had been unveiled by the local Chief Justice, Lord Cornwallis was able to represent the family by a visit to Halifax in 1949, when he laid a wreath at the foot of this intrepid ancestor's memorial.

Nor was that all that he was able to do during this visit. He presided at the opening of a new school bearing the family name. He was able to visit not only the Canadian naval station called H.M.C.S. *Cornwallis,* but also the famous Cornwallis Inn at Kentville, Nova Scotia. Another link with hospitality on that continent is the Cornwallis Hotel in Cornwall, Ontario. The mention of such establishments should remind us that there was the Lord Cornwallis Inn at Tunbridge Wells, now demolished, and still more recently the Abbey House hotel at Brome in Suffolk renamed the Cornwallis Inn after the family.

Yet if that was a link that was renewed there was a link that was now severed. As already the owner and occupant of his own home at Plovers, Horsmonden and, following the death of his father, and the previous loss of his eldest brother there was no reason, other than payment of death duties, to hold on to the Linton estate. Accordingly, after a tenure of just over 200 years, the successor of the Mann and Cornwallis families sold Linton to Mr. Olaf Hambro in 1938. All the estate employees had to be given notice and many of them moved out of the district.

Olaf Hambro was the grandson of Charles Joachim Baron Hambro, a Dane, who founded the Bank of C.J. Hambro and Son in London. The present setting of the house, even after occupation by others, is one in which the family can take some pride as part of their past, and the willingness of the present owners, once Eastern Produce (Holdings) Plc, but now Linton Park, plc, to maintain and exhibit many family portraits following the time of the 5th Earl is appreciated. Just as one can enjoy the array of another generation of portraits at Audley End so also a more recent clutch of ancestors now impress the visitor in the rooms at Linton.

It was in the church at Linton that there was raised the memorial to Lady Cornwallis after she died in 1957. Besides the dates of her life it reads: "Remembering with gratitude her great devotion to her family and home, and her gracious life of service to others". That stands beside the one to her husband as well as the one to their oldest soldier son.

There are also, of course, the earlier mentioned memorials to Sir Anthony Mayne and his wife, Dame Briggatt, as well as the alabaster urn commemorating Galfridus Mann. Here too are those to Laura, Countess Cornwallis, the young Viscount Brome, and Julia Mann, Viscountess Holmesdale.

One of the persistent interests of Lord Cornwallis, beginning even before he assumed the title, was the Association of Men of Kent and Kentish Men. He became President in 1932 on the death of Lord Sackville, and from the start this new and much younger leader threw himself wholeheartedly into the task. "Kent is my native County", he once remarked, "and I was brought up to respect it."

Certainly his feelings were often expressed in well-chosen words and at the various banquets of the County Society, at not a few of which The Duke and Duchess of Kent were the principal guests, he was able to give voice to what he knew Kent could and would do for the nation. His words in 1936 seem specially momentous bearing in mind the events that were soon to follow.

"We treasure traditions, we are proud of our history. We do not forget that Men of Kent defended their rights against William the Conqueror and retained their ancient laws. Our coastline, which is first in the defence of our Country, makes us fully realise the full value of the sea and the Navy that protects us . . . We in the Association are pledged to maintain our heritage and we mean to keep the 'Garden of England' as fair as we can . . ."

His deeds did not belie his words as one or two examples show. In August 1940 a British pilot in that other dramatic line of defence, the Battle of Britain, parachuted into a field by the family home. The pilot was duly offered a bed for a well-earned rest. When he awoke his host was able to inform him that he had just received a cheque for £5000 from a Mr. Stanley Johnson, of Bearstead, who wanted it earmarked for a new Spitfire. This led to the appeal for an Invicta Flight of Spitfires. The appeal was so well supported that a full County of Kent Squadron was procured and the leader's plane was named "Spirit of Kent, Lord Cornwallis."

The pilot was Wing Commander Stanford Tuck, well-known in the Battle of Britain, who, until his death, maintained his links with the village of Horsmonden. He was driven back to Biggin Hill, after his rest and food, by the present Lord Cornwallis who then spent a very uncomfortable night at the aerodrome which had been badly bombed that afternoon.

Whilst such things might be up in the air there was urgent work to be done on the ground. Appointed Chairman of the Kent War Agricultural Committee with the task of organizing 11,000 farmers and nearly 170,000 acres of arable land he presided over the achievement of raising that acreage to over 290,000 and evacuating 125,000 of the best sheep and 20,000 cattle from the exposed and tempting invasion area of Romney Marsh. What is perhaps easily overlooked is the fact that this was done as the evacuation of Dunkirk was also being undertaken. Two immense projects that needed and received widespread and careful management. Yet the Chairman was quite plain: "Mark these two words – voluntary and unpaid – farmers, landowners, farm workers, Land Girls and railway officials – they should never be forgotten." The Chairman himself was never a serious farmer before he bought Ashurst Park in the 1950s. He was always terribly pessimistic about his own crops – there being in existence a well known photograph of him standing, hands over his eyes, in a field of oats. It is captioned "The Gentleman Farmer surveying his oat", because there wasn't going to be more than one.

As part of this all-out effort there was not to be forgotten the part played by his first wife. She was a true blunt Yorkshire woman. She was well known for what her children called her "soot bags". These were delivered with unbelievable accuracy on someone who had made an unfortunate remark or acted in a stupid way. One of her triumphs was when she was sitting on the benches at Canterbury Cricket ground as her husband was captaining Kent. A man sitting in front of her was being extremely uncomplimentary about her husband. Why did he play – he couldn't bowl, bat, or field. He was useless. A very high catch went up into the deep field and her husband ran and caught an absolutely stunning catch. The critic was enthusiastic about this wonderful catch – who caught it? who caught it? "Only my rotten husband" was the response from behind him. The man got up, went to his car, and left the ground. She and her husband were a very devoted couple, and if apart, wrote to each other every day. She was the Chairman of the Kent Women's Land Army and though she knew her heart was weak she was tireless in her efforts. On one occasion her response to someone who expressed concern for her was: "There are better men than I being killed every day. I carry on." In 1943 she could carry on no longer and she died in October.

With his appointment in September 1944 as Lord Lieutenant of the County in succession to John Charles, Marquess Camden, GCVO, Lord Cornwallis rightly became the leading personality in Kent and was to preside over some heartening occasions as the war came to an end. In October he took the salute as the Home Guard stood down after a service at Canterbury Cathedral; the Women's Land Army stood down in 1945 and at a location not unknown to His Lordship, the St. Lawrence cricket ground in that city; whilst on two occasions H.M. King George VI and Queen Elizabeth visited parts of the county which had suffered greatly from bombing and were enthusiastically received both by their official representative and the people of the area. One occasion he would never forget was the installation of Mr. Winston Churchill as Lord Warden of the Cinque Ports and the words which the latter addressed to those in the ancient Court of Shepway.

"We are moving into a new age. Secrets have been wrested from nature which ought to awe and prevent the quarrels of mankind, even if they do not allay suspicion . . . Far wider combinations than cooperated in the defence of the English Channel will be needed to save the future peace and happiness of mankind." As was so often the case with this speaker his prescience and foresight were remarkable.

The start of the post-war years was specially marked by his marriage to Esmé, Lady Walker of Slinfold, Sussex, which is where they were to live until they purchased Ashurst Park in 1956. The marriage was graced by the presence of the Duchess of Kent, who was received by Lord and Lady Harris and the Bishop of Rochester shared the service with other clergy. The couple spent their honeymoon in Bermuda and with friends in New York.

Then began again the seemingly ceaseless round of military, agricultural, sport and civic occasions, with Mr. Churchill again appearing at the County Show, Queen Elizabeth, now the Queen Mother, being introduced to the best of British apples, the Duke of Edinburgh visiting Kent's cricket team and H.M. the Queen spending a whole day touring the Weald.

In 1952 the red and white flag of Denmark flew over the West Gate of Canterbury when H.M. King Frederick IX of that country came with H.R.H. Prince George to unveil, in the Warriors' Chapel of the Cathedral, a new Regimental Memorial Window. His Majesty came as Colonel-in-Chief of the Royal East Kent Regiment, 'The Buffs', and in the Cathedral the scene was enriched by the presence, alongside the King, of the Bishop of Copenhagen, the Rt. Revd Fugisang-Damgaard and two other Danish clergy dressed in their medieval gowns and large ruffs.

Lord and Lady Cornwallis attended the present Queen's Coronation in 1953. Later that year, and by the Queen's express command, Her Majesty's Lieutenant for Kent went down with the Swedish ambassador to welcome H.M. King Gustav who had arrived on a normal passenger boat and wearing a trilby and brown overcoat. It is hardly surprising that his fellow passengers were not aware of their distinguished travelling companion.

Something of the same informality was present when it came to bidding farewell, in the Queen's name, to the then ruling monarch of Iraq, King Feisal. He left Lydd airport dressed, not in the now familiar attire of Middle Eastern leaders, but a well-cut lounge suit. His brother was similarly attired. This was a fateful farewell as within a matter of weeks the King had been assassinated and regimes leading to the present state of affairs had been inaugurated. There must have been rather similar feelings after sharing with the Duke of Kent an official welcome to President Trubman of Liberia in 1962.

Numerous as were the occasions on which he welcomed members of the Royal Family. There is the record of some special banter that occurred during the tour of the Queen and the Duke of Edinburgh in south-east Kent in 1958. After a tour of Dover castle and other civic locations the royal couple moved on to Folkestone, and received members of the Town Council in the Leas Cliff Hall. When the Queen asked Councillor Mrs.

Panting how many women were on the Council the reply was "Five". "You are still outnumbered", said the Queen, but The Duke joined in with, "Oh, five good ones will keep everyone in order."

We know how devoted Lord Cornwallis was to his native County. It was of no surprise therefore when in January 1960 he rose in the House of Lords to council caution in permitting the extension of "that sprawling development of a great octopus", the London County Council. For him the proper geographical boundary of Kent included Woolwich, Greenwich, Catford, Blackheath and other boroughs. In 1962 he was concerned about the water policy of Kent. Three years later he raised the whole matter of the county's rural heritage threatened by excessive planning permissions. If anyone might have any questions about the part played by the hereditary peers in maintaining the best and preparing for the continued prosperity of county community life then the work of this man merits careful consideration.

One outstanding example of his interest and application is the encouragement and establishment of the idea of a University for Kent at Canterbury. Education was not one of his least interests. In 1966 when acting as Pro Chancellor for this new addition to England's Universities he admitted H.R.H. Princess Marina, albeit herself the Chancellor, as the first graduate with the Hon. Degree of Civil Law. He had chaired the Interim Committee that oversaw all the necessary preparations for such an opening and he had seen the target of the appeal which he had organised finally achieved. It was only right that the central complex should be called 'The Cornwallis Building'. On 12th July 1968 he himself received at the Duchess's hands his own Doctorate of Civil Law. Sadly again, within a month H.R.H. Princess Marina died after a short illness. Her successors as regular visitors to Kent now included Princess Margaret, Princess Alexandra, the Duke of Gloucester and the Duchess of Kent.

The Lord Lieutenant was also honoured with the Freeman of Maidstone. He was also the principal guest at a dinner in the County Hall given by the Chairman and Aldermen of the County Council.

One of his principal interests was the Kent County Show of which he was President first in 1932 for one year and later on for 34 years from 1947 to 1981 when he retired. At the same time in 1932 he became the President of the Association of Men of Kent and Kentish Men, an office he held until May 1960. For his services to them and to the County he was awarded the Edward Hardy Gold Medal.

Looking always to the future there were two other areas of county interest that claimed part of his time and attention. The first was the work of the Scout Movement and as County Association President he was plain spoken about the value of such work. "The Scouts have no colour, no creed – just an ideal. As an organization it is a tremendous character builder and I think it is one of the most important organization for youth in the world." He had welcomed the Deputy Chief Scout, Lord Somers, in 1939. On behalf of both the Queen and the Chief Scout, he was himself making awards to both senior and junior members of the Movement. The measure of his sense of service was underlined by his having come from Scotland specially to perform this task.

His other great concern was that children should have safe and pleasant places in which to play. Lord Luke of Pavenham, Chairman of the National Playing Fields Association paid a glowing tribute in 1960 to the Kent Branch of which, perhaps to noone's surprise, Lord Cornwallis was again the President. As if he could have foreseen the situation that would still prevail in the next century he said, on this occasion:

"These children need somewhere where they can go to play and let themselves go. Somewhere where the exuberance of the British race can get a chance to find a proper outlet in something that is healthy, happy, and competitive, and which gives them some incentive to become a little better than when they started."

As Chairman of the Reed Paper Group he was a keen supporter of the popular 'Kent Messenger' and Mr. Pratt Boorman, its proprietor, whilst as Chairman of Fremlin's Brewery he was no less eager to promote 'Kent's Best'. These business interests only served to show how he understood the importance of an all-round national economy.

There remains but one more aspect of this remarkable 'all rounder' which has to be mentioned before we pass to the present generation. Like his father and several forefathers he was a dedicated Freemason. Having attained the rank of Grand Warden in the United Grand Lodge in 1933 he succeeded his father as Provincial Grand Master of Kent in 1935. In his time the number of lodges doubled. Before he ended his notable career in that office he was to see Kent divided into East and West Provinces with himself as the first PGM of both. Such was the foundation that he and his assistants established that both Provinces are still in good heart 25 years later.

When he visited Nova Scotia for the Halifax Lodge Bi-centenary his Masonic connections there should also be commemorated. He was invested as Past Deputy Grand Master of that Province and also given the Henry Price Commemoration Medal by the Grand Lodge of Massachusetts. As Pro-Grand Master the present Lord Cornwallis also visited the Halifax Lodge on the occasion of its 250th anniversary.

At home the constant series of church services and Cathedral events that marked his tenure of office reveal the then happy relations that constantly prevailed between Church and Craft, and the fact that an Archbishop and Bishops were both Kentish neighbours and Brethren compares sadly with what has transpired since.

What a delight it must have been for him in 1970 to see in his Provincial procession his own son and heir, the Hon. Fiennes Neil Wykeham Cornwallis, OBE, as Chairman of the Management Committee of the Boys School, and to know that before long the family name would once again grace the ranks of the chief Rulers of the Craft.

Lord Cornwalis died on 4th January 1982 at his home, Ashurst Park, Tunbridge Wells. In 1968 another royal recognition had been made with his appointment as Knight Commander of the Royal Victorian Order in the Queen's Birthday Honours, and happily he had lived long enough to both enjoy and justify the new dignity he bore. He received this further distinction before the death of his second wife on 5 June 1969.

The title of 3rd Baron Cornwallis of Linton was proudly taken up by his eldest son who now lives in Goudhurst, Kent. Born in 1921 and educated at Eton where he won the School Racquets. The present peer was commissioned in the Coldstream Guards and served with them between 1940 and 1944. In 1942 he married Judith Lacy Scott by whom he had one son, the Hon. Fiennes Wykeham Jeremy Cornwallis, and a daughter, Anne, who died in her early twenties. This marriage ended in 1948. In 1951 he was married Agnes Jean Russell Landale and they had another son and three daughters. Sadly, after a long illness, she died in 2001 after nearly fifty years of married life. All of these children, like the son of the first marriage, are married and there are several grandchildren. (See family tree on page 274).

Of his children, his daughter Mary Clare, ran a very successful school for 3 to 7 year olds for 19 years in London but has now retired to Scotland to become a fulltime artist. Vanessa has emigrated to Brisbane, Australia, where she runs an excellent Art gallery. She was given an Australia Day award for service to her community. Rosie is running a project in India helping wives to provide for themselves in one of the poorer areas.

The nine grandchildren and two great-grandchildren have not yet each been able to make their mark. However, Charlotte Cornwallis is the Real Tennis Ladies World Champion. She won the title first in 2001, lost it in 2003, and regained it along with the British, USA and French Championships in 2005. By the time this book was about to be printed she had also secured the Australian title and so she became the first lady to win the Grand Slam. She entered in 2005 for the Browning Cup, the British Professional Competition and was the first woman to have won that. Amongst the other grandchildren he can boast a chef, a potter and a promising cricketer and golfer.

The present peer, having a father who was involved in almost everything in Kent, perforce turned his attention elsewhere. He focused his activities on agricultural and related subjects, on finance and Freemasonry in London.

After learning farm skills in Shropshire and a short spell with Strutt and Parker he went into farming on his own account at Ruck Farm, Horsmonden, which had been handed over to him by his father. Apart from cattle, pigs and fruit he set up one of the earliest garden contracting firms. This led to his becoming a founder member of the British Agricultural Contractors Association in 1949 and its second President. On its amalgamation with the National Tractor Engine and Tractor Association in 1958 and the formation of the National Association of Agricultural Contractors, he became, and was, the first President holding office until 1963 and again from 1986 to 1998.

In farming his first love was his Guernsey Cattle, a prize-winning herd which he built up himself from an original herd of five house cows. In the early fifties he was appalled by the Danish domination of the British bacon market. He founded the County Quality Bacon Federation which was an association of bacon producers based on regional groups and names. This received wide support in both England and Scotland and helped substantially to improve the quality of, and awareness about, British bacon. It was also the first organisation to introduce ultrasonic quality testing on live animals before marketing. He was supported by Prof. Ian Lucas, Principal of Bangor University and later the Principal of Wye College.

This enterprise led quite soon to the development of locally produced enterprises in other things such as Dorset and Welsh lamb, to mention only two. From there eventually developed the farm shops selling local produce with which we are all familiar today. Between 1956 and 1963 he was provided by the N.F.U. with an office in Agricultural House, Knightsbridge.

During the same period he joined, as a founder member, a new fruit cooperative called Checkers, based in the Cranbrook area of Kent. This was established in co-operation with one of the leading London fruit salesmen in Covent Garden Market.

In 1958 he joined the Kent branch of the CLA and was its Chairman in 1971. Together with John Warde of Squerreys Court, Westerham, they rejuvenated the branch. In 1964 he joined the CLA executive in London and, in consequence of various assignments that he carried out on their behalf, he remained a Nominated member of the Council until 1999. He had been a member in unbroken service for 36 years.

These various assignments led him into a varied career of considerable interest. In 1970 the CLA appointed him as their representative on the committee set up to assess the effect on British Horticulture of entering the Common Market. While serving on this committee he was approached by a representative of the Federation of Agricultural Cooperatives to assist in drawing together organisations involved in various commodities. This led to the formation of the Fruit Forum, an organisation representing every cooperative in Top and Soft Fruit growing, and he was their first Chairman.

When the representative for British cooperation in Brussels retired in 1974 he was appointed to that post and held it until 1986. During this time the Chairman of the Ministry of Agriculture's Quality Apple scheme, known as the Kingdom Scheme, indicated that he wished to retire. Although the Chairman was paid by the Ministry he was elected by the growers and then approved by the Minister. Lord Cornwallis was so elected to the post which he held until the growers voted out the Apple and Pear Development Council.

When this occurred the fruit industry was left bereft of any organised body. He immediately stepped into the breach with the support of a number of major growers and two of the main co-operatives. He set up English Apples and Pears as a coordinating and promotional body for the Industry. He chaired the organisation during its formative years and then became President, finally retiring in 1996. English Apples and Pears has ever since remained the main promotional body for the Industry.

In 1971 the CLA was offered a casual one year vacancy on the London Regional Committee of the Confederation of British Industry. Lord Cornwallis was asked to take up

Fiennes Stanley Wykeham Cornwallis -- Mabel Leigh

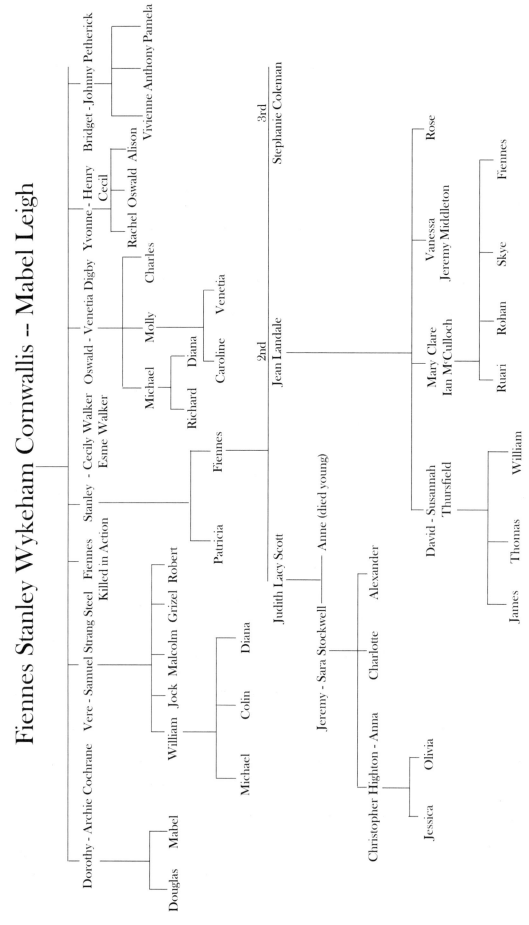

the appointment. At the end of the year he was re-elected by the CBI members onto the National Small Firms Committee of the Council. In 1978 the President of the CBI approached him to become the Chairman of this Committee and thus onto the President's Committee, the main body of the Industry. He served thus for three years until 1981, an unusual job for a farmer.

On inheriting the title in 1982 he took up several briefs on behalf of the CLA in the Lords, notably the Waterways Bill. On this occasion he obtained 19 agreed amendments to the Bill which considerably improved its drafting. He also spoke on matters affecting the Fruit Industry and the County of Kent in particular. He did not, however, stand for one of the elected places in the House under the Labour Government.

In November 1955 he was initiated into Freemasonry. He was to rise quickly through the ranks being appointed Junior Grand Warden of the United Grand Lodge in 1963.

In 1966 he was appointed Chairman of the Masonic Institution for Boys which then supported the Masonic School for boys, who had lost one or both parents, and needed help. The Charity, however, needed a re-focus for its overheads were burdensome. The new Chairman decided that charitable money should not be used to maintain bricks and mortar but ought to be directed to the support of those people who needed it. He proceeded to close the Junior School against great opposition, and to use the money released to send pupils to schools near where their relatives and friends were living. He gave up this post on being appointed Assistant Grand Master in 1972. His successor as Chairman closed the Senior School.

The Duke of Kent asked him, as Assistant Grand Master, to chair the Grand Master's Committee to look at the Masonic Charities and to report back to him. His report recommended the establishment of a Grand Charity which was then brought into existence, the separation of some of the duties of the Grand Secretary into independent hands, and a realignment of seniority in certain lodge offices. The latter recommendations were not brought in until some years later.

He held the office of A.G.M. until 1976 when he became Deputy Grand Master. In 1982 he was appointed Pro Grand Master (The Grand Master's alternate), an office twice held by members of his family in earlier generations. In this role he thought that Districts and Lodges overseas had not been visited enough by the rulers in the Craft. Over the next 10 years he and his colleagues travelled extensively across the world, not only to lodges owing allegiance to England, but also to Europe and the United States.

He also had to deal with considerable adverse publicity from the churches, the police and the press. He realised that Masonry was not open enough about itself and its activities, so he established a Public Relations campaign and began loosening the perceived secrecy of the organisation.

He was also able eventually to secure a resolution of the serious problems relating to the Royal Masonic Hospital. His last achievement, before retiring in 1991, was the setting up of the New Masonic Samaritan Fund which is now a thriving institution.

Going back once again to 1968 he joined the Board of the Planet Building Society. This Society amalgamated with the Magnet and then the Town and Country Societies. He was Chairman of all three at some stage of their development. He negotiated the eventual takeover of the Town and Country by the Woolwich in 1991.

In 1979 he was appointed by Mrs. Thatcher as one of the Government's nominated Trustees of the Chevening Estate outside Sevenoaks, with responsibility for the lands and farms owned by the Estate. The farm houses and buildings had not been well maintained because all the money had been spent on the restoration of the House. Within a restricted budget he set about remedying the situation.

Such money as there was left had been invested in long dated Government Securities. In agreement with his colleagues, Lazards were appointed to re-organise investments and a disposal of some of the outlying houses, and a giant attic sale was able to help to bring the finances back into balance, and enabled the property to become viable and run at a surplus.

The Chevening Act, originally passed through Parliament by Lord Stanhope, had to be amended and brought up to date. This required negotiation with the various beneficiaries under the Act; the American Ambassador, the Canadian High Commissioner and the National Trust. Power to let land had also to be introduced.

Lord Cornwallis always thought that the re-establishment of the Chevening property as a viable enterprise was the best achievement of his life, and the most enjoyable job he ever had. It could not have been done without the help of the brilliant Estate Administrator, Captain David Husband, R.N., O.B.E.

Lord Cornwallis was also a Founder Governor of Cobham Hall School from its opening in September 1962. He was appointed Deputy Chairman and Executive Governor, and as such, was responsible for the construction of the first new classrooms and the development of the School over its first 10 years. He was also, later on, a Governor of Sevenoaks School for some years.

His main interests now are his extensive stamp collection and he is a Fellow of the Royal London Philatelic Association. Much time is spent in supporting charitable activities. There are two Cornwallis Charitable Trusts and he is involved in local charities at Horsmonden and the local branch of the Alzheimer's Association.

In 2002, he married Stephanie Coleman, the widow of Antony Hinds Coleman, and mother of four daughters.

He now lives at Goudhurst and continues to enjoy life as the present head of the line going back nearly 800 years.